FOOTLOOSE
IN
JACKSONIAN
AMERICA

FOOTLOOSE IN JACKSONIAN AMERICA

ROBERT W. SCOTT AND HIS AGRARIAN WORLD

by Thomas D. Clark

THE KENTUCKY HISTORICAL SOCIETY

Copyright © 1989 by the Kentucky Historical Society

Library of Congress Cataloging-in-Publication Data

Clark, Thomas Dionysius, 1903-
Footloose in Jacksonian America: Robert W. Scott and his agrarian world / by
Thomas D. Clark
p. cm
Includes The diary of Robert W. Scott.
Includes bibliographical references.
ISBN 0-916968-19-7: $29.95

1. United States—Description and travel—1783-1848. 2. Scott, Robert W. (Robert Wilmot),
1808-1884—Diaries. 3. Plantation owners—Kentucky—Diaries. 4. Agriculture—Southern
States-History—19th century. I. Scott, Robert W. (Robert Wilmot), 1808-1884. II. Title.
III. Title: Jacksonian America.
E165.C586   1990   90-4067
973.5—dc20   CIP

*To Beth, my collaborator
for more than a half-century*

Contents

Illustrations

Acknowledgments

IN THE EDITING of a journal which covers as many places and events as Robert Wilmot Scott's does, the editor becomes obligated to many persons and institutions. First, I must express deep gratitude to the late Mrs. S. I. M. Major of Versailles, Kentucky, for entrusting me with a sizable portion of the Scott-Major papers and the journal in 1960. Unfortunately, the Special Collections Department of the Margaret I. King Library allowed the journal to get away from it. After considerable search I discovered that James Ferguson of Madison County had sold it to Yale University. The Director of Rare Books and Manuscripts at Yale agreed that the journal should be returned to Kentucky, and today it is a valuable part of the Special Collections Department of the King Library. William J. Marshall, of the Department of Special Collections, has generously granted me permission to have free access to the journal, to edit, and publish it.

It is a miracle that so much of the Scott documentary collections has survived numerous divisions. An important body of the Scott-Major papers passed into the hands of Mr. and Mrs. Harley Ferguson of Madison County, and they in turn deposited them in the Townsend Collection of Eastern Kentucky University Library. Sharon McConnell graciously granted me full access to these important papers. There is also a collection of Scott manuscripts, including the earliest Locust Hill farm book, in the Filson Club in Louisville. James Bentley and Nettie Watson were most helpful in making available these materials.

Over the years the Greene family at the Falls of Rough, Kentucky, accumulated a large volume of Greene-Scott manuscripts. These were transferred by the estate of Jennie Greene, a Scott granddaughter, to the Kentuckiana Collection of Western Kentucky University. The second Locust Hill farm book was preserved by Miss Greene. I am indebted to Riley Handy, Penny Harrison, and Nancy Baird not only for arranging access to the papers, but for duplicating many of them for me.

Henrietta Scott Mitchell preserved the important body of intimate Scott correspondence, and in turn her daughter Henrietta Mitchell Wiley of Buffalo, New York, kept the papers intact. She, however, wished them

destroyed upon her death. Fortunately indeed, her attorney did not have
the heart to destroy them and arrangements were made through Mrs. Louis
Cox of the Society of Colonial Dames of the Commonwealth of Kentucky
to return them to Frankfort. Happily, the papers are now deposited in
Liberty Hall, the former home of John Brown. My indebtedness is to
Pamela Metcalf who called my attention to the existence of the papers
and arranged my access to them. I am, of course, indebted to the Society
of Colonial Dames for their preservation of the papers, for access to them,
and for the privilege of photographing the famous livestock award silver
pitcher.

No one can use the manuscript and rare book collection of the University of Kentucky Library without becoming deeply indebted to Clare
McCann. She has indeed been patient and helpful in making not only the
Scott journal but other manuscript materials available. Anita Gentry of
the Franklin County, Kentucky, clerk's office went to considerable efforts
to locate the deed to Locust Hill, only to discover that it had been pilfered.
She, however, produced evidence of its antecedents. William Metropolis,
assistant curator of the Harvard University Geological Museum, confirmed
for me the existence of the mineral collection Scott described. Albert Muncy
of St. Augustine, Florida, supplied me with important leads describing
Governor William P. Duvall's archaeological discoveries. Finally, my wife
Elizabeth Turner Clark was of indispensable assistance in helping me copy-
read the journal and in deciphering many of Scott's blurred words.

One

THE DIARY OF
ROBERT W. SCOTT

Robert W. Scott, circa 1840

An Introduction

ROBERT WILMOT SCOTT, an eager young Kentuckian, saddled his horse just a month and a half before his twenty-first birthday and set out to see the world, or at least that part of it which lay east and northeast of Kentucky. He had attended Transylvania University and had studied law under the tutelage of Haggin and Loughboro in Frankfort. Scott was a student in Transylvania when conditions were unsettled over the resignation of the liberal Horace Holley as president. He had represented the student body in delivering an address of regret that the president was leaving, and expressed sympathy for him in the senseless controversy which had forced his resignation. At Frankfort, in the law offices of "New Court" partisans, life was more peaceful. Judge James Haggin had served as a justice on the so-called "New Court" bench until the legislature dissolved that body on January 1, 1827.

Out beyond the pale of politics-ridden Kentucky in 1829 lay the broad expanse of Jacksonian America. The country in that era was undergoing fundamental changes and making almost revolutionary technological, economic, and social advances. Immediately on Scott's itinerary was a visit to Virginia, which had briefly been the home of his father's Scotch family before it came out to Kentucky in 1785. The Wilmots had emigrated westward from Maryland, so in a sense this part of his visit was in the nature of a sentimental journey.

Departing Frankfort on September 17, 1829, with a word of wisdom from Grandfather Wilmot, and one of deeper sentimental meaning from Elizabeth Brown, he rode away on what amounted to a *Wanderjahr*. His saddlebags bulged with letters of introduction from Kentuckians to Virginians, and to politicians and others in the newly installed Jacksonian administration. He chose a somewhat circuitous route in departing Kentucky, riding by way of Lexington, Paris, Cynthiana, Vanceburg, and Greenupsburg on the Ohio. On this leg of his journey Scott recorded no impressions of the countryside or the Kentuckians whom he met on the way. He surely must have met with a "mean" tavern-keeper or two, some local politicians, and other persons worthy of his attention. He did describe passing the scene of the Battle of the Blue Licks, mentioning only vaguely a knowledge of the historical event which had occurred there.

Along the Little Sandy River in present Greenup County, Kentucky, there were numerous iron furnaces in operation. Scott visited some of these but failed to describe them in the careful detail he was later to use in describing New England industries. It would have been interesting to know what people he saw at the furnaces and the nature of their work, or something of the iron trade. Perhaps he felt these things were commonplace and too close to home.

Once beyond the boundary of Kentucky the young traveler became more explicit about the passing scene. The Kanawha Valley with its waterfalls, salt works, and wild mountain scenery excited him. Following along the famous hog drover's road across the Gauley Mountain, Scott not only encountered rugged terrain and scenery but "mean" landlords as well. He carried in his pocket two hundred dollars and with determined Scotch frugality he meant to make it stretch as far as possible.

In his heart Scott bore a zeal for the rising temperance movement in America, which in 1829 saw the creation of local chapters with almost the same rapidity that malarial and smallpox epidemics occurred across the land. At Lewisburg on top of the mountains the young Kentuckian first encountered this movement. Again in the tiny village of Lexington, Virginia, he sensed a rivalry between the clergy and the temperance leaders as to who had first claim on men's spiritual emotions.

In western Virginia Scott traveled along the route of the grand tour of the chalybeate springs and natural geological wonders. Water bubbling up from the bottoms of sulphureous basins at temperatures too hot to be tested with the naked hand stirred his curiosity. He attempted to learn about the chemistry, physics, and geology of these natural phenomena. He had a good eye for location, physical sizes and manifestations, and settings. The springs interested him far more as natural wonders than as popular gathering places for Virginia and eastern seaboard society. Natural Bridge, for instance, was far more fascinating than Lexington, the seat of struggling Washington College and a newly formed temperance society. Not only was this natural wonder a picturesque physical landmark to be viewed and wondered about, it also had staggering physical dimensions, a history, and a practical use. Scott was fascinated by the fact that George Washington had carved his initials high up on one wall and that Thomas Jefferson had once owned the bridge.

Ahead of him after Natural Bridge were the famous Virginia caverns. Scott observed these not as great underground cavities, but as grand naturally formed chambers which possessed many of the characteristics of public assembly rooms. At the famous Weyer's Cave he visualized the joyous assemblies which were said to have gathered there.

Across the Blue Ridges along the rim of the upper Virginia piedmont the University of Virginia at Charlottesville was in 1829 more of an architectural accomplishment than a significant center of learning in America. To a young Transylvanian who had been a student during the invigorating Holley years, the university was struggling to find its mission and a sense of intellectual direction. The institution had only a small library, no scientific museum or laboratory, and no art collection — not even a row of portraits of illustrious past presidents. These things were to be found in Richmond.

On October 10, at the end of a 695-mile ride, and at a cost of $32.75, Scott rode into Richmond. At this date "all roads led to the Capitol." He could not have chosen a more exciting time to visit the city than this stirring moment. Gathered there were the delegates to the famous revisionary constitutional convention, among them nearly all the famous and near-famous sons of the Commonwealth. There were James and Dolly Madison, James Monroe, John Marshall, John Randolph of Roanoke, and almost the entire Virginia congressional delegation. Scott set out to present his letters of introduction and no doubt to garner others. He observed closely the physical features, personal appearances, and gesticulations of the persons whom he visited and then went away and made a succinct, photographically detailed description of them. One almost feels that he sees Dolly Madison peeping out from behind the curtains at the Stevenson home, her slightly dowdy appearance, and then the almost wax museum-like appearance of James Madison. In his precise physical descriptions Scott almost unconsciously sensed the great transitions which had occurred in personalities, modes of dress, and casts of minds in the opening years of the Jacksonian Era.

For a month the Kentuckian lingered in Richmond to savor its society, learning, as he said, the customs of the people and listening to the debates in the convention. He visited all the notable places, including the capitol with its gallery of paintings and statuary, the somewhat tawdry museum, the arsenal, and the penitentiary. His father, Joel Scott, was then serving as keeper of the Kentucky penitentiary, in an era of the most pronounced sensitivity to date for care of the state's prisoners. Throughout his journey Scott was to present himself to penitentiary wardens with virtual official requests that he be allowed to inspect their institutions. Whether or not he had been asked to do this by a father in search of ideas for improving management of the Frankfort institution is not clear.

Unfortunately, for all his close attention to minute details, Robert W. Scott left some glaring gaps in his journal. What were the taverns actually like, what did he eat and under what surrounding conditions, whom did he meet in these places, and to whom did he sell his horse in Richmond and for how much? Surely he did not part with the faithful animal which had borne him so far overland without some pain and sentiment. Too, how much money did he carry aboard the steamboat when he set out down the James River to face the alien world of the East Coast? At Norfolk he visited Fortress Monroe, saw the Rip Raps at the moment this vast marine engineering project was involved in scandal, and observed a bit of the rest of the Norfolk area.

Up until the time he went aboard the coastal vessel headed for New York, Scott had never encountered rougher water than that in the wake of a Kentucky River ferry crossing. Before he had partaken of his second meal, the somewhat rough sea had unsettled his whole physical being; he spent much of the passage up the coast trying to gain his sea legs. Ahead lay New York with its wonders. Amazingly, however, either the city failed to fascinate Scott or he found it too large and overwhelming to linger. It perhaps was too expensive for him. Out of all the places of wonder he might have visited, he seems only to have seen an unusually large child who was on public display, to have viewed the normally invisible world of wonders through a new and powerful microscope, and then to have made a visit to the Brooklyn Navy Yard. Like every other visitor to New York Scott went out to view the great ships of the United States Navy then in station and to see the place where the much-publicized *Fulton* mishap had occurred. On his way through Brooklyn he recorded a brief impression of its houses and streets.

It was to be New England which held fascinations for the young traveler. Doing little more than passing through New York, he left that city for New Haven and its somewhat chaste urban-rural surroundings. In the emergent years, 1820-1830, the East Coast and New England was a wonderland for the intellectually alert Kentuckian attuned to a purely agrarian tempo of economy and society. Scott had an eye for mechanical innovations as well as personalities. In this area technological advances were being made in manufacturing, transportation, and the arts. The nation was expanding its influence in international trade and diplomacy, and at home people were beginning to tackle the staggering task of settling vast reaches of the continent, building new cities, exploiting natural resources, creating new cultural institutions, and undertaking social reforms. In Washington the political era extending from Thomas Jefferson's administration to that of John Quincy Adams had ended. Nevertheless, it had left behind a legacy of progress and an emergent thrust of national might to be expressed in terms of great ships, canals, railroads, and factories. A good part of the nation's power and pride was expressed in the great ships which Scott either saw afloat or a-building. The early naval experiment with the use of steam lay aground in the Brooklyn Harbor in the wrecked hulk of the catamaran ship *Robert Fulton*. As inefficient as this vessel was in design and operation, it had come to an inglorious end as the result of gross carelessness. Scott was to view the hulk of the vessel shortly after the explosion which had wrecked it. At the time, United States naval authorities still thought basically in terms of the British man-of-war design, and the ships which Scott saw in Brooklyn, Boston, and Philadelphia were as much symbols of national ambition as instruments of defense.

Nearly every traveler in this age who reached the eastern coast of the United States went to the naval yards to marvel at Yankee ingeniousness in building the great vessels, with their long rows of gun ports perforating their sides. Beyond this it took tremendous organization to assemble the mountains of materials necessary to construct a seventy-four-plus gun ship. This necessitated the procurement of approximately eight hundred thousand board feet of lumber, hewn oak timbers, masts, and cross-arms to outfit a ship of the *Pennsylvania* class. As impressive as the assembled volume of wood was, it became far more impressive when it was known that much of it had to be of a specialized nature to be shaped and fitted by master craftsmen. In its finished form the mammoth ship was truly a floating forest. More than this, it was a floating exhibit of nineteenth-century American advancement in metal, wood, and design work. Before these naval masterpieces Scott shared the excitement of all other visitors, especially the British travelers who came to make critical comparisons of American marine engineering capabilities with those of England.

When Scott arrived in New Haven, Horace Holley's old Yale University beckoned. The year before he visited that city, the Yale faculty had issued its famous report of 1828. In this searching analysis of the state of education generally and particularly at Yale, the old classical-theological curriculum had been brought under serious questioning. Over the years it had become solidified into a rigid and sterile classroom exercise without much practical application to the educational demands of the times. Yale's physical location and plant impressed the young visitor. He was especially attracted to the library, museum, and the collection of artifacts on display in cabinets. It seems strange that Scott, the student spokesman in defense of Holley at Transylvania, did not refer to his friend's days at Yale.

There was on every hand a Yankee tidiness about both New Haven and Hartford which appealed to the visitor. The commercial, public, and residential buildings all reflected an eastern feeling for dignity and order. Connecticut's two statehouses had about them a simple charm which reflected only a minimal amount of their political nature. Throughout his journey Scott climbed up into domes, to the tops of monuments, and into every other high structure from which he could get a panoramic view of the countryside. This he did in the capitols in New Haven and at Hartford. It is difficult to determine to whom Scott talked in many places and what information he gleaned from newspapers, from the Worcester *Gazetteer* which he carried, and from the local guides. He gave attention to the historic past, but only casually so in many instances. His erroneous reference to the Charter Oak incident seems to indicate limited knowledge of the local history of the places he visited.

Jostling over the rocky Connecticut-Rhode Island roads in a stagecoach gave Scott moments of reflection on the sterile countryside through which he passed. Providence no doubt had genuine appeal for the Kentucky Baptist. He arrived just in time to savor that city's piety in the celebration of Thanksgiving. He was made aware of the role of organized religion in the city by the ringing of church bells, the governor's Thanksgiving Proclamation, and the crowds flocking into churches. There was also a visible display of affluence in the bountiful dinners served about the city. Providence and its various institutions made mixed impressions on visitors. Scott viewed it as a mixture of religious devotion, humanity, and a hard-driving commercialism thriving on growing textile industries and shipping. Two colleges gave the city a cultural tone almost equal to that of New Haven.

In Boston in 1829 a visitor found an exciting variety of attractions. None, however, was more appealing to the physical being than America's premier hotel, the Tremont House. As frugal as he was with his funds Scott indulged himself in the luxuries of this establishment. Nearby the hotel was the Tremont Theater, which offered a varied playbill, thus giving the youthful visitor an opportunity to exercise his critical powers.

Across the Charles River in Cambridge was Harvard University with its stately buildings, library, museum, and faculty. This institution was of genuine interest to Scott, but he seems to have been more impressed by Yale. There were also the shipyard, the Bunker Hill Monument still under construction, and the famous Massachusetts Penitentiary which commanded his attention. Actually, he seemed more interested in the penitentiary and its inmates and operational procedures than in Harvard, Josiah Quincy, and the student body. In the City of Boston the Statehouse, the Marine Railway, the Boyleston Market, and the historic Commons caught his eye.

Scott left Boston sometime early in December. He was precise in giving the day of the week and the exact time of his departure, but not the date. His ultimate destination was Albany, New York. On the way he visited the industries clustered about Chicopee Falls. His descriptions of the manufacture of guns by machines guided in their operation by templates is historically significant. The inventions of Thomas Blanchard were to become in the long range of military history as important as Eli Whitney's introduction of detachable parts. The paper and textile mills were interesting. Scott looked upon the textile mill with its attached dormitory as being something of a young lady's finishing school, precisely the impression millmasters wanted visitors to carry away with them.

Albany in December was not the most salubrious place to visit. Scott spent most of his stay there indoors. His descriptions of the New York Statehouse — with its interior decorations and walls lined with portraits — are vivid. Outside he got a close-up look at a screw dock, a device which then was exciting canal boat operators and builders. This device greatly facilitated the handling of boats in and out of the water. Throughout his visit Scott gave meticulous attention to mechanical things. In his growing up he had been associated with a milling industry in Georgetown, Kentucky. He knew first-hand about the principles of machine operations and could understand the innovations made by the improved technologies of production.

Apparently Scott remained in Albany only two and a half days before he turned southward down the Hudson. Along the river he viewed the farms and was especially attracted to that of General John Armstrong. (It is doubtful, however, that the young Kentuckian knew the general's personal history. Armstrong had served briefly and most ineffectively as James Madison's secretary of war; his muddling, said his critics, had resulted in the British capture of the capital.) In addition to the farms were the rising hills along the stream which formed the famous Hudson Valley Palisades. Before him was West Point and the seat of the United States Military Academy. To Scott this was a place of romance and exciting history. In late 1829 there were nine Kentuckians enrolled in the Academy, among whom were Henry Clay, Jr., Albert Taylor Bledsoe, Aylett Buckner, Humphrey Marshall, Henry Walleck, Camilla C. Daviess, John Waller Barry, and Thomas Ludwell Alexander. The visitor almost seemed to view the famous academy and its surrounding Revolutionary War sites more as historical landmarks than as an institution for the training of officers to command military forces on the expanding American frontier. Scott did savor slightly the routine of barracks life, with its moments of pomp and ceremony.

The journey from West Point to New York City was made mostly at night, which accounts for this vague gap in the travel diary. The canal-stagecoach journey from New York to Princeton, New Jersey, was little more exciting. When Scott arrived in Princeton, the College of New Jersey was in a desperate financial and educational plight: its whole organization was undergoing a revamping, its faculty was exceedingly small, its library suffered for lack of books, and the student enrollment was at a minimum. Nevertheless, Nassau Hall was attractive as were the grounds. He gained a sense of the Revolutionary War past of the town and campus when Washington's frayed army was on the move.

The journey from Princeton to Philadelphia offered more excitement than that from West Point to Princeton. At first, Scott was traveling over the unfinished canal system which in time was to connect the Hudson River with Delaware Bay and the Atlantic Ocean. The method of operating the slender canal boats piqued the interest of the mechanically minded Scott. The accident he described created a bit of comedy which caused passengers to ignore the niceties of social decorum aboard the vessels. Near the termination of the canal-river journey, back from the Delaware River, Scott viewed the home of Joseph Bonaparte, or Count de Survilliers, former king of Spain. Nearby the Kentuckian also saw the home of the famous actor Thomas Abthorpe Cooper.

Scott arrived in Philadelphia on December 11, and spent eight days in the city, departing it on the morning of the nineteenth. He found the city an exciting place, and almost frantically set out to visit every institution, public and private. His description of the new Eastern Penitentiary is as precise as that contained in the visiting British delegation's report to Parliament. Scott visited schools, the United States Mint, Peale's Museum, and attended several theatrical performances in the famous Philadelphia playhouses. One senses in this part of his travel diary an almost insatiate desire to learn what went on in one of early nineteenth-century America's oldest and most important cities. As in other cases the reader is given a near-photographic description of institutions and their procedures, but, with the exception of the schoolchildren, human faces come less clearly into focus. Though lacking the quality of sophistication and maturity of overall institutional observation of James Silk Buckingham, Thomas Hamilton, and Basil Hall, Scott's descriptions are nevertheless more intimate and human. On the way from Philadelphia to Baltimore, Scott met the James Brown family, who were returning to Louisiana from Paris, France, where Brown had served as John Quincy Adams' minister plenipotentiary. At that time Mrs. Brown was suffering from an incurable cancer.

Baltimore proved almost as exciting to the young Kentuckian as Philadelphia. If he had willfully chosen to arrive in that city in one of its most dramatic historical moments, he could not have done better. He saw Charles Carroll of Carrollton riding away in the first car to run over the short link of completed track of the Baltimore and Ohio Railroad. Scott was able to secure a seat on the second car and to experience the thrill of dashing over the rails behind a galloping horse. He was intrigued by the mechanics of the railroad and described the great fill and bridge over the Gwynne Falls. The Carrollton Viaduct then — and now — represented a masterpiece of American engineering.

Scott examined and sketched the mechanisms of the Winan's Car, which was to introduce to American railroading a departure from the ancient carriage tradition. Back in the city of Baltimore he visited the

Washington and Battle monuments, Peale's Museum, a glass factory, the Maryland Penitentiary, the Medical College, and an iron foundry, all in three days' time.

Scott arrived in Washington on the evening of December 22, and set out immediately to find his Georgetown family friend, Colonel Richard Mentor Johnson, then a member of the House of Representatives. He remained in the national capital a month and ten days. This was the end of the first year of the Jackson administration, and social and political affairs were on the eve of rather complicated entanglements. Armed with a formidable packet of introductory letters, the young visitor set out to see the sights, to visit with the great men, and to enjoy the pleasures of Washington society. Being thoroughly social he made the round of the embassies, leaving his calling card as an indication that he wished to be invited to receptions and other public functions.

None of the receptions and levees in Jacksonian Washington, however, equaled those held at the White House to celebrate the new year and the anniversary of the Battle of New Orleans. These were brawling social mixers and equalizers which gathered in the socially prominent, the climbers, the curious, the seekers after political favors, the "unwashed," and the thirsty. They were largely shoving matches by unruly milling throngs that moved like a great and ponderous body from one room to another. Punch bowls and confectionary tables drew the mob of hungry and thirsty constituents more interested in their offerings than the prospects of shaking Old Hickory's hand. Scott had never seen anything like this in simple, democratic Frankfort, where governors held plain, back-slapping, hand-shaking public receptions and invited a favored few to private dinners and parties. Fortunately for the record there were other visitors who also recorded in journals their impressions of the open levees of this era.

Scott arrived on the Jacksonian scene in a magic moment, 1829-30, when stirring events either were occurring or were about to occur. The Jacksonians had been in office long enough to create factions among themselves, to be torn apart by social jealousies, to engage in capital politics, and to feel the impact of stirring national issues. There was little surface evidence of the rising social storm among the crowds that swarmed into the White House to jostle diplomats, judges, congressmen, high-ranking military officers, and the wives of officialdom. Scott was well acquainted with William T. Barry from both Lexington and Frankfort associations. From him he obtained entrée to the most important homes in the city. With little or no show of partisanship he visited with all factions and viewed the mores of Washington through the dual lenses of humor and criticism. He gave attention to the most minute details of dress and beauty (or lack of it), social graces, and general decorum, nearly always contrasting the social affairs in Washington with those back on the banks of the Kentucky. His good Baptist eye viewed social departures and innovations with a strong vein of puritanism.

Scott noted the details of dress, and any awkwardness of form, among the crowds that thronged into the White House and the embassies. He was quick to spot any lapses in personal appearances and the lack of what he considered social discipline. He seems, however, not to have sensed the impending social rift among the people close to the president over the O'Neale-Eaton affair, nor the ground swell of political rivalries and conflicts between the administration and the Supreme Court.

There was plenty of excitement in other parts of the Washington scene. The arrival of Sam Houston, accompanied by a delegation of Cherokees to protest the manner in which annuity payments were made to the Indians, set tongues a-wagging. Dressed in tribal garb, baubles and all, Houston added further sensation to his erratic career. Houston's dramatic visit, however, was tepid when compared with the furor stirred up over the Foote Resolution appended to the Public Land Bill then before Congress. The emotionally charged issue was a clarion call to battle. At the historic debate which ensued, Robert W. Scott was present to hear Daniel Webster and Robert Y. Hayne in their momentous confrontation over the Foote Resolution. He conveyed in his journal entry a sense of appreciating the significance of the debates. His precise physical descriptions of the famous orators are among the best first-hand observations on paper. To Scott, Washington, like Richmond during the Virginia Constitutional Convention, was a veritable gallery of personalities who challenged him to record their features and personal characteristics with photographic precision. He seems to have been driven to record for posterity as accurately as possible the appearances of the politicians then in office. He portrayed them in much the same manner as he in future years would describe his purebred farm animals. Every detail from drooping eyelashes to balding spots was described in human dimensions. One feels after reading his descriptions that he has come virtually face-to-face with Daniel Webster, John C. Calhoun, John Quincy Adams, Andrew Jackson, and Thomas Hart Benton. They literally stand forth on the pages of the Scott journal.

Scott does not describe the procedures he used in recording such precise details of individual appearances, but he hinted that he took notes and then rushed back to his room to organize his impressions into formal pen-and-ink narrative portraits. In some cases he gives the impression of having made a standard list of personal features which he checked while making notes. Whatever the technique, the gallery of faces, including character notations, gesticulations, and stature, constitutes the next best thing to a solid chapter in biography. Even Anne Royall, the "unconscionable scold," appears on Scott's pages in far gentler light than that which she turned on public personalities in her own acerbic descriptions.

Especially fascinating was Scott's visit with John Quincy Adams and the topics of their conversation. Adams was interested in the fact that President Jackson had asked Congress to dispose of a presidential gift. He also referred to the Russian succession in a somewhat nostalgic tone. At that moment the ex-president was already making plans to reenter politics. Too, he was nearby, so he could keep a critical eye on the Jacksonians, one more critical than he was willing to confide in his young visitor.

The sights and places of interest in Washington were numerous. Scott was physically equal to the task of walking miles during the day and of attending receptions by night. The Patent Office, the Potomac Canal, the Library of Congress, the Navy Yard, the Supreme Court, all beckoned. In the somewhat musty and disorganized Patent Office, Scott was able to savor an exhibit of both American mechanical ingenuity and whimsicalities in the search for ways and means of lightening man's daily tasks.

It is difficult to ascertain the precise case which was being argued before the United States Supreme Court on the day of Scott's visitation. But from the assembly of counsel he indicated was present, it seems likely that it was the famous case *United States* v. *Missouri*. Yet the presence of William Wirt would also seem to indicate it was one of the complicated *Cherokees* v. *Georgia* cases. Certainly Scott was not privileged to hear the court publish a significant decision. Hum-drum decisions characterized the renderings of the court during the year of the Kentuckian's visit.

By the coincidence of the times, Scott was most fortunate to be in Washington when three major controversies were approaching the point of explosion. He seems either not to have heard any gossip about the Eaton-O'Neale social commotion or to have been unwilling to repeat it. Obviously his good friends the Barrys were highly conscious of this impending social blow-up. Without question he was thoroughly cognizant of the sectional issue involved in the Foote Resolution and the resulting Webster-Hayne Debate. He gave close attention to the appearances of the three principals in the debates. Likewise he gave close attention to the seating arrangements of the justices of the Supreme Court, without indicating that he sensed the conflict between President Jackson and Chief Justice John Marshall. He gave no evidence of knowing about the political turmoil and emotions revolving around the appointments of Justices John McLean and Smith Thomson.

Even though Scott failed to sense the undercurrents and political stresses and strains of Jacksonian Washington, he did better than several more sophisticated foreign visitors in this era. His descriptions of the kaleidoscopic social scene are informative. In many respects they are more adequate than those of the famous Ben Perley Poore. Too, he was accurate in his descriptions and use of facts. This is true of the entire journal.

Turning homeward, January 31, 1830, Robert Scott retraced much of his route back to Baltimore, and then to Philadelphia. He spent a day and a half in Baltimore visiting buildings and places which he missed when he was there in late December. He departed that city on the afternoon of February 2 by stagecoach and traveled eighteen hours by way of Elkton, Maryland, Wilmington, Delaware, and Darby, Pennsylvania. He saw by the way sites of some of the famous grain mills along the Brandywine which had figured so prominently in supplying breadstuffs in the American Revolution.

Back in Philadelphia Scott returned to Mrs. Catherine Yohe's "sheepish" boarding house, and from there set out to complete his visit to the city. This time he went to the Navy Yard, where he saw several vessels under construction. The queen of the lot was the much-heralded 140-gun *Pennsylvania*. This ship was to become the pride of the American navy. Historically it was to become more of a noble exhibit of American materials and workmanship than a practical fighting vessel. An astonishing amount and variety of woods were used in its construction, and the man-hours of labor were almost beyond calculation. Scott's second visit to Philadelphia was of short duration; aside from the visit to the Navy Yard he attended a night lecture given by Federal District Judge Hopkinson on the principles of the law.

In dead of winter the stagecoach journey from Philadelphia to Pittsburgh over the old Forbes Road was drab, this despite the fact that the route passed through the rich German or Pennsylvania Dutch farming country about Lancaster. Scott was aware that this was fertile farming country and that he also traveled through areas served by the growing network of Pennsylvania canals. In time these inland waterways would form a somewhat tenuous connection between the Ohio River and the Delaware Bay.

At Harrisburg the stage crossed the Susquehanna on the extraordinary covered bridge over the river. The slatting on this bridge admitted enough light to give the tunnel a bizarre appearance, a fact which at a future date was to intrigue Charles Dickens. Beyond Harrisburg at Carlisle, Scott took time from his travel to visit the starveling little Dickinson College and to call on an equally straitened chapter of the Union Philosophical Literary Society. His journal seems to indicate he visited the Society more as an inspector than as a passing brother.

Beyond Carlisle the country became mountainous and the towns were less attractive. From inside a stagecoach, a traveler could see little to captivate him. However, at McConnelsburg an object of interest appeared on the scene in a sixteen-year-old college girl who was returning to her home. Scott was attracted to this lass, whom he discovered to be both cultivated and intelligent. She was a true daughter of the hills who "had a heart to love & a taste to admire their beauty and grandeur." This young lady was the last thing of beauty and seduction Scott was to see on his journey home. Pittsburgh could be sensed a-far off by the pall of coal smoke which hovered over it. When Scott entered that city he fell into a bad humor, and he left it pretty much in the same frame of mind.

Nevertheless, the young traveler did sense the rising industrial importance of this famous western river city. He visited the waterworks, the Western Pennsylvania Penitentiary, and the glass factories. He saw iron rolling mills in operation, a paper mill, and a damask factory. One of the wonders of the city was the Allegheny Canal Aqueduct which passed canal traffic over the river and directly into the city.

Scott viewed Pittsburgh as a dreary, soot-stained, emerging industrial town whose streets were filthy and its humanity of a coarse and unattractive appearance. He wrote, "In truth during the two days and a half I have not seen one genteel & lady looking woman, in the city, but I have seen more slatterns than I could have imagined." These women, however, appeared to be prolific from the numbers of children on the streets.

In mid-February the Ohio River was iced over, and steamboats could not move in or out of Pittsburgh. Scott took a stagecoach to Steubenville, Ohio. Down river was Wheeling, West Virginia, the western main town on the National Road and a smaller carbon copy of industrial Pittsburgh. Farther down Marietta, of Ohio Associates fame, was a town buried behind a muddy front and difficult of access for the traveler on foot. Gallipolis with its spacious public square appeared to be a more attractive place. As the *LaGrange* plowed its way down the Ohio, the ice began to disappear, and in almost record time the vessel swept past Cincinnati and reached Louisville. Apparently Scott arrived on February 20, though he neglected to make specific note of the date. He seemed not to have deemed anything in Kentucky worthy of mention; he made only the briefest notes of his outward journey and none of his return.

When Robert Scott died in 1884, after a long and successful career as a farmer, stock-breeder, and concerned citizen, the personal part of his estate was distributed among his heirs. This included correspondence, library, and farm records. Mrs. S. I. M. Major of Frankfort and Mrs. Willis Green of the Falls of Rough came into possession of much of this material, and Dr. Preston Brown of Louisville probably also received books and papers. Mrs. Major's papers and those of her famous editor-husband were inherited by their son Commander S. I. M. Major of Versailles. This extensive collection contains a number of Scott letters and originally held the two-volume journal. These passed from Mrs. Major's estate to James and Mrs. Harley Ferguson of Richmond, Kentucky. After being unable to find a purchaser in Kentucky, James Ferguson sold the journal to the Yale University Library in the late 1960s. He turned the correspondence over to the John Wilson Townsend Library of Eastern Kentucky University. In July 1980, the Special Collections Department of the Margaret I. King Library, University of Kentucky, purchased the journal from Yale; in October 1980, it arrived back in Kentucky.

I first saw the Scott journal early in 1960 when Mrs. Major asked me to come to Versailles to deliver some books and manuscripts to the Margaret I. King Library for possible sale. She gave me permission to have the journal duplicated and reserved for me the privilege of editing and publishing it. I was unaware that the University of Kentucky had not obtained the journal until I was well along with editing it. I now have special permission for a third time to publish it in the present form, permission having come first from the Yale University Library and more recently from the Special Collections Department of the Margaret I. King Library of the University of Kentucky.

It is a remarkable fact that Robert W. Scott's perceptive journal has existed so many years untouched, and that the Scott-Major papers have survived so many divisions and exchanges. The Kentuckiana Collection at Western Kentucky University has acquired the Willis Green papers, and the John Wilson Townsend Collection of Eastern Kentucky University has acquired the Major papers. Mrs. Harley Ferguson of Richmond is in possession of some of the genealogical records of the Scott-Major families, and the Kentucky Historical Society has acquired the collection of photographs.

In editing this journal I have exercised care to present it as nearly as physically possible in its original form. Scott wrote a fairly clear and bold hand, although he exhibited some eccentricities in expression and when forming certain letters; there are abundant inconsistencies in spelling. Nevertheless, his style is clear, concise, and descriptive. It is at once discernible that the journal was recorded in running narrative form, which indicates the author brought it up-to-date periodically, often using the past tense. Scott was consistent in his extravagant use of punctuation marks, especially the semicolon. In places he may have intended his marks to be colons, but it is almost impossible to determine this fact. Too, there are places where it is difficult to distinguish periods from commas.

It seems clear from the outset that Scott traveled alone, yet on the journey from Philadelphia home he speaks of a companion named Brown. This may have been no more than a casual acquaintance whom he met aboard the stagecoach, or it may have been one of the Browns of Frankfort who joined him along the way.

The route which Robert W. Scott traveled was generally a part of the northern section of the American "Grand Tour." Contemporary maps indicated the roads and water passages. Somewhere along the way Scott bought Joseph Worcester's *Atlas* and *Gazetteer*. It is difficult, however, to imagine his lugging these voluminous guides around with him. The

Gazetteer contained considerable statistical detail about all the places which the youthful traveler saw, but not all the information which he recorded from first-hand viewing came from a published source. There were reasonably satisfactory guides to Philadelphia, Baltimore, and Washington, and it seems clear Scott used them.

As full and perceptive as this journal is, its author left unanswered some intriguing questions. When the steamer *LaGrange* backed away from its landing at Wheeling, Scott ostensibly was through writing in his journal. He landed at Louisville but there is no indication as to the time or the date. Did someone meet him or did he board a stagecoach or a steamboat for Frankfort? An examination of the list of books which he purchased along the way, aside from the Worcester *Atlas* and *Gazetteer*, reveals some of his other sources of information. Two are especially interesting, Basil Hall's three-volume *Travels in North America in the Years 1827 and 1828* and the *Guide to Washington*. Scott no doubt grew more contemplative on his way home as he pored over the contents of his twenty-two-cent investment in a booklet which described marriage ceremonies.

Faithful to Elizabeth Brown's admonition, he "took good care of his heart." The bold society ladies of Washington who floated about ballroom floors baring their "thick" ankles, clad in new-fad bloomers, and otherwise flouting the staid Kentucky social code had not alienated his affections. Before him in Frankfort, upon his return, were the challenges of establishing a law practice, getting married, and rendering heroic services to the sick and dying during the devastating cholera epidemic of 1833.

The law made only tentative claim on the imaginative and industrious youth. At heart Scott was wedded to the land. Soon after his marriage he purchased the Locust Hill Farm of Benjamin Hardin. It was located five miles east of Frankfort on the Versailles Pike, in the best farming area of Franklin County. There he built the palatial Greek Revival-style house Locust Hill, now known as Scotland. There he settled down to raise a family and to become one of Kentucky's most progressive farmers and livestock breeders. In time his cattle (cross breeds of Durham and Kentucky shorthorns), sheep, cashmere goats, and cross-bred hogs became nationally famous. Over the years Scott developed a premium market for his livestock.

In 1835, now married and a landowner, Scott traveled south by steamboat, evidently with the intention of purchasing a cotton plantation in the newly opening lands in the delta region of Washington County, Mississippi. This was the period when many Kentucky slaveholders bought plantations and transferred their surplus labor from hemp and tobacco fields to the cotton lands of the Lower South. Almost as a continuation of his 1829/30 journal, Scott described the down-river scenes, conversations aboard the steamboat, the land, and entertainment along the way. The Daniel Boone story which the aged John Brown told him may or may not have been true. There was a historical lapse of a year or two in the life of Daniel Boone which apparently failed to clear up in his autobiography published by John Filson. The Duval story of the Spanish remains can be documented rather fully as Scott described them from hearing the governor's account.

Scott, just beginning his long career as a successful bluegrass farmer, can be forgiven his erroneous observation that his host-relative Worthington in Mississippi was feeding his hogs cottonseed. These are deadly to hogs because the linters on the seed clog a hog's respiratory system. The editor of this journal was reared on the strict Mississippi admonition, "Keep the hogs away from the cottonseed!"

The New Orleans interlude was fascinating and in rather sharp contrast to what Scott had observed in the eastern part of the country five years before. Nevertheless, the Kentuckian had the rare opportunity to take lodging in the famous Bishop House, which catered only to male guests. The room charge of $2.50 a day including "found" appealed to his thrifty nature, but he was irked by the demand of a fifty-cent tip for uncorking a bottle. His hurt feelings, however, were assuaged by his delight at seeing George "Yankee" Hill give his world-famous impersonation of a "Yankee in Spain" in the fabulously ornate Caldwell's Theater.

Scott returned home without having bought a cotton plantation in the opening Mississippi delta country. He hinted at the reason in his second journal, but one can well imagine the contrast which presented itself between his bluegrass lands and the swampy flat lands of the Delta. One was thoroughly adapted to the raising of livestock, the other to the production of a staple field crop of which the author had no personal knowledge. He bought instead on October 11, 1838, two small tracts of land adjoining his property.

Robert Wilmot Scott was an intelligent, creative man. Throughout his life he exhibited a curiosity about persons and things. He was a closely observant man, fully dedicated to the causes which he espoused. He made almost innumerable contributions in the fields of agriculture, livestock breeding, journalism, and public education. Almost every contemporary regional agricultural journal contained scores of articles and reports on a wide range of subjects written by the Master of Locust Hill. None of his contributions, however, was more historically significant than his descriptions of what he saw in Jacksonian America. At that time the Jacksonians were hurtling headlong into an era of change in every field of national endeavor. One senses in the journal an appreciation of the phenomenal mechanical and scientific changes which were coming over the nation. There is also a sense of the burgeoning new culture which was to make radical departures from the past in many areas of human relationships.

There may be no other first-hand source which presents so precise a view by an ordinary citizen of national personalities and scenes in this fermentative era. Because of his intimate Frankfort associations, and his subsequent law partnership with Judge James Haggin, it is evident that Scott was a Jacksonian partisan. Judge Haggin had served on the New Court during its brief existence from 1825 to 1829, when the regularly constituted Kentucky Court of Appeals decided the New Court was without legal status or jurisdiction and that its decisions were null and void. In his comments on the nation's capital, Scott never once mentioned Henry Clay. It is true that Clay was not in the city at the time, having left the office of secretary of state and returned to Kentucky and his Ashland farm to recoup his political and economic fortunes.

Fortunately there were several travelers abroad in 1829-30 who published extensive journals and who viewed many of the same things Scott saw. His observations compare most favorably with those of Tyrone Power, James Silk Buckingham, Thomas Hamilton, Basil Hall, and even Frances Trollope. His youthful and inquiring mind led him deeper into many areas and subjects than was true of the accounts of more experienced travelers. This journal of an eager American gives fresh and youthful dimensions to the fairly good volume of contemporary sources relating to an expanding America at a time when fundamental political and judicial issues were thrusting the nation headlong into major political and sectional conflicts. Scott saw the principal actors of the times and has left graphic descriptions of them on the stage, in legislative and judicial halls, and in quieter private moments in their homes.

Memoranda Itineris
September 17, 1829 to February 19, 1830;
January 1 to 28, 1836

LEFT FRANKFORT on Thursday the 17th of Sept. 1829 with $200. a horse, clothes &c.

Received various good words of advice among which are the following; the first from my Father. "Act well my son and all will be well with you." The next from a single lady and a particular friend. "Take good care of your heart." The next from my old grandfather "Be as wise as a serpent & as harmless as a dove."[1]

Passed through Lexington, Paris & Cynthianna arrived at the Lower Blue Licks on the evening of the 21st of Sept. Saw the ground where the Battle of the Blue Licks, was fought about the year 17[82] between about 100 whites, commanded by Col Todd, with Daniel Boon in company, and about 500 Indians; the whites were decoyed between two parties of the enemy and defeated with much slaughter; Col. Todd being among the slain.[2]

Passed through Vanceburg on to Greenupsburg,[3] the county seat of Greenup County which is verry broken, the hills abounding in iron ore in inexhaustible quantities. In the county there are seven furnaces and six forges for the manufacture of castings and bar iron. The principal building of a Furnace is a hollow stone tower about 80 feet in height, 15 or 20 feet square at the bottom tapering to the top. The ore when pulverized is thrown into the top together with charcoal and some limestone so that the tower is full from top to bottom. The fire is kindled by means of a wind pipe applied at the bottom, the wind to blow the fire is made by water power on an enjine of about 30 horse power. When the ore is melted it collects in a bason at the bottom of the tower, where it is separated from the dross (which has the appearance of glass,) and is then either dipped from the bason with ladles and poured into the moulds for making castings, or it is suffered to run out into ridges made in the sand, and there cooled and called pig iron. If it is designed to make bar iron, the pigs are again melted, purified & moulded; then heated in a coal fire blowed by a bellows, then placed under a cast iron hammer weighing about 700 pounds & there drawn into any shape. The hammer & bellows may be driven by either steam or water power. The hammer is raised by a wheel, the cogs of which strike under the handle near the hammer and having raised the hammer up it is thrown down by means of a spring with great force & celerity. Two fires are requisite to supply one hammer with hot iron & when in complete operation will draw about nine tons of bar iron in a week; which is exported from Greenupburg to various towns on the Ohio River. The furnaces work day and night on all days, sundays & Mondays, & employ about 40 men each.[4]

Travelled up the Ohio, reached the boundary line (big Sandy river) on the night of the eighth day. Passed through Geyandalt [Guyandott] and Barbourville in [Cabell] County;[5] passed through Charlestown on the Great Kenhawa about 50 miles from its mouth,[6] a few miles above which on the same river are the numerous salt works. There are about sixty furnaces at the Kenhawa Salt Works. The water is obtained at the depth of about 400 feet, is pumped by horse power, boiled in long rows of 15 or 20 gallon kettles heated by fires made of stone coal dug from the adjoining mountains. Each salt work makes about 10,000 bushels of salt annually, it is principally bought up by a company of Merchants of Kentucky, who give 25 cents a bushel for it at the works, and export it to various towns by means of flat boats. The expense of establishing a Salt work is about 3,000 dollars. They are profitable.[7] The Kenhawa River is navigable for small steam boats several months in the year as high up as the Great falls; where the river is one third of a mile wide & is suddenly pricipitated about 25 or 30 feet over a sand stone extending irregularly & diagonally across the river making the falls a half mile long. There is a griss or saw mill on either side; also a house for building flat boats which are launched into the beautiful bason beneath; it is about 60 feet deap & is formed by the water falling over the rocks.[8]

Paid 18 cts. tole at Gauley Bridge, which is a handsome flat wooden structure supported by six stone pillars. Ascended Gauley mountains, ascent two miles long, perpendicular hight between 800 & 1,000 feet. Travelled on a turnpike made by throwing up the earth on each side & graduating it: paid 12½ tole.[9]

Detained a day and a half on Gauley Mountain at old Mr. Kinslys by rain; lived excellently on fried venison &c. Reached Lewisburg the county seat of Greenbriar. Was visited by the President Mr. _____ of the Lewisburg Temperance Society; which was established in Jan 1828, has about 80, members, principally not professors of Religion, some young men; no ladies; some members have been expelled; total abstinence is enjoined; auxiliaries are about to be established in other parts of the county; the society has been much opposed, not patronized by the preachers of the place.[10]

Visited the White Sulpher Springs, kept by M. Caldwell accomodation good, much frequented, two springs of strong sulpher water without salt under saloons. Situation of the place delightful & romantic, a small valley surmounded by mountains covered with oak, pine & other ever-greens.[11]

Saw the Falling Spring, where a small stream dashes over an irregular sirface of 80 yards, falls in some places perpendicularly about 200 feet, the water when falling resembles snow, the stream below abounds with petrifactions of various vegetables, obtained some of moss &c, the stream rushes with much irregularity & rapidity over other & less falls & among craggy rocks covered with a crust of petrifaction, scenery wild & roman-tic, place difficult of access and but little visited, though a tasteful com-bination of picturesque sublime & beautiful.[12]

Visited the Hot Springs,[13] kept by Mr. Boggs improvements inferiour, accomodation but common situation not remarkably fine, high moun-tain on the east, valley & distant mountains on the west. three or four springs of diferent temperatures, three bath houses, used by both sexes at different hours, took a warm bath, remarkably pleasant but enervating soon after, the pools of various sizes about 5 feet deep &c, paid an enor-mous bill to a mean landlord and departed for the Warm Spring, had a pleasant change, good accomodation &c, two large streams of warm water rising in a low & marshy meadow in a valley. Warm spring mountain immediately on the East, others all around, verry cold water running spon-taneously from a hydron within ten feet of the warm spring, several large & commodious bath houses, grounds not handsomely improved, build-ings not conveniently & tastefully situated, place not as much visited as formerly. About sun rise ascended Warm Spring Mountain elevation con-siderable, covered with shrubs & trees, in the East the prospect is truly grand & sublime the verdant mountains stretching to invisible extent & endless variety above & around each other, like the seats of some vast amphitheatre, every scene of which proclaims the majesty & power of him who curtained the mountains with sublimity & spread the valleys with beauty.[14]

Passed by & examined, the Blowing Cave: a great phenomenon but a curiosity of little interest, consisting of three apertures about the size of a large barrel in the south eastern side of a small mountain, the air passing in at some & out at others the current varying, but the strongest in warm weather, the cave small rough & dry inside; used to preserve fresh meets in the summer season, access much confined; external appear-ance not attractive nor curious.[15]

Visited the Natural Bridge in Rock Bridge County, on sunday the 17th day of my journey & the 4 of October. The spectacle was grand by descrip-tion, the arch over Cedar creek of hard & solid limestone, length about 90 feet, a stone is 7 seconds in falling from the top to the water below, height about 150 feet, breath 80, thickness 40 feet[;] could not throw a stone from the bottom to the ceiling of the arch, rocks and trees in all parts marked with names. I ascended the almost pricipitous rocks about 20 feet, stood where Washington stood when he marked the initials of his name, saw the letters, remarked them, then marked the initials of my own about 12 inches under them, descended in safety.[16]

Pine, Cedar, Oak & the Arbor Vitae grow spantaneously on and around the Bridge. Revisited Lexington small town of most beautiful situation, surrounded on all sides by distant and verdant mountains, abounding in high and commanding situations, having an arsenal with 30,000 stand of arms, & being the seat of Washington College now fallen, having three large & handsome brick buildings, the principall with white columns in front, all three buildings well situated on the hill to the North West of the town.[17] The inhabitants chiefly Presbyterian having a Temperance Society which has doubtless diminished the manufacture & consumption of ardent spirit in the whole county, similar Societies exist in almost all the churches in the neighborhood.[18] Passed on to Staunton, which contains an hospital established by the State for lunatics, it is a most beautiful edefice of brick; having a principal & wings on an elevated situation, and containing about 30 invalids. When visited Weyer's Cave near Madison's Cave, both of which are in Cave hill, two miles distant from Port Republick; the last is not now visited, the first is about half a mile in length, with many rooms of various sizes. The chrystalization of limestone water has ceiled the whole interiour of the cave, and formed in many instances curious imitations of natural objects, which are designated by their appropriate names, such as the "Rising Moon, Washington's Monument" &c. The falling of the water from the roof has variegated the floor with immense quantities of spar of various colours and sizes from that of the "Sewing needles" which are stuck in "lady Washington's bedcurtains," to the size of Pompey's Pillar & the "Pyramids of Egypt." "The Ball Room" is spacious and elegant, in this the beaus & belle in the vicinity sometimes assemble & dance, on which occasions the whole cave is splendidly illuminated by thousands of candles.[19] Visited Charlottesville, seat of the Virginia University, having a most splendid suit of brick buildings, the designing and erection of which were superinted by the Honourable Thos. Jefferson, they are situated on an eminence about a mile from town, the principal building being a Rotunda, three stories high, having on each side of it two rows of two story brick buildings running parallel to each other about two hundred yards in the rear. The Rotunda contains the Lecture Rooms and a splendid room with a circular gallery illuminated from all sides and from above; this room contains a fine library of 7000 volumes and a small Museum chiefly lithotick. The two exteriour rows contain 6 hotels; (three each) for boarding the students, & the rooms for the students; the two interiour rows, contain the dwellings of the professors & rooms for the students. The buildings are calculated to accomodate 200 students, at present the number is 120 including the students of Law & Medicine. There are 6 professors, but no President. The course of study thorough & extensive. Degrees are confered by each department, upon application & rigid examination, notwithstanding the number of graduates is few in proportion to the number of students. The salary of the professors is 1500 dollars each.[20]

Arrived at Richmond the seat of Government of Va, on saturday the 10th day of Oct 1829 the 23 days after leaving Frankfort, having rode 595 miles, & spent $32.75 leaving me in possession of $167.75 & my horse &c.[21]

Boarding at Hallam's Eagle Hotel[22] price $8.00 a week Convention in session Hon. Jas Monroe President, it consists of 96 members assembled to amend the constitution of the State.[23] After the election of its officers &c it proceeded to resolve itself into several committees. Mr Madison was appointed Chairman of the Legislative Com. to which was refered that part of the existing Con. which relates to the Legislative department of the government. Chief Justice Marshall was appointed chairman of the Judiciary Com. to which was refered so much of the existing Con. as relates to the Judiciary. Govenor. Wm. B. Giles was appointed Chairman of so much of the existing Constitution as relates to the Executive, & was appointed Chairman of the Residuary Com. to which was refered the Bill of rights & all other parts not refered to the other committees. They met daily in the Captol, consulted in conversational style & on the 24 of Oct the Legis. Com. which was the last, made its report, the others having reported previously.[24]

Subsequently visited Messrs Kerr, Forbes, Green, & the Hon. Mr. [John] Taliaffiro, & the Hon Mr P. P. Barbour of Orange county, Member of the Convention & of Congress, now about 48 years old, rather below the common statue & spare, has light hair, a high & full forehead, eyebrows heavy and projecting, cheek bones prominent, mouth small, lips thin & inverted, chin sharp & prominent, voice strong, shrill & disagreeable, manners easy and becoming, conversation appropriate & agreeable, some what inclined to a display of literary knowledge.[25]

Oct. 26, 10 o'clock A.M. visited the Hon. Jas. Madison a member of the convention, residing with his family with the Hon A. R. Stevenson.[26] As I approached the house I saw Mrs Madison upstairs standing before a mirror adjusting her cap and hair: rung the bell, was invited to the drawing room, 'asked for Mr M. sat a few moments, when Mrs Madison entered & politely apollogised for Mr M.'s delay said he was writing, but would soon finish & come down, she alluded to my name, seeming to know me, I told her who I was & what my object, she then commenced a familiar & agreeable conversation on common place topics & after a few moments retired. She is a fine looking old lady, carrying her age remarkably well, having a fair skin & pleasant countenance; her person large much exceeding the common size; her dress was rich tasteful & comely, but evincing more care & regard to fashion than is common with ladies of her age.[27] Mr Madison soon entered, I addressed him politely & delivered him my letters, he seated himself in a large cushioned arm chair, read them & expressed a pleasure on being acquainted, he inquired for Rev. Bryce & Col. Johnson,[28] the authors of the letters & then of my family & ancestors, with whom he said he was well & intimately acquainted; conversed easily & agreeably on various subjects; his enunciation was clear & distinct though his voice was coarse & seemed to be much improved, his manners were easy & dignified & he was polite to condescention, having proffered his attention and kind offices I retired.

The Hon. James Madison,

is in the 85 year of his age,[29] in tolerably good health thin of flesh, rather under the common size, wears a black broad brimmed hat, black broad cloth dress coat, with pockets under the flaps behind, black cloth vest & black cloth pantaloons extending only to the knees, with long black stockings, knee buckles and shoes; a white cravat & ruffled shirt with the collar under his cravat; his form erect, his step firm but somewhat slow, walks without a staff, his visage pale, & abounding in small rinkles, his features well proportioned but not striking, his head bald on the top, but excessively powdered, showing a point in front & circular recesses at the sides of the forehead, his hair behind also much powdered & tied in a que which is worm under his coat collar; his forehead of common size, his brow grey, heavy, & projecting, his eyes small & faded, his nose of ordinary size, & straight, his mouth rather small, his lips well proportioned his ears obscured by his whiskers & hair, his sight & hearing both somewhat impaired.[30]

Visited the Hon Chapman Johnson,[31] an eminent lawyer & member of the Convention, of large & well proportioned person, about 50 years of age, his hair entire, but grey, his countenance dark & pale; his forehead of common size his nose a little aquiline, his eye faded his mouth small, his lips thin & inverted his chin sharp & prominent, wears short whiskers, genteel in his dress, agreeable in his manners & conversation though he seems to be somewhat affected.

Visited The Hon John Marshall,[32] now a member of the Convention, Chief Justice of the U.St. resident of Richmond, in the 74th year of his age about 6 feet two inches high, remarkably straight, rather spare & slender, remarkably active and fond of walking in a firm and brisk gait; wears a black broad brim hat, dress coat of black cloth with pockets under the flaps behind, black cloth vest & short black cloth pantaloons, with long grey yarn stockings, knee buckles and shoes, plain shirt, with the collar worn under his white cravat, which is tied before; his hair is entire, equally mixed of black & grey, wears it combed down before & trimmed short around his forehead, long behind, plaited and tied in a que with a black ribband, wears a pair of short whiskers & has a thick black beard, his complexion dark, his face full, round & much rinkled, his countenance mild, pleasant & intelligent, forehead full, eyebrows greyish, heavy & projecting, his eye dark, (but little faded) & sprightly, nose a little turned up at the end, mouth & chin of ordinary size & appearance, his whole appearance venerable & imposing, his motions easy & graceful, in his manners polite affable and agreeable, his voice low, coarse & feeble.

Hon. James Monroe,[33] now a member of the Convention & citizen of Loudon county, in the 73 year of his age, health rather delicate, about 5 feet 8 inches high & well proportioned, his dress neat & genteel consisting of a black cloth dress coat with pockets under the flaps behind, black cloth vest & short black cloth pantaloons & long black stockings, plain shirt, collar concealed under his white cravat, which is tied behind; a broad brimmed black hat & shoes, his hair is somewhat grey & thin on the crown of the head, he wears it combed back, showing large recesses on the sides of his forehead, which is of good size, receding & much rinkled, his eyebrows projecting, eyes faded, sunken & flighty, nose straight & rather large, his mouth & lips of common size & well proportioned, his chin dimpled, he walks without a staff, his step being somewhat feeble & sluggish, his head is inclined a little forward: His conduct & manners evince strong marks of bodily & mental ability and decay, his gestures ungraceful undignified & often improper, stands in the chair with his hands clasped before him & is constantly rubbing his fingers one with another, his voice is coarse & feeble, his enunciation thick & often speaking unintended words.

Hon John Randolph[34] now a member of the Convention, about 58 years of age, in delicate health, spare & of middling stature, his person indifferent & unprepossessing, being a little hump shouldered & having a very short neck, his head considerably inclined forward, wears a common black hat, a complete suit of black cloth, white cotton socks & large coarse shoes resembling over shoes, walks with a plain hickory stick with the bark on it & a knot on the handle end; his hair is entire, a little grey, is parted on the top of the head & combed down the sides, is tolerably short & worn without a cue; his face is rather too small & is unprepossessing, his forehead rather narrow & low somewhat obscured by his hair, his eyebrows thin & smart, his eyes small, dark, sparkling & intelligent, nose straight & of ordinary size, his mouth small, his chin somewhat obscured by his shirt collar & cravat, which is a blue & white fancy handkerchief exactly like his pocket handkerchief; he sometimes wears plain spectacles with black frames; his beard is of a light colour & remarkably thin, his voice clear, shrill & pectoral, his left leg is a little shorter than his right, which causes him to limp & in addition to his short neck & stoop shoulders, renders his mein uneasy & ungraceful; his head is rather flat & his face much shrivelled, wears coarse buck skin gloves, a watch with large gold seals.

Hon. Wm B. Giles[35] now the Governor of Va and a member of the Convention, in delicate health & in the decline of life, about the middle size having a frame once robust & compact, walks with crutches on account of infirmity in his hips & legs, careless of his person & dress, his countenance indicating care & study, being somewhat gloomy & melancholy, his hair is entire, somewhat grey, is worn short carelessly & naturally; his face full & his forehead of good size & receding; his eyebrows grey, heavy & projecting, his eyes dim & faded, his nose straight & large, his mouth & ordinary size having a large rinkle on each side.

Rev Alex. Campbell,[36] a Baptist Minister, now a member of the Va Convention, in the prime of life, having a robust & well formed person his countenance lively, animated, & intelligent, his manners easy, graceful & by no means grave, his features pleasant & expressive, his hair light & somewhat grey, worn naturally & of common length, his forehead of good size a little receding, his eye blue, his nose a little aquiline, his mouth of common size his chin a little dimpled, has a thick light coloured beard, wears short whiskers, his pronunciation imperfect, his dialect not purely English, his voice strong & shrill.

Visited the Richmond Museum in a large stuccoed building in the south east corner of the Capitol square, contains a tolerably large & valuable collection of various curiosities, & also a collection of paintings & statues, the last are made of plaister of Paris in imitation of the Belvidere Apollo, Venus de Medices &c. The whole establishment is owned by a painter & owing to his neglect it presents strong marks of disorder & decay & is but little frequented.[37]

Visited the Virginia Penitentiary situated about a mile west of the Capitol, buildings of brick, outter wall 20 feet high & nearly square in its form, domitories three stories high & in the form of a semicircle the ends terminating in the front side, having an hospital, work shops &c, contains 160 prisoners, the number once exceeded 200, employed in the various mechanic arts; unnecessary intercourse & conversation forbidden; work many in the same shop during the day; confined apart at night; the cells clean & comfortable; convicts somewhat squallid in their appearance; wear caps of various colours, their heads being shaven on the top once a week, the institution is kept by Saml P. Parsons employed by the state at a fixed price $2000. It presents the appearance of business & economy, it involves the state several thousand $ in debt.[38]

Visited the Virginia Armory, situated about half a mile west of the Capitol the bank of the canal buildings of brick, laid out in the form of a hollow square; manufacture of arms now discontinued; saw about 300 iron cannon of various sizes, & six large, long, brass cannon presented by the French government, also two brass mortars & many shells &c.[39]

Eagle Hotel, No. 80 City of Richmond[40] November 2nd 1829, on this day the writer completed his twenty first year; in the morning went to the capitol, where among others, the Hon. Jas. Monroe addressed the convention: visited

The Virginia Library, kept in the second story of the capitol, containing about 4000 volumes of new & valuable books, Law, Political, Historical &c Miscellaneous and cost about $9000 paid from the State treasury and revenue. The library has been collected within the last eighteen months, is kept in good order & neatness.[41] Previously had visited the Theatre, &c Monumental Church which last is owned by the Episcopaleans & is so called because it is built on the scite of the former Theatre which was burnt in & in its front is a white marble monument surmounted by a funeral urns, erected in memory of the persons who were burnt in the Theatre. The monument is about 7 feet high & covered by the portico of the church.[42]

The Capitol contains a white marble monument & full size statue of Washington & a marble bust of Lafayette executed in Italy & also a full length portrait of Mr Jefferson. The court house contains a full length portrait of Washington & a similar one of Lafayette, suspended, one on each side & over the seat of the Judge.

Visited Ford's paintings & also those of Harding, saw the portraits Madison, Marshall, Judge Washington, Judge Trimble, Peter Francisco, Daniel Boon & the present Duke of Sussex &c.[43] Attended a meeting of the Richmond Temperance Society which has about 80 members all males, been established since January 1828. David P. Burr is the President.[44] Left Richmond on the morning of the 8th of November, having been three weeks; having seen its interesting objects, learned the manners & customs of the people, became acquainted with some of the best families & heard some of the greatest men speak in the Convention, from which I learned some of the politics of the State. Expenses about $100.

Embarked on the Steam Boat Richmond, Chapman at 6 o'clock A.M. & reached Norfork at 9 o'clock P.M.[45] Price of passage $4 and found.

Passed Fort Powhatan[46] on the route now in ruins. Next day embarked on the Steam boat Hampton & visited Fortress Monroe on Old Point Comfort, due East of Cape Henry & between the mouths of James & York rivers. The fortifications consist of a high & thick stone wall along the coast; within the wall are rooms for artillery & the lodgings of the soldiers; the wall is in the shape of a polygon, enclose 120 acres, 72 being within the inclosure & not under the wall; in the inclosure are five gardens & the residences of the married officers. Fortifications when complete will mount about 5 or 600 guns all 24 pounders, the fortress has cost about 4 millions about 300 soldiers & officers are stationed there & there are about 400 workmen now employed in building the walls & filling them in with sand.[47] Col. House is the commander in chief.[48] Returned to Norfolk on the same day by the same boat, price of passage one dollar. Distance from Richmond to Norfolk 115 miles, from Norfolk to Old Point 14 miles.[49]

Left Norfolk on the morning of the 10th Nov. in the schooner Roman, for New York[;] price of passage $8. Captain Hart. As we sailed out of Norfolk harbour left the Navy Yard & Dry Dock on our left, also the Marine Hospital situated on an island built by the U. St. for infirm sailors,[50] being a large 4 story, stone, building not yet finished. Also passed, on the left, Crany Island, on which troops were stationed & a battle fought during the late war, also passed, on the right, Fort Norfolk[51] now neglected & abandoned, its use being superceded by Fortress Monroe which commands the entrance into both James and Elizabeth Rivers. Passed between Old Point & the Rip Raps,[52] which last is a small island containing about 9 acres formed by sinking stones &c in Hampton Roads; the Island is situated one mile South East of Fortress Monroe, has cost about 800 thousand dollars & is intended as the situation of an United States Fortress.

Sea Sickness.

After having passed the Capes of the Chesepeake Bay about 12 o'clock, vessel going about six miles in an hour, sea a little rought, felt a little sickness at the stomach, head somewhat giddy; about 3. o'clock went below to dinner, eat a few mouthfulls, became quite sick, nerves trembled & my cheeks became verry pale; sickness increased untill at length by inserting my finger in my throat I procured an envisceration of my breakfat & dinner over the side of the vessel, felt somewhat relieved; during the evening had several discharges of bile from the stomach at irregular intervals from one to four hours each being succeded by weakness & intense sickness; after dark it being cold on deck went down into the cabbin; laid down in my birth, about supper time taken suddenly with something; there being several other passengers sick in the same room & four ladies & five children passengers in an adjoining room all sick; ate no supper, after 10 o'clock P.M. the wind change became unfavourable; became a Blow, a Gale & a Storm, during the night witnessed many novel & interesting scenes, enjoyed & observed, though I was quite sick. On deck the Captain Hart & some of the sailors were dressed in oil cloth over clothes; each strictly engaged at his peculiar duty; the wind blowing hard, the waves running high, the spray braking over the forepart of the vessel & washing it from stem to stern, the captain shouting his commands & the sailors singing and hallowing as they executed them; below some of the sea sick were groaning & some vometing, children were screaming & the women sighing, together with the rattling of dishes & chairs & the falling of the stove. The rolling of the vessel excited the stagnant salt water in the hold of the vessel which occasioned a most unpleasant odour, rendered more offensive by the copious discharge of foul stomachs. The wind was so strong as to tear & disable a main sail, & by six o'clock next morning it had driven the vessel many miles back to a station which it had occupied on the preceding evening; had occasional spells of sickness & discharges of bile; on the following morning after I was taken, ate no breakfast took some high seasoned soup for dinner, felt much better, took but little supper, being a little sick, felt sick on going on deck next morning, after breakfast was quite well, the sea sickness having lasted about 30 hours. Then went on prosperously. Saw many porpoise, sea Gulls & wild ducks, &c. Fourth day saw many skiffs containing men fishing for cod & other fish; almost becalmed off Sandy Hook Light houses. Carried into port by a gintle wind & flood tide which rises about 6 feet & runs 6 or 7 miles in an hour. Landed at Coffee House Slip N. York at 9 o'clock, friday night being the fourth day of the passage & thirteenth of the month and took boarding at the American Hotel,[53] price $10. a week fires, blacking & washing extra.

Visited Peale's Museum & Gallery of the fine Arts. Broadway, opposite the Park. Saw the portraits of many distinguished American & foreign persons, among the rest, that of the founder of the Museum, a full length portrait drawn by himself, when far advanced in life.[54]

Saw a Mammoth Child, from Ductchess county New York, three years old, weighs 124 pounds, three feet 4 inches high, three feet ten inches around the waist, fifteen inches around the arm and seventeen inches below the knee. The child was in perfect health, and exhibited a surprising degree of mirth playfulness & activity, running all over the rooms & playing familiarly with other children. She has a sister who is six years old, weighs two hundred and five pounds, 3 feet 11 inches high, 4 feet 2 inches around the waist, 15 inches around the arm & 17 inches below the knee. The name of the older is Susan & that of the younger is Deborah Tripp.[55]

Saw also a Solar Microscope, an optic instrument contrived so as to magnify the shape and appearance of objects, beheld through it, more than three million times; the animalcular in vinegar appear to be cels five or six feet in length.[56]

Visited the United States Navy yard, on East River, on the North side of Brooklyn & opposite to the City of New York; enclosing 60 or 80 acres of ground & many valuable buildings the handsomest of which is the residence of Commodore Chauncey commander in chief at that station.[57] There are two large frame houses near the water, which have neither division walls nor columns, the sides & roofs being supported by studds

& rafters, in one of the houses or docks which is about the height of a four story house, is a large vessel intended to mount 100 guns, now building & nearly finished & ready for launching.

Went on board & examined a 74 gun ship called the United States,[58] now used as a receiving shipp, or a vessel in which U. S. sailors not engaged in duty, are deposited & kept under military discipline. There were about 80 men on board; of a tolerably decent, healthful & cheerful appearance. Near the hammocks of the sailors were new & neat bibles which generally appeared entirely unused. Many of the sailors were engaged in cleaning the ship which presented the appearance of order & decency.

Boarded the Man of War Ohio,[59] lying at anchor near the States & close to the shore, a new ship, only about 8 or 10 years old; lately launched; not yet finished, being a vessel of the largest class, exceeding 300 feet in length & pierced for 110 gunns all to be 36 pounders; it expected she will be compleated & called into service next spring. Saw two other vessels of war closeby, lying side by side at anchor. Also the far famed Friggate Brandy Wine.[60] Also the wreck of the steam Friggate Fulton,[61] which was accidentally exploded in May last, aground & burnt almost to the waters edge.

Brooklyn, the Village near the Navy yard is large, & once was flourishing, the houses are principally framed & painted white, having tasteful & spacious yards, gardens & greens, so that in summer it must be a most beautiful & pleasant retreat to those residing in New York.[62]

Left N. York on Saturday 4 o'clock P.M. Nov. 21st in the steamboat U. States,[63] passed by the Navy yard & dry Dock, Hell-Gate & the State Prison & the Marine Hospital, & reached New Haven on the following morning about 12 o'clock, distance about 65 or 70 miles, price of fare $3 & found.

New Haven[64] contains about [10,180] inhabitants, houses principally of frame work weatherboarded & painted white, having spaces between them planted with shrubs & grass; the principal streets are shaded with sugar & large elm trees which give the town a most rural & delightful appearance. The handsomest street is Church street running nearly east & west on the North side of it & about the centre of the City are two beautiful grass lots or public squares, each containing eight acres, the one immediately on church street is entirely vacant, the other immediately in the rear, contains 4 churches & a state house, Two of the churches belong to the Presbyterians, large handsome, of brick having tall white cupolose & one of them a clock, on the left of which & immediately in a line with the other two is the Episcopal church, a large Gothic church of stone & having a Gothic cupola of dark stone also. In the rear of these is the state house, not yet finished, a large three story building, having six fluted columns in each end, which (together with the whole building) are to be stuc-

coed in imitation of marble. In the rear of all these are the buildings of
Yale College,⁶⁵ 7 in number all in a row having a lawn in front which
is towards the town, the building of brick & chiefly 4 story high. Met
with some Kentuckians was most kindly received, formed some acquaintances among the college students who accompanied us in visiting the Dining room Rhetorical chamber, (which contains the portraits of the benefac-
tors of the college & some of the present & former presidents & professors)
& Philosophical Apparatus & also the Cabinet of Minerals, said to be the
best in the U.S. & next to best in the world, formed principally by a dona-
tion of a Mr Gibbs worth 10 or 15 thousand pounds; there are more than
50 cases containing the minerals &c. There is a Library of _____ volumes
in the college, also two others of _____ volumes each, the property of
the Coliopean & Brothers in Unity Societies. This city is remarkable in
several respects & on the whole is one of the most picturesque and pleasant I have seen, notwithstanding the houses are scattered, the streets
unpaved & business declining. Remarkable for many churches, 2 clocks
& large bell.⁶⁶

Left New Haven on Monday Nov 23, at 3 & reached Hartford⁶⁷ about
12 o'clock P.M. having passed Middletown on the Conn. River which is
the seat of a manufactory of swords & fire arms extensive & owned by
individuals, country generally level, tolerably fertile & handsome. Con-
veyance by Stage, distance 40 miles, fare $2. Hartford resembles New
Haven in many respects, is one of the Capitols of the State, but not the
residence of Gov. Tomlinson,⁶⁸ is the seat of Washington college, situated
about a mile from town in a S.W. direction, the principal buildings being
a large 4 story stone buildings, presenting a large plain front on its left
is the college chapel of stone, ordinary size & workmanship. The State
House in which the famed Hartford Convention⁶⁹ sat is a large 3 story
brick building whitewashed, situated about the centre of town, double
front, one to the principal street & the other at the termination of a street
leading directly to the river Conn. which about ¾ of a mile distant. In
the south end of the 2nd story is the chamber of the convention; it is entered
by one door in the side, occupies the most of that end, is large & commodious. In front of the door, and on the middle of wall of the south
end, is a full length portrait of Washington, delivering his inaugural
address, a fine painting by Stewart above the painting which is an elegant
guilt frame, are the arms & insignia of the U. S. in gold leaf, slightly shaded
& concealed by a set of handsome purple curtains. On the opposite wall
is the printed letter of Washington on declining a re-election to the presidency; all as they were during the sitting of the Convention, the chairs
& settees are of handsome workmanship & of antique & odd forms, that
of the speaker is small, but larger than the others & is ornamented with
crimson & is situated immediately in front of W's portrait on a platform

of 18 or 20 inches elevation, on each side of the chair is a long circular table, parallel or ranging with the side of the house. Went up into the Dome, which is surmounted by a statue of Justice bearing the scales in her left hand & sword in her right; from the windows of the Dome had a most extensive & delightful view of the whole town & country around for 15 or 20 miles. The town & county the meadows of the Conn. especially present a most delightful appearance not inferiour to & resembling Lexington Kentucky.

Saw from the same place the Hospital the Deaf & Dumb assylum, Washington College, the City hall the Bridge & several churches & heard the time of the day announced by 4 large clocks. Also saw the old oak tree south of town in the roots of which the charter of the state was concealed when about to be taken by the British During the Rev. war.[70] This place is the seat of a Temperance Society which was then bearing all things before it. I was informed that about 1000 persons had joined at a late meeting.

Left Hartford about 7 o'clock on Wednesday morning & reached Providence R. I.[71] about 8 o'clock P.M. in the stage the distance being about 90 miles, fare _____ roads rough, country barren, rocky & broken. Stopped at the Franklin House,[72] having stopped at the U.S. Hotel in Hartford & at the Tontine Coffee House in New Haven. Providence like the former places is remarkable for the number, size & elegance of its churches, large bells & fine large clocks.

Spent Thanksgiving day in Prov. it being Thursday the 26 of Nov. Pursuant to a resolution by the Legislature the Gov. proceeds to appoint the day & to recommend that on that day the citizens abstain from all unnecessary labour & unbecoming recreation & that they do assemble at their usual places of worship & unite in rendering unfeigned gratitude to him who is the source of all power & goodness, for continually extending over us a protecting & paternal care, for having bountifully bestowed upon them the highest temporal blessings & for diffusing the benign influences of that pure & holy religion which enjoins the practice of every virtue and promises eternal life, in short to give thanks for all present & past blessings & to implore a continuation of them. About 10 o'clock divine service was announced in all the churches by the simultaneous ringing of all their immense bells; the sounds were almost deafning & my feelings were novel deep & devout.[73] A[t] dinner on that day the tables are loaded with the most delicious viands & rare & choice luxuries of all sorts which can be obtained, the remainder of the day is spent in benevolent engagements, social enjoyments or publick amusements. The same day is commonly observed throughout N.E. When the bells had ceased to ring we ascended the cupola of a church situated on a hill near the college on the [N.W.] side of the city, the height was immense & the view delightful &

extensive. One of the greatest attractions in the city is the Arcade[74] which is a long spacious & splendid building, its front, lower floor & lower steps & the columns in both fronts being of granite.

It is three stories high with the front doors of all the apartments opening in the same passage which extends its whole length & is brilliantly illuminated by glass windows on the comb of the roof. It was intended for merchants fancy stores &c but at present is little used, many apartments being "to Let"

Brown University[75] is located in this City. The principal buildings two in number of brick about 30 feet assunder nearly in a direct line, presenting nearly the same appearance, each being about 4 stories high & of neat but simple construction; in front of them in the same enclosure is the dwelling of the Pres. an ordinary frame building painted white.

About ¾ of a mile from this college is situated the Quaker College[76] also an hospital or Assylum, both spacious & handsome edifices, could gain no information concerning their internal regulations.

Prov. is a sea port & has no inconsiderable shipping; at the wharf I saw & examined the superb steam boat Chancellor Livingston,[77] now running hence to New York.

Left Prov. on Friday at 7 A.M. in the stage & reached Boston at 2 o'clock P.M. same day, distance [approximately 70] miles fare _____ turn pike road through a barren & broken country the chief products, rough stones & pine trees.

Passed a manufacturing town called [Pawtuckett] in which the famous Sam. Patch[78] was once a labourer. The factory in which he worked is situated on the brink of a creek from the roof of this factory about 60 feet high he began to jump, the same leap is now performed by other boys.

Stopped at Tremont House[79] unquestionably the best house of entertainment in the Western Continent.

On the night of arrival went to Tremont Theatre (nearly opposite to Tremont House). The building is most spacious & splendid, has four tier of seats for the audience besides the pit[;] the stage is large enough for any play, well furnished with splendid curtains & scenery. The audience was large & respectable but not fashionable the play was Shakspeare's fine tragedy of Hamlet.[80]

Mr. Booth[81] personating the character of Hamlet for the [play]. His performance though somewhat defective, was characterized by his usual excellence. A few nights after saw him personate the character of King Lear in which he surpassed his priour performance, the company was not in general good & of course Mr Booth was not well supported. Miss Rock & Miss Eberle were the most admired actresses. The stage inferiour but less licentious in Boston than in New York.

Visited the New England Museum[82] one of the largest in the U.S. much of it is in disorder & decay the rooms small & obscure, the preservation defective & the arrangement injudicious. The most important object was a white marble statue of Venus by Canova.

Saw a monument to Franklin in Franklin place & another erected over the remains of his ancestors in a burial ground near Tremont House; the last is a pyramid 25 feet high formed of blocks of granite of about six tons weight each, the former an urn of large size.[83] Went to the state house, the finest I have seen, saw a full size statue of Washington of white marble executed by Chantry; inferiour to that at Richmond ascended the dome of the state house, dome about 50 feet in diameter at the base, my high view almost boundless & verry beautiful, the bay is said to resemble the bay of Naples.

Churches are numerous; Boston said to be the paradise of preachers. Markets verry good one house built of granite is spacious & splendid.

On Monday Visited Cambridge the seat of Harvard University.[84] Went in an hourly coach, fare 25 cents, distance 3 miles. The principal University buildings are 6 or 7 in number, 4 stories high, situated in an enclosure of 10 or 15 acres, bordered by several rows of young pine trees; buildings chiefly of brick, of an antiquated appearance; one called the college is of granite, three stories, contains the Chapel, dining & other halls.

First visited the Library, collection large, in two room, which are also well furnished with the busts & portraits of great men, among the rest a white marble bust of Washington & a plaister bust of John Adams both mounted on marble pedestals. Obtained a conductor & visited the Philosophical Chamber, containing the philosophical aparatus which is numerous & valuable; thence visited the Cabinet of Minerals, the collection is large & exceedingly valuable deposited in about 50 cases with glass fronts. The two last chambers are immediately under the Library & are in a front building which has a clock & bell on it.[85]

In connection with the College is a Botanic Garden. The number of students about 500. Josiah Quincy Pres.[86] The college is chiefly governed by the Unitarians, but is open to students of all denominations, who are permitted to attend service in any of the other churches in the place. Returned to Boston same day & way, saw the ruinous walls & ditch surrounding them of an old fortification built during the Revolution, walls about 60 feet square. In front of the colleges is a large common or green.

On Tuesday Dec. 1st, travelled on foot almost over the whole City. Went in the hourly stage to Charlestown for 12½ cents. Visited Bunker Hill Monument situated on Breeds hill to the North of Boston.[87] The Mon. is of large blocks of granite from the Quincy Railway[,] is unfinished, is about 25 or 30 feet high in form of a Pyramid in side which is a circular cavity around which a flight of stone steps wind to the summit. It is situate on the top of the Hill, with in 15 or 20 feet of the relics of the old fortification a shallow ditch & low mound are still to be seen, the hill is covered with grass & is clear of permanent buildings. Extensive & delightful view from the top.

Thence visited Bunkers hill which is joining on the North is a green, bears traces of mounds & trenches, joins the main land on the North by chars [Charles] Neck.

Thence visited the State Prison in Chas.town[88] at the end of Bridge, partly enclosed by water, surrounded by a granite stone wall about 3 feet thick and 15 high, has a wooden railling on the top of it, five guards are employed in watching in day time on the top of the wall which contains several acres, upon which are many building chiefly of stone, the principal a new stone house 4 stories high, containing 304 dormitories each for one prisoner around this building are three rows of porticos into which the cells open, around these at the distance of 5 or 6 feet is a thick stone wall as high as the prison & under the same roof with it. The cells are small but large enough for one bed & box &c they are neatly white washed & kept quite clean. Their beds consists of a sack sowed to a compact frame, which is attached to the wall by two iron hinges thus being closed up to the wall or laid horizontally at pleasure, the beds are furnished with blankets &c but no feathers or straw.

William Austin is the Warden or Principal. The number of prisoners about 270 of which about 30 are blacks, prisoners sent chiefly from Boston for theft. There are no females in this prison. Notwithstanding the prisoners are industriously employed at the various mechanic arts the institution brings the State about 65 or 70 thousand dollars annually. The principal employments are coarse tailoring, brush making, picking oakum, black smithing & dressing stone, at the last about 100 men. The stone is Quincy granite for tombs, sills, steps, & building. The bellows were stationed on the heads of the blacksmiths. Observed in the brush making room a curious saw, made like, resembling & running like a Whirley gigg. I.E. fixed upon an axel & revolving in its place perpendicularly.

In the cook row saw a rare & valuable Steam Boiler for cooking. It consisted of a cast iron cilendar 4 or 5 feet high, an inch or two thick & 18 or 20 inches in diameter. About one third the way up this cilender was a door, under which a grate to sustain the fuel & under this a flue or draught about a foot from the top & on the opposite side from the door was a hole for a pipe to carry of the smoke. In the plate which covered the top of the cilender were four holes from which ran four metallic pipes to conduct the heat to the bottoms of four casks or tubs which contain the water or other substance desired to be boiled or cooked. The objects gained were a saving of room, fuel & cooking aparatus.

Each convict was supplied with tin pans &c for eating. Principal food, beaf, soup & potatoes, rice, coffee at breakfast & supper. Prisoners shave twice a week put on clean shirts once a week. The Hospital of the prison was rarely crowded with invalids.

Thence visited the Navy Yard[89] having three large 5 or 6 story frame houses for building ships & one for a store house for ship timber many inferiour. Saw three vessels of war of large size, dismasted, at anchor side by side near the Navy Yard Wharf, one of which the Columbus[90] used as a receiving ship. Saw about 100 men employed in constructing a dry dock. It consists of a large reservoir near the waters edge, is built of quincy granite, is large enough to admit vessels of the largest size, it is intended to draw vessels into this place, then to let out the water so that the ship will be entirely dry & then while they are bare to do whatever repairs may be necessary, when the repairs are complete the water will be let into the dock through flues extending through the walls quite round the ship, so that she may be floated gradually an[d] then glide out to sea again.

The work thus far is executed in a nice, strong and substantial manner & will be several years in completion & at an immense cost. At present a small steam engine is employed to keep the hole clear of water & to turn grind stones & turning Lathes. About 500 men were employed during the last summer.

Saw at the Navy Yard about 200 iron cannon of various sizes & a quantity of balls & cast iron blocks for ships ballast.

Thence crossed to Boston & visited the Marine Railway in the North part of the City.[91] It is the property of the Marine Railway Company & cost about 100 thousand dollars. Three parallel rows of timber extend with a gentle inclination from the dry shore to deep water so that one end of the railway is dry & the other in the water; Upon these timbers are iron grooves, upon which is fixed a frame like a waggon body, resting on iron rollers fitting upon the grooves. Upon this movable body the ship is drawn while in the water and when it is fastened to the body this body is then drawn up, the wheels rolling upon the grooves, by means of large chains attached to machinery propelled by horse power, the horses turning a draught wheel in the second story of a house. Three or 4 horses can draw up a ship of common size with ease; Merchant men only. When a vessel is thus drawn high & dry its copper & it may be taken off & any other repairs done applicable & then the ship is restored to its element by the same means. There are two railways.

Thence went to Boylston Market thence to Boston Neck & thence to Boston Common. Thence to Tre. [Tremont] House & thence to Hannover St & engaged a passage inn the stage to Worcester, distance 40 miles, fare $2. Left Boston on Wednesday at 2 o'clock A.M. & reached Worcester at 9 or 10. Thence to Springfield 20 miles, fare $2.50, reached the last place about 7 or 8 o'clock; having passed over 90 miles, country a little broken, soil rocky & sandy, forest trees chiefly pine & scrub oak, saw many fine country seats among the rest one which is the scene of an anecdote in the life of Jerome Bonaparte & Miss Patterson, it was the place where he shot a horse &c. Saw many beautiful manufacturing & country villages[92] remarkable for their order, decency, & beauty, houses chiefly of frame work painted white & having green window shutters; each dwelling house is commonly surrounded by a handsome yard & garden in fine cultivation & each village well supplied with fine churches. The Commons, or publick greens in their villages add greatly to their beauty & health & give them a picturesque appearance. Springfield is pleasantly situated on the Connecticut, & well furnished by the Phelp's Hotel at which we stopped.

On the road to Springfield fell in with Mr. Shepherd a manufacturer of Northampton Mass.[93] Who gave us letters to Col Lee[94] superintendant of The United States Armory about 1½ or 2 miles east of Springfield on Mill River which place we visited on Thursday morning, in a gig hired at _____. The mills are four in number. In one is a furnace & hammers for heating hammering & rolling the iron, all propelled by water power. The handle of the hammer is poised in the middle, on one end is the hammer of cast iron, with a movable steel face the other end is faced with metal & is struck by the cog of a wheel which revolves horizontally on its axis, the cogs of the wheel being towards the ground; the end of the handle which is struck by the cogs, rests upon a frame to which a lever is attached by raising which the handle is applied to the cogs & by depressing it the handle is removed. The number of blows of the hammer is regulated by increasing or dimenishing the quanty of water power on the wheel.

Near this is a saw to saw the barrel of gunn stocks, it consists of a circular plate of steel with teeth like a handsaw revolving on its axis with amazing velocity, to this saw the wood is applied fixed fast in a frame which is driven to the saw by means of a cogwheel running on a horizontal row of permanent cogs.

Near this is a machine for turning gun stocks. It consists of a circular saw, revolving perpendicular upon its axis, The stock with a moving frame of iron about 6 feet in length, fixed by means of seven rods to move along in front of the saw from one end to the other of the frame which moves horizontally; the stock in its rough state is fastened in this frame & turns horizontally upon pins so that it can easily be applied to the saw, in the oposite site of the machine is fixed a nice gun stock of iron (which is used as a pattern) and turns horizontally upon pivots, a brass wheel is so fixed as to touch this pattern, the wheel also revolving upon its axis but perpendicularly, one side of it against the pattern & the other against the frame which contains the stock, the form of the pattern regulating the motions of the wheel & it the motions of the frame by which the gunn stock is applied to the saw. The small end of the stock is applied to the saw first & whilst it revolves slowly upon its axis it is carried along & applicats the saw from one end to the other. The stock is then taken out[,] the frame is slid back & another stock put in.

And thus the exact shape is given to the stock & it is rendered ready for the irons & for polishing in about 5 or 10 minutes. Any other articlle may be turned or sawed by the same principles, the form of the article to be turned being regulated by the form of the pattern, if it be a shoe last the wood will be sawed in the form of the shoe last &c. One man with little skill can attend with the last machine. Saw a machine for fitting in the wood, the mountain on the butt end of the musket. An augur bit of a semi circular form is turned perpendicularly & is applied to the wood so as to cut according to a pattern which regulates its motions, by confining the stem of the auger. The machine for turning gunn barrels is as follows. The barrel after being inlaid & bored is placed fast upon a rod, laid horizontally in a machine & turns upon its axis & not otherwise, the bit which cuts the iron is placed in a frame which moves from one end of the gun barrel to the other by means of cogwheels & slides, when the bit is fastened in the frame it is applied to the pallet, the machine is then put in motion the barrel begins to turn upon its axis & the bit to move with the frame from one end of the barrel to the other, cutting with its side & not with its front. The former method was grinding[.] The advantages of the latter are chiefly dispatch saving the cost of grindstones & saving the metal, as the turnings are taken up, melted & hammered. The screw turning machine is as follows. The coarse wire is placed in a vice & turned like the spendle of a wheel in front of it are two dies each having a semicurcular hole with teeth like a file, the two dies being placed together form a hole into which the wire is thrust & it is thus instantaneously turned or filed round & smoth. The wire is permanent & the dies fixed in a frame which can be moved to or from the wire with ease & despatch. The gunn mountain locks &c instead of being hammered & filed as in Ky. are cut by strong machinery out of plates of rolled iron or else the warm metal is applied to a mould or die & is struck with a hammer & cut from the sheet by the mould. The barrels after being turned are smoothed on grindstones & polished on wheels covered with leather straps upon which emery is made to adhere by means of glue. About a mile distant from the Mills is the Armory at which the remaining & more delicate operations are performed. These buildings are of brick whitewashed, two stories high beside the basement, regularly laid out, three being on one street, & one on each flank of this row, in the rear of which are two handsome lawns of 15 or 20 acres, the Lts house being situated at the far side. These buildings contain finishing shops remarkable for their order &

neatness, the floors[,] benches, tools & operatives being all nice & clean & the windows ornamented with rose bushes, orange trees, chrysanthensis in fine vegetation & bloom. The labourers at the Armory appeared more decent industrious & Temperate than those at the Mills. They are all paid by the day & earn from 1 to 2 dollars per day according to their industry & skill; from 3 to 5 hundred being employed. Muskets only being made at this establishment.[95] Visited a Paper mill on the same stream, working from 50 to 80 persons chiefly females from 12 to 20 years of age. The paper makes its appearance upon a piece of flannel stretched upon rollers, whence it is connected to a cylender around which it is rolled to infinite length if desired; the operation being performed by machinery.

Thence had a merry ride over a sandy plane 3 miles to the Chickapee Manufactory[96] of cotton cloths at the falls of Chickee river, owned by a Company[.] Had a letter to Mr. Henshaw superintendant, about half a million dollars bein invested, employ about 800 labourers, consume about 2½ tons of cotton & make about 100 dollars worth of cloth daily. Factory houses four or 5 inn number & as many stories high, in the lowest the cotton is run through picking machines & rolled into mats, in the next the mats into roving in the next the roving is spun in the next it is woven in the next the yarn is sized &c, the goods being passed from one story to another by means of cupboards sliding perpendicularly, the machinery all propelled by water power. The Looms some what after the following fashion. The slay on the frame containing it which beats up the filling was moved by means of a crank, the frame standing upon two legs like a horse & working upon pivots. The treadle were sprung by means of an axle on which were fixed wheels or rather plates of irregulary forms (have &c), the plates projecting from opposite sides of the axle & touching the treaddles in proper order. I saw machines with four treaddles.

The shuttle was made of two thin iron plates pointed & joined at the ends, in form of common shuttles, the bobbin was placed upon a stem in the shuttle & held to its place by a spring which caught the bobbin in a groove on its large end. The shuttles were thrown by means of strings, one end of which were attached to slides on the rods & the other to a piece of wood in the form of a cut ninepence playing on its sharp end like a pivot, the strings attached to the corners terminating the circles & all under the web, these ninepences are moved by strings attached to the two outer treadles, so that when the treadles spring the shuttle flies.[97]

If the strings & batton attached to the looms in Ky. were turned under the webs, they would hang in the form of the above described fining. If the handle with which the shuttle is jerked was then fixed so that the small end would play on a pivot & strings were attached to the leather & then to the outer treadles, it would further illustrate the plan used in the Chicy. Fac. The lever or gear or harness were made of wire. In the Sizing room the web is rolled from one cylinder on to another, in its passage passing between two firm rollers, the lower of which is completely immersed in the sizing, the rollers run horizontally, one above the other & in opposite directions, so that by the compression of the rollers the web passes off being entirely free from a surplus quanity of the sizing. It then passes by a stove which dries it & then on cylinders. The goods after being washed is put into large tubbs 10 to 15 feet long open at the top & a frame work at the bottom & in these tubs it is steamed & sprinkled and kept moist by bleaching waters & curious compound as it is improved in whiteness it passes from one tub to another & is then rolled dry between two rollers & is then sized between two rollers & is then ironed between rollers.

The operatives are almost all females from 12 to 20 of fine moral character, jealous & careful of their reputation, many of remarkable beauty, good educations & of respectable parents some of whom are worth 20 or 30 thousand dollars. They are paid by the job & earn from 2 to 3 dollars a week besides their board, some earn more & some less according to their industry & skill. They are boarded in families attached to the Factories.[98]

Springfield[99] a handsome white housed green yard, fine churched & large commoned healthy looking village, country sandy, product of the soil chiefly rice, some cu[l]tivated without fences, hogs kept up & cattle rare.

Left on Friday morning at 2 o'clock in the Stage for Albany[100] distance about 80 miles fare $4.37½. Passed over a rough barren & sandy country the face of which was enlivened occasionally by a handsome N.E. village; passed over the southern end of the Green Mountains & also some others.[101]

Arrived at Greenbush about 8 o'clock P.M. & crossed over the Hudson in a skiff, the weather extremly cold, the water freezing & the ice running & put up at Drake's American Hotel.[102] Next morning bought a pair of Indian rubber over shoes price $1.75 the snow being 2 or 3 inches deep, walked over the city built chiefly on a hill & plain running along the river. Saw the Canal & basin full of ice snow & canal boats. Went to the State House a fine large square building of hewn stone of a spanish brown colour having four tall large & handsome Ionic Columns of white marble in front. Saw the Council Chamber containing the portraits of the State Governor.

Saw the Library containing 3 or 4 thousand vols in two rooms ornamented with engravings & portraits of Great men. Went to the Assembly Chamber, a handsome room richly carpeted & curtained & ornamented by a bad likeness of Washington delivering his inaugural address copied from Stuarts by Ames, placed immediately behind the Speaker's chair. Went to the Senate chamber, adorned by the Portrait of George Clinton[103] placed under crimson curtains behind the speaker's chair & a portrait of

T. Van Vetchen,[104] a great Lawyer of Albany on the left of the chair. All the rooms almost the Declaration Independence, engraved in splendid style & placed in elegant gilt frames. Went into the Dome of handsome form & size, surmounted by a white marble statue of Justice holding the scales in her left & a naked sword in her right hand, execution not superiour. From the Dome had a fine view of the City its suburbs & environs the State house having a commanding situation at the end of State street, immediately on the left of it is the Albany Academy[105] a large & statly edifice of brown stone, having like the State house a fine park in its front, saw the several churches for the Dutch &c. In front & beyond the Hudson on the hill which rise like the seats of an Amphitheatre, are situated the barracks & other buildings of Cantonment Greenbush at which place troops were stationed during the late war. The buildings are numerous & spacious, look white & from their situation on the hills among the ever green pines present a handsome & romantic Appearance.

Saw a Screw Dock[106] near the Canal Basin & on the border of & on a level with the River. Small boats are drawn from the river into the dock and rested upon a frame sunk into the water, after the boat is fastened to the frame the screws & 8 in number are turned perpendicularly & by then the frame & vessel are raised out of the water so that the vessel may be repaired.

Publick amusement in abundance. Theatre Atheneum Amphitheatre Circus & Museum all in active operation. Went to the Circus & saw the play of Timorer the Tartor.[107]

Left Albany on Sunday morning at 10 o'clock in the steam boat Constellation & reached West Point about 10 o'clock P.M. distance about 102 miles, fare the same as to New York one dollar and found. Passed many fine residences and much splendid scenery on the banks of the Hudson, among the former the residence of General Armstrong. The river is a deep, straight & beautiful stream, its banks two thirds the distance from Albany rising into hills gradually from the shore, the lands particularly on the Eastern side being barren & sandy, producing pine & ceder, about one fourth in cultivation. The width of the river varies from 3/4ths to more than a mile in breadth. On the west side 58 miles from its mouth is West Point in Orange County N. York, the seat of a strong fortress during the Revolutionary War & the present seat of a U.S. Military Academy established in 1802 on an appropriation of 25,000 dollars.[108] From Newburg to the Point, a distance of seven miles the river runs due south in a direct line, the Point the River passes through the Highlands, and winds its course in a south westward direction, thus rounding two sides of the Point while the third the plain being rather in the form of a triangle, is bounded by the high hill on which is built fort Putman. The plain which is the scite of the Academy is about 80 feet above the river & contains about _____

The plain is of a smoth & even surface, sandy soil producing pine, cedar
& hickory, is not in fine cultivation nor important.[109]

On the West side of the plain, on the brink of the hill immediately
above the landing is situated a new & splendid three story frame tavern
painted white, well kept & built at the expense of the U.St. At this, the
only tavern on the Point, I stopped, upon its summit is a square cupola
with glass windows, to this I ascended & turning my face towards the
West I saw immediately in front 3/4ths of a mile distant I saw the three
principal buildings of the Academy, the centre one & that on its left are
two story & that on the right is three, on the flank of these in front is
a large 4 story building, like the others built of rough grey stone. The
centre building contains the Chapel on the lower floor & the library on
the upper floor, the building on the left is used as a mess house & that
on the right & flank as the dormitories & study rooms of the Cadets. The
library contains several thousand volumes of valuable & scientific books
judiciously selected & well arranged. The cadets & almost all required to
eat at the mess rooms & there only, the fare is uniform tolerably holsome
& far from sumptuous, & so tired do the cadets become of their fare that
they not unfrequently risk summary expulsion, to obtain something better.
(Col. Thayer is Superintendant)[110]

To my right & on the North side of the Barracks are the residences
of the Professors, they are chiefly of brick two stories high & in a line
running East & West 6 or 8 in number, three of which are white washed,
near the corner of this line & fronting the river are two others of rough
stone & two stories high, in front of the three last & on the descent to
the river is the magazine & barracks for the regular troops, musicians &C.
Immediately in rear of the barracks is a long frame house containing an
excellent park of artillery, & about 100 yards still further in the rear is
the Hospital not yet finished, of rough grey stone, two stories high & fronting the river to the southwest.

To the left of the Tavern & on the southwest point of the plain are
the relics of Fort Clinton[;][111] though much decayed the relics of its ditch
walls & cells are still quite visable; these ruins are the scite of the handsome white marble monument erect by the corps of cadets in 1828 to the
Memory of Kosciusco,[112] who resided on the point during the Revolutionary contest & who after having signalized himself among the friends
of Liberty in America died in obscurity on the continent of Europe. The
mon consists of a handsome fluted column about 8 feet high, mounted
upon a base also of white marble, 5 or 6 feet square encompassed by a
handsome grass plat enclosed by an iron railing. On the North side of
the base is the inscription "Erected by the Corps of Cadets 1828," & on
the opposite side "Kosciusko."[113] It is intended that the column shall be
surmounted by a furneral urn or a bust of Kosciusco & when complete

will have cost about $2,000. Between this place & the Barracks is the camp ground where the cadets spend the summer months in camp west of this & on the bank of the river in the Kosciusko garden, a small plain of ¼ of an acre about halfway down the descent to the river, said to have been cultivated by himself now tastefully planted with trees, furnished with benches & having a fine marble fountain of clear bubbling water in the middle of it.[114]

On the high hill to the Northwest of the Point is Old fort Putman[115] to which I ascended it is now in ruins & is fast tumbling to decay. The works though seemingly intended to be temporary only since great strength & permanency a part of the walls being 10 to 18 [feet] in height & some of the cells being almost entire, one was pointed out as that in which Major Andre[116] was imprisoned or confined.

The students dress in a gray uniform appeared healthy & genteel, though their rooms and the entries & balconies were exceedingly dirty & in disorder. I saw a guard parade in the morning & a general parade in the evening & having spent a pleasant time with some of my Ky friends & paid a high tavern bill. I embarked on the North America for New York, arrived same night & left New York on Wednesday Nov. 29, for Princeton by the Union line fare $1.25. The passengers having arrived by steam at Brunswick were placed in 10 four horse coaches each taking 9 passengers & so taken to Princeton &c which is the seat of a Theological seminary containing professors & students, the building 4 stories of rough grey stone, in the form of a parallel ogram, situated in the south west part of the town & fronting the west. It has a small library consisting chiefly of large, old and valuable Theological books. The seminary is in the direction of the Presbyterians. The College in this place is a building of the same character but larger & situated on the far end of a lot on the South side of main street which runs east & west. This institution is in a feeble state, having two professors & seventy students & a President.[117]

Princeton though pleasantly situated is inferior to most N. England villages in its appearances. The country around is rolling soil thin, timber chiefly oak, beech & pine, saw some fine orchards. From the cupola of the Seminary had an extensive & pleasant view of the surrounding county.

Revisited the College the principal building called Nassau Hall, venerable for antiquity & consecrated by revolutionary occurrances, the same into which the British retreated when pursued by the Americans who compelled them to stack their arms in the College lawn, after discharging a few volleys of Artillery into the College house. The injury which the building sustained is not now perceptable but the balls taken from the walls are still preserved, Saw the dining hall of the students Refectory, neat & clean. Saw the library of 8000 volumes & an Orrery constructed by the great Rittenhouse.[118] Left Princeton on Thursday morning & after passing over a level & cultivated country of thin soil & passing by some revolutionary scenes, among the rest a hill upon [which] Washington built his fires before he fought the glorious battle of [Trenton],[119] passed through Trenton; embarked on The Delaware in steam B & passed Joseph Bonapartes Residence,[120] situate about 200 yards from the Delaware on a high bank, near Bordentown: his two dwelling houses are so built as to look up the river & fronting a Tower, 4 stories high, of quadrangular form, with a handsome cupola, intended as a wing to a French Chattheau now used as an observatory. The Ex King of Spain is now employed in agricultural pursuits, is very wealthy & keeps bachelors hall, his wife and children being in Europe.[121] Passed many handsome country residences on the banks of the river among the rest that of Cooper[122] the great actor, it is of odd construction, situate on the bank with the yard extending down to the water, of a yellow or ocre colour, low three stories in rear with a piazza towards the River, embosomed by shrubs & trees. & having a row of 5 or 6 marble busts between the house & river, and on the Pennsylvania side. Passed the little town just below Cooper's[123] Residence & several others & reached Pha. about 7 o'clock distance 50 miles, fare $1.50; 25 cents more than is charged by the same line from New York to Philedelphia, Competition has reduced the fare on this line. The other the Dispatch.

Friday morning Dec. 11 then got in a carriage & went to see the New penty[;] its being inaccessable went to the Pagoda 7 stories high & 60 or 80 feet encompassed by a circular Labryinth garden having seven circular walks, the sides planted with various evergreens pine, cedar, arbor vita & in the interour of the Pagoda is a winding stair case around the mast of a ship extending from the bottom to the top at which the stairs are so narrow as to scarce as to admit by squeezing.

It was built by a Lawyer who having but little legal business, turned his attention to building air Castles & Chinese Pagoda's it is fashionaly attended as a summer retreat & pleasure ground admittance 25 cents, a drink of liquor to boot.[124]

Saw there a riding machine called Velocipide consisting of two small carriage wheels, coupled together & running in a straight line one wheel after the other about three feet apart. The back or cupling pole is mounted & the machine is propelled by the feet of the rider its course being regulated by turning the fore wheel to the right or left. It travels with considerable rapidity & ease to those [with] will to ride it, not exactly so to me.[125]

Went to Fairmount Water Works, owned by, & situated in the North West part of the city on the banks of the Schuyikill. The water is thrown from the Schuyikill by means of two double force pumps, propelled by four water wheels each about 45 or 50 horse power, each pump raising about 1000 gallons of water per minute up an ascent of 95 feet perpen-

dicular into a three reserviors containing 1,000,000 gallons, 12 feet deep
& square, all enclosed with a paling, the water is conducted thence by
means of one main cast iron pipe to the City thence by many branches,
to almost every house for a fee of $5 to a family. The water power to
turn the water wheels is obtained by erecting a dam across the Schuyikill
the dam 6 or 8 feet high & long with an elbow projecting up the river
& near the opposite shore where there are locks through which the boats
pass, chiefly tow boats drawn either by horses or men. The axel of the
water wheels has a crank attached to a pistens which works in the pump
of cast iron verry like the pistons & cilender of a steam engine, save that
the pumps work & lay horizontally & are about 18 inches diameter.[126]

On the precipitous & rocky side of the hill up which the water is conducted to the resevoir stands a white marble statue of Ceres supporting
on her right shoulder a stork with extended wing & neck out of its open
mouth the water is made to spout several feet in an upward direction.
The whole works are erected in a strong, substantial & remarkably neat
manner. The same object was formerly accomplished by steampower, the
engine and pumps are still standing but unused. From its beauty & novelty
it is made in the summertime a place of fashionable resort.

Thence went to the shot Tower & manufactory. The tower which
is of brick is about 12 or 18 feet square at the bottom & half that at the
top, 160 feet high ascended by a staircase along the walls having in all
232 steps. The metal is melted near the top in kettles & poured through
seives & falls to the bottom in water, the seives divide the hot lead & give
the size to the shot, they are perfectly round when they reach the water.[127]
From the top of the Tower had an extensive view of the City, the rivers
& adjacent country for many miles around.

Went to The Porcelain Factory the only one in the U. S. the property
of [William Ellis Tucker] well conducted. The stone & earth are obtained
chiefly in New Jersey & Delaware, the earth is purified by washing &
passing it through seives & strainers having been mixed with a certain
portion of white stone like clay is put upon a horizontal wheel & is turned
into the rough form of the article, is then partially dried, again put on
the wheel & with a sharp instrument is cut and trimmed into exact forms.
It is then glazed, then burned in a kiln, then the ornaments are put on
with a brush, the colours all being metalic; the ware is then exposed to
a moderate heat in order to make the colours penetrate the ware, which
is then polished & ready for sale. All ware of an oval form or of an
embossed form must be moulded in moulds prepared purposely. Saw an
abundance & variety of ware in all stages, it was tasteful, handsome &
seemingly of strong & durable texture, & high reputation of ready sale,
reflecting much credit on Mr. [William Ellis Tucker] the proprietor who
undertook the business on experiment without much knowledge & begins

to be handsomely rewarded.[128]

Visited the New State Prison situated 2½ miles in the northwest suburbs of the City. Samuel R. Wood Inspector, a bachelor, a Quaker of middle age & size, clever, & communicative. The outer walls of stone, & near a half mile in circumference, inclosing nearly ten acres of ground, the wall 30 feet from the surface & extending _____ feet below the surface, 12 feet thick at the bottom tapering to 3 at top which is covered with a shingle roof slanting only & projecting on the inside. The southside towards the City is the front which has five towers in it _____ feet higher than the wall, one at each corner for guard houses, and one which is the highest & largest in the center above the gait & over the gait way. Joining this on the right is a tower in which is the Inspector's office & the Infirmary for sick prisoners & on the lift of the center tower is one containing the office & private apartments of the Warden handsomely finished and furnished. In the center of the exterior wall which is a quadrangle & nearly a square, is an octagonal three story house for an observatory. From this building as a center branch out of rows of cells like the radii of a circle, which extend almost to the outer wall. At present but three rows are built, & there are but eight prisoners as yet in the prison. A person can sit in the basement of the observatory and look all along the ailes which lead by the cells, & from the second story he can overlook the cells & the yards which are attached to them in which the prisoners are permitted to exercise one hour each day. They are kept employed at various trades according to their skill & capacity. Neither stripes or chains are used, misconduct or laziness is punished by diminishing the quantity & deteriorating the quality of the prisoners food: they are taught to look upon their imprisonment as intended to improve & not to punish them & as intended for their own good, to look upon labour as pleasant & not as punishment. Their food is much the same the whole year around, viz 1 lb. rye bread & ½ pint of each boiled milk & ½ pint water for breakfast. 1 pint soup & 1 lb. meat & ½ pound bread for dinner besides some vegetables. 3 or 4 potatoes. Supper 1 pint indian mush & half a gill of molasses.

Their heads are closely shaven & they wear wollen caps & other clothes according to the season, change their shirts twice a week & shave twice. Change their towels & sheets once a week. Their bedding consists of sheet, converlet, blankets & a hair matress spread upon a bead stead made of iron, sheet iron strips about half an inch broad extending from the frame cross wise like a bed cord, smoother & equally as elastic; one side of the frame is fastened to the wall by hinges so that the bedstead containing the bed can be raised up close & parallel to the wall & there confined by a hook, the legs which support the bedstead when let down are made of small bars of iron with joints near the frame so that they will lay close when the frame is raised & fall when it is let down. The cells are lighted in day by a hole through the arched roof, large on the inside & tapering to the outside to the size of _____ inches in diameter the hole being covered with a pane of glass. The rooms are ventilated through a cast iron pipe on each side the door near the ground as large as one's fist & by many small holes on the opposite side of the cell near the top of the wall & thence communicating to the top of the house in open air. Their excrement is dropped through a cast iron funnel of large size, situated in one corner of the dormitory into cast iron pipes of large size & filled with water, one large pipe _____ inches in diameter running under the passage of each radius with branch pipes of smaller size communicating with the funnels in the cells; at certain periods the water will be drawn off all at once & with it the excrement, the pipes cleaned & again filled. The cells are to be warmed in the following summer. A heater is built under the passage floor of each radius & perhaps one at each end of it. This heater or oven is built of brick one thick, quadrangular & about 6 or 8 feet square, with many cast iron pipes extending from the inside of the oven to the fresh air on the outside, entirely within the square oven is a cylindrical stove of large size, having one place to put in the coal, one to take out the ashes & a pipe to take of the smoke; so that the fresh air is admitted into the oven by the afore said pipe & when heated by the stove is conducted off through pipes to the cells. The ceiling of the cells is arched & of brick about _____ feet high the cells about _____ feet square, inside white washed, the floor of smooth plank. The doorway is but _____ feet high & _____ feet broad & has two doors, the interior of bar iron laid cross ways & bolted together, resting upon pivots, not hinges, let into the top & bottom of the cast iron door facings the outer door is of strong plank; the construction of the two doors is such that the interior door can not be opened from the inside unless it is opened first.

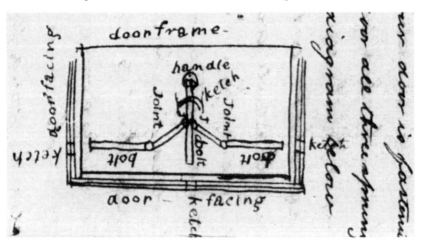

This desirable end is accomplished by the following snug contrivance, the breadth of the doors is precisely the same as the thickness of the wall & the outside door is hung upon the right (as you enter) & interior door upon the left, both doors opening inward towards each other, so that when both are open the outter door will occupy the right facing & the interior door the left facing, from this it is obvious that if the interior door was opened first there would not be room or sweap for the outter door to open, & the outter door must be shut or if open must lay close to the jam or facing otherwise there will not be room the interiour door to open. Q.E.D. The interiour door is fastened by three bolts on the outside of the door all three opening in one instant, as explained by the diagram below. The bolts represented as unsprung, when sprung the bottom & top bolts will lay in a straight line & the middle one at right angles, they are confined by a sort of house lock passing throug a hole in the handle of the middle bolt & the ketch which surrounds it & which is fastened to the door.

The washing & cooking for the prisoners is done by persons employed for the purpose, their victuals are administered to them by the assistant keepers, through a hole opening into the passage, the form of the hole is similar to one formed by joining the spouts of two funnels, the sides of it being faced with cast iron. The cells of the prisoners are rarely entered by anyone except the warden & he only is allowed to converse with them, but the law in this respect is relaxed in favour of the Physician (who is required to visit each man twice a week) & some other persons on particular occasions. & for extra purposes.

When a prisoner is first brought he is conducted to the Inspector's room thence to a small house containing three rooms, in the first the prisoner is searched shaved & stripped, in the next purifies in a warm bath, in the next he puts on the prison garments & is thence conducted blindfold to his cell. The cost of feeding a man 10 cents per day & it is estimated that their labour will clear about _____ per week. The cost of bedding & bedstead about _____. The cost of the whole buildings about 3 hundred & 30 thousand dollars & when complete will cost about 400 thousand dollars.[129]

Visited the House of Refuge Dec. 14, 1829, Situated in the N. West part of the environs of Pha. Designed for the reformation of juvenile delinquents supported & established chiefly by charity & partly by appropriations from the state, Contains about 90 males & about 20 females all under 21 years of age. The cells remarkably neat 3 rows high & running parallel to about 6. or 8. feet from the outter wall & under the same roof with its side, The wall encloses 6 or 8 acres in all & are built of stone, prisoner chiefly orphans or the offspring of worthless parents, when sentenced to the House they may be kept untill they are _____ but are discharged or bound out as soon as they evince honest & industrious habits. They are kept employed at study or work. The boys chiefly at shoemaking, wicker work, tailoring & carpentering & girls at sewing, punishments chiefly stripes in the hand.

A library of good size and quality is open to the use of the delinquents, education being much attended to. They lodge separately, play & work & study together & eat at two tables in the same hall, 20 minutes is the time allowed for a meal, no one is allowed to speak during meal time. The quantity & sort of food various, soup, beef & vegetables & molasses &c.[130]

Visited an Infant School in the South part of the city in company with Mrs. Aerstein one of the managers; the school house is the basement story of a Presbyterian church, when I arrived the children had a recess & in all my life I never saw a more cheerful & frolicksome company, they were singing, pratting, & running in every direction, while their Instructress was watching over them; we were invited into the school room, at the sound of a whistle the children the girls first, began with much alacrity to fall in a ring one close after the other & to march slowly around it at the same time singing in loud & animated strains several short hyms, marking time by stamping & claping their hands, having marched round once or twice the formost led the way to their seats which are raised like an amphitheatre the largest girls occupying the highest, the boys then took their seats on the other side or ends of the seats & they all so joined in the same song. A whistle was sounded & the instructress in a pleasant tone asked them to be so silent that they could hear the pin which she held in her fingers fall on the floor they were silent & she commenced questioning them on Geography, they replying in rhyme & song.

One little boy was scratched by another, the offender was informed on & began to cry, the instructress took him from his seat, turned the attention of the class to him by some questions & then asked him if he was sorry for his offense, he replied no promptly, he was made to stand idle while the mistress continued her questions, presently she was informed that he was sorry, he said he was sorry, kissed & embraced the little boy whom he had scratched & they sat down together in good humour & friends. They sung many lessons some to the tune of Auld Lang Sayne & I want be a Numi to the latter "I am so fond of Infant School I should not stay away." Those who can read learn the answers from the books & the others are taught by the mistress & learn from hearing the recitation of the others. To teach them the multiplication table a frame about a yard square is suspended in the middle of the room, this frame contains 12 wires running horizontally from one side of the frame to the other, upon each wire there is a row of 12 wooden balls about the size of a turkey egg each row painted of a different colour. The mistress stands by the frame & with a rod passes the balls along the wire two at a time begin-

ning at the left hand & proceeding from top to bottom, the children singing as she counts, "twice one are two" & so on until 12 times 12 make
144. Hung all around the room are paste boards on which are pasted sheets
containing the alphabet & easy lessons, ornamented & explained by objects
& hieroglyphics.

The number I thought to be about 100; 60 being girls the others boys
or in that proportion all between the ages of 2½ to 6 years old, chiefly
between 4 & 6 years and managed by two instructresses. Chastisement
is very rare & then very mild. The children are chiefly orphans or the
children of poor parents of all denominations, the children had clean faces
and hands & generally clean clothes & check aprons. The school is supported by charitable donations the room rent books & services of the
Teachers being the objects chiefly of expense.[131]

Lines addressed to a Friend

Oh thou whose image haunts my loneliest hour
Whose presence can dispell with majic power
The gloom which can condemn my heart to know
And from my spirit drive all gloomy woe
Permit my humble muse to speak a train
Of feeling truths in unaffected strain
Nor blame the band if his weak love should prove
Unfit to wake a strain for generous loves
His muse unpracticed in poetic art
But feebly speaks the language of the heart
If warm affection bright as morning's beam
And love as pure as ever poets dream
Could make amends, for genius, every line
Would breathe the language of the tuneful nine
As some lone traveller from his nation home
In foreign climes an exile forced to roam
Less smiling nation all her charms display
To please his eye and cheer his lonely way
Meets generous souls whose minds possess the art
To please the fancy and to win the heart
Yet all but serves to bring before his mind
The view of forms & friendships left behind
Tis so with me; though through the world I roam
I'm pulled by duty from my heart's "dear home"
When kindred souls the social unath entwine
And wit and poetry all the powers combine
Mid the gay scenes of festive mirth and glee
My heart in lonely sadness turns to thee
Nor stops the influence here, if changed the scene

And awakening clouds of sorrow intevene
If other friends forget the scared tie
And cherished hopes butwither droop and die
To thee I turn and in thy influence find
A balm to sooth the sorrows of my mind
Oh Friendship! soother of life's gloomy way
Without thee who on earth could wish to stay
Without a friend in joy to share a past
In   shade to bind the broken heart
Our pathway through this scene of hopes & fears
Would well deserve the title "ode of tears."

Receipts
A List of Introductory Letters

Blake, James	Drayton, Wm.
Gunnell, James	Williams, Lewis
Rockhill, Thos. C.	Webster, Daniel
Riggs & Company	Smith, William
Marshall, John	, John
Madison, James	Barney, John
Johnson, Chapman	Van Renseliar, L.
Calhoun, John C.	Bunges, Tristam
Brown, Obeo B.	Macon, N.
Brantley, N. B.	Ingensol, Ralph L.
Frame, Joseph	Green, Thomas E.
Forbes, John	Dearborne, Hret. L.
Caswell, A.	Berryman, Edwin Upshaw
Parkerson, Wm.	Grigg, John
Barlow, P. B.	Campbell, [Alexander]
Kerr, John	Crowningshield, B. M.
Bryce, Arch A.	

Expenditures
Catalogue of Books we bought between Oct. 10, 1829

Johnson & Walker's English Dictionary	$2 12½
Halls Travels in America	1 50
French & English Vocabulary	50
Polloks Course of Time	40
Tablet of Memory	1 12½
Blank Book	37½
A large Geographical Atlas	6 50
Views of American Scenery	40
McDonald Clarke's Sketches	12½

Telemachus in French	1	
Federalists		75
Leotts Life of Napoleon	2	50
Worcester's Gazette	2	80
Botta's history of Amer. Revolution	1	95
Picture of Boston	1	25
Don Juan		75
American Constitutions		75
Marriage Ceremonies		22
View of the World		40
Life of Rich'a. H. Lee	1	20
Reid on the Mind		30
Ballantine on Linistarion	1	5
Bucks Theological Dictionary		95
Washington Guide		50
Gibbon's Rome	5	85

Words of advice from parting friends
The battle of the Blue Licks
Iron Works in Greenup County
Kenhawa Salt Works
Great Falls of the Kenhawa River
Lewisburg Temperance Society
White Sulphur Springs
Falling Spring
Hot Springs & Warm Springs
Prospect from Warm Spring Mountain
Blowingbarn
Natural Bridge
Lexington & Washington College
Staunton & the Lunatic Assylum
Meyers Cave
Charlottesville & Virginia University
Virginia Convention
Hon. P. P. Barbour
Visit to the home of Jas. Madison
Chapman Johnson
Chief Justice Marshall
Hon. James Monroe
Hon. John Randolph
Hon. Wm. B. Giles
Rev. Alex. Campbell
Museum, Penty., Armory, Library & Church

Capitol Paintings & the Temp. Soc.
Norfork & fortress Monroe
Passage to New York Sea Sickness
Mamouth Children & Solar Microscope in P.M
Navy Yard & Dry Dock

   Philadelphia Pa. Dec. 16th, 1829, visited the Walnut Street Prison,
a city & county establishment, situated on the neat square south of the
Old State house; the principal building in front & the entrance; three stories
high, of brick, with wings of stone; the outter wall of stone, topped with
brick, having a row or roof of planks projecting inwards, the height of
the wall about 28 feet, 4 feet thick at bottom. The interior buildings are
various & iregular in their location. Though this prison is the property
of this County, yet other Counties can send convicts, they being bound
for the expenses of the prisoner. The interior of the wall is divided into
three divisions; one for females, one for grown men & one for young men.
The number of males about 400 & of females 60; but 16 of which are white;
among the youths the number of blacks greatly exceeds the number of
whites; they are generally convicted for Larceny, they are employed in
dying & weaving check & other cotton cloth, in sawing & dressing stone;
some in tailoring &c. The prisoners in the men's department cook for all
& the women wash for all, their coats & pantaloons of thick coarse linsey,
their shirts of coarse linen, all made in the prison; they shave twice &
change shirts once a week. The spinning weaving & carding are all done
by hand. The prisoners, males, are lodged in rooms containing from 18
to 30, their mattress bed, being rolled up and hung to the wall during the
day & spread upon the floor when in use; The females lodge several in
the same room, but have rough bedsteads in some of them. The three
departments have each a dining hall where the prisoners eat, the blacks
& whites apart. Their chief articles of diet are rye coffee for breakfast,
soup & meat & vegetables for dinner & thin corn mush with some molasses
in it for supper; their bread and mush is made of rye meal, as they say
it is more healthy than indian meal. Their principal table plate is a coarse
earthen shallow crock, answering well for either soup, mush or coffee.
Their hair is long, their appearance generally decent & healthy. Their work
shops tolerably decent, & their dormitories quite so. Though I observed
no loud talking or laughing yet the prisoners seemed cheerful & busy &
looked at us boldly & fearlessly. The punishments for offenses committed
in the prison are solitary confinement, with less or worse food & other
comforts; the lash or chains not being authorized by law. It is contemplated
to abolish this institution when the sentences of the prisoners now in shall
have expired, as the system is thought to be deficient and the expenses
of are 15 or 20 thousand dollars annually. The prisoners are tasked & a

fixed price allowed for their labour to be credited to the account of the County from which he comes. Saw a prisoner keeping the Record of Convictions in the following way. The names, age, residence, crime, description, trade, &c. of the prisoners were recorded in lines running regularly from top to bottom of the page, & neatly done. The "warping bars" was made as follows, The yarn was wound round a drum (made like one of the drums of a pair of winding blades) standing & revolving perpendicular upon its axis; round the top pole was wound a string communicating with a small frame which guided the yarn on the drum, as the string unwound the frame carried the yarn down & vice versa, the drum was large 5. or 6 feet in diameter & 8. or 10 high, it was turned by a band passing round the bottom thence on a flat wheel turned by a hand crank & running perpendicularly. The yarn was wrung by means of a crank, to which it was hooked. The prison is visited by Preachers, volunteering their services on the sabbath; and furnished with Bibles. There is an apothecary shop well supplied, and a hospital well kept connected with the prison.[132]

Visited the New Prison a second time. Learned that criminals only from the Eastern district could be sent to this prison; that, at Pittsburgh being for the west district.[133] The Prison is situated 2½ miles North West of the State house. The warden obtained the privilege for me of seeing & conversing with the prisoners, as this is contrary to the rules of the place, the privilege is rarely granted & then for special & particular purposes. This favour was another proof of the gentlemanly cleverness of Mr. Wood the Warden; Of the 8 prisoners I saw 7,[134] none of which had been there more than four months. Their rooms were warm & decent, the air pure & fresh. I think they were about 10 feet long & 6 broad with an arched ceiling 8 or 10 feet at the highest point. Two of the prisoners were engaged in shoemaking, one in weaving, one in quilling for the weaver, one in carpentering, one in tailoring, others not known. They were of a healthy, robust & cheerful appearance, conversed readily, smiled & laughed pleasantly when I spoke to them; when questioned regarding their situation they all said it was comfortable & preferable to a residence in Walnut St. Prison. One young man who had been in W. St. Prison told me he would prefer the New Prison because he would get no worse there if he got no better, saying that he was much worse when he went out of the W. St. Prison than when he went in. Though all but two said they were quite lonesome, yet none expressed much displeasure of solitary confinement or much desire for society; & though all said they would prefer to be out, yet one said he would be well content to remain, if he could pocket the proceeds of his labour; he had just learned the shoemakers trade & had been in prisons before. None seemed oppressed with melancholy as if brooding over his situation; but several told me that they sometimes thought & reflected on their past life & present situation & one hoped that by industry & good conduct his sentence would be shortened. So far from being averse to labour it was agreeable & they took but little exercise except in labour; they resorted to it to make the time pass off more pleasantly. They all said that they were fond of reading & one on being questioned as to the amount said he read more than 20 or 30 chapters per week, of the Bible, which is the principle & perhaps only book they have. They said that they ate with good appetite & slept but tolerably when they exercised but little. They receive the warden with seeming pleasure rather than the reverse, & were pleasant rather than melancholy. The diet of the prisoners is as follows. For breakfast half a pint of skimmed milk with half a pint of water, the two boiled together, & one pound of rye bread. For dinner a piece of meat weighing one pound when raw, one pint of soup made of it, half a pound of bread and three or four potatoes boiled with the soup. For supper one pint of indian mush & half a gill of molasses. The warden thinks this amply sufficient. To reward the industrious and obedient the same quantity is prepared in a more nice & palitable manner. Each man is supplied with a small tin water pitcher with a top to it, a tin wash basin & a tin bason or mess pot, suiting for soup, coffee or mush. They, like the prisoners of walnut Street Prison & all others in the East, receive instruction from ministers of the gospel gratuitously. The warden thought that $1 per week would find a prisoner in food, clothing & bedding & that they will earn about 30 cents per day on an average. The cost of a bed is about $20, the iron bedstead $9, the hair mattress $5, the blankets & sheets $6. The warden & other officers have fixed salaries to be paid by the State. In the weaving room a common hand bow was fixed so as to draw the frame containing the sleigh to the webb with greater force.[135]

Visited the United States Mint, on North Sixth street; buildings numerous, irregular, and uncomely.[136] Between 20 & 30 men are employed & about 8000 dollars are coined in a day or two thousand half dollars per hour. The first operation is to melt the silver (commonly Mexican dollars) in an iron crucible in a coal fire & then pour it into cast iron moulds making silver bars about 12 inches long one inch or more broad & half an inch thick; these bars are then put between to iron rollers of great strength, laying horizontally & running one above the other in the same direction they are about 6 inches in diameter & 12 or 18 in. length. The bars are rolled out to the length of 6 or 8 feet to the thickness of half a dollar & a little broader, these strips are then taken to the cutting mill where the coin is cut or punched out, by means of a punch fitting in a hole just the size of 50 cents; the coin being punched out of the strip in about 3 seconds; these blanks are then taken to another machine where the letters &c are put on the edges; the blanks are then whitened & taken to the stamping mill formed as follows. A large steel screw works perpendicularly in a screw tap, to the top of the screw is fixed an iron lever about 10 feet long, the screw to the middle of the lever, which works horizontally like the needle of a compass, propelled by manual labour. It is worked or vibrated back & forward describing about one fourth of a circle; to the lower end of this screw is fixed a round bar of steel about 4 or 5 inches long & of the same diameter as a half a dollar, on the lower end of this bar is the die or impression, just below this bar of steel is fixed another bar upon the upper end of which is fixed or engraved the other impression, the blank piece of silver is thrown by machinery between these two dies, is rested or laid upon the lower one, the screw is then turned which drives the upper die down upon the coin with much force & thus the impression is made; the coin is pushed by machinery from between the dies & another blank put in. This operation is performed with much facility & expedition impressing two thousand half dollars in an hour. The dies cost about $150, the machine is operated by three men at hard labour. The coin is then scattered with much care over the floor of the counting room, mixed, counted, deposited in vaults & thence is conveyed to the United States Bank. Throughout all the rooms, silver in various forms is laying about like so much iron in a blacksmith's shop, much care is taken of it notwithstanding. The rolling mill is driven by steam I think. Yes, true.[137]

Visited the Deaf & Dumb Asylum situated on Broad Street in the western part of the City, the building large, three stories high, of hewn grey stone with columns in front, the building respectable, but not handsome.[138] It is a charitable institution but is assisted by appropriations by the State. Invalids are received from any State some are supported & instructed gratuitously & others pay $170 per annum & others in part support themselves by the profits of their labour, there being a shoemaker's shop & weaving shop for weaving check and cotton cloth &c connected with the Asylum.

The invalids are first taught to denote physical objects by signs, then letters by signs (having an alphabet of signs) then to join the letters or signs & form words denoting physical objects first, they are then taught that physical objects have properties. On presenting our Permit on Thursday evening (it being an examination day) we were conducted into the Chapel; of good size; the spectators seats elevated one above the other; about 20 ladies & 15 or 20 gentlemen as spectators. The class 2nd was called, (had been under instruction two years) when five girls, made their appearance from the door next the female side of the Asylum and 5 boys made theirs from an opposite side. They were all decently clad, more or less genteely; of cheerful & healthful aspect & between the ages of 12 & 18 years, each took a stand by a large chalk board, a row of which was along the side of the house opposite the spectators, while the Instructor an intelligent gentleman of 25 or 30, took his stand at the side between the scholars & audience. His first made signs of physical objects & the pupils wrote their names on the boards; he then gave them historical & other sentences which they put in writing; then made them tell the various parts of speech & partially define them; made them write original sentences in which particular parts of speech must be used. The instructor told how such invalids were first taught what an adjective was by Abbe Licard. He showed them a piece of blank paper, then painted it & asked them if they could take the colouring away, they thus learned that black was an adjective to the paper. The pupils exhibited much dexterity in committing their ideas to writing & spelt with their fingers, with much facility & held familiar converse by signs. The exhibition gave general satisfaction & all were convinced of the quality of the Institution.

Visited the Museum in the Arcade, one of the best in the U.S.A. founded by Peale[139] the same who founded that in New York. The principal curiosity was a complete set of the bones of the Mammouth (dug up in the State of N. York) put together in their natural position & placed with a complete set of the bones of the Elephant set up after Nature, the latter standing with ease under the head of the former. The objects are well arranged & in good preservation.

Visited the Academy of Fine Arts,[140] the best collections of paintings, engravings, busts & statues, that I have seen, arranged in four rooms. A painting of the revival of a corpse on touching the bones of the prophet Elisha, a marble bust of Franklin, the Graces, in plaister, & a colossal, decapitated, white marble, statue of Ceres, from the ruins of Megara in Greece, were among the greatest curiosities.

Visited the Atheneum,[141] where the principal periodicals &c of the day are kept for the inspection & entertainment of subscribers and their friends not resident in the city. Attended the Fair held in the Masonic Hall for various charitable purposes, the collection large & splendid, many beautiful & ingenious. The room not tastefully decorated well attended vast crowds of Gentlemen & Ladies some quite handsome. Profits handsome, prices high, large as so. Visited Arch Street Theatre, saw Mr. & Mrs. Pearman, Mr. & Mrs. Sloman, Miss George, Mr. Jefferson &c perform the Play of Guy Mannering or the Gypsies Prophecy & the Farce of The Happiest day of my life.[142]

Went to a party at Mr. Boggs' danced, a cotillion, no waltzing, but few handsome girls, one sprightly one, many with short dresses, & large ankles, gentlemen very clever, not burdened with grace or elegance, music various & good, no tea, sweet meats in profusion, little drinking of wine & less of ardent spirits, assembled about — & rose at 12.0[.]

Visited the Criminal Court, looked like a mob, wenches, pickpockets, negroes & rascals have complete possession. Visited the Supreme Court, very respectable tribunal saw several of the greatest lawyers. Saw the hall in which the declaration of Independence was signed, &c.

Much pleased with the Churches went to 2. Paid a bill of a dollar a day, left on the 9th day. Mrs. Yohe's being rather a sheepish (punning!) establishment;[143] embarked on the Steam Boat William Penn, for Baltimore fare $4: distance about 100 miles. In descending the Delaware our Steam Boat ran afoul of a Schooner under sail in the same direction, the gib Boom of the Schooner ran through the Stewards room, the barber shop & passing through the boiler room, barely missed the boiler of the Steam boat, penetrated to the stairway of the gentlemen's cabin, then broke about its middle and was drawn out by the rigging of the Schooner, the sails & rigging of which were much injured. The accident originated in carelessness, was done & over in a minute or two & the steamer proceeded on her journey. As the boom passed over the boiler it opened a valve from which the cabin was instantaneously filled with steam which together with the shock threw the passengers into the greatest consternation, the steward had well nigh fallen upon his carving knife, the barber droped his box & razor in the greatest agitation, the subject ran upon deck with his clothes half off & his face lathered. The passengers in the gentlemens' cabin forgot their gallantry & rushed abruptly from the steam through the ladies' cabin up the stairs to the deck, some with their hats left behind & others just as they jumped from their berths with their coats off in their stocking feet & others with one boot & one slipper. In a few moments the danger was over & the various characters collected in groups to talk about the disaster. In a short time the Steamer reached the Eastern end of the Canal having passed in her route the towns of Wilmington & New Castle both on the Western side of the Delaware, the banks of which are chiefly low & sandy. At Delaware City we were marched over land about 200 yards & embarked on board a large barge on the Canal which 14 miles long about 8 feet deep & 60 feet wide in the channel, a tow path only on North side the other being broken & irregular the canal being in some places ½ a mile wide.[144] The Barge would carry 200 passengers, had no births, was drawn by two teams of three horses each, having a driver on each hinder horse, they drawing in a row by tow lines about 70 yards long, attached to the top of the boat & on the side (not the bow) next the towpath. The canal has a lock at the East end & one about ⅓ the distance from the East end, which raises about 10 feet, and two at the West end, their sides & bottom of stone. We passed & ascended the second Lock as follows. The lock was about 100 feet long, 15 broad & 30 feet deep, or just large enough to admit one Barge or sloop, at each end of the lock was a double door, the pannels of which were hung upon oposite sides of the lock all opening upsteam, when in about 20 yards from the Lock our tow lines were detached from the boat, the lower doors or gates were thrown open (one opening on each side), & our boat glided into the Lock, the water in it being of the same elevation as the water on which we were just travelling, when the boat was fairly in the lock, the doors by which we entered were closed fitting together like a forceps, the point up stream, the flood gates at the bottom of the upper doors were then raised through which the water rushed from above & thus we were gradually raised up to a level with the water in front of us, the upper doors were then thrown open, the tow lines were attached & we were thus drawn out & so on.

We passed several low bridges over the Canal constructed so as to be ballanced upon pivots on the side of the canal & to be turned round on the pivots with much celerity & ease. We passed a dock & bridge & changed horses in 10 minutes. Passed a schooner (towed by three horses), in the following manner. The schooner being spoken, put herself on the outside of the canal, slacked her tow line & stopped her horses on the outside of the tow path so that our horses & our boat passed over their tow line between their horses & their boat, while they were still.

Passed the deep cut, where the banks of sand & gravel were excavated about 85 feet; where a frame wooden bridge was thrown across the canal from one bank to the other & was so high that a sloop with its masts could pass under. In changing teams at this place one horse became entangled in the gear & commenced kicking, which frightened the others so that one of the old teams & one of the fresh teams broke off & ran several miles along the tow path; one team was at length stopped by the exhaustion & falling of a horse, the others by men working on the canal. The banks of the Canal are preserved in some places by walling them with stone & in others by graduating them from top to bottom & covering them with thatch & sowing them with grass to prevent their being washed by rain, cut by torrents, or broken by the waves; the tow path is made by laying a stratum of Earth then one of hay & then earth &c. The horses drawing the barge proceeded in a brisk trot & sometimes in a gallop at the rate of 5 or 6 miles in an hour, had three changes in the 14 miles. The barge moved generally about 4 feet from the shore & ran remarkably smooth & easy, but had nearly run out on shore at the western end of the Canal. There we embarked on a steamer in a creek & thence went into Elk river thence to the Chesapeake down to Baltimore & were safely landed at Barnum's City Hotel by 9 o'clock.[145] Saturday night Dec. 19, 1829, the same day we left Philadelphia. Among other passengers was the Honourable Jas. Brown, a Minister to France & his family.[146]

Monday Dec. 21st, 1829, hired a carriage for 50 cents & went about a mile west of the City, to see some experiments on the Baltimore & Ohio Rail Road, of which about 26 miles is nearly completed at a cost of about $20,000 per mile, the road is made by levelling & graduating the earth & laying & confining two parallel rows of large scantling upon which are fastened two parallel rows of iron bars, about one inch thick & between two & three inches broad, upon these iron rails the wheels of the Cars run, between the rows of rails the earth is turnpiked & on this the horses travel. I saw one & a half miles of the rail road, a part of which was on a level with the adjacent earth, a part was cut through a hill 30 feet & a part over a branch was raised 40 or 50 feet. At the Western end of the section there was a superb stone bridge over a creek built of hewn stone, with an arch the span of which was 80 feet, from the water to the top of the bridge was about 60 feet, the length 310 feet, breadth about 30 feet, cost of the bridge $60,000 dollars. The country over which this part runs is of a sandy soil.[147]

The sides of the road were thronged with visitors some on foot some in carriages & some on horseback. Among others was the venerable Charles Carrol,[148] When I saw him he was seated in one of the cars with 20 or 30 gentlemen & was travelling at the rate of 9 or 10 miles in an hour, his hands were crossed before him & resting on the top of his staff, his long white silver locks were streaming behind in the wind, his dress was black, his complexion sallow, his visage much rinkled, his face long & large, nose large & prominent a little aquilene, his whole countenance was manly & seemed much enlivened by the scene to which his presence imparted so much interest. This car was loaded with 27 gentlemen, was drawn by one horse & performed the route of one mile & a half in seven minutes & a half. The frame of the car was of wood; the wheels of the same size before & behind; 4 in number made of cast iron and almost 3 feet in diameter, the car so fixed that the horse could readily be attached to either end. Together [with] two sprightly, intelligent & respectable ladies & 21 gentlemen I embarked in this car, drawn by one horse & proceeded 1½ miles in 10 minutes, the passage being very pleasant, the motion rapid but smooth & steady as well as safe, the horse performing with much ease.[149] Tis part of the road almost a perfect level.

When we returned a new and splendid car of Winan's plan & invention was on the railway filled with passengers & just ready to start.[150] The chief diference between this & the other is that in winan's the running wheel & axle are solid & turn together the doll extending quite through the hub of the wheel & fitting in to the rim a friction wheel upon which the body of the carriage rests, thus placing the friction on the extreme end of the axel, which works into the friction wheel & rests on its rim.

In this car, which was handsomely finished, the seats being cushioned 6 or 8 in number & the whole nicely painted, I obtained a seat with 36 others and we proceeded about half way on the road at the rate of about 9 miles an hour, drawn with perfect ease by one common draught horse; as this was only an experiment he sometimes walked now trotted & now galloped with perfect ease his traces being slack half the time; when we wished to return, the carriage was stopped by pressing a wooden leaver against the wheel, the horse was unhitched, taken round & hitched to the other end of the car; we turned about our faces & the driver who this time rode the horse, put off in a long trot, &c.[151]

Winan's Rail Road Carriage

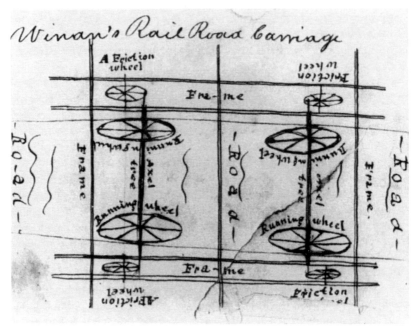

We visited a factory for Glass Blowing where I believed that all glass ware except window glass is made; this operation though quite simple is yet more difficult of description. We entered a large frame workshop, with a large brick furnace, in the form of a sugar loaf, in the middle of it, the base of the furnace is ten or 12 feet in diameter, the top extending out of the roof of the house; Within this furnace was a large crucible, containing the molten sand, under which an immense coal fire was kept constantly burning. Around the furnace & above the top of the crucible were 5 or 6 small holes from which the workmen took the glass, They held hollow iron rods of about 5 feet in length & not unlike the barrel of a shot gun, in their hands. These they thrust into the molten glass, so much of which as adhered to the blow pipe was taken out red hot, turned over & over on an iron thus rounded like the head of a cane, the workman then applied his mouth to the other end of the pipe, blows gently swells it to the form of a bladder, then strikes the end of the glass on the ground to flatten it, then holding the pipe in a horizontal position he turns it rapidly, at the same time applying an iron, not unlike a pair of sheep shears, to the warm glass he fashions it to his liking. In making a common tumbler the glass first assumes the form of a bottle by the above process, the mouth being attached to the pipe is broken off from it & the bottom of the bottle is stuck to the hot glass on the end of the blow pipe, the bottle is again heated & while hot is turned in a horizontal position, an iron being at the same time thrust into its mouth & which is thus expanded as desired, an even iron is applied to the mouth of the tumbler to flatten it, it is then broken off the blow pipe & is complete. During the operation it passes through the hands of several persons, each performing his proper part & requiring from three to five minutes of time according to the skill of the men or boys engaged. While the ware is yet hot from the hands of the artists it must be put in pans in a large furnace of moderate heat where it is permitted to cool gradually, otherwise it would be liable to crack.[152]

Thence we waded through mud & water about a mile & a half to the Penitentiary, situated on a plain, west of the Alleghany river in the remote edge of Alleghany town. Its first appearance evinced the munificence of the State in its erection; but is a monument of the dullness of the architect who planned & of the folly of the legislature which adopted the plan of the building & had it executed.[153]

Tuesday December. 22nd. 1829, visited the Maryland Penitentiary, of which Mr. Joseph Owens is keeper. The principal & front buildings of brick, 4 stories high, the wall chiefly of rough stone, topped with brick, but 18 feet high, enclosing about 6 acres of ground; divided into three apartments, one for men, one for youths & one for females; the whole number of prisoners about 360, about 230 of which are blacks, & about 45 females, but two of which are white.[154] Two of the prisoners, a black man & woman are confined for life, for murder. The chief employment is dying and weaving striped cotton cloth; there being about 110 looms employed, each weaving from 12 to 20 yards per day according to the capacity of the labourer & the length of the day; a man is taught to weave in three months & then like the rest he receives a task which he must perform, & is paid for what he weaves over it. The yarns are bought, (being spun near Baltimore) &c are died & woven in the prison at a total cost of about 7 cents per yard & readily sold, chiefly in the Western country, for 14 cents per yard thus making a neat profit of 7 cents. The goods of good quality & in much demand. Coarse linsey for garments for the prisoners is also made in the prison, stone is sawed extensively but not dressed otherwise.[155]

Twenty or 30 persons were employed in making horn combs, of good quality & ready & profitable sale. The horns are first sawed in the middle & then the circle is divided or split on one side, then boiled in oil & water then opened out, with irons for the purpose, then pressed flat between hot plates of iron well oiled, the pressure applied by a horizontal screw, the horn then pressed & coolled between cold cast iron plates, is then marked then sawed into proper sizes, then rasped with broad raspes, is then softened by warming, is then cut into two pieces by a machine making the teeth as it cuts them, the teeth after being cut with this machine are rasped & trimmed, the combs then polished with brick dust, then coloured with various preparations, again polished, then warmed & while warm applied & bound to a round piece of wood which gives them their shape when cooled. The raspings & shavings are sold to chemists to make prussian blue, or to gardners for manure. The operation required but little skill & little information.[156] The prisoners lodge separately, eat in a common hall, work, many in the same shop, intercourse & conversation being prohibited, as far as possible. Their rations are fixed by Law.[157] Their beds are hammocks or linnen suspended by strings at the end from the wall. Their faces are bathed their heads are shaven once a week. Their linnen changed once a week, well supplied with towels, have three meals a day; are furnished with bibles, prayer & hymn book & tracts; hear preaching 2 or 3 times every sunday, preachers volunteering; have a sunday school, 10 or 15 young men of Baltimore attending the prison every sunday & given instruction gratuitously.[158]

Within the walls is a prison on a new plan, 4 stories high, of brick, in an oblong circular form, the cell doors opening into the interior of the building, each story having a circular portico, the whole having but one great entrance; each cell having a small window over the door & one on the oposite side of the cell; the porticos or passages illuminated by windows at the ends & top or roof along the comb of the building; all executed with much strength & neatness.[159] The whole prison indicated order decency & good management; the prisoners working industrously; corporeal punishment, though in use, rarely resorted to. The women were employed in sewing, spinning & weaving. The officers evinced much cleverness & attention to me, furnished me with the last year's reports & promised those of the present, giving at the same time, all desired information readily.[160]

Visited Washington's Monument, the most superb work of the kind that I have ever seen, consisting of a Greek Doric column built of white marble blocks 20 feet in diameter at its base & 130 feet hight. The column is surmounted by a colosseum statue of Washington, executed by Carici of Verona in Italy, at a cost of 10,000 dollars; the statue 15 feet in height, composed of 3 pieces of white marble, originally of a solid & detached mass, found in an open field about 40 miles from Baltimore.[161] I paid 12½ cents to the Keeper, got a lantern & ascended a flight of 200 self supporting white marble steps, winding around a solid pillar of brick & from the top of the monument; had an extensive & delightful view of the Patapsco river, the Bay, the city & adjacent country; among all the interesting objects Fort McHenry was not the least important. The design of the statue represents Washington surrendering his commission at Annapolis, holding the roll in his right hand, arm half extended, the left covered with a profusion of drapery representing a sort of cloak; the statue is roughly executed, unpolished & not an excellent likeness, his nose being rather short. The height of the whole, statue, column, base & elevation of the hill amounts to about 182 feet & when entirely complete will have cost not much less than $200,000. The funds raised chiefly by voluntary contributions of the citizens of Baltimore.[162]

Visited the Battle Monument, various City Springs, Medical College, Cast Iron Foundry, Glass works &c. Paid a bill exceeding $5.[163] Took stage for Washington about two o'clock on Tuesday Dec. 22nd 1829, distance about 37 miles, fare $2.50, road very fine, arrived same evening at Gasby's Dec. 23rd called on Col. Johnson[164] & in company with him went to the Palace & called on President Jackson about 10 o'clock, found him upstairs doing business with a countryman; at the front door found a servant who showed us to his room. When presented, the Pres. rose & shook hands in an easy & familiar style & having taken his seat commenced a conversation in familiar style on common topics. Sat about 15 minutes rose shook hands & departed, entertaining more favourable opinions of his manners as well as of his appearance.[165] Thence went to call on Sec. Van Buren,[165] found him polite & affable, in tolerable health, complaining of ill health caused by confinement & the labours of his office. Thence called on Sec. Eaton,[167] & found his wife extremely gay, pretty & clever. Called on Sec Ingham[168] found him plain & careless of his dress, common in conversation, polite but ungracefully so. Called on Vice Pres. Calhoun,[169] found him remarkably polite & genteel conversed in sprightly, lively & familiar tones; tall in his person & elegant in his manners. Called on Postmaster Barry[170] & found him absent;

Tuesday, Dec. 23rd 1829 left Gadsby's & took lodgings at Mrs. Blake's Pen. avenue, price $8. a week.

After visiting the halls of Congress & calling upon several gentlemen, took a circuit & according to the customs of the City called at the residences of the Foreign Ministers & delivered my card to servants at the door, this being the method by which persons wishing to be invited to their entertainments first introduce themselves.

Dec. 31. went to a party at Mr Clarke's,[171] clerk of the House. The company was received & presented at the door, was so large as to crowd 4 spacious rooms; it was a perfect squeeze, of persons of all ages, both sexes & many nations, French, German & English being spoken. Many a fantastic dress was rumpled, many a shoulder bow & breast knot was broken, many an ugly face was seen & but few handsome ones. The only amusements were observation, & squeezing about through the crowd from one room to another, having room for an occasional conversation, & the final amusement was eating a Splendid, rich & various set supper & those who chose indulged freely in champaign while the Temps took a lemonade.

January first 1830, a beautiful clear sunny day, not warm, nor yet cold. Called upon Miss Louisa Hunter & with her & others went, like a thousand others of all classes & ages to pay our new years respect to the President, upon common custom & general invitation. After passing a host of carriages, entered the great gateway, reached the portico, pressed through a motly crowd, passed the front door, at which a guard was placed to keep off the more ungenteel of the rabble; passed through an ante-chamber in which a fine band of musicians, with red dresses & various instruments, was stationed & performed; entered the front drawing room, passed through an avenue opened through the dense crowd of visitors by a guard & then found the Pres, already much exhausted, receiving his company standing, shook hands with him, passed the usual compliments & continuing a few steps was presented to the ladies of the family; they dressed in splendid attire, rising from their splendid sofas, gracefully bowing & resuming their seats. After squeezing through groups of handsome belles & beaux, motly mechanics, & splendidly dressed Foreign Ministers & U.S. Officers winding round large round marble tables & gilt chairs with cushioned seats, & backs, we reached the Famed East Room, the splendour of which by no means answered my expectations, its form is oblong, its ceiling high, with broad & handsome cornice, the walls & windows adorned with handsome curtains, not splendid; the carpet was of ordinary richness, the ground colours being dark, chiefly a dusky green & blue; several large mirrors with gilt frames were on the walls. The mantle pieces & facings were of handsome polished marble & were ornamented by many splendid jars containing artificial flowers incased in glass ovals. Upon the whole the East Room was not superiour to several private parlours I have seen & I think not superiour to H.R. hall in the capitol.[172] Having amused ourselves for about an hour we retired. The house was open from 12, to 3, during which time several interesting occurrences & humorous anecdotes took place. A lady leaving the East room held her mouth & eyes aghast in admiration, the Pres. meeting her enquired how she liked it. "Oh"! she replied, it is most splendid indeed. "Yes", said the Pres. "Its *splendid* but still its *verry plain.*"

Among other officers in uniform was Com. Hull,[173] of low stature & very portly, now Com-in-chief at the Wash. Navy yard; he was pushed by a company giving marching orders from his seat, until he found himself against a marble table, his feet were untripped & he fell sprawling upon the polished marble surface. Among a number of persons crowding around the parlour door was a tall dirty looking backwoodsman, with his mouth open & his eyes stretched, pushing toward the Pres. Come & speak to the Pres." said the guard, "if you wish, if not, give back." Well, said the visiter drawing in his neck & thrusting his hands in his breeches, If Ginel Jackson wants to speak to me he must be purty quick about it. I jist wanted to ax if you had anything to drink in yonder" pointing to the E. Room. I did not see the drinkables but heard that they were served in such abundance that many visitants became riotious & that a battle took place.[174] The foreign Ministers were in attendance, their court dresses though peculiar & rich were not gaudy as they are represented on the Stage. Speaking of the Stage reminds me of the Washington Theatre which I attended on christmas evening. Cooper[175] was the chief attraction, he appearing in the character of Mark Anthony in one scene of the tragedy of Ceasar; his performance was excellent, the harrangue producing similar effects on the audience that it had upon the Romans in the play. He subsequently recited the Legendary Tale of Alphonzo & Imogine, during which the attention of the audience, their listening ears, open mouths & loud applause, spoke well of his performance. His is far advanced in the years, being about _____ years of age, his performance is said to have waned with increasing years. He looks remarkably young & retains his vigour astonishingly for one of his years & intemperate habits; he is nearly 6 feet high, stoutly built, manly & vigorous form, face round & full, features look bloated, as by intoxication, showing few marks of age, his whiskers sandy, hair grey but artifically black, a little bald on the crown of the head, his voice still strong, rather shrill when exerted, but capable of considerable variation in its tones.[176]

At this time Cooper attracts but little attention, the audience being like the house rather small & shabby.

Jan. 2nd an exceedingly lovely day, clear sunny & pleasant. At 10 o'clock hired a carriage for 25 cts. rode a mile & a half & paid a visit *in effigie* to Baron Huygens Dutch Minister[177] living in a fine brick house on the banks of Rock creek near Georgetown, to which place I then waked & examined the Canal Chessapeak & Ohio yet in its incipient state.[178] When complete it will extend from [Wheeling] on the Ohio to Georgetown on the Potomac a distance of 366 miles. At Geo.town it will empty into Rock creek about ¼ of a mile from its mouth, by means of 4 stone docks, each of considerable height, they are in a forward state & many miles of the canal are under contract & underweigh.

Visited a Cannon Foundry above Geotown, & immediately on the banks of the Potomac. It is a private concern, the metal is brought down the river, cast into cannon, Mortars, ball & shells & sold chiefly to the government of Mexico & the South American republics. The first step is to cast or mould it from a pattern, to cut off the muzzle end, then to bore out the calibre, then to turn & otherwise polish the exterriour surface. Saw 20 or 30 of various sizes from 24 to 36 pounders some remarkably thick & strong.[179]

Returning heard the sounds of revelry among the students of the Catholic College, the principal building a large, 4 story, oblong brick house, on an eminence fronting the North, with the River in the rear, near this is another large brick house, like the other looking old, dreary & desolate. Congress authorized it to confer degrees in 1815. At present it has a library of 700 vols. & about 80 students.[180]

Walked through Geo.town, but a common place & thence home in all five or 6 miles.

January the 8th The preceding evening was celebrated by a Levee of the mansion of the President, the company was large & with a few exceptions was genteel in appearance & decorous in behaviour, promenading & pushing the chief amusement.

Jan. 8th, 1830 was a clear & pleasant sunny day[.] About 1 o'clock went with a cicerone to the top of the dome of the Capitol, had a fine view of the interior of the Dome being 115 feet above its base; for the first time had a proper idea of the large size of the building, it covering more than an acre of ground, & costing about two million of dollars, had a fine view of the armory, where the National Banner was displayed & cannon were roaring in honour of the battle of N.O. also saw the Navy yard &c had an extensive view of the River & adjoining country which gradually rises within 5 or 6 miles many feet above the valley in which Washington is situated, the face of the country is rolling & somewhere is hilly, is chiefly sandy & barren, the timber being chiefly pine & cedar.

On the night of the 8th went to a Grand Ball. $5. The entertainments were prepared by dancing master Carusi[181] at his assembly rooms (formerly a Theatre was then bought by Carusi & repaired for a ball room) the upper room used for dancing while in the lower one was spread the supper table; the ball room was entered on the South side by 3 doors, the centre door used by the gentlemen & a door on each side opening from dressing rooms for the ladies, the room was lighted by three large circular chandeliers, handsomely hung with evergreens & each containing 25 candles, other lights were arranged along the walls in circles & festoon, &c. Over the doors was a small gallery containing the musicians, the marine band 10 in number dressed in red coats & performing well on a variety of instruments, making loud, animated & harmonious music. On the opposite side of the hall was a large recess in the wall, in front of which was an awning or canopy of rich cloth partially exposing to view a coarse painting, executed by [Thomas Sully] representing Gen. Jackson in military dress standing beside his horse with his arm resting on the shoulders of his horse;[182]

immediately in front of this painting were several rows of seats occupied by those ladies who did not dance.

The company consisted of about 300 gentlemen & 200 ladies a great variety in their dress & appearance, several ladies of exceeding beauty & very many who were shockingly ugly, the company generally seamed well entertained with dancing cotillions & reels the figures of which were very simple & the steps of the dancers not uncommon or uncommonly graceful. About the middle of the evening the Waltz was introduced by about 20 ladies & gentlemen chiefly foreigners, while the rest of the company formed a circle around & looked on with much interest. The figure of the Waltz as there performed was simple, chiefly consisting of turning round. The Gen. having his right arm around his partner's waist, her left arm resting on his right arm & shoulder, while with his left hand he held his partner's right & in this position they whirled each other around with so much rapidity as to cause the head to swim, turning with a regular & graceful step & undulating motion. Though the Waltz did not seem to the performers to be in the slightest degree repugnant to delicacy, yet to strangers the motions & positions seemed rather amorous as was fully testified by the reluctance which the most of the fashionables evinced in participating in it. About an hour after the company had assembled & was fully engaged in dancing, all of a sudden the music stopped & the dancers were left to return to their places without music & in blushes & disorder; the coming of the Pres was announced, the bugle struck up a martial air in loud & animated strains, while the company with much eagerness forsook their seats & cotillions and arranged themselves in two rows, leaving a passage between from the door to the Canopy. Jackson's march was played by the whole band, while all eyes were turned with much anxiety towards the door in momentary expectation of the Pres the door was thrown open, but lo! he appeared not! "False alarm", was sounded by almost every tongue & pictured in every face, the ladies frowned, their beaux muttered in mortification & the mannagers blushed for their bad management. While the musicians suddenly turned the tune from "Jackson's a coming" to "pray young doctor can you tell" what caused the disappointment I don't know. But in the course of an hour the same preparations were again made & the Pres entered followed by the V.P. & speaker of the H.R. Sec of State Secretaries of &c, & bowing gracefully to his admirers on either side he walked up to the pavillion, where his eyes brightened to see his portrait & that of his warhorse. After the more consequential & ardent of his admirers had there fatigued him with their caresses, he ascended to the highest seat under the pavillion & placed himself between two ladies whom he discoursed quite eloquently & who seemed flattered with his attentions, he soon after descended & in about half a hour made his exit I know not how.[183] The Officers of Government

Foreign Ministers, officers of the US. army & Navy were chiefly in attendance in their military & other dresses. About 11 o'clock the company
adjourned to the supper room, the repast was various, abundant & splendid, was served in a large room the sides & ceiling of which were tastefully decorated with wreaths & festoons of evergreens & candles, the room
containing three long rows of tables at which all the ladies sat down at
once; as soon as they had retired the gentlemen took their places at the
tables.

Upon the whole the Ball was most splendid & went off in fine style
affording general satisfaction. As to myself, after examining the room &
quizzing the dress, faces, & manners of the various characters, my thoughts
were unfortunately turned toward Frankfort & the less brilliant but more
beloved assemblage which I imagined was then figuring away at Mrs.
Price's[184] or somewhere else; from the depth of my soul I longed to be
there & my absence filled me with melancholy, which neither animated
tunes nor sprightly dances, no not handsome gay & amorous partners
could dispell. After dancing six or eight times with some of the belles &
closely observing others from all parts of the country, I left the ball &
reached home about one o'clock well tired & better satisfied that fashionable society was no where superiour to that of Frankfort Ky. though it
is true that the belles had more accomplishments, that is immodest airs
& fantastic millinery, about them in Washington than in Ky & what is
more my suspicions were confirmed that the ladies of Washington were
not the most pure in soul & chaste in deed of all the Fair which I had seen.
P.S. several of the most fashionable young ladies wore short dresses &
pantaletts.

Jan. 12th went to the House of Representatives & heard the Hon. Mr
Burgess[185] of R. Louisiana make a speech in favour of distributing the public
lands among the several states having become acquainted with him a few
days previous, I was enabled to take a description. He is of middle stature
& well built, in the decline of life, his complexion & features bearing the
marks of age, his head bald on the crown & front, his hair & whiskers
quite gray, his forehead of good size, his eye dark animated & penetrating
& deeply set under a projecting eyebrow, his nose a little aquiline, his
mouth & chin corresponding with his other features, the whole indicating
intelligence, but being rather cold & repulsive. In speaking his language
& reason were good, his voice full & loud, his manners & gestures a little
theatrical, while his tones resembled those of a pulpit orator, his enunciation was indistinct on account of the loss of his teeth & decline of his voice.
In private his manners were not polite & easy. On the whole he seamed
worthy of his reputation.

Jan 14th heard Mr Buchannan[186] of Pennsylvania speak in favour of
extending the circuit court system to some of the Western states &c. His

language was appropriate & perspicuous, his reasoning sound & very clear, indicating much care & previous preparation, his voice was shrill loud & clear & from being incapable of much variation & modulation soon became tiresome, his principal gesture was throwing his right hand & arm up & down, having all his fingers closed but the forefinger. In politics he is a Jackson Republican Federalist. Having met him frequently at balls where he danced & at private parties where he was affable & pleasant. I took a description of his person, he is of midling stature, portly in his form, quite broad across his shoulders genteel in his person & easy in his manners, his head large, having light hair a little thin on the top, sandy whiskers, a fat, full, trey face, looking in good humour & rather blank his forehead rather small for the rest of his face, his eyes grey & unexpressive, his nose short & small, his mouth & chin rather long for the rest of his face, the former not broad, the latter projecting as far as his forehead, he looks to be about 40, carries his head a little inclined to his right shoulder, with his left eye open & the brow of it a little turned up, which gives him rather a common, careless & quissical appearance.

On the evening of January 14, went to a grand Party at Secretary Inghams,[187] arrived half after 7 o'clock, found Mr Ingham near the door paid my respects to him & was by him presented to his wife & daughter who stood in the middle of the floor to receive the company & then like the rest I put off to make my way through the crowd to & amuse myself the best way I could. Three large rooms were open & all were excessively crowded by gentlemen & ladies of all ages frequently brought in the closest contact & not in the most delicate positions. Dancing was introduced & towards the close of the evening waltzing also, but there were few to participate in the latter amusement, few being acquainted with it some thinking it indelicate. Among other visitors was Mr Houston[188] late Gov of Tennessee of a tall & remarkably fine person & fine full open countenance genteel in his dress & elegant in his manners; he was treated very respectfully by both gentlemen & ladies; He wore a large & full wig of black hair, rather dark for his complexion & the colour of his eyebrows, & this gave him rather an unnatural appearance. He came to the city in company with a deputation of Cherokees, coming on business of the nation & wearing Indian dress.[189]

Commodore Hull; commander of the Washington naval station was also there, wearing his military dress; he does not exceed 5 feet 8 inches in height, built verry portly, having a full round face, dark hair his head a little bald on the top, & seamed rather silent & backward.

The company amused themselves in crowding & dancing and dispersed gradually about 11 or 12 o'clock. As the crowd was verry great the party was verry pleasant.

Jan 16th 1830, a fair & pleasant day, visited the Capitol about one o'clock. The House of Representatives not in session, but their Chamber was crowded with a very fashionable assemblage of ladies & gentlemen. This being the Anniversary of a verry respectable association, for the promotion of literature & the sciences, called the Columbian Institute[190] (of which J. Q. Adams was last President) the Hon. Edward Everest[191] was, according to previous appointment, about to deliver an address. I located myself at a convenient station in one of the soft arm chairs of the members & soon after the Orator ascended the Speaker's chair & commenced in low tones his address, having his manuscript before his eyes, but so familiar to his mind that he did not find it necessary to refer to it. After making some fine remarks upon the utility & efficacy of voluntary associations generally he proceded to advance many opinions & theories worthy of a highly cultivated genius & a philanthropic heart, supporting them by historical illustrations the most forcible & happy, showing himself to have an extensive acquaintance with the sciences & the history of Chem. The matter of his discourse (though he did not give any information of the Institution which he addressed) pleased me much more than the delivery of it, his voice not loud, neither was it musical or capable of much variation, having a great uniformity, dwelling almost entirely on the middle tones, his articulation was generally rather slow & though distinct was a little stiff. Though the occasion did not permit much animation yet his discourse suffered for the want of it; his principal gestures were with the right arm & hand the forefinger only being generally oppen, while his left hand was too much behind his back; his stature was too low for a great orator not exceeding 5 feet 6 or 8 inches, his person was well formed, clad in a genteel dress showing nothing of the dandy or divine; his features were pleasant, not remarkable in any way, rather inclining to the Roman character & having light hair. He seemed to be about 35 years of age, born in Boston of obscure parentage, fostered by charitable institutions, entered early in literary pursuits & labours graduated at Cambridge, studied Divinity, took charge of a church in Boston, was much beloved & admired, visited Europe, turned his attention to politics, & at this early age, has distinguished himself as a gentleman, a scholar, a divine, & a politician. On this occasion the opinion was unanimous that he acquitted himself well, evincing an acquaintance with literature & science & the same showing nothing of the pedant & making no display.

The Supreme Court commenced its session in the Capitol about the First of January; several days after I set out to pay them a formal visit; ascending Capitol hill on the Western side. I walked under an arched passway of strong masonry & entered the Capitol by the basement front door; proceeding a few paces I found myself in a passage exiting through the principal building, at one end of which I perceived the National Banner in miniature hanging out from a room door, here it struck me was a sacred place of deposit for the papers of the Nation or more probably a Committee on the state of the Union was here in session, curiosity led me to the place where to my utter astonishment I discovered — what think you! — "Oysters, roasted, stewed, & fried". I turned short about & at the other end of the passage I saw "Oysters as you like them"[.] I liked them out of my sight! hurried up a flight of stone steps, & soon found myself in a large rough stone room among a forest of 50 stone columns about 12 feet high supporting innumerable arches, having a common centre & all supporting that grand structure the Rotundo; this chamber was quite dark & gloomy the doors only admitting solar light, looking through the rows of columns I discovered on each side of the room a small bright light, shining in that darkness with a festoon as dazzling as the sun, attracted by their brilliancy I approached one & on examination found them to be air holes through which were shining the fires in the large brick stoves or ovens used in heating the Rotundo; pipes conducting the warm air from the ovens to the room. With my eyes dazzled by these lights & my brain bewildered by the numerous arched pillars & passages, I almost forgot my direction but set out & after wandering along dark passages, winding staircases, & arched galleries I at length hit upon the room in the North east corner of the basement floor.[192] I entered (after passing several doors) "the dark vaulted chamber" (as Mr Buchannan called it), & took possission a sofa just in time to hear the Sergeant at arms pray "God save the United States & this honourable court"[193] This room was of moderate size in form a semi-circle, the Judicial Platform occupying the diameter, while the periphery was occupied by the Lawyers & spectators. The ceiling was arched, similar in its form to half an oval. On the west side of the Chamber, high upon the wall was Justice & several other figures in basso relivo of mean execution. The room was decently finished & furnished but it was dark, its structure was curious & compact so much so that it little corresponded with the majesty & dignity of the Supreme Judicial tribunal of "these great United States."[194] (The U.S. Telegraph No. 20. Vol 5.)

A few days after visited the Court & found the whole seven judges in attendance, dressed in their flowing black silk robes, seated in their cushioned, arm chairs behind a bar or desk covered with green cloth & curtains; they were engage now in listening, now in reading the printed briefs & now in listening, now in reading the printed briefs & now in taking notes of the arguments. They all sat in a row & in the following order.[195] Judge M'Lean on the extreme right, the youngest looking man, tall person fair skin, lean face, dark hair & fine large forehead, eye large & penetrating nose aquiline, mouth & chin of common appearance. Judge Story of Mastts next; of middle stature, portly person, venerable appearance, of a ruddy complexion, face full & round of little expression, his hair verry grey & his head almost bald on the crown & front. Judge Johnson of S. Carolina next, about 60 years of age of large fine & vigorous person, genteel appearance, having a full round & fat face, complexion ruddy, hair considerably grey, head a little bald on the top & crown. C. Judge Marshall of Va next, (see elsewhere) Smith Tompson of N. York next, rather tall & spare in his person, dignified & venerable in his appearance, his complexion a little ruddy his features much marked by age, yet intelligent and imposing, his hair verry grey thin on the crown of his head, worn combed up in front or cued behind, his face is of the form of a parallelogram, his forehead being high & square, his cheeks lank on the sides of his face & full towards his chin which is broad & prominent, his mouth is a little inverted, having deep rinkles on each side of it. Gabriel Duval of Mary. next, of middle stature & stoutly built, but not corpulent, his complexion is a little dark, his countenance rather sour, his hair is of a light colour, a little grey & thin in front, his forehead is full & high & round, projecting over his eyes & nose which is straight large & full at the nostrils, his chin & mouth of good proportions, his cheeks rather lean & without whiskers. Judge Baldwin sits on the extreme left, of middle stature & compact form, he looks younger than any except M'Lean, has a dark skin, his countenance not open nor expanded, his hair is dark, thick & verry little grey, is worn short & trimmed round the forehead, which is not very high is broad & square, his eyes dark; his nose of common size & full at the nostrils, his mouth broad, his lips square, chin rather sharp & dimpled. All the judges wore black cloth coats & all wore spectacles except M'Lean & all seamed industrious & attentive.[196] The arguments of counsel were purely legal, no rhetoric, no oratory, the Judges having more regard for sound authority & argument than for fulsome harrangues. Among others heard Ky. Berrien & Coxe of the District & Ogden Webster Wirt Wickliffe & Bronston, (Att Gen. of New York,) from a distance.[197]

Washington City January 19th 1830.
    Portraits of Persons.

Thomas H. Benton[198] Senator from Missouri is about 45 or 50 years of age, nearly 6 feet in height, stoutly built, erect in his gait & genteel in his person, his appearance manly and imposing, his complexion ruddy, his countenance intelligent, his head of good proportions, his face full & round, his hair light, thin on the crown of his head, combed on the sides toward the eyes & combed up in front & over the top of his head; his forehead high & broad, his eyebrows light & thin, his eyes grey sunk deep in his head, sprightly & penetrating, his nose a little aquiline & sharp at the end, his c[h]eeks full & ruddy, supporting a pair of bushy red whiskers, his mouth rather small, lips thin, his chin sharp & more prominent than his mouth, his voice is strong shrill & monotonous, soon becoming unpleasant. In debate he is too apt to be violent & personal, wanting suavity & winning manner, his language is chaste and grammatical as well as forcible, his gestures are principally with the right hand with the forefinger prominent, he occasionally in argument, throws back his shoulders turns his head a little to the left, arches his eyebrows & looks askaunt giving his countenance the appearance of archness, penetration or dignity. He is remarkable for uncommon industry & untiring perserverence.

Edward Livingston,[199] formerly of New York, now a Senator from Louisiana, is about 80 years of age, but looks much younger & is quite vigorous, his person is tall, exceeding six feet in height, not very good, rather spare & raw boned & a little knock kneed; his appearance genteel but indicates but little attention to dress; his head is rather too flat, his face is too flat & long for its breadth, his hair is dark or rather black, but very little grey, but a little thin on the crown of the head is worn combed back on both the sides & top, his complexion is dark, his countenance is rather dull & grave, indicating care & study, his forehead is full & round, receding at the sides, his eyebrows thin, dark & thrown up at the outter ends, his eye is dark & covered with heavy eyelids, his nose is long & straight full at the end, having broad distended nostrils, his cheeks are rather thin on the sides of his face, but too full & wrinkled near the mouth; his mouth is large his lips thin & fitting closely; his chin is small & a little tinged with his beard, he wears no whiskers, which makes his cheeks look too lank & the lower part of his face too large for the upper part.

Jan. 20 heard him in the Supreme court, his delivery was confused, occasionally halting in his speech, stammering a little & miscalling words, his voice strong & full, his enunciation a little lisping from loss of his teeth.

Hon. John C. Calhoun Speaker of the Senate from S. Carolina, about 45 years of age, tall and commanding in his person, exceeding six feet in height, slender, spare & raw boned, he is plain but genteel in his person, in his manner graceful easy & dignified in conversation, he is fluent sprightly & affable rapid in his delivery but distinct in his enunciation, his voice is strong but rather harsh & unpleasant, his head is small & flat, his hair is thick coarse & black is worn carelessly, sticking out on all sides, his countenance is generally smiling & sprightly though the features of his face are irregular and diminutive, his forehead is low, narrow & square, skirted by thin & dark eyebrows; projecting over the eyes & deeply indented where it joins the nose, which is straight short & ugly, his eyes small, of a hazle colour & sprightly appearance, his cheeks are hollow & a little wrinkled, his mouth of common size, not broad nor having thick round lips, his chin is broad & rather to prominent, it & his mouth are too long to be in proportion to his nose & [o]ther parts of his face; he wears short whiskers.[200]

Hon. Daniel Webster[201] a native of New Hampshire now a Senator in congress from Massachusetts, is between 40 & 50 years of age about 5 feet 10 or 12 inches high, his person of good proportion, quite genteel in his personal appearance & rather distant in his manners, his head is of common size, his hair is very black & quite entire, being neither thin nor grey, his complexion is very sallow & his countenance is cold & rather dull than sprightly. His hair is worn carelessly, standing up loosely on the top inclining a little to the right, his forehead is remarkable, broad & round, though not high yet not meeting the hair until the middle of the top of the head, as if from loss of hair, his eyebrows are smoth, turned up at the outter ends and very black, his eyes are dark & full, his nose straight, tolerably large, full & prominent at the end, his cheek bones rather prominent, his cheeks not plump, supporting a pair of small black whiskers his mouth of good size, under lip too small & wears a pouting & sour appearance, his chin is a little dimpled & prominent the lower part of his face deeply tinged by his thick black beard, when he smiles his sallow countenance & white teeth give him quite a gastly appearance, his voice is full & susceptible of much modulation, strong in argument, easy in delivery, clear in expression, in gesture sparse but ungraceful.

Hon. Littleton W. Tazwell,[202] a Senator from Virginia, about 55 or 60 years of age, with good health & constitution, of large stature, exceeding 6 feet in height, robustly formed, rather inclined to be rawboned, not careful of his dress & person, his complexion is dark & his features large & manly, his countenance, when not engaged in conversation or active business, is rather stern & melancholy, he is often observed sitting with his body inclined forward, his legs crossed, his right hand in his breast, his brow wrinkled, & his eyes fixed on the floor as if in deep thought. His head is large, his hair dark, & worn combed from the front & sides to the rear of his head, his forehead is of moderate height & breadth, exceedingly wrinkled, his eyebrows heavy & dark, his eyes hazel enclosed by heavy eyelids, his nose is large & prominent, his cheeks rather lean & wrinkled, his lips square, mouth of common size, chin a little dimpled & covered with dark beard, wears short whiskers & shirt collar turned over. He is profound in wisdom & independent in sentiment, participating but little in the proceedings of the Convention, & not having appeared in the Senate at this date.
Washington Jan. 29th, 1830.

Hon. Andrew Stevenson[203] from Va. Speaker of the H.R. Looks to be about 38 years of age is probably older, of a tall erect, elegant & well proportioned person, exceeding six feet in height, is genteel in his dress, easy in his manners & sprightly in conversation. His complexion is fair & his countenance agreeable but not indicative of greatness. His head is of good size, his hair is dark, a little grey, worn very short & combed

up in front, his forehead is high & full, his eyebrows thin smooth & of
a light colour, his eyes blue, his cheek bones high & prominent, his cheeks
not very full & without whiskers which circumstance combined with the
fairness of his skin give him a youthful appearance, his mouth of common size, his lips round, his chin of due proportion & common appearance having but little beard. His voice is full strong & tuneable. He discharges the duties of the chair with promptness, ease & ability.

Hon. George McDuffie[204] of S. Car. in the H.R. is about five feet,
eight or ten inches in height, his form erect, person rather spare & inclined
to rawbone, looks to be about 35 or 38 years of age, genteel in his dress
and prepossessing in his personal appearance, his complexion is fair, his
countenance is pleasant & intelligent, the features of his face are fine particularly in profile; his hair is thick, dark & entire, worn combed down
at the sides & in front, being trimmed round his forehead forming a point
in the centre of it, his forehead is high, full & broad, his eyebrows are
thin & lighter than his hair, his eyes are blue, small & deeply sunk under
his forehead & obscured by his cheek bones, which are rather too prominent, his nose is a little aquiline, long & sharp at the end, his mouth is
of good size, his lips a little contracted at the corners as in a smile, his
chin is of common size, rather prominent & a little dimpled, his cheeks
are full near the cheek bones, tapering to the chin, & having no whiskers,
from this circumstance & the fairness of his complexion his appearance
is very youthful.

Hon. John Randolph, of Roanoake, now a member of the Va. Convention, & of the aristocratic party, a bachelor, in delicate health & about
58 years of age; he is of midling stature; in his person, spare & uncomely,
being a little hump shouldered & having a very short neck; his left leg
a little shorter than his right; in his mein, though supported by a cane,
he is limping & ungraceful. His dress is a common black hat; a complete
dress suit of dark olive cloth, white cotton socks, large coarse shoes,
resembling overshoes, a plain linnen shirt, dark olive vest buttoned up
to his cravat, which is a blue & white fancy handkerchief of silk & exactly
like his pocket handkerchief; plain spectacles with tortoise shell frames,
which together with a large coarse pair of buff buckskin gloves make his
entire dress. His head is small, flat, & inclined forward; his face is rather
small, shrivelled & effeminate; his forehead is rather narrow & low, somewhat obscured by his hair, which is entire, a little grey, worn short parted
on the top of his head & combed down on the sides; his eyebrows like
his hair are of a light colour, & are thin & smooth, his eyes small dark,
brilliant, sparkling, penetrating & intelligent; his cheeks fair, thin & unen-
cumbered by beard or whiskers; his chin is small, almost beardless, &
obscured by his collar & cravat, his voice is shrill clear & pectoral striking upon the ear & sounding as if passed through a tube from the mouth

of the speaker to the ear of the hearer. His feminine appearance & the cast of features are such that they invariably recall the image of Mrs. Ann Royall to my view.[205]

Hon. P. P. Barbour of Va. member of the H. R. of him see vol. 1st page 92. therefore let this page be dedicated to her ladyship, Mrs. Ann Royall.[206] Saw her several times on the street and in the gallery of the H.R. She is a lady of ordinary size & common appearance, wearing a brown bombaset cloak, callico gown, white muzzlin ruffle & a silk scoop or folding bonnet, she wore & cap & had a profusion of dark curls laying on her forehead & hanging about her face, they did not soot her complexion her face was round & full, a little shrivelled, her complexion fair & her countenance was humorous & pleasant; her eye was small, dark, very intelligent & sprightly, her mouth was small & pouting in playfull good humour. When she would come into the Gallery she wold salute & return salute with the members whose notice she drew. She was very communicative & approachable, talking & laughing with anybody who would permit her, her language was vulgar & a little profane but indicating nothing of spleen or malignity. She commonly brought pencil or pen ink, & paper to take notes &c, one morning a person let the door fly when she was entering which knocked her ink over her book & clothes, she was considerably dashed but not vexed, "burned him for an awkward fellow & swore she would put him in her black book. Wished to know what we thought of her in Ky saying we had reason to be proud of her &c.[207]

Jan. 18th 1830. In company with a Member, visited the Library of Congress, was introduced to Mr. John S. Meechan,[208] the Librarian, a polite & sensible gentleman, it seemed, who invited me to examine the room and contents at pleasure. The room is a long parallelogram, about 30 feet broad & extending the whole western front of the principal building, the ceiling is semicircular the whole length & has three circular windows in the top of it. The walls & ceiling a[re] plaistered with white lime, (the ceiling being handsomely wrought) & the wood work is painted white, the floor is of stone or other solid substance & is covered with a handsome carpet, the room is well supplied with chairs tables & cushioned settees or lounges, is warmed by a fireplace for wood at each end having handsome white marble mantle pieces supported by white marble columns, & by two tall & large cylindrical sheet iron stoves for stone coal near the middle, these stoves do not show the pipes which conduct off the smoke & add rather than detract from the appearance of the room. The room is ornamented also by busts in plaister of Jackson & Moultree placed on one mantlepiece, a mantle clock on the other over which is a portrait of Columbus; near the middle of the room is a fine white marble bust of La Fayette executed since his last visit to America & bearing engraven on its side the memorable blessing which he invoked on our country on taking a final leave of our shores. The room is also illuminated by several windows on the wind side one of which raises high enough to permit visitors to walk out upon an extensive balcony which commands an extensive prospect including the City &c. The Library is under the direction of Congress is free to the use of its members, the Judges of the Supreme Court Heads of Departments, Presidents & Ex presidents of the U. States residing within the District, strangers must be introduced by a Mem. of Con. or by the Lib. & can not have the use of books out of the room without leaving a pecuniary deposit with the Librarian. The room is open almost all day during the session of Cong. & thrice a week in vacation. It is divided into upper & lower stories or galleries; below along the wall on each side are six partitions, making in all 12 recesses for books below, & 14 above, but three sides of these recesses contain books, the front being open & each is supplied with a chair, table & stationary. The Library contains about fourteen thousand volumes & cost about sixty four thousand dollars, several thousand being annually expended in its improvement. The books are in various languages & on all subjects, being arranged in fourty four chapters or classes, many of the works being large rare & valuable consisting in great measure of the Library presented by Mr Jefferson to Congress.[209]

Jan. 20 visited The Patent Office kept in the East end & second story of the building containing the Gen. & City Post Offices. John D. Craig is the Superintendent. As this is the house of Uncle Sam, & is free to the inspection of every one I went without conductor & Letter, & after ascending a flight or two of dirty & new stairs, I reached a room about 60 or 70 feet long & 20 broad in the area of this room 12 cases, each containing 5 shelves placed about 3 feet apart in parallel rows across the room from one end to the other of the room. These cases contain the various models & when the cases are finished they will have wire doors to defend the models from the intrusions of the meddlesome. Cases are also arranged in cases placed against the walls around the room. The whole number of models is about seven thousand, many hundred being added each year, they are arranged in fourteen classes, one for Agriculture, one for Fine Arts &c. The models [seemed] to be too small, imperfect in their structure & frail in their materials easily to be put out of order. Among the most remarkable were the numerous wooden bridges & a churn the dasher of which was attached by a crank to a horizontal wheel propelled by a weight like a clock, Another was propelled by Dog power, the animal treading an inclined plane invented I suppose by men who milk the quows [cows].[210]

Jan 21st a clear sunny day, accepted the invitation of the Hon B. M. Crowningsheild former Sec. of the Navy, now a member of Congress from Salem, Massachusetts, to accompany him on a visit to Ex Pres. John

Quincy Adams now residing with his wife at the residence of his son about 600 yards north of the Pres's house.[211] We got into a carriage & having reached his residence, a handsome 3 story brick building, & ascertained that Mr Adams could be seen we alighted & were conducted through a passage ornamented with orange, Lime & other trees growing in boxes into a small but very neat & handsome parlour, took our seats & in a few moments he came in & we were introduced as Kentuckians. The conversation began with the weather & then turned to the news of the day. Mr Adams asked if the morning papers contained anything further concerning the health of Nicholas Emperor of Russia,[212] Remarking that he considered his life of more importance to the world than that of any other man now living, in as much as the peace of Europe, the prosperity of Russia & the national existance of Turkey all depended upon it, that in case of his death the crown would devolve upon his offspring now in minority & that the regency would devolve upon Michael, the brother of Nicholas. He told an anecdote illustrative of the facility with which the Russians get rid of an obnoxious prince. A Russian nobleman told him in a humorous manner that it was against their Constitution for one to ascend the throne, alluding to the Con. of the U.S. Russia in fact having no constitution, the Nobleman intending to convey the idea that an obnoxious or incompetent prince would be dispatched. Also spoke of the abdication of Constantine, confessing his incompetency to the duties of the sovereignty & his fear of assassination.[213] The conversation then turned upon the _____ medal lately sent from Colombia to Pres. Jackson & by him sent to the Congress to be by them disposed of, he having refused to accept it, owing to a clause in the constitution prohibiting an officer of the U. St. to accept presents from foreigners &c;[214] Mr Adams observing that during his Presidency a portrait of Bolivar was sent to the Pres. of U.S. & that he had it hung up in the Pres.'s house, where it still hung if not removed, observing that he did not see proper to send it to Congress for them to dispose of, he then remarked that the portrait was executed by a native artist, & though it was said to be a good likeness yet it exhibited a total want of acquaintance with the art, being greatly deficient in perspective, light & shade; judging from the backward state of the arts in that country he presumed (for he had not seen the medal) that it was badly executed; & so it was;[215] he then made several remarks concerning the composition & construction of medals, saying that France, England & even Russia had obtained proficiency & superiority in the art, that they were valuable in commemorating important events, that the Europeans had them in series showing important historical information, that a medallist of Geneva had executed a great many in fine style, likenesses of the great men of Europe, that an historical account of the French Revolution, on a series of medals had been sent to the U.S. by Mr Irving;[216] but unfortunately they were lost in their passage. He said that the U.S. was greatly deficient in this branch of the arts, that Maurice Turtz was the only tolerable medallist among us &c. His whole conversation was exceeding easy & interesting, rich with historical events & evincing extensive erudition, but not showing the sleightest marks of display or pedantry, though he seamed rather fond of long speeches. His dialect was a little remarkable being strongly & plainly that of a man of Massachusetts. After sitting about 25 or 30 minutes, we rose, gave him a shake by the hand & bade him good morning. His stature is rather too low, not exceeding 5 feet 8 or 10 inches in height, broad shoulders & a little inclined to corpulency; his dress was a frock brown cloth coat buttoned round him, blue pantaloons, white yarn socks & shoes, the whole not evincing much neatness, or attention, his head is tolerably large, the top & fore half is almost entirely bald, his hair is dark, considerably grey, of common length & is worn naturally, his complexion is a little dark, his countenance is not imposing or prepossessing & except his bald head & grey beard indicates but little of years, his face is full & round, his forehead is full & round, his eyebrows dark, thin straight & elevated at the outter extremes, his eyes are hazel, full round & very watery owing to the obstruction of the duct leading from the eyes to the nose, his eye lids are heavy & reddish, his nose is long, large, straight & prominent, his cheeks are full of a ruddy complexion almost entirely free from wrinkles & entirely without whiskers, his mouth of common size, lip a little rounding & when smiling disclosing a fine set of fore teeth, his chin of ordinary appearance less prominent than his nose. His manners were rather cold & ungraceful[,] his salutation being rather a sudden jerk than an easy shake of the hand. His voice is strong & rather harsh & unmusical. He is engaged in literary labours, probably the biography of his father.[217]

Visited King's Gallery of the Fine Arts[218] a two story frame building kept by an individual. The principal attraction was Sully's Capuchin Chapel. The artist is of Phila & has gained much reputation by this specimen of his skill. The Capuchins were monks of the order of St. Francis, were extremely vigorous, are said always to have worn brown or grey, never wore shoes, never go in a bath or shave their beards. This painting is about four feet broad & six feet high, representing the interiour of the Chapel, the room a long parallellogram, with a vaulted and variegated ceiling, the walls being adorned with paintings, the room is shown in perspective, and contains 32 persons engaged in divine service, I think in prayer, near the far end of the room is an altar surmounted by a cross, a venerable monk clothed in flowing robes of a reddish colour seamed to be engaged on the altar at prayer, another standing near him is holding a smoking censor, while two children stood near each holding a candle, in the nearer end of the room a monk was kneeling with his head & hands resting on his seat, while another sat opposite in a listening attitude, all the rest, dressed in flowing brown robes were standing near the walls around the room, grave & reverend in appearance. The painting exhibited light & shade & perspective more naturally & strikingly than any I ever saw.

This gallery, though the collection is not the best or most extensive, contains several heads & bust in plaister of distinguished American & Foreign personages. There are also several paintings of considerable merit, several portraits among the rest those of McDuffie, Webster & Ex. Pres. Monroe. The paintings are chiefly in the second story of the house, the room being illuminated by a dome in the centre of the ceiling; the busts &c. are in a room immediately beneath.

On Thursday night, Jan. 21st about half after 8 o'clock went to the President's Drawing room. The crowd was considerable, several rooms were open, the company promiscuous & ceremonies conducted as on former occasions. Refreshments, such as ice creams cake &c were served sparingly, toddy & whiskey punch seemed to be the most fashionable drinks. Among other distinguished visitors were Chief Justice Marshall, & some of his Associates, several Governors of states & territories visiting the Capitol, also several Indians, dressed genteely behaving properly & attracting but little attention.[219] The amusements consisted chiefly in prominading through the crowd, in squeezing quizzing & conversing. The Foreign Ministers were generally in attendance, having observed them on former occasions also, I am enabled to give some description of them.

Baron de Krudener,[220] Minister from Russia, of a low stature not exceeding 5 feet 6 or 8 inches, fair complexion, light hair worn combed over his forehead which is very receding, his eyes blue his nose long straight & prominent, mouth & chin of ordinary size & appearance, dresses tolerably genteely & looks like a common man in point of talents; 45 years old.

Baron Stackelberg[221] from Sweden & Norway. Is tall & commanding in his appearance, near about 50 years of age, very lively & jocose, his hair is very grey, a little thin on the crown of his head, is worn sticking out from his face at right angles all round, his complexion is swarthy or rather ruddy seemingly affected by intemperance, his features are good, his forehead high & broad, his eyebrows & whiskers grey, his eye blue, his nose large, his mouth & chin well proportioned; he is fond of amusement, speaks broken English, affable in conversation, drinks deeply of champagne & waltzes remarkably well. These Representatives dress & look like Republicans, except on extra occasions when they wear their Court dresses.

Among others was a foreigner high in command, at the Battle of Navarins wearing uniform dress of blue cloth with medals, stars & crosses, on his left breast, insignia of the orders of societies of which he is a member.

Jan. 18th 1830 attend the Capitol at night to witness the Annual Meeting of the American Colonization Soc.[222] Pres Washington being dead C. F. Mercer of va[223] took the Chair[;] after prayer the report was read by the Sec. General, resolutions were proposed, supported by eloquent & animated speeches & adopted. The society was attended by delegates from many distant auxilliary Soc. among the rest four from the State of Ohio.

The chamber of the H. R. crowded to overflowing with an audience of both sexes, the most intelligent & fashionable that the city could afford paid the most profound attention & remained to a late hour thereby showing an intense interest in the subject notwithstanding its stateness. Charles Carrol was chosen next President, & the Soc. adjourned.

The hall was brilliantly illuminated & looked most magnificent & splendid, the spacious chamber, its vaulted & variegated ceiling, the lofty columns, the brilliant curtains stretched in rich folds from their capitals, the large & brilliant chandelier, the vast concourse their intense interest & the importance of their object, involving benevolence philanthropy & patriotism, all combined formed a scene at once beyond imagination & description.

Jan. 26th attended the Senate to hear Mr Webster reply to Mr Hayne of S. Carolina who had spoken on the day previous & then concluded a long & animated speech commenced a few days previous,[224] and being a part of a debate arising out of a Resolution introduced by Mr Foot of Connecticut, to enquire into the expediency of suspending the surveys of public lands & of abolishing a land office it being suspected that the final effect of the Resolution might be to discourage emigration to the west, it was warmly opposed by Mr. Benton, in reply to Mr. Foot (a Mr Kane of Illinois also having spoken against the res.) for four reasons because first it would check emigration to the new states & territories. Secondly limit their settlement, Thirdly deliver large portions of them to the dominion of wild beasts. Fourthly to remove all land records from the new States. These reasons were ably set forth & substantiated by eloquence of a rather forcible & threatening character. Mr Benton accusing the East of entertaining feelings hostile to the prosperity of the West.[225] Mr Hayne soon after made a speech on the same side, in which he lost sight of the resolution the drift of his speech being to show that the East had been hostile while the South had been favourable, refering to many acts of the Eastern Legislatures & of their representatives in congress & also many acts of the Southern Legislatures & of Southern Reps. in Congress to prove his position. The question thus having become whether the South or East was most partial to Western interest. Mr Webster rose in vindication of N. England particularly of Massachusets showing by argument that Southern policy opposed the western interest while that of N. England fostered, he like Mr Hayne speaking highly in praise of the western states, from which a stranger might have supposed that the West was in market & was to be bought by extravagant compliments the East & South being the bidders. This speech of Mr Webster was extempore & of about an hour's length was followed in a short speech by Mr Benton, he rising arrogantly & presumptuously as the champion of the West, disclaiming the alleged partiality & rejecting the profered kindness of the East.[226] By this time the question again began to change, the propriety of negro slavery, the policy of the Tariff & constitutionality of Congress making roads &c, now coming before the views of the speakers. Mr Hayne again replied to Mr Webster in a speech two days long a saturday and sunday intervening between the first & second parts of it giving him time to prepare & me an opportunity of describing his person, manners &c.

Robert Y. Hayne,[227] Senator of South Carolina, looks to be about 38 or 40 years of age, in fact much older, about 6 feet high & well proportioned person, neither delicate nor corpulent he is genteel in dress & personal appearance, his complexion rather dark, his countenance open & youthful, rather prepossessing yet showing no marks of superiour greatness; his head of good proportions, his hair black, entire, a little grey, worn with considerable care & attention, combed towards his face & forehead in front, combed up over the forehead & turned over to the right with much care, his forehead is high & broad, his eyebrows dark and smooth, his eye round tolerably full & hazle, his nose of good size & straight, his cheeks of proper fullness & without whiskers, having little beard, his mouth & chin of common size & appearance, the latter a little dimpled & having but little beard; his whole face is rather long than broad & rather handsome than great or intelligent. He is married & has several children. In speaking his tones are loud & animated, his voice being full & strong, his chief gesture is with the right hand, the elbow being lifted higher than the shoulder or hand in an ungraceful manner, his emphasis & modulation are generally good except at the close of sentences when they are whining & disagreeable & though studied are unnatural, his lanuage is chaste & grammatical on the whole he may be truly called a good speaker. I[n] the last speech he justified southern men & measures, vindicated African slavery in the south as morally & politically justifiable, censured the Tariff as obnoxious & unconstitutional, assailed the East as wanting patriotism in last war in refusing loans to government, spoke of the treaty concerning the navigation of the Mississippi, the embargo, the Hartford convention & the "Coalition of 1825" charging the East as wanting to sever the Union at one time & to "consolidate" it at another, vindicating his own political course & consistency & assailing that of Mr Webster with some acrimony & personality. The debate in the meantime

turning upon the consistency & the litigating parties & the sections & states
which they represent & the policy they advocate & their loyalty to the
Union & desire for the general welfare, the debate all the time rising in
importance & becoming more animated & personal. He concluded his
remarks yesterday & this morning a dense crowd of the most respectable
gentlemen & ladies assembled as on yesterday, crowded the floor &
galleries, the ladies ousting the senators & besieging the speaker's chair.
They listened for two hours & a half to Mr Webster in the grandest &
most interesting specimen of parliamentary eloquence which it has ever
been my good fortune to hear. Like Hayne Benton & others he spoke from
notes previously prepared; while taking them yesterday, the unusual
redness of his face evinced excitement, but this morning he appeared calm
& rising proceeded in a temperate & calm, yet firm & dignified manner
to defend himself & his country, & to assail his antagonist with the most
ingenious satire & penetrating & cutting sarcasm, refuting his facts &
attacking & subverting his arguments; his manner & countenance now
sickening as from disgust & contempt, now smiling in ridicule, now fired
by his subject his countenance brightened while his attitude & voice rose
with eloquence the most impassioned & convicting. After replying to some
personal remarks in which he said that the bow of the hon. Member was
too weak to send an arrow to his breast, he alluded to the wide range
which he had taken, having said something about every thing else but
the subject under consideration, refered to the Resolution & then proceded
to vindicate his course during the debate, then the policy & acts of his
state, showing the the Tariff policy originated in the South & that Mr
Hayne once supported it &c.[228]

Jan. 27. Mr Webster concluded his speech after occupying nearly three
hours in the most convincing argument & forcible eloquence. His remarks
chiefly related to the nature of our government; & were intended to show
the impropriety & unconstitutionality of a State resisting the Gen. Govt.
& closed in appropriate & eloquent terms invoking Union, happiness &
glory upon our common Country.

Mr Hayne made a short & forcible reply, the debate all the time
assuming a more amicable cast. Mr Webster again spoke a few moments
& the Senate adjourned.

Jan. 27. Walked from Land's End to Gizzard's Point, i.e. walked to
Geo. town, but did not see Miss _____[.][229] Then walked back to the
Capitol, but not to hear Mr Benton, then walked to the Navy Yard but
would not see Miss Hart, then to the Marine Barracks[230] where nothing
could be seen & thence to Mrs Blake's[231] & saw a smoking dinner; having
walked in all about 10 miles.

The Navy Yard is an extensive & business establishment. There are
two houses for ships on the stocks, in one of which was a vessel about

half finished & near it was a friggate but near the close of the last war, now lay in the water without masts or rigging never having been in service. The inclosure contained several other houses some for dwellings, others for stores, shops & timbers. Saw a quantity of iron cannon & mortars & balls & shells. Saw the machinery for putting masts in vessels. Near the shore of the River two large poles, of the size of large & high trees, formed of various timbers bound together, were raised into the air in the form of a forceps, their lower ends resting on the ground considerably asunder, while the upper ends were bound together by a cable extending thence to the ground, attached to an immense anchor; the upper ends of the poles projected over the water & above the ship, the mast was raised & lowered by ropes & pullies attached the upper end of the poles. But the most interesting object about the Yard was the Monument erected to the memory of several brave officers who perished before Tripoli.[232] The structure is small & tolerably handsome, not pretending to grandeur. It is situated near the principal entrance & is surrounded by cannon, two of which are large brass pieces. The basement is of coarse dark freestone & is nearly 6 feet high, upon this rests a higher base, also square, of handsome white marble & is about 12 or 14 feet square, the corners supporting funeral urns of Potomac marble, the base is also ornamented with 4 or 5 figures. Fame[,] History[,] Children of Am. in white marble, the statuary & good workmanship, the figures & the design are explained by an inscription on one side of the higher base & just beneath the shaft of the column; it runs thus, speaking of those whose memory it was erected,

The love of Glory inspired them
Fame has crowned their deeds
History records the event,
The Children of Columbia admire
And Commerce laments their fall.

This base supports a round, emblematical, white marble column about 10 or 11 feet in height, bearing an eagle & the American arms on its summit. The monument exhibits marks of decay & also of Brittish barbarity, the conquering soldiery, during the late capture of the Navy Yard, having taken the pen from the hand of History & broken off the fingers & of several other of the figures.

Commodore Hull is the Commander of the station.

The Marine Barracks are of considerable extent, being a principal building & two wings, encased in a high wall including one or two acres of ground; a place of little interest; situate on the East side of 8th Street a little north of the Navy Yard.

The Armory is situated on Greanleafs Point & contains considerable quantities of cannon. The Penitentiary is erected near the Armory is extensive, built on an appropriations of $40,000.[233]

Jan. 29th Visited the Supreme Court for the last time, saw their Honours on the bench & heard the Chief Justice deliver an opinion.[234] Among other lawyers in attendance was the Hon. William Wirt ex.Att. Gen of U.S. He looks to be about 50 years of age, has a manly robust constitution, about 5 feet 10 or 11 inches in height, portly person, broad shoulders & short neck, dresses genteelly & looks lively intelligent & happy, he has a large head, his hair of a light colour, is curly & worn carelessly & fuzzy, his forehead is neither verry broad nor high is considerably wrinkled, his eyebrows light, his eyes grey, his nose is larg a little aquilene & is very full at the end, his mouth a little receding, his under lip & chin jutting out a little, the last a little dimpled & thickly covered with beard, his cheeks are tolerably full, short whiskers.[235]

Jan. 30. took a parting look at the Court & that noble edifice the Capitol. The city is laid out on a grand scale, but as yet is comparatively small, the houses are of various materials, sizes, colours & constructions, is uncommonly scattered. The city is remarkable for innumerable beggars, dogs & grog shops.[236] The citizens are the subjects of a despotism, that is they are governed by a body over which they have no control, but they are not oppressed & do not complain of their situation as a great number of the citizens are officers of Government & are dependent on the caprices of their respective superiours for the tenure of their officers, they are considerably servile & fawning, so much so as to affect the character of the city generally. Nothing more is necessary to make respectablity in Washington than to have patronage power and wealth or any of them. The people are formally polite, but not cordially hospitable on a short acquaintance; devoted to fashion & fond of display, extravagant in articles of dress & house furniture. As there [are] always many strangers in the city of various countries & habits & as there [are] always many men in the city at a distance from their families & wives, the sexes are not scrupulous about illicit intercourse.

Jan. 31. Took a passage in the Union Line of Stages, fare $1.50, started about 10 o'clock & reached Baltimore in about 6 hours, distance about 36 miles. Passed by Bladensberg the scene of an interesting skirmish during the last war, the town consists of a few shabby houses.[237] Passed a quantity of iron ore dug from the banks along the road; passed also a quantity of red coloured earth of a sandy nature, dug & sold for red paint of a secondary quality, passed numerous huts & cabins the miserable residence of the Railroad men & their families; as the road advances the huts are demolished & erected again further along the road, & by the time it is finished some of the families may have performed a pilgrimage equal to that to Mecca, or equal to that of the Children of Israel.[238]

Feb. 1st. 1830. Visited the Catholic Church,[239] a spacious stone building of uncommon form, the principal attractions were the paintings, chiefly of European artists; presented to the Church. One about 6 feet square was a scene from the holy wars, presented by the King of Spain Chas. X. Another of the same size represented Christ taken from the Cross, presented by the late king of France. The whole number of paintings were 15 or twenty, the scenes taken from sacred history, the paintings not so large or so good as those mentioned.

The church was ornamented with several statues carved of wood & presented by the Pope. The altar was splendid, well supplied with crosses & candles according to the custom; behind the cross was a figure about 4 feet long of Christ on the Cross. We were attended by the wife of the Sexton[;] an intelligent Irish lady & a zealous catholic, she told us much about the faith & ceremonies & sold us some catholic books for which we paid liberal prices, after passing the numerous charity boxes in the Church & paying the lady 28 cents for showing the church. Visited Peale's Baltimore Museum, the collection various & extensive, contained in three or four room on the second & third floor; the arrangement was good & in good order.[240]

Visited the Baltimore Exchange[241] a spacious & superb edifice built of brick & stuccoed, three or four stories high, the extensive reading room well supplied with Paintings, newspapers &c, those paintings of Washington delivering his inaugural & a full length of La Fayete were the most remarkable. The room is free only to subscribers & strangers introduced, we were politely invited in by the keeper who discovered us to be strange visiters, also invited to the Rotundo, very spacious & lofty, at the top we found numerous spy glasses & telescopes, this being a telegraph station; saw the numerous county seats in the vicinity of Baltimore & the public buildings &c through the spy glasses. Saw the flags & figures &c which are hoisted &c placed in view at the different stations to convey information by telegraph.

Visited the Council Chamber in the second story of the Exchange, the room spacious & handsomely furnished, containing 15 or twenty portraits of eminent men connected with the history of the City & a white marble bust of Washington placed in the curtains behind the chair of the presiding officer.

Left Baltimore in the stage for Philadelphia at 4 o'clock Feb 2nd fare through $10 distance about 106 miles. Beltzhouvers tavern[242] being only tolerable, but redeemed by the low charge of $1.25 a day. On the route passed over good roads, an undulating country, soil chiefly sandy & barren, timber scrub oak, some pine & cedar & some maple & sugar tree. The inhabitants chiefly poor, settlements sparse, fare very mean & tavern bills high. The stages &c were inferiour for that part of the country. Struck the Susquehanna at a small & shabby village called Havre de Grass,[243] the river being frozen hard enough to bear a horse & gig, we left the stage

& walked over the river (at this place a mile or more in width & 60 feet deep in some places) on the ice & again took the stage on the other side. Saw a quantity of Canvass back ducks, large fine & fat, they abound in this vicinity & sell for $1.50 a pair. Passed through a small town on the head of Elk river, called Elkton.[244] Passed New Castle.[245] Passed through Wilmington also on the Delaware, large & tolerably comfortable, formerly a commercial place. Passed through Darby[246] a small place famous for its butter, having previously passed the Brandywine Mills,[247] situate near Wilmington, famous for their flour & connected with the history of the Revolution. Reached Pha. in safety having passed 106 miles in about 18 hours including all stoppages. The whole face of the country was covered with sleet the trees & shrubs were covered with ice & pendant with icicles, transparent & brilliant as glass when lighted by the rays of the sun nothing the splendour of the spectacle, resembling so many diamonds & rubies.

Mrs. Yohe's Philadelphia. Feb. 4th 1830.[248]

At half after 7 o'clock P.M. visited the Franklin Institute to hear Judge Hopkinson,[249] of the U.S. district Court, deliver one of a series of Lectures on Commercial Law. He is of middle stature, plain & genteel in his personal appearance; exceeding 60 years of age, head bald on top, countenance intelligent & prepossessing; his manners and delivery were simple, unpretending & exceedingly interesting; he stood behind a high desk & read his manuscript in audible but not loud tones. The particular subjects were the Law of Principal & Agent embracing the Law of Loan, Auctions Carriers & Balements generally. His discourse evinced an intimate acquaintance with the subject & the best authors on them. During his discourse he spoke of the necessity of Lawyers being acquainted with their profession & passed some just & severe censures upon the Drones & Quacks who disgrace the Profession & concluded with some invaluable remarks upon the judiciary, showing their importance & eulogizing their worth. At all times he had the profound attention of his audience & some applause. Audience all males, chiefly Merchants, respectable & decorous. Admission for single nights 50 cents.

Feb. 5th. Visited the Navy Yard in the south part of Phila. Several acres of ground are enclosed by a high brick wall within which are 15 or 20 houses some of brick & some frame, being the residences of the officers & the deposits of timber & other stores. There are several buildings for work shops, but nothing of the kind is now in progress. Near the banks of the Delaware are two large, six story frame houses each containing a vessel. The smallest house contains a 64 gunn vessel called the _____ so nearly finished that she could be fitted for sea in the months. The other house contains the Pensylvania[250] pierced for 140 gunns, arranged on four decks, she is the largest vessel owned by the U.S. & is one of the largest in the world. The coarser part of her work is complete & she could be fitted for sea in 6 or 8 months, her joiners work, masts, sails, rigging & gunns, have yet to be put on her. The river at Pha. is to shallow to float her with her guns & they will be put on board lower down. Saw also many cannon for ships, also numerous balls & anchors.[251]

Saw several other vessels anchored in the vicinity. Several of the officers of this post under arrest. Admittance from 9 o'clock P.M. to 3 P.M.

Feb. 9th 1830. Took the stage for Harrisburg at 2 o'clock A.M.[;] stage fare $4.50 distance about 100 miles. A fine snow was on the ground and as we passed out of the City we met numerous sleighs with tinkling bells full of ladies & gentlemen travelling with considerable rapidity & not suspending their pleasure during the whole night. After leaving the City the Stage struck up a good turn pike road, along the east bank of the Schuylkill, running through a handsome, fertile and gently undulating limestone country & passing through the small & shabby villages, Norristown, Pottsgrove and Reading at which last place we crossed the Schuylkill & thence passing through Lebanon reached Harrisburg on the east bank of the Susquehanna about 8 o'clock P.M. the same day.[252] In the course of the day we passed several times the Schuylkill canal,[253] a small work for the improvement of the river & intended chiefly for the transportation of the Schuylkill coal the mines being situated on the head waters of that stream. Also passed the Union Canal[254] designed to connect the Schuylkill canal at Reading with the Susquehanna at Harrisburg. It seemed to be a superiour work to the Sch. canal, & is nearly complete as far as Lebanon; the work now suspended while the state Legislature is tardily proceeding to raise funds for their continuance. This is esteemed one of the best parts of the State, the soil is good, best adopted for the culture of small grain, & producing excellent & abundant crops of wheat & rice. If the New Englanders were in possession of the country the banks of the Schuylkill would be a paradise, but the Dutch are in possession of it; originally rude & ignorant & now possessing little of information or refinement, speaking reading & writing the Dutch language as their mother tongue; both the men and women being coarse, ugly, dirty & careless of body & mind, knowing or caring little of good living & good breading, being careless of the intercourse of the sexes, living in mean and tasteless houses, but having good farms. Indeed I think I may [write] it down as a general sign in Pa. that wherever the farm & barn are larger & neater than the dwelling house & the cattle & stock more decent in their personal appearance than their owners, there the people are Dutch. Some other things struck me as being their characteristics Viz. a fondness for staves, barns of a red colour, confectionary, large horses & bake ovens.[255] At Harrisburg I saw both branches of the Legislature in session & I never saw a more common, or coarser collection of Representatives; heard several speeches in both houses, some of them evincing ignorance, but none showing superiority in fluency or a knowledge of politics or of general topics. The Capitol is pleasantly situated on rising ground in the north edge of the town; it is a plain high two story brick edifice, a rotunda in the centre & the halls of legislation on each side, on the basement floor, of the same size & arranged somewhat semicircularly, in front of the Rotunda there are several high & large white columns in somewhat semicircular order; on each side of the building there is another also two story & of brick, about 60 feet from the main building & seeming as wings to it & used as publick offices; all situated in a large & naked lot & inclosed by an iron railing. The legislative halls have no galleries the members & spectators sitting on the same floor. Harrisburg is a small town with a few good houses & many mean ones, its situation is almost a plane & it is surrounded by handsome scenery. It contains an arsenal; situate near the Cap. From H. went to Carlisle, crossed the Susquehanna at H. on two bridges built of wood & supported by stone pillars, each nearly half a mile long, the channel of the channel of the river being here divided by an island containing a few acres & a house the bridges extending from either side of it.[257]

Carlisle is a small & tolerably genteel village situated upon an extensive & fertile plain[,] the country rising in the distance to a considerable height; the houses are chiefly of brick & coarse stone, the latter presenting a sombre appearance.[258] It is a county seat & has several respectable buildings among which are one or two churches. But the principal attraction is Dickinson College;[259] situated on the road side in the western part of the town. The building is plain three story rough stone house, with a sleight projection in the centre. It has no pretension to beauty & little to symetry, the front door being a deception & the entrance being from the rear; it is surrounded by a large level & naked grasslot, with a small building or two in the rear. At present the College is at a very low ebb, having but 2 Professors & but 18 students. Sam B. How, has lately been chosen Pres. is shortly expected, & it is hoped will partially at least restore it to prosperity. Its enemies charge it with being a sectarian institution, the Presbyterians having controul. This college is the seat of two rival Societies, the Belleslettres & the Union Philosophical Soc. the former having 14, the latter but 4 regular members, of which last two are Juniors & two Sophomores. Being a member of this society, I desired to know its particular circumstances, accordingly I called on one of the regular members, introduced myself to him & subsequently others, who by their kindness & polite attention evinced that they were not fellow members in name only, but also in feeling also. The Soc. hall was shown me, a room of moderate size of an oval form & very genteel appearance; the walls were covered with handsome paper & were mainly occupied by book cases arranged around the room; the number of volumes exceeding two thousand chiefly octavo, seemed to [be] in very good order & good condition. The chair of the presiding officer was a handsome structure, covered with red velvet tastefully disposed, above it hung a large & handsomely ornamented engraving of the Dec. of Independence, mounted in a splendid guilt frame. In front of the chair of the presiding officer was the rostrum, slightly elevated & covered with green baise. I inspected some of the numerous records of the Soc; they seamed to be well executed & carefully preserved. From a member I learned that the U. S. was established by some seceders from the Belleslettres.[260]

From Carlisle we proceeded through Chambersburg to McConnelsburg which last place was first seen from the summit of Cave Mountain. The ascent is four miles & the descent from the Tavern on its summit to the village at its base is also 4 miles.[261] The prospect from this elevation is remarkably fine, the little village is situated in the centre of an extensive plain between two ranges of mountains & when seen from a distance looks not unlike a parcel of old pine boxes disposed on each side of the road, the houses being chiefly old & of wood. In descending the Mountain on this side of the last named village, we stopped at a mean house to take in a female passenger; after taking in the band boxes &c the stranger entered by my assistance & to my astonishment proved to be a lovely young Maid of the Mountain, about 16 of a fine person very fashionable & genteel appearance, features, very fine, countenance sprightly & intelligent. I cautiously commenced a conversation which on her part proved that her mind and feelings were as highly cultivated & refined as her person was enchanting; I learned that the mountains were her home & that she had a heart to love & a taste to admire their beauty & grandeur.

After riding several miles by her side feasting my eyes on her beauty & my intellect on the productions of hers, we reached a large white tavern house on the right side of the road surrounded by an extensive farm. This was the residence of her father & here she left me, much to my sorrow; The smiling domestics who came out to greet her on her return from her visit, showed that her merit was duly appreciated by those around her. Subsequently I learned that she was Miss Reamer & that she had been educated in Hagerstown, Pa.[262]

We proceeded, the country continuing mountainous & covered with snow, variegated by the appearance of evergreens, the principal growth being Pine Laurel some cedar & some scrub oak. In some places the mountains spread out into extensive plains, now they branched into numerous divisions, now rose majestically high & now sunk to a depth which was sublimity itself. We continued & soon passed the wooden bridge over the Juniatta a little beyond which the road is partially overhung by a high free stone cliff, covered with icicles & presenting a craggy & frightful appearance, while the delightful Juniatta rolled calmly in the valley below its bosom now cased with impervious ice then clad in a mantle of snow.[263]

We next reached Bloody Run[264] a small shabby village the seat of an Indian Battle which made a little stream run blood, from which the village takes its name. Here I attempted to quiz a Dutch Dame, who here joined us, about her bake oven (in the mouth of which 2 large white cats were then seated & seamed to hold their winter quarters) but Brown[263] discovered my mood laughed out, I could not contain myself & was thus betrayed & foiled in my purpose. After passing the small towns Bedford, Somerset & Mt Pleasant we at length, on the sixth day after leaving Phia, struck the Alleghany River & after passing a fortress & garrison on its bank, we proceeded down its bank, the country & sky beginning to assume a dusky hue, several coal mines were seen on the sides of the hills, the people began to wear sooty clothes & smutty faces, even the cows, sheep & geese were tinged. Proceeding rapidly we soon saw in the distance the dark, lowering & gloomy cloud which eternally rests over this the most filthy of all places which I have ever seen. The soot & smoke this moment settles on my paper, thickens my ink[,] dirties my clothes, darkens my skin, fills my nose, gathers in my eyes, obstructs my breath, gives me the head ache & puts me out of temper, in fact I have been angry & peevish, since 20 minutes after taking lodging at Griffiths & expect to be so until I leave the city. But notwithstanding my ill humour I have been busy to see what is to be seen, to see what causes this disagreeable atmosphere. I have groped my way through the darkness, wound among the dark houses & obscure streets, clambered over piles of ashes & cinder deposited in the streets, waded through the black streams of slop water & melted snow & have found some interesting objects. The first of interest was the Cut Glass Manufactory. The Machinery was propelled by stream & the operations simply beyond my conception; a great number of coarse & fine grindstones were arranged on various axels & turned with considerable rapidity; to these the glass ware was applied by the workmen & was readily ground according to his wishes, the coarse work being done the ware was applied to a finer stone & therein polished as smooth as desired. The work was done by men and boys, seaming to require but little skill & only steady nerves to place & hold the ware properly on the grindstone. Saw decanters, tumblers &c cut.[266]

The outter wall [Western Pennsylvania Penitentiary] encases 3 acres of ground[,] is of free stone of a light colour, in the form of an octagon & is 24 feet high & covered with a shingle rooff & ornamented by four gothic towers. I saw ornamented because they are useless, not being strong enough for cells, too inconvenient for dwellings & not necessary for storehouses. One side of the octagon constitutes the front looking towards the river & city & having a fine & extensive yard; planted with ornamental trees, before it, with a gravel walk leading from the front gate to the front door, the whole front is occupied by a three story gothic building (the sides being terminated by towers) used as the office & residence of the Warden & other officers, on the top of this building in the centre of it is a small & handsome cupola. Within this wall is a single story brick building erected about 15 feet from the outter wall forming an entire circle & containing a double row of cells, one row opening towards the outter wall & the other towards the centre of the circle. The cells are 190 in number of the proper size for one person, & each cell has a small ante chamber with doors opening from one to another & when all are open forming a passage all around the row of cells. The space within the row of cells is divided by converging brick walls, serving only to conceal the rascality of the prisoners, & to prevent inspection by the officers.[267]

The prison has been in operation 3 years, the original cost of the building $185,000. at present contains 55 prisoners of which 6 are females, the expenses of the prisoners being defrayed by the counties sending them. Solitary confinement without labour is the design of the Institution, but on account of the improper construction of the buildings or the relaxation of the discipline the design is not affected. The females have a small yard to themselves in which they hold free & unreserved communication, occasionally seeing those of the opposite sex. The men can converse freely through the doors of their ante chambers (which are kept open by a stove pipe running through them) besides a certain number have the privilege of the whole yard every day for the performance of domestic duties, which gives all an oppertunity of seeing & conversing with each other once a week.

The females do the washing & the males the coking for the establishment, with this exception the prisoners are entirely idle or engaged according to their fancy in talk or song of which last I heard a specimen in which several participated in loud and animated strains. I saw several of the prisoners males & females, they were both dressed in striped linsey & looked very hearty & healthy.

The diet of the prisoners is varied every day & consists chiefly of broth, bread, mush, molasses & potatoes. They change their clothes but once a week. They are furnished with bibles & tracts by the Bible & tract societies but have no preaching nor other instruction except as they teach each other. The punishments for disorderly conduct are the dungeons, confined in chains, dieted on bread & water &c stripes not entering into the system.

The officers of the Institution are a "watch man" a Warden (Mr John Patterson) & an assistant; paid by the State & chosen by the Inspectors of which there are five, appointed either by the Gov. or Ligis.[268]

Returning we took a look at the Alleghany Canal & the Aqueduct by which it is carried across the river Alleghany to the City of Pittsburg.[269] About 70 miles of the canal are completed the latter place terminating the southern & Blairsville the Northern end of it. The river when the Aquaduct crosses it is broad[;] the aquaduct is built of wood similar to a bridge & is supported by six stone pillars with timbers bent in the form of a segment of a circle fastened together & spanning from one pillar to another; in the middle of the bridge there is a warterproof passage for navigation broad enough for a single boat & also a foot way for men or beasts on each side of it. The whole work is under a shingle roof, the sides of it also being protected from the weather; it seamed to [have been] executed with much skill & taste, having a beautiful & permanent appearance. It was built by _____ and cost about _____.

Prefering to look at the Aquaduct from below we crossed the river on the ice, then about a foot thick, & had it and the fine bridge below it, within view at the same time. The bridge has six stone pillars also, is similar in the principles of its construction & resembles it in appearance. Thence we crossed the majestic Monongehala bridge to see the Window Glass works, they were not blowing & we continued our walk to the Iron Rolling Mills just below.[270] The works like all others in this vicinity are driven by steam stove coal being the fuel, the coal used in this factory is dug out of the bowels of the hill just above & is rolled down almost to the door. Two large iron cylinders were confined in a horizontl position & turned in opposite directions. These cylendars had grooves cut in them, at one end of the cylendars the groves were large & their size diminished gradually to the other end, the groove in the upper cylendar was exactly above the groove in the lower one. The large hot bars of iron were applied to these gro[o]ves, was passed through first the larger & then the smaller ones, the iron growing longer & smaller each time until it became the desired size.

Sheet iron was formed by passing through rollers with smooth surfaces & without grooves, the rollers being pressed closer together by a screw as the iron was passed through them sucessively. At this place were also numerous machines for cutting nails of various sizes. The labour in thes factories is divided between men & boys there being almost an equal number.[271]

Visited Hamilton Stewarts Domestic cloth Hall, the proprietor of the Factories for the manufacture of cotton & Damask table linnen, saw various specimens, among others a piece intended as a present to Mr Niles editor of the Register, the cloth had his name woven in it & also a motto recognizing him as the friend of Domestic Manufactures. Visited a flowered Paper Manufactory. The colours are all water colours; the figures are carved upon flat bords of hard wood, about 18 inches broad & as long as the paper is broad, these boards are taken in the hand of the workmen the carved side is laid upon the table covered over with colouring which adheres to the mould & is then placed upon the paper & pressed, the paper receives the impression, is then hung up in a warm room, the paint is dried in half a day & when dry is ready to receive another set of colours from another set of moulds. The colours are laid on & dried successively, the moulds being changed as often as the colours are; the whole operations being so simple that the workmen wondered that we had come to see them.[272]

The Pittsburg Water Works are inferiour & of little interest. A steam engine draws the water from the Alleghany & deposits it through pipes on the top of a high hill in the East part of the town in two reservoirs faced with stone, 12 feet deep & about 110 feet square, & from the reservoirs is conducted through the city in iron pipes.[273]

Feb. 16th Being anxious for the opening of the River, I walked down Wood Street to the Steam boat landing where several boats were standing enclosed in the ice & like myself awaiting its thawing. The sun was shining warm & fair, & the filthy streets were pouring their murky torrents in profusion upon the ice bound stream & blackening its snow clad surface with their Stygian waters. Seeing such quantities of filth I became curious to know something of the health of the place & according took a Perigrenation through the city & to some of the factories to observe the countenances of the people; though in the course of the walk I saw several flourishing burial grounds, heard of a funeral & saw a bier, yet my opinion is in favour of the health of the place, the people have dark & dirty complexion, but generally look healthy. Of the ladies I can not make many pleasant memorandum, their dirty pavements covered with frozen dish water & soapsuds, speak a truth which I can not contradict. In truth during two days & a half I have not seen one genteel & lady looking woman, in the city, but I have seen more slatterns than I could have imagined. From all appearances they are exceeding prolific; I stood in one place & counted 40 children, none of which seamed to exceed 12 years; thinking that I might be in the vicinity of a school house I walked a few squares further & at one sight counted 18 or 20 more about 6 years old & under, all looking dirty, but very sprightly & healthy. I no longer wondered that I should see a tasteful & spacious stone edifice rising among these dark abodes, already called an Academy.[274] After remaining in Pittsburgh three days & a half despaired of the river's opening; paid a bill of $3.87½ to Griffith,[275] he keeping a mean house but probably the best in the place, & took the stage to Steubenville at 6 o'clock A.M. Feb. 18 distance about 37 miles & fare $2.25.

Country mountainous, roads muddy. Crossed the Ohio river in a ferry boat about a mile above Stuebenville, which is a small & dirty place, abounding in mills & factories propelled by steam, stone coal being the fuel. The country in the vicinity is mountainous, exceeding romantic & tokenlly fertile. The large flocks of merino sheep which we saw as we approached the town gave notice that this was the seat of the best cloth manufactory in the West, we reached town in time to visit it; a fine three or four story brick building in the west part of town. Eight or ten power looms were in operation weaving broad cloth, of a tolerably fine quality. A carding machine which disposed of the carded wool in the form of a coarse thread was one of the chief peculiarities. The card from which the wool was taken by the comb was divided into many rows of cards, each row disposing of a bat of wool about one inch & a half broad, these bats passed through the axes of short & hollow spindles, running horizontally & were thus twisted & then were wound on large spools. The labour was generally performed by boys & girls of a dirty & slovenly appearance. The factory being chiefly owned by Mr. Basel Wells, who has a hand-some brick residence on the bank of the river, a little below town. Disap-pointed at the size & disgusted with the smoke & dirt of Stuebenville, left it next morning, crossed the river & went down it through Wellsburg &c to Wheeling,[276] At Wellsburg we took in a stage companion who by his good sense, long experience & kind manners rendered the passage highly pleasant. He was a soldier in the Revolution & one of the few who kindled & kept the large fires which deceived the senses of the British on the heights of Trenton just before the capture of the Hessians & the defeat of the British at Princeton; He was then a boy of 14 years, has since served in N. Western army & now resides on the banks of the Ohio which he assisted to gain from the Indians & whose majestic rolling he has observed for 35 years. He lives in the vicinity of Alex. Campbell[277] who he told me bears the name of a good citizen neighbour & preacher, that he has been twice mar-ried acquired property by his last wife, has augmented it by the printing press in operation at his county seat Bethany, with which the newspaper aided by him is printed, also, his translation of the bible, his controversy with several persons among others that with Mr Owen who was lately entertained in hospitable manner by M Campbell.[278] Passing down the River we saw four or five coal mines in the hills & also the Railway ways on which the coal is conveyed from the mine down the hill to the river. The hill is graduated the descent made regular to the base of the hill & four rows of wooden rails are laid in parrallel from top to bottom, one rail way for descending & one of ascending waggons (which are small & resemble the waggons for children). By means of a large roap wound round a beam roling horizontally, with a waggon attached to each end of it, the loaded waggon in its descent is made to draw the empty one to the top of the hill, the speed of the descent being regulated by a man holding the crank or handle of the leading; the empty wagon ascending one rail way while the descending & loaded waggon occupies the other. Passed a small Salt Works & also a well where a man had penetrated the earth to the depth of 900 feet with an intention of getting water or bore to the sea, but operations were unfortunately suspended by getting the auger fast & though 6 months were spent in efforts to extricate it it could not be effected.[279]

Passing down the River our veteran companion pointed us to a bottom on the other side, the banks much washed by the river, with a small old frame house now tottering on the brink. "There said he", pointing to the bottoms, "once stood a fort & the residence of Mr Carpenter one of the earliest settlers on this river, whose wife was one of the most remarkable women of her day, having among other feats not less remarkable produced seven children at three births, all of which she raised to manhood except one, all of them well known by me, She & her husband were once employed in hoeing corn near the fort when they were attacked by several Indians who shot her husband down but missed her, she gathered her clothes around her waist to expedite her fleight which she instantly commenced to the Fort, which though closely pursued she reached in safety & as she sprung into the door she smacked her hand on *satins* the fineness of the pass & bade them kiss it damned sons of bitches.[280] She soon mustered the forces of the station & stallied out in pursuit of the foe, found her husband & restored him to health & safety. There they lived & died, their posterity occupying their dwelling untill the encroachments of the river deprived them of it, they then sallied out to seek their fortunes elsewhere.

In the course of the route we saw on the River many flocks of wild ducks which our companion told us were called Dippers or Divers from the great skill & quickness with which they dived under the water, he told us the method by which the Eagles catch them, two uniting they place themselves in the air above the duck, one pounces down to sieze it, it of course dives into the water & the eagle rises into the air, while the other eagle pounces down to meet the duck on its ascent & thus they proceed alternately until they worry down & catch the duck.

Reached Wheeling & stopped at Jone's City Hotel which thus far is the best tavern seen for many months.[281] The town is situated on the west side of the Ohio with a high hill on the other side of town, so that it lies on a strip of bottom land with an island near the other shore. P.S. the boat shakes too much for me to write.

Feb. 19. 1830. Among other institutions mechanical visited a new Paper Manufactory upon the same plan with that near Springfield Massachusetts. The machine is patented being invented in the above named state & may be thus described. A large vat contains the ground rags & water, near one end of this is a hollow cylindar of fine wire about 18 inches or two feet in diameter, revolving horizontally with the axes resting on the opposite sides of the wooden vat, the wire cylender has nearly half of its lower side immersed in water & ground rangs, so that as the wire cylin-

dar revolves the water runs through the wire to the centre of the cylendar
& is thence conducted entirely off, leaving the outside of the wire cylendar covered with ground rags; as they rise out of the vat they fall in with
another wooden cilendar of the same size, rolling on the top of the first
named, this top cilender has a canvass cloth passing round it & kept
extended by other rollers at the middle & ends, as the ground rags in passing between the two cylenders come in contact with the canvass they
adhere to it & are thence wound round another large cylinder in a broad
& infinite sheet, the fineness of the rags & the wire cilender regulating
the fineness of the paper. The machinery was simple in construction easily
made & kept in order, two or three could be asily tended by one person
each machine saving the labour of many. The machinery is built & put
in operation by the inventors at a cost including the patent right, of 800
or 1000 dolls. accord to the finish of the work.[282] After spending a day
& a half in Wheeling looking at all its parts traversing its muddy streets
to see its factories &c paid a bill of $1.43, heard the pleasant intelligence
that the Lagrange would leave that evening for Louisville the river having broken up & the ice partially ceasing to run. At 8 o'clock was snug
in her commodious cabin, The firemen therein the wood & coal, rushed
the fires & raised the steam, the engineer gave a few fizzes & when the
landsmen pushed off he plied the wheels, the pilot turned the helm & struck
up the departing song, the whole crew joining in chorus with much animation. ["]I'm gwine away I'm gwin away from Wheelin Town; I'm gwine
away I'm gwine away to Louisville" So we put off, occasionally much
jared by striking the wheels against the ice, but are now stopped on the
far side of the Island to take in loading.[283]

    The beautiful & fertile island is the place of resort for the fashionables
of Wheeling,[284] that night it afforded us a harbour & the next morning
we put off by times, & after struggling with the ice for three days at length
arrived safe at Cincinnatti. The journey though tedious & barren of
remarkable incidents was nevertheless quite pleasant, having good company & good accomodations. We called at & passed several small towns
on the River, of all which Marietta[285] will not be forgotten[,] I having spent
a considerable time in the night in a fruitless search to find the town wading
half leg deep in the mud. Was also in Galliopolis,[286] a small & tolerably
handsome town, having on the bank of the river a level & spacious public
square now in grass & not enclosed, when planted with trees it will be
quite handsome. At Cincinnatti heard the small pox was raging to a considerable extent, took a turn through the City,[287] marked considerable
improvement in it & then departed for Louisville, the boat crew singing
a song on departing as they had also on arriving. Saw several handsome
& well improved residences on the banks of the River, particularly a handsome white brick house on the left hand side a few miles below Cincin-

natti. As the river was not in fine order, the ice having melted or disappeared, we passed rapidly down the river at the rate of 10 or 11 miles per hour reaching Louisville in almost 14 or 15 hours. Distance from Wheeling about _____ miles price of passage $.13.

January 1st 1836.

Having returned to Frankfort I formed a partnership in the practice of Law with the late James Haggin[288] & pursued the profession with tolerable success until Jan. 1834 when on account of delicate health I removed with my wife and child to Locust Hill, a farm which I purchased 5 miles E of Frankfort for about $9000.[289] Haveing business at Lake Washington, M.J. I am again on the highways & rivers, and having found the foregoing Memorand of much interest to me I have determined to continue it on this second Excursion. Leave on Saturday evening.

Dec. 26 1835, took passage on the Steamer Clay for Lake Washington fare $25, had a pleasant run and agreeable (arrived at Washington's Wednesday 10 o'clock A.M. Dec. 30)

FLORIDA

company. Among the passengers was Governor Duval[290] late of Florida a gentleman of urbane manners kind heart & extensive information. He is of the opinion that Florida was once inhabited extensively by the Buccanneers, who, driven from the Gulph & seas by the united fleets of Europe on account of their predatory depradations upon the commerce of all other nations besides Spain, were compelled to fly to the interiour for safety, were cut off from the rest of the world they built fortifications to sustain themselves against the natives of the country, erected dwellings & cultivated farms, and thus sustained themselves for a long period, until at length they were over whelmed by a grand combination of all the Indians in that region. He is fortified in these opinions by the historical fact of the expulsion of the Buccaneers, and their sudden disappearance from the civalized world & from the high seas; and by the constant discovery of implements of war & husbandry, fortifications & landmarks being frequently discovered. On one occasion he & his son fatigued with the chase sat down upon a small green mound under a spreading shade, & his son carelessly stuck his butcher knife into the mount & found it struck against iron; this led them to examine the mound which proved to consist of several hundred hoes and some axes covered with earth; they were much eaten by rust, but still showing a shape not much discordant from those now in use, but apparently of superiour workmanship.

On another occasion whilst exploring the woods he stopped at a spring for refreshment & whilst it was being cleaned out, a large and substantial box of live oak, which was undoubtedly put in the spring by some former inhabitants, was discovered in the mud, excavated & replaced for the use of the inhabitants of another century. From this spring he could plainly trace by scattered bricks & fragments of masonry what had been a covered way from the spring to the fort nearby the works, banks, ditches, walls in part, of which were indistinctly to be traced. Near this spring also he discovered in the mud an old rusty barrel of a twelve pounder cannon, which was subsequently dug out & taken to Tallahassee wher it is still to be seen & in actual use on occasions of anniversaries & festivals.[291] He named the discovery of many similar things too tedious to mention. He supposes that the Buccaneers by the expendature of their ammunition lost the superiour advantages of fire arms & being thus reduced to an equatily with the Aborigines were so unfortunate as to gain their displeasure & be destroyed by their superiour numbers in one simultaneous effort.

DANIEL BOON.

Amg the Passengers was also my venerable uncle by marriage Hon. John Brown,[292] who informed that the last time he saw Dan. Boon whom he well knew was in Phia. during the session of the old Congress there, Boon with his wife had travelled on foot in Indian style to that city on business.[293] Whenever he travelled he was in the habit of taking his much loved spouse on account of a lesson which she once gave him for leaving her behind. During one of his first trips to Ky. Boon began to be anxious to see his wife for whom he had provided a rude hut & sent his brother Squire Boon to bring her out to Ky. But squire was rather fond of ease than enterprise & of love than glory. Dan Boon becoming anxious that his brother did not return after the lapse of about a year returned to Va. to see what had befallen his wife & Brother. As he rode up to his old home-stead covered with bear & Buffalo skins his wife discerned him & know-ing him ran & embraced him with much warmth & tenderness, but soon began to weap & cry. Old Dan. being surprised at her weeping on such an occasion asked the cause. Oh! said she, I have been unfortunate since your have been gone; Why what's the matter? asked Boon; I have had a child!! Ah! says Boon, but tis no matter never mind, tis my fault, I ought to have staid at home — But who's the father of it? Your brother Squire", answered she; Tis all the better, exclaimed he in good humour, till all in the family; And thus the small affair was easily accomodation by his happy & forgiving disposition. But he took care after that either to take her with him or else to stay at home.[294]

Having arrived at Worthington's Point[295] on the 30 of Dec. just 3 days from Frankfort I spent several days in examining the farm & adjacent coun-try being charmed with its unbounded fertility and inviting situation. We had near 3000 head of excellent cattle all raised & sustained with no other expense or trouble but occasional salting. They range at large in the cane brakes & swamp coming home in lots of 30 or 40 occasionally for salt, as soon as the mosquettos become numerous & troublesome all the cattle come home & stand in the open & sunny ground (when the musehettos do not come) until night when they go out to feed. W. killed this year about 140 fine hogs also raised with little trouble or expense save fattening on corn; stock hogs subsist on acorns, cotton seed & muscadine grapes upon which last they are quite fat when put in the pen to fatten, some corn is given only in wet times when the country is overflowed with water &c. Though the country presents these great advantages for raising stock still but few farmers attend to them, the employment is raising cotton being so much more profitable; upon an average a hand will tend 8 acres of cotton & 2 acres of corn, producing about 450 lbs. of cotton or 10 bls of corn to the acre, the average profit on the hands ranging between 2 & 4 hundred dollars. The culture of Cotton does not seem in any manner more difficult than grain & not so much so as of hemp, & upon the whole a cotton farm seems less difficult to conduct than a farm of the same size in Ky. This arises from the fact that but 2 crops are raised cotton & corn.

The country generally is settling & improving exceedingly fast, more attention is paid to comfort in building & housekeeping, planters are getting in the habit of having their families with them & the society is improving as a matter of course. My prejudices against the life of a planter, so far from being augmented were rather transformed into partialities for it.[296]

After two days, enduring cold & smoke on the bank of the river we got aboard the Siam, a small bad steamer from St. Louis & went to Donalsonville,[297] fare $12.00. On the route we saw nothing of much interest ex[cep]t a cemetary & tomb which were situated on the bank of the River immediately in front of the mansion house of a French sugar plant.

The grave yard contained a single tomb with a high paling enclosure of 20 or 30 feet square & was most beautifully ornamented with roses, Crocus's, palm cedar, honeysuckles & Magnolias all blooming & beaming with most luxuriant vegetation, these together with the painted seats, flower pots & beds & plants indicated as a spot as highly favoured as it was lovely. To the eyes of Kentuckian just as it were turned from dimming wintry snows & piercing winds this green & blooming spot was most lovely indeed. As I plucked the blooming flowers & inhaled their delicious perfumes my delight was exquisite, but soon was tempered by the regret that my beloved wife was not by my side to participate with me in the pleasure but I culled a bouquet of sweetest flowers & now that she should see at least their faded beauties when I reached home.[298]

As we approached New Orleans for many miles above Donaldson-ville the river was lined on both sides with contiguous cotton & sugar plantations, generally presenting the appearance of comfort & in some instances of splendour & affluence.[299]

Arrived at N. Orleans on the morning of the 28th of Jan. 1836 put up at Bishop's hotel an immense establishment, bearing the highest reputation of any tavern in the city, though in all respects inferiour to the best hotels of the Eastern cities.[300] Fare $2.50 per day, with extra charges for all occasions even to unstopping a bottle, for making you a fine 50 cts.

Went to *Caldwell's Theatre*[301] a very spacious & splendid establishment, not yet finished. The play was the Yankee in Spain personated by Mr Hill, the company was indifferent.[302] The orchestra was composed of about 30 musicians performing on all manner of instruments, the band so unwieldly, the music so scientific & precise & the instruments so discordant that the whole effect was unpleasant to my ears. Good order was preserved, gentlemen not allowed even to sit with their hats on during the performance, still it seemed not to be honoured with the presence of the fair sex.[303]

Visited the *Catholic Burying* Ground truly the city of the dead,[304] a large area in a remote part of the city is enclosed by a high brick

Memorad of the life of R. W. Scott

Waller Fund, in 1853-4 a organization was effected among the Baptists of Ky. for the relief of Rev. John L. Waller from his indebtedness, & R.W.S. was made the Sec. & Financial Agent, & collected & paid out nearly $2000, for the object to the entire satisfaction of the Society called the Waller Relief Asn.[305]

Com. School System in Ky

In May 7, 1838, I was commissioned by Rev. J. J. Bullock, Supt., a Commissioner of Com. Schools for Franklin Co. & by B. B. Smith in 1841, & put 7 schools in operation out of 13 districts, & the first in the State.[306]

see papers, School in operation in 1841.

Lines in imitation of "Were's not a joy"

Think not because the eye is bright and smile
The heart that beats within is light and free from pain

THE LIFE OF
ROBERT WILMOT SCOTT

1

The Master of Locust Hill

THE DECADE from 1820 to 1830 was one of political and religious turmoil in Kentucky. For a sixteen-year-old Georgetown student at Transylvania the troubles of that institution made unusual calls upon him. Robert Wilmot Scott was a dedicated scholar fascinated with the English language, and especially with its poetic use. He prepared meticulously two poetry notebooks, one of which still survives.[1] In adolescence young Robert revealed that hunger for knowledge which characterized the tenor of his whole life. Some of the poems he recorded in copperplate script were of his own composition; others were selected from the classics. For him the world of learning was drawn into focus by his Transylvania professors, and by access to the books in the growing library. He was enchanted with the thought that the study of philosophy stretched the human mind as Socrates had promised. Even the world of science beckoned seductively.[2]

If delving into the broad fields of classical learning challenged the ambitious young Scott of Georgetown and supplied his mind with intoxicating nourishment, the fundamentalist storm which raged about him was emotionally and intellectually distractive. Transylvania in these earlier years had shown bright promise of becoming a major university in the rising new West. The New England clergyman Horace Holley had brought to its campus fresh and invigorating intellectual stimulus. He had stirred staff, students, and community with new visions of liberal learning.[3] Never before had Kentucky minds been awakened so vigorously, nor had so many old moral and social values been brought under questioning. Quickly, narrow and bigoted clergymen and laymen brought the Yankee president under fire.[4] The resulting fundamentalist storm concerned Robert Wilmot Scott and his fellow students. He was chosen to speak for the students, who had just begun to savor the fruits of learning, in expressing their sense of satisfaction with their experiences on one hand, and to protest against the senseless martyrdom the bigots were imposing on their dedicated leader.[5] This disastrous moment in the history of liberal education in Kentucky no doubt had its profound effect on Robert Scott throughout his life.[6]

In spite of the growing storm of conflict brewing between president, trustees, clergymen, and public, Robert W. Scott's year at Transylvania was a truly seminal one. He gained insights not only into the great world of learning, but also into the workings of Kentucky practical politics in the opening of the Jacksonian Era. His family were Jacksonian Democrats, and so were his close friends. For instance, he was intimate with the famous William T. Barry family, and he knew Amos Kendall, John Adair, Joseph Desha, and others.[7] Lexington in those years was still the cultural and legal center of Kentucky. Its newspaper press had wider than mere local influence. There were, for example, Thomas Smith's *Reporter* and N. L. Finnell's *Observer*.[8]

The Fayette County Bar included in its membership Henry Clay, George Robertson, William Taylor Barry, Robert Wickliffe, and Thomas A. Marshall. The fertile lands and bluegrass farms of Fayette County were tended by prosperous farmers and livestock breeders who exhibited a wide category of field crops, animals, and home crafts at the early fairs.[9]

Politically, a revolutionary change was coming in the Commonwealth. A biting financial panic had wrecked the state's ill-conceived banking system, had bankrupted thousands of debtors, and even threatened the foundation of state government itself. The old Republican-Federalist party alignments were rapidly deteriorating, and new ones were emerging. A penurious and incompetent Jacksonian, Joseph Desha, occupied the governor's office in Frankfort, and these partisans were pushing their way into other offices.[10] Nevertheless, this was a challenging time for a serious-minded young Kentuckian to come of age and to seek career directions. On a much broader canvas America was entering a fermentative era which was to sweep the nation to new technological and intellectual heights, political realignments, and international power.[11]

Robert Wilmot Scott was born on his maternal grandfather Robert Wilmot's farm in Bourbon County on November 8, 1808. His father Joel Scott and Sarah Ridgely Wilmot, Joel's second wife, were either visiting on that farm when Robert was born or they were living there only temporarily.[12] The Scott homestead was located on the waters of the North Elkhorn Creek in Scott County near the Great Crossings. This famous bluegrass valley of the triple-pronged Elkhorn had long held a magnetic attraction for Virginians who came across the mountains in search of rich farmlands. John Scott, a second-generation Anglo-American and a veteran of the Battle of King's Mountain, had moved west in 1785 with his wife Hanna and their young son Joel.[13] The Scotts were originally from Culpepper County, but in their latest move they came from Madison County.[14] The Kentucky land on which John settled his family was some of the most fertile in the western country and promised almost unlimited returns to a diligent farmer.

The Wilmots arrived in Kentucky a year behind the Scotts.[15] They came by way of the second great immigrant artery, the Ohio River. From the well-established landing point at the mouth of Limestone Creek they traveled south over the well-beaten frontier trail to the Stoner Fork of the Licking River near Paris in Bourbon County. Captain Robert Wilmot, later promoted to colonel by popular acclaim, was a revolutionary war veteran who throughout the conflict had commanded the Baltimore County Artillery Company. Once settled in Kentucky, he quickly became an important local political figure.[16] He served as a delegate to the state House of Representatives from Bourbon County, 1796-1802, and in 1799 was a member of the Second Kentucky Constitutional Convention. This convention was made up largely of conservative landholders who had been chosen over an opposing slate which favored emancipation of slaves, direct election of major state officials, public support of education, and the distinct separation of powers of state government.[17]

Thus Robert Wilmot Scott had strong frontier and colonial ties with both Kentucky and the eastern seaboard. He was to visit the latter region in his twenty-first year. His years of growing to manhood on the North Elkhorn and in Georgetown had fundamental bearings upon his future life. First, he fell under the seductive spell of the land, which instilled in him an unwavering love of farming. Both his grandfather John, and his father Joel, were successful farmers. With Anglo ingenuity and managerial ability, John Scott ran a fulling and dressing mill on the waters of the Elkhorn, and later his son Joel established a woolen mill and store in Georgetown. On his visit to Chicopee Falls, Massachusetts, and its textile mills in 1829, Robert was intrigued by the whole manufacturing operation. He was comparing the bigger and more sophisticated operation with his family's modest Elkhorn mills.[18]

Joel Scott, however, was not to carve out his niche in Kentucky history as a Scott County farmer-storekeeper and mill master. In 1824, he applied for the job of keeper of the Kentucky Penitentiary in Frankfort with the patronage blessing of his fellow Jacksonian, Governor Joseph Desha. Scott was awarded this position by the General Assembly in an extensive legislative act which was more nearly a business contract than a law. He was appointed director on January 10, 1825, having based his candidacy upon the fact that he had successfully operated a mill and textile machines and could bring definite moral and labor reforms to the institution.[19]

In 1835, there were eighty-four prisoners huddled in the Frankfort penitentiary, placed there for the commission of crimes which ranged from felonies of counterfeiting and horse, hog, and Negro stealing, to forgery and burglary, with horse stealing the most frequent charge. Convicts had been worked largely to produce a personal profit for the keepers, with no thought of correction and reform. Joel Scott's immediate predecessor William Hardin was a good example of this abuse.[20] The thirty or so cells were crowded, filthy, and cold. Clothing was shabby, health conditions abominable, and punishment harsh. Few Kentuckians, including the governor, were aware of the medieval barbarities which prevailed in this hellhole of social neglect.[21] All the politicians wanted was to get the prisoners out of sight and out of mind — and to save the public treasury.[22]

Joel Scott built a woolen and cotton mill his first year as keeper, and returned to the Kentucky treasury a profit of $5,720. Governor Desha reported to the General Assembly that year that for the first time the Penitentiary had not been a financial burden to the taxpayers. In time, Scott was to develop wagon, cooper, chair, carpenter, shoemaker, and blacksmith shops, and to engage his "horse thieves" in a vocation rather than planning the next siege of bridle snatching.[23] The Penitentiary soon became in fact one of the most efficient manufacturing enterprises in the state. It was a source for well-made objects which found ready sale to the public. Aside from these industries Scott engaged the convicts in the dressing of the Tyrone limestone blocks cut from the bed of the Kentucky River for the construction of Gideon Shryock's elegant Greek Revival capitol.[24] This preoccupation of his father with the Kentucky Penitentiary caused Robert to give special attention to the penitentiaries he visited in the East during 1829 and 1830.

When Robert W. Scott joined his family in Frankfort after his year at Transylvania University, he found Joel busily engaged in rebuilding the horrible old pesthole of a penitentiary, organizing the trades and shops, and participating in the political pullings and haulings of the capital. The demanding activities associated with the prison's operation obviously became a central interest of the family. Robert, however, had determined prior to leaving the University that he would read law preparatory to entering upon a professional career. He began this process in the offices of Judge James Haggin and Preston H. Loughboro, both strong Jacksonians and local relief and New Court partisans.[25]

The decade between 1819 and 1829 was an exciting time to be in Frankfort, with all the cross-currents of economic crisis, bitter partisanship, and clash of personalities. The ruinous banking crisis and panic of 1819, the passage of ill-considered legislation aimed at the protection of debtors, and shaky state banking currency stirred a revolution in Kentucky politics. Adverse court reviews of this legislation created a near-disastrous constitutional issue to be argued by extreme partisans on both sides.[26]

In the presidential election of 1824 Henry Clay had failed of election but had become a kingmaker in the United States House of Representatives. For this act Jacksonians burned him in effigy in several Kentucky towns. Early in January 1825, the General Assembly voted to remove from office the judges of the regularly constituted Court of Appeals and to replace them with a new court which would rule favorably upon relief legislation that had been enacted on the untenable grounds, "If it [the constitutional court] shall inflict upon the community such injury as the legislature may deem reasonable cause."[27] In the middle of that decade General Lafayette visited Kentucky, including Frankfort, in May, and in the following November Colonel Solomon P. Sharp, a former congressman, legislator, and Kentucky attorney general, was assassinated by Jeroboam Beauchamp in a sensational political murder. The assassination and trial, followed by the execution of Beauchamp and the love-pact suicide of his female paramour Anne Cook, created a sensation which has lingered on in American literary writing.[28]

In the midst of the latter years of this public unheaval Robert W. Scott applied himself assiduously to the reading of law. Just as he had read and written poetry to be recorded in his notebooks, he digested the contents of *Kyd on Awards, Selwyn on Evidence, Chitty on Bills, Roberts on Frauds, Newland on Contracts,* and *Teller on Executives.* There seems to exist no record of the reactions of his mentor to all his careful briefings, or whether Scott did all of his reading in Frankfort. In some of his autobiographical notes he hints that he spent considerable time in Lexington reading law in the offices of members of the Fayette Bar.[29]

At nineteen years of age Scott impressed people around him as being a studious, philosophical young man. His twelve-year-old cousin Priscilla Wilmot wrote him in 1827 about her academic problems. She was enrolled in Miss Spencer's School in Georgetown and was having both curricular and maternal problems. She was studying history but had dropped geography and astronomy. Miss Spencer had suggested that she substitute for them rhetoric and botany. Her mother wanted her to drop out of school and take lady-like private lessons in music. She needed Cousin Robert's moral support to enable her to remain in school and to study "something more important."[30] At nineteen, Robert had impressed his adolescent relative as being a man of genuine intellectual maturity who understood the mysteries of philosophy.

Not all of Robert Scott's time was spent burrowing through rusty volumes of legal wisdom in Haggin and Loughboro's offices. He enjoyed thoroughly the sedate parties and dances which were so popular among the older Frankfort societies clustered around the great bend of the Kentucky River in a secluded social cul-de-sac. He attended suppers, joined in the celebration of holidays, and courted Elizabeth Watts Brown, the fourth daughter of Dr. Preston W. and Elizabeth Watts Brown.[31] The Browns were among the first families of both Frankfort and Kentucky. Dr. Brown was the eleventh child of the Reverend John and Elizabeth Preston Brown of Virginia, and was a brother of John, Samuel, and James

Elizabeth Watts Brown, daughter of Elizabeth and Preston Brown

Brown, who distinguished themselves in politics and medicine. Dr. Preston Brown was a successful medical practitioner in his own right, having practiced in Woodford, Franklin, and Jefferson counties. He died in Louisville in 1826, and his widow moved the family back to Frankfort.[32]

That wintry day in February 1830 when Robert Wilmot Scott traveled from Louisville to Frankfort on the last leg of his long visit to the East, his mind may have been preoccupied with plans to begin immediately the practice of law as a partner of his former mentor Judge James Haggin.[33] For the next two years he practiced this profession, but the record is deathly silent on how well he succeeded. Curiously, this is the most inadequately documented phase of his life.

Outside the law office Scott's life is almost an open book. He courted Elizabeth Watts Brown with ardor, entered into the swirl of social affairs in the capital city, and watched the changing tides of state politics. He and Elizabeth terminated their courtship on October 28, 1831, in a fashionable wedding. How much the bride was influenced by the book on weddings which Robert had bought in Washington is unknown. There, however, has survived more tangible evidence in the form of a truly elegant wedding gown which had been designed and sewn by Louisville seamstresses. Its slender and tightly fitted bodice was for the figure of a comely lass, and the multifold flowing skirt and generous train have the appear-

Elizabeth Brown, just prior to her marriage to Scott, 1831

Elizabeth Brown Scott, attending a picnic at the Forks of Elkhorn, Franklin County, Kentucky

ance of being lifted directly from the pages of an early nineteenth-century fashion magazine. Following their marriage Elizabeth and Robert either moved directly to the Browns' country home, Sumners Forest, in Woodford County, or they were living there when their first-born of nine children, Preston Brown Scott, arrived on September 24, 1832.[34] As a new family man Robert Wilmot Scott forsook the practice of law on the grounds of failing health and returned to the land to become one of Kentucky's most progressive farmers. The once-dedicated student of poetry and philosophy, and later of the law, now focused his eternally inquiring mind upon the challenges of horticulture, agriculture, and livestock breeding.[35]

However vigorous the industrious Scotts, father and son, may have appeared in the conduct of their affairs in 1834, both claimed to be beset by failing health.[36] Joel Scott resigned his position as director of the Kentucky Penitentiary halfway through his second contract, and Robert gave up his law practice for the same reason. Through the years Joel Scott purchased and sold land in and about Frankfort, but in 1834 he went across the Woodford County line to purchase a farm near the Frankfort-Versailles Pike.[37] Robert purchased the poorly managed and run-down farm of Martin D. Hardin from the latter's heirs. This 205-acre tract, which

Locust Hill

Scott immediately named Locust Hill, lay astride the Franklin-Woodford County boundary directly off the road to Versailles, just east of the village of Jett, and southwest of Ducker's Station on the pioneer Lexington and Ohio Railroad.[38] He purchased a second farm from the heirs of William Churchill in a second-stage transfer from a revolutionary war land grant.[39] This latter purchase filled out the Locust Hill Farm to the main road on the southwest. In time Scott was to increase the Locust Hill Estate to more than a thousand acres.[40]

The farm land of Locust Hill was located in the westernmost fringe of the Inner Kentucky Bluegrass, almost halfway between the waters of the Forks of the Elkhorn and the Kentucky River. It was of a rolling nature, sometimes steeply so, well-drained, but not so fertile as some of the "asparagus bed" lands of Woodford County immediately to the east. Careless practices of cultivation had resulted in serious erosion and leaching of the soil, and portions of the farm had been allowed to grow up in scrub brush and trash trees. Nevertheless, there were back areas which were still covered with respectable stands of near-virgin oaks, black walnut, ash, cherry, hickory, and sugar maple suitable for the production of furniture-grade lumber.[41]

The record is unclear as to whether the famous lawyer-legislator-secretary of state ever lived on the farm. It is doubtful that he did because he was too occupied with politics and an active practice of the law. There stood on the property a dilapidated log house of early pioneer construction and a scattering of run-down outbuildings hardly adaptable to the Hardin life style.[42] Robert Scott and his family may not have moved directly to the farm from either Sumners Forest or Frankfort for some time after it was purchased. In 1845, Robert Scott began the construction of an elegant two-and-a-half-story brick-limestone Greek Revival mansion. This twenty-room structure was placed atop one of the steepest points on the farm, facing toward the village of Jett and Frankfort to the northwest. In order to get full advantage of the striking rural panorama of the Elkhorn-Kentucky river swales, Scott had an observatory constructed atop the tall house.[43] The mansion was completed in 1847 at a cost of $25,000.[44]

Surrounding the imposing Greek temple of a house was a carefully platted eight-acre garden and orchard area, and in front of the house Scott dug a reflecting fish pond. In future years he wrote essays about this intensive use of the plot, and he took deep satisfaction in its continuing bountiful yields of fruits and vegetables for his family table. There were few commodious Kentucky bluegrass farmhouses better located or so tastefully surrounded by trees and shrubbery.[45]

When Robert W. Scott purchased the Hardin land he also acquired part or all of the famous lawyer's livestock holdings of sheep, cattle, and hogs. These animals comprised a foundation for a distinguished livestock breeding career.[46] As a farmer the ex-lawyer Scott proved as alert and industrious as he had been an inquiring student and traveler. Just as he had recorded full and descriptive notes in his poetry books at Transylvania University, legal notes in his law study books, and his incisive *Wanderjahr* journal, he kept meticulous records of his farm operations. From his farm books a current agricultural historian can go far toward reconstructing a picture of a Bluegrass farm operation in the years 1834-1884.[47] In that half-century Robert W. Scott was frugal in expenditures. He also kept meticulous records regarding labor and costs, the calendar of plantings, methods of breaking the land, cultivation, and harvesting. Scott maintained an equally precise record of his livestock husbandry.[48] Although there are numerous notations of payments and advancements of furnishings to cash wage laborers, they were not sufficient numbers to have operated intensively so large a plantation.

Robert Scott owned slaves. In 1850, he had twenty-six, who ranged between the ages of one and fifty. There were fourteen females and twelve males, most of whom were under twenty years of age. This number had increased to thirty-three in 1860, with thirteen males and twenty females. The average age had advanced a decade.[49] There existed at Locust Hill after 1849 living accommodations for "fifty to one hundred persons." In addition to the slave laborers there were wage hands who received ten to twenty dollars and keep per month. This type of Kentucky farm labor in the antebellum years seems to have been no more dependable than the modern seasonal farm workers. There was a constant coming and going of these people, with none of them remaining more than a year; some, in fact, departed within the month they were employed. They missed work because of illnesses, drunkenness, and apparently plain shiftlessness. Typical of these transients was John Pitcher, who "set in to work on the 13th of June and quit on April 15. . . ." Pitcher came and went over the years, never improving his devotion to duty. So it went from one crop season to the next.[50]

There were overseers, but it was chiefly Robert Scott who kept Locust Hill laborers performing their duties. There is no hint of his having to discipline slaves. Some of the wage hands occupied the tenant houses and were supplied rations from cribs and smokehouses. From detailed accounts it is possible to reconstruct a notion of the diet of antebellum bluegrass farm laborers. Again, John Pitcher was charged with requisitions of corn meal, fatback and middling meat, salt, tobacco, and corned beef. Scott also furnished his wage hands, in lieu of cash, cloth, pantaloons, boots, sugar, and other merchandise, most of it bought on account from Knott's store in Frankfort.[51] Though it is hard to isolate the fact in the farm book accounts, Robert W. Scott did employ overseers, and he apparently had the usual experience with this functionary as did farmers in the Lower South. There appear notations in Elizabeth Scott's correspondence which indicate this was the case.[52]

Just as Robert Scott kept a close account of supplies issued to farm hands, he made a record of family purchases and doctors' bills. For the numerous Locust Hill fireplaces he bought firewood by the wagonload at seventy-five cents each, as well as boxes of candles and sugar in the bulk. He and the feminine members of the household bought velvet, cambrics, silks, calico curtain materials, bed ticking, pantaloons, bonnets, and other clothing. Much of the Scott open store account with Simon Cone, Frankfort merchant, seems to have been for cloth and other clothing supplies for slaves. Frequently there were entries for "shoes for Nef," "dress for Louisa," and "pantaloons for Bartow." There is further evidence of the presence of slaves who shucked corn each fall. There are entries in this category for "Anderson," "Clayburn," "Louis," "John," "Holly," "Caesar," and others. They were paid at the rate of approximately $3.75 for 31 shocks of corn. It may have been that these were the slaves of neighboring farmers who were placed out seasonally for hire.[53]

2

The Complete Farmer

THE MASTER OF LOCUST HILL was a complete farmer. He planned his orchards and field crops with obvious knowledge of the physical capabilities of the land. Before he built his mansion he had surrounded the site with gardens, orchards, and grape arbors. In the six-acre orchard he planted five varieties of apples, sixteen of pears, eighteen of peaches, one or two of violet nectarines, five of cherries, and almost as many of grapes. In the two-acre kitchen garden he planted a wide variety of vegetables, and in the open fields and between orchard rows he planted Irish and sweet potatoes. Scott described in his farm book the location of fruit trees, the garden plots, the processes of grafting fruit cuttings, the time required for fruiting and maturity, and the comparative qualities of the various varieties.[1]

The Locust Hill Plantation became, in fact, a model demonstration of good husbandry. Robert Scott was an ardent disciple of diversification, a practice he followed throughout his active career as planter. The serious purpose of Locust Hill was production of crops and livestock. Main crops were corn, wheat, hemp, oats, and red clover for hay. There appears no mention of tobacco in the farm book. On August 19, 1835, Scott noted the fact that he, four men, and two boys had spent almost a month cutting and stacking hay in "a meadow which was remarkably clear of cheat & weeds & fully ripe."[2] Always the experimenter and innovator, he planted eighteen acres to rice in 1835, but the next year reduced this to eight acres. There was no further mention of this crop, which no doubt was too exotic for the Bluegrass.[3]

If Scott's rice experiment was less than a booming success, his annual corn crops were eminently productive. Just as he had been selective in choices of several desirable fruit tree and vegetable varieties, so he was in the use of various corn varieties. He planted everything from popcorn to the favorite Bluegrass Crittenden main crop variety.[4] Evidence of the productivity of the Locust Hill lands was indicated in the prodigious amount of corn which Scott had shucked every harvest season and in the amounts which he fed to animals. He recorded the wagonloads which were

Robert Wilmot Scott, circa 1850

harvested from the various fields and which were fed to livestock and sold to neighbors.[5]

In the process of becoming a recognized corn planter, Robert Scott became involved in 1839 in a stormy controversy over what was called by a shyster New York promoter an extraordinary variety of Oriental corn. It was said that a New York tea importer in unpacking a shipment from China had discovered several grains of corn. He planted these to compare the Oriental maize with that grown in North America. The import from China was said to sprout limbs like a tree and produce an ear at the end of each branch. A large ear crowned the central stalk as an extra dividend. An entrepreneuring seed dealer named Thornburn advertised this new wonder which returned a thousand grains for each one planted at the premium price of twenty-five cents an ear. Robert W. Scott procured an ear through a congressman, and later a Pennsylvania friend sent him an ear. He planted the seed in a test plot and kept a detailed record of its growth and yield. In August 1839, he reported the results in a letter to the *Franklin Farmer*. He was convinced that both Thornburn and his highly touted "Chinese Corn" were humbugs of the first order. He charged the New Yorker with peddling the poorest variety of "nubbing" seeds at an outrageous price. Thornburn had other attackers, but none so convincing as the Master of Locust Hill.[6]

From his observatory atop the Locust Hill mansion Robert Wilmot Scott could view daily during growing seasons the waving grain and corn fields of his estate. When he had traveled in the East in 1829-30, he was tireless in climbing into the domes of state capitols and to the top stories of other tall buildings and monuments in order to get a clearer perspective of the lay of the land. Undoubtedly, no panoramic view, however, produced in him so much inner satisfaction as that of his own well-tilled and mowed fields and pastures. The grazing herds which dotted his pastures reflected well-being and good breeding.

Robert W. Scott became an important second-generation livestock breeder in Kentucky in the 1840s. This industry had already reached a rather high degree of excellence by the time he purchased Locust Hill. At Sandersville in nearby Fayette County, and later at Grass Hills, in Carroll County, Lewis Sanders, dean of early breeders and importers, had established a fine herd of purebred Durham cattle. Even closer by Locust Hill, at Woodburn Farm on the waters of Elkhorn Creek, Robert Aitcheson Alexander owned Kentucky's finest herds of cattle and sheep and bred superb race horses. Over the years this famous farm was to produce such notable breeding stock as El Hakim, Sirius, Vellum, Duchess of Athol, Mazurka, and Lady Valentine.[7] In Bourbon County Brutus J. Clay almost rivaled Alexander as a breeder. His neighbor Jeremiah Duncan also produced highly esteemed prize animals. At Pleasant Hill on the south bank of the Kentucky River, the community of Shakers bred top-quality cattle, sheep, and hogs. In Fayette County Dr. Elisha Warfield was an importer and breeder, along with Henry Clay and David Sutton. This was an age in which central bluegrass farmers were establishing Kentucky's reputation for the production of finely bred farm animals in every category.[8]

Robert Scott in 1835 purchased at the sale of Judge Haggin's livestock several heifers, among them the famous Durham shorthorn-milker Hetty Haggin. Hetty had in her lineage the deep impress of bovine aristocracy which all but rivaled the proudest lineage of the Kentucky human aristocrats. She traced her ancestry back through the earliest Lewis Sanders importation of purebred Durhams to the pastures of England and Scotland.[9] In a reminiscent letter to John Duncan, editor of the *Farmers' Home Journal*, Scott wrote from Lexington on October 17, 1883: "Judge James Haggin, formerly of this county, purchased some of Col. Sanders' best stock, of pure Durham blood, & he was regarded as one of the most skillful breeders of that day, his stock being generously known as the 'Haggin Stock.' At his death I purchased at the public sale in 1835 some of the best females, especially a cow known as Hetty Haggin, & I now have a bill of sale of his Executor, Harrison Blanton, and of William Rogers of Bourbon County, (who has kept Mr. Haggin's cattle for him) that she was one of his best and purest Durhams, especially for milking qualities, which I have now fully realized, as she once required milking four times a day. She was very prolific (as is shown in the pedigrees of my stock, published in several of the volumes of Allen's American Short Horn Herd Book) and that quality has been carefully preserved in her descendants, no other breed having been required to substitute their deficiencies."[10]

When the early breeder David Sutton disposed of his cattle herd, Scott purchased for $1,300 the promising young bull Frederick as herd sire. Like Hetty Haggin this animal had an illustrious lineage reaching beyond the Atlantic, which accounted for Scott's willingness to pay the highest price a bull had sold for in Kentucky. Frederick's dam had the record of producing forty quarts of milk a day, enough to supply the numerous Scott brood and to spare.[11] There exists correspondence between Robert W. Scott and Lewis Sanders in which the latter discussed the history of the breeding of the Kentucky shorthorn cattle which were brought to America in the famous 1817 importation of purebred Durhams. This date stands out in Kentucky cattle history as equally important with the political one of the admission of the Commonwealth to the Union in 1792.[12] Any cattle bloodline which could be traced back through the famous imports Cornplanter, Tecumseh, and Mrs. Motte was solidly based.[13]

Robert Scott was well aware of the historical importance to Kentucky of the importation of 1817. There were twelve head of Durham and Teeswaters in this original herd, eleven of which reached Kentucky in good breeding condition. The famous herd sire Prince Frederick's pedigree traced back to the Durham bulls San Martin and Tecumseh and to the dam Mrs. Motte. In laying the foundatin for his herd Scott sought out the descendants of this early stock.[14] Judge Haggin, though never a dirt farmer outright, was a cattle fancier and had established one of Kentucky's finest herds of prime Durham shorthorns.[15]

Remarkably soon after Scott began acquiring the properties which eventually comprised the Locust Hill Plantation, his name began appearing in the annals of Kentucky livestock breeding. Not only did he gain possession of one of the finest dams in the first half of the nineteenth century in American cattle breeding, he came to own other animals who were almost as productive. From his expensive bull and the prize dam Ruby, he bred Fair Maid of Frankfort, who helped to line his trophy case with first ribbons won at central Kentucky livestock exhibits.[16] The Fair Maid of Frankfort was a source of great Scott family pride. In one of Robert Scott's absences, Elizabeth wrote him on January 11, 1859: "Simon, Lewis, Claiborn and Cesar took the two hoggs, Ruby, Fair Maid, and Constellation to the fair on yesterday, and they were very much admired, for a very good reason, there were none to compete with except one Harris' of Elkhorn, but Simon says they made a heap of fuss over them and a great many men came up and looked at them. The fat hog was left there, Lewis thinks Mr. Tibbles bought him. I have not seen father since to know about it."[17]

Charles Foster, the well-known agricultural artist from the staff of the *Western Farmer and Gardener,* visited Locust Hill for the purpose of painting the Fair Maid, an honor which was almost akin to having Matthew Harris Jouett paint a portrait of the lady of the household. Looking about him on the farm and observing its operation, he wrote, "It is necessary to repeat, that the whole of that portion of Mr. Scott's stock springing from Old Hetty are fine, it is a fact so notoriously attested that it needs nothing here to give it force."[18] Later, Foster was back at Locust Hill to paint a group portrait of Old Hetty and seven of her offspring and another of Constellation.[19] Wherever Scott exhibited his Locust Hill cattle after 1841, they were respected as strong competition to the best animals bluegrass breeders had to show.[20] Scott's bull Constellation was exhibited in the Woodford Fair in 1840 and won first place over eight competitors chosen from the best herds of Durham shorthorns in central Kentucky.[21]

The Locust Hill farm book records the breeding, calving, and milking performances of the more notable members of the Scott herd. The arrival of a well-formed and marked bull calf was a joyful event. Scattered among the aristocrats of the herd were the lesser dams entitled to the utility names Big Red, Muley, Brindle, White, and English. They were not in a class with their sisters, but it was they who supplied the milk and butter for the family. Unlike Hetty Haggin, Kentuckian, One Teat, Fair Maid of Frankfort, Fortune, Black Taylor, Princess, Frederick, and Constellation, they were never honored by posing for visiting artists and cattle fanciers.[22]

The Scott cattle, 1832-1883, filled columns of pedigree records in Allen's *American Short Horn Herd Book*. When the herd was dispersed in 1884, there was still in the pastures at Locust Hill a distinguished herd of descendants of the 1817 Durham-Teeswaters importation, plus the side-breedings from the best herds of later bluegrass importations.[23]

Throughout the years after 1832, Robert W. Scott continued an impassioned interest in the up-grading of his cattle herd. He took immense pride in his success in producing animals which yielded bountiful returns in both milk and meat. Though he exhibited scores of animals at livestock fairs and exhibitions, he never specialized in the production of animals solely for show purposes. In the closing weeks of his life he was still able to exert enough energy to prepare a brief catalog of the number of superb Durham shorthorn cattle which still grazed his pastures. In this valedictory listing he revealed deep satisfaction in the fact that in the past half-century he had made an impact on the improvement of Kentucky and southern livestock. In the pastures and feed lots where once his brag stock Hetty Haggin, Fair Maid of Frankfort, and Constellation had cropped tender red clover and bluegrass, their descendants Florence, Rosalie, Galla, Meta, Prince, and Senator 2nd carried on a proud family tradition, and there was still tender red clover and bluegrass for them to crop.[24]

As in the planting of field crops, orchards, and gardens, Robert W. Scott operated a highly diversified livestock program. There is no record of a thoroughbred racing entry having come from the stables of Locust Hill, but there were plenty of good-quality workhorses and mules of home raising. Scott had no ambition to challenge such distinguished thoroughbred breeders as Robert Aitcheson Alexander and Colonel Abe Buford, a fact so eloquently reflected in his farm book No. 1. This record contains the dates mares were bred to stallions and jacks, and the dates they foaled. Entries from year to year read, "Mary Davis foaled a mule," "Orphan bred to my jack," "Fairy bred to W. Ayres' horse," and "Diamond foaled a mule by Innes' Satan." Scott made a permanent record of what was a common workhorse and mule breeding history on many bluegrass livestock farms.[25]

There was a rising demand for work stock in which Scott was increasing the acreage of his plantation and engaging in more intensive farming. Operation of the near-thousand-acre tract in the growing of crops, tending gardens and orchards, haying, and clipping weeds and briars required a generous amount of horsepower. Besides providing for his own needs for draft animals Scott found a profitable return for his mares and jacks in the sale of mules to drovers on court days. This was an era when blue-grass drovers herded their droves southward to supply cotton plantations in the Lower South. There were designated court days in most of the Kentucky counties when farmers brought in their surplus mules for sale.[26] Indicative of this trade was an undated entry which reminded Scott that he had "Sold my mules to W. C. Blackburn for $25.00 each to be delivered on the 12th of October 1846 in good condition, & [he] pays $75.00 down on a credit on note for negro hire which he holds & the rest is to be paid on delivery of the mules."[27] This entry does not make clear whether Scott was hiring slave laborers from Blackburn, or Blackburn was hiring from Scott. Throughout the farm journal there are labor entries which seem clearly to be for hired slaves at Locust Hill.[28]

The rolling hills of Woodford and Franklin counties were ideally suited for the breeding and pasturage of sheep. Locust Hill was reasonably well isolated from a thickly populated area to reduce that bane of sheep grazing in Kentucky, the "family" dog run wild. Sheep could range with considerable safety in its pastures without the constant watchcare of shepherds. As the sheep ate one range free of weeds and nipped grass short, they were moved to another area to repeat their weed-control browsing.[29] There is an open question as to which excited Robert W. Scott the most, his fine cattle herd or his experimentations with improving his flock of sheep. Nothing in his academic background or practical experience indicated that he had any special training in eugenics and heredity, but his persistence and common sense enabled him to experiment successfully in sensitive biological areas. Clearly, Scott did intensive reading in all areas of the agricultural sciences, and especially animal husbandry. He subscribed to farm journals, bought specialized books, attended lectures, and entertained visiting agricultural writers and speakers, including Judge Adam Beatty, Solon Robinson, Thomas Afleck, Charles Foster, R. Vandusen, and others.[30]

In the closing year of his farming career, Robert Scott wrote that when he began farming in 1832 he was determined to bring about an improvement of the quality of his farm animals. He had observed at the outset that all farm animals tended to regress in quality when no active effort was made to breed-up their bloodlines. A good case in point was the western sheep which had stocked most Kentucky farms. These animals, it was true, were hardy, fecund, and thrifty, but they were deficient in both carcasses and fleece. Wool shorn from their backs was demonstrated to be suitable for the spinning and weaving of coarse cloths, for the making of linsey-woolsey and coarse jeans, and the famous Kentucky comforters. Their wool had clothed at least three generations of Kentucky countrymen. But in spite of this, it was unsuitable for the manufacture of fine textured fabrics.[31]

Early in the nineteenth century, and in a burst of enthusiasm, Kentuckians imported Southdowns, Cotswolds, Leicesters, Oxfordshires, and Teeswaters rams and ewes from England and Scotland.[32] Briefly they experienced a rage for the more delicate merinos from Spain. This animal cloaked itself in a fine silky fleece, but its carcass was undersized. Some Kentucky sheepmen seemed to think that this latin import would quickly supplant the old rangy natives who had braved the Wilderness Trail, Indians, wolves, and all other hazards and establish itself west of the mountains. None of the imports impressed Robert Scott as being ideal for Kentucky and the West. They all lacked the qualities which fitted them to thrive on the land and in the Kentucky environment. He sought an animal which was hardy enough to live off the natural forage of Locust Hill meadows and to adapt handsomely to changing environmental conditions, and which would produce not only a fleshy carcass of well-flavored meat, but, above all, a finely textured fleece.[33]

Sometime in the latter 1830s Robert Scott focused his attention seriously on breeding the ideal type of sheep, not only for Kentucky, but for the entire West.[34] He is known to have kept a sheep book, but a search for it has gone unrewarded. He embarked upon a complicated program of cross-breeding and back-breeding. In all he used at least a half-dozen breeds of animals in making his basic crosses. He kept records of characteristics, desirable and undesirable qualities, and the eugenic stability of each generation. By 1850 he had a flock of two hundred breeding ewes and fifty yearling rams. He changed rams with each breeding season to introduce new strains. By 1856 he was satisfied that he had stabilized a bloodline which could be depended upon in future generations to maintain its vitality. To this new composite breed he gave the name "Improved Kentucky," a name which he was proudly able to establish in the annals of American sheep breeding.[35]

Scott's patient experiments with sheep began to reward him when a pen of "Improved Kentucky" in 1856 won special awards at the Kentucky Agricultural Fair, held that year in Paris, Bourbon County.[36] The next year he sent a pen of selected animals to the United States Agricultural Society exhibition in Louisville and again captured awards. In 1876, Scott sent several fleeces to the International American Centennial Exhibition in Philadelphia, for which he received a special gold medal and a diploma.[37] Five years later he sent fleeced skins to the Cotton States and International Exhibition in Atlanta. He was ill and unable to accompany them to describe the history of the breeding of the animals, but nevertheless they won awards.[38] No notice of his accomplishments, however, pleased Robert Scott more than the publication in 1866 of a rather full history of his sheep husbandry in the *Annual Report* of the United States Bureau of Agriculture, illustrated by two of R. Vandusen's drawings.[39]

This New York animal painter came to Locust Hill to paint specimen of the farm's prize sheep, one of which was a two-year-old ewe and her male and female offspring. These beautiful animals were slaughtered immediately after being sketched in order to record precisely their body weight and the weight of their fleeces. Vandusen portrayed these magnificent animals as having clean, open faces and lower limbs, with square, blocky bodies covered with deep piles of wool of even silky qualities, which were said to meet the most exacting standards for the making of fine woolen fabrics.

With missionary zeal Scott promoted his "Improved Kentucky" sheep throughout the Commonwealth, the South, and even the Far West. To him a farm without a flock of sheep was unthinkable. In an article published in the Frankfort *Yeoman* he wrote: "Every consideration corroborating the fact that the sheep is one of the most valuable of our domestic animals, and no farmer should be without them. Like cattle and hogs, they produce meat and fat and hides and also wool. Their flesh is, of all others (the goat, perhaps, only excepted), the most wholesome, as they are not generally subject to parasitic and other diseases, as in the case of the hog and the ox. In size they are the more convenient for domestic use than the ox, and are more convenient for slaughter than the hog. They will gather their own feed at all seasons of the year without shelter, and develop all of their valuable products without grain feeding, which is not the case with the hog and the ox."[40]

Spending fifty years of careful experimentation and cross-breeding to produce a superior type of sheep was a long step. Robert Scott, in cooperation with Polk Prince of Guthrie, Kentucky, realized considerable income from his goat herd. On occasion he said he sold a small flock of mixed bloods for two thousand dollars. As in the breeding of the "Improved Kentucky" sheep, he cross-bred several breeds of angora stock and common hillside goats to produce a superior animal. The Locust Hill animals were magnificent with their long, woolly coats and fine, twisted long horns. At the height of his breeding experiments he had sixty fine cross-bred nannies, and almost as many of lesser stock. Scott became an authority on the production, care, and marketing of angora wool. In an article prepared for publication in the *Second Report* from the State Bureau of Agriculture, Horticulture, and Statistics, he described the nature of the goat, the texture of its coat, his breeding procedures, and the modes of shearing and packing the wool for sale.[41]

Scott built up a clientele for his angora breeding stock all over the country. Almost every month shipments of selected kids departed Ducker's Station for farms far removed from Locust Hill. Interestingly, he received more orders from the South than he had animals for sale.[42] In describing his experiences with angora goats Scott gave an insight into the nature of fencing on his farms. Some of the fields and pastures were enclosed by rock fences, some by plank and post, and some by rows of Osage oranges. He warned that it was unwise to pasture goats inside the latter enclosure because they would eat the "fencing."[43] He kept his pastures free of burry weeds and other plants which might shed debris to become entangled in the angora's fleece. He boasted that his pastures were so free of noxious weeds that his angora wool was clean at the time of clipping and required no washing of either the animals or their wool.[44]

Locust Hill became a universal livestock center. Robert Scott made his broad acres as nearly self-sustaining as possible. Since 1834 he raised hogs in prodigious numbers. Under the raised heading "HOGS HOGS" in his farm book, he noted that he had bought forty-seven stock hogs from Brutus J. Clay of Bourbon County.[45] This in an age when Kentuckians were in competition with their corn and hog growing neighbors north of the Ohio for a profitable foothold in the pork trade. By 1830 they had almost replaced the hardy old long-snouted and thin-haunced pioneer who had rooted his way from Virginia and Pennsylvania to the Bluegrass with purebred imported stock. Just as cattle breeders had among them their famous stockmen so did prominent hog raisers achieve fame with their imported animals. Among these were Dr. Samuel D. Martin, the dean of hog breeders, Robert Allen, Lewis Shirley, Benjamin P. Gray, W. P. Curd, Edward Allen, James E. Letton, and W. R. Duncan. All of these, along with the Shakers at Pleasant Hill, established regional reputations for producing superior purebred swine.[46]

Robert W. Scott was not inactive in the field of hog breeding. In 1838, he butchered thirty-three hogs which yielded six thousand pounds of cured pork with which to feed his family, slaves, and hired laborers. The next year he butchered and processed seven thousand pounds, and set aside four thousand pounds specifically for family use.[47] Throughout his farm accounts Scott entered notations of cured pork in the form of middlings, shoulders, and hams. Often he used meat in lieu of cash to pay the wages of farm laborers. He sold his surplus meats to neighbors and storekeepers. Steadily the hog droves at Locust Hill yielded a profit. As with all his livestock ventures, Robert Scott bred for hardiness and capability to forage for much of their livelihood in his bluegrass pastures.[48]

Kentucky importers and breeders experimented with almost a dozen breeds, among them Woburns, Irish Graziers, Poland Chinas, Yorkshires, Chester Whites, Tamworths, Essex, Guineas, and the domestic Shaker-bred Berkshires. Scott made a careful inventory of the characteristics of these breeds and divided them into two general classes. In the active and thrifty self-reliant group he placed the Woburns, Irish Graziers, Yorkshires, and Poland Chinas.[49] The remaining he described as indolent and content to remain closeby the feed trough and depend on their masters to rustle up the feed to pile soft fat on their lazy carcasses. He finally settled on a cross-breed of Woburns-Irish Graziers-Poland Chinas, which, like his famous "Improved Kentucky" sheep, became an established type. After 1840, Scott fed from one to two hundred hogs annually for pork. In addition he established a flourishing market in a large number of the neighboring states for his composite breed of pigs.[50]

Hog killing time at Locust Hill was a long and tedious seasonal process which demanded the labors of most everybody from Elizabeth Scott to the youngest housemaids and boys. Elizabeth wrote her absent husband in December 1858, "We are killing hogs today about fifteen and will make three killings between this and Christmas. Mr. Bell said the hoggs weighed a great deal more than he expected one weighed 575 pounds and instead of paying $50.00 he handed me $60.00, a right nice sum." In order to process such large amounts of pork Scott had to maintain elaborate slaughtering and meat-curing equipment. This particular farm operation necessitated the possession of kettles, boilers, tubs, butcher blocks, salting troughs or boxes, tables, racks, sausage mills and stuffers, properly sealed smokehouses and fireboxes, and supplies of hardwood to burn in slow, smouldering heaps. There was constantly a threat of spoilage from changing weather conditions and from skipper infestations. These things had to be guarded against throughout the year, because once a smokehouse became infested it was nearly impossible to eradicate the pests. An interesting by-product of pork butchering at Locust Hill was the making of soap from fatty meat scraps. Again Elizabeth Scott wrote, "Ellen had been very busy making soap out of soda ash it is not near as strong as potash but makes very nice soap with the assistance of lye."[51]

3

An Idyll of the Land

AS PLEASANT AS LIFE WAS most of the time on the Locust Hill Plantation, the intense occupation with livestock breeding and grazing required almost around-the-clock concern. Even though Robert Scott was firmly committed to the breeding of hardy animals, pastures had to be watched, mowed, and bushed. Fences had to be built and maintained, including gates, which Scott considered the symbols of good or poor farming. Unlike most Kentucky farmers, Scott had to make rather elaborate provisions for shipping his sales animals. This meant he had to maintain a carpenter shop for fabricating crates in which to ship pigs, sheep, and goats. These were so constructed that they would contain sufficient feed and water to last throughout an uninterrupted journey. Cattle were shipped equipped with strong head halters to control them. These were made of loosely woven grass or jute which fitted well back from the base of the horns. Scott contended that any injury to the tender area about the horns would cause the animal to sicken and die. In 1884, he looked back upon a half-century as a successful cattle breeder saying he had shipped animals, and especially the Improved Kentucky sheep, to most of the states of the Union.[1]

Not all the responsibilities for managing the Locust Hill livestock operation fell upon its master. Often when he was absent on sales ventures, orders poured in for animals, and Elizabeth had to oversee selections and the making of crates and attend to shipping details. As she revealed in her letters to Robert, these chores caused her deep concern.[2] She no doubt managed these matters in expert fashion because her husband boasted that he had never lost an animal in transit.[3]

Robert Scott visited country fairs and agricultural society and farm meetings with the enthusiasm of an evangelizing parson. He made speeches and wrote special articles on the breeding and care of sheep, hogs, and cattle. He gave farmers information on removal of weeds and brush from the land and discussed field crops.[4] On his visits to the Lower South he was often appalled by the slovenly indifference of the region's farmers in the upkeep and management of their land and animals. Cattle mortal-

Elizabeth Brown Scott, circa 1855

ity was high, a fact he attributed to improper acclimatization care and
to incorrect feeding procedures in their shipment. He said he had shipped
Locust Hill animals into the cotton South at all seasons of the year without
loss. Cattle brought in from the West, he wrote, were taken directly from
green pastures and put aboard steamboats and trains without even a day's
preparation. They were fed a diet of timothy hay in passage, which caused
constipation and accompanying fever. A further aggravation was the rough
handling en route.[5]

Once imported cattle arrived in the South, farmers appeared to be
indifferent, if not reckless, in the management of their herds. They fed
them cottonseed, bagasse from sugar cane, and corn in the ear. Often
purebred cattle were turned out on the range with native cows to browse
in canebrakes and swamps where they had to reach overhead for forage.
Pedigreed Kentucky animals had been raised in bluegrass pastures where
they had abundant food underfoot, and their necks and muscular systems
were not adapted to reaching upward.[6] Scott lectured southerners on their
sloppy ways. He said flies, gnats, and mosquitoes found the larger carcasses of purebred Kentucky Durham cattle more enticing than the thick-
skinned native canebrake rangers. The tails of Kentucky Durhams were
several inches shorter than those of their scrubby cousins. "The splendid
Durham bull," he wrote, "is an artificial animal, of the greatest value in
cross-breeding, produced by consumate skill through the years, and his
excellence can only be sustained by a continuation of the same care."[7]
He advised his southern patrons to take reasonable and intelligent care
of the animals he shipped them and they would be well rewarded. If they
did this and an animal should die, he would replace it at half the original
price.[8]

Robert W. Scott was not only a traveling encyclopedia of the science
of animal breeding, he was also a master salesman. He traveled extensively in both the Ohio Valley and the Lower South promoting his strain
of Durham cattle, "Improved Kentucky" sheep, angora goats, cross-bred
hogs, and mules. During his absences from Locust Hill, life sometimes
became hectic for Elizabeth and the overseer. On December 9, 1858, while
he was away in Mississippi and Louisiana, Elizabeth wrote her husband:
"I could not get any plank in town, or crates either and he [lumber dealer]
advised me to write Hyatt Higgins to send down five crates, to send Mr.
Beal's sheep in, and finding I could not yet get any plank for a week concluded to trouble him in a business way sent for the crates this morning
at the depot but they were not there and will send to Frankfort this evening
to see if there is a letter, did I do right? I feared Mr. Beal would be hurt
at the delay for he wrote that he had been waiting three weeks to hear
from you or his sheep."[9]

The operation of Locust Hill and its somewhat complex personnel organization was a demanding responsibility for both the Scotts. Elizabeth in her letters reflected the tremendous pressure under which she labored when left alone to manage affairs. Daily operation of the plantation and the servicing of orders was an almost overwhelming chore. She wrote on one occasion, "I suffer more from headache than I ever did. I dreamed the other night that a man came for his hoggs and sheep and I could not get the boxes made, so I arose this morning with a very bad headache." In a thinly veiled pleading for assurance she urged Robert, "Do write me a loving letter for I am low-spirited and would write how much I miss you if you did not know it before."[10]

For Elizabeth Brown Scott, reared in a proud family largely removed from the nagging cares of an operating farm, the demands of motherhood, a large house, a constant turmoil of young slaves underfoot, and ceaseless activities of farm hands was at times almost too frustrating to be borne with grace. At times she expressed envy that Robert enjoyed opportunities to travel well beyond Kentucky and to mix with attractive people in pleasant surroundings. One Sunday morning when a combination of envy and depression beset her, and she was momentarily free of immediate demands for sheep and hog crates and impatient customers, and especially was out of the clutches of the insufferably inefficient F. C. and L. Railroad, she bespoke her mind in letter. "I can see you pleased and delighted with everything around you," she told Robert, "good company, good sleeping, and good eating — don't you wish you had been blessed with such managers and accomplished ladies as you meet with at these fairs — query I wonder if they had as many children, as many sickly darkies — and cross workmen if they would do any better than your humble servant. I am sure they are welcome to try it — for 25 years I have tried to do my duty toward you, your family and my own and somewhere I have been misunderstood by everybody — and am not half as much beloved as you are who never tried so much."[11]

Elizabeth may have been momentarily harassed but she was never cowed. With the iron of Brown blood flowing generously in her veins, she was not to be "sassed" by anybody — husband, children, or biting, fighting, and kicking slaves and hired hands. There was a kicking incident either at Locust Hill or in the neighborhood in which a man kicked a woman. She wrote, "The woman aggravated him and he kicked her & the men all take up for him. Well I know one thing if a man ever kicked me I will kick back again. There is no scripture for it, there is something about smiting the cheek but nothing about kicking."[12] Unfortunately, Robert did not keep a journal describing his experiences on his travels nor did he record his thoughts on the tribulations of keeping up with a large family, of entertaining an almost ceaseless stream of visiting relatives and strangers, and of disciplining quarreling slaves and workmen. His letters, however, reflect a man of even temper, keen judgment, and a thorough dedication to farming and livestock breeding. His writings contain a strong element of self-assurance without being offensively didactic.

Most obviously Robert W. Scott was a man who built trust and respect in other men. In 1840, he was appointed a member of a distinguished committee composed of Dr. Samuel D. Martin and Captain Benjamin Warfield to decide the exceedingly delicate questions of qualifications of animals for entry into the registry of the *Kentucky Herd Book*. The decisions of the committee were not materially revised in future debating on the issues.[13]

Through Civil War, emancipation of slaves, a confusion in postwar Kentucky politics, and depressions, Robert Scott remained a model farmer, keeping up-to-date his bull, sheep, and farm books, writing enthusiastically about the art and science of livestock breeding and the planting and growing of field crops. His essays reflected the same observant and meticulous insights and qualities which distinguished his descriptions of people and scenes he had visited on his travels in the East as a neophyte lawyer.[14] In 1879, William J. Davie, the commissioner of the Kentucky Bureau of Agriculture, Horticulture, and Statistics, wrote that Scott, after forty years of successful operation of Locust Hill Plantation, was "one of the best educated and most scientific farmers in the state."[15] This perhaps was not a too extravagant Kentucky hyperbole.

Throughout the decades when Robert W. Scott operated the livestock and farming program at Locust Hill, visitors were impressed with the careful husbandry and generous hospitality of the master. Thomas Afleck, the well-known Ohio agricultural traveler and editor, visited the Franklin County farm early in 1841 and observed, "This is one of the best farms in the state."[16] Afleck was convinced the owner knew his business and operated as a seasoned farmer and businessman. Scott had begun farming poor, badly worn, and disorganized tracts of land and molded them into a showplace. Before him the Hardins and Churchills had been indifferent, if not downright miserable, farmers. They had cleared away much of the virgin forest growth and then allowed the brush and gullies to take it over. Fields and pastures were largely unfenced. Buildings were dilapidated and unfit for efficient livestock management, drainage was poor, and there were lacking connecting roadways.

In quick order, the younger owner Scott constructed barns and sheds, divided the land into fields and meadows, built good stone and wooden fences, and in places planted osage orange hedgerows. (There appears in the farm book one of the few documentary notes in Kentucky concerning the building of stone fences. Scott paid Duncan Thompson 37½ cents per yard for building a stone fence. It perhaps is significant that he advanced

Thompson $4.00 to join the Sons of Temperance and another $5.00 to go to Lexington — which may have actually nullified his conversion to temperance.[17]) At every entry way Scott erected good and operable gates, a sharp departure from the usual Kentucky farm tradition. In fact, good gates was a passion with Robert Scott. He was disdainful of the sloven device called a "Kentucky slip-gap" which seemed to be as much a part of the bluegrass farm as iron weeds. He designed a light, well-made gate for general pasture and field use, giving a precise engineering step-by-step procedure for its construction. These he published along with an essay which was one part directions for construction and the remainder an expression of the philosophical importance of farm gates which could be manipulated with ease.[18] As in all other details of his farm operations, Scott had his gates painted, numbered, and recorded in an operational file.[19]

In an age when scientific information about farming in general, and in the Bluegrass in particular, was difficult to come by, Scott had a remarkable amount of knowledge: the science of the soil. For example, he saved the manure from his expanding livestock herds and droves and spread it on the land. He refuted the old Kentucky folk adage that hemp grew poorly on manured land; his hemp was superior in both growth and quality. Characteristic of all central Kentucky-Elkhorn bluegrass lands, there were on Locust Hill tracts of soggy and wet lands, limestone sinks, and other naturally untenable culs-de-sac. Scott drained these and planted locust and walnut trees which grew into fence posts and premium-quality lumber. Like every southern farmer he battled blackberry and bramble briars and iron weeds in his meadows and pastures. He described in an essay procedures for the destruction of these noxious weeds, admonishing fellow farmers to be diligent in their warring because it required hard work, proper timing, and patience. To him, once-a-season cutting of weeds and briars was an almost useless operation. Triumphantly Scott wrote that he had practically eradicated these nuisances from the fields and pastures at Locust Hill.[20]

As on an English manorial holding, Scott maintained his vegetable gardens and orchards in park-like condition. He pruned fruit trees on schedule, kept the grass and weeds cut, and followed other good practices.[21] Nowhere, however, did he mention following a spraying schedule to check insects and scale infections. He took pride in his handsome farm seat. As mentioned earlier he constructed a fish pond near the front elevation of the house as a well-stocked reflecting pool. "In short," said Thomas Afleck, "the whole business of the farm is carried on as it ought to be."[22]

The bountiful fields, pastures, gardens, and orchards supplied the Scott family and the Locust Hill cadre of slaves and workmen with fine-quality grains, vegetables, fruits, and meats. There seems never to have been a shortage of pork, including hams, lean bacon, and fatback. There was always an ample supply of poultry, beef, mutton, and kid.[23] Gardens were productive of vegetables in some form for year-round consumption. Those of a highly seasonal and perishable nature were staggered so as to ripen in succession. On July 5, 1841, Robert Scott wrote Thomas Afleck, "We were feasting on strawberries, I believe when you were here; raspberries succeeded in equal abundance; and new cherries, and early apples and pears, and a few apricots are taking their turn. We have finished cutting wheat and rye and are now cutting a forty-acre meadow, as usual without the aid of spirituous liquors of any sort — coffee, buttermilk, or sweetened vinegar and water have been the substitute."[24] Ever an ardent temperance man, Robert W. Scott was unwilling to relent even to get his wheat and rye harvested in the traditional Kentucky way.

In the ample Locust Hill kitchen, the cook Siddy (or Sidney) could be counted on to prepare good and hearty Kentucky country dishes. Working more from instinct than formal recipes, she successfully blended ingredients in conjugal proportions to achieve pleasing results. Occasionally things beyond Siddy's control went awry, and her best efforts went for naught. Elizabeth wrote Robert, "I went in the kitchen this morning to see Siddy work the biscuits. She did it well, and when they came up they were decidely *mean* — it is not good flour."[25] Almost the same day, Siddy stewed around the kitchen preparing a sumptuous dinner without accomplishing the main purpose. Elizabeth Humphreys and Cousin Mary Harrison gave every indication that they were inching their way out from Frankfort to spend three or four days at Locust Hill, and Elizabeth and Siddy had industriously prepared dinner for them daily. In desperation Elizabeth hustled Simon off to Frankfort to inquire why they had not come and when, if ever, they might be expected to arrive. They sent back word that they would be on hand "tomorrow if it did not rain or snow." The next day dawned fair and dry, ducks and turkeys were killed and roasted, vegetables were prepared, cakes were baked, and the table was set in readiness for the guests, but again they lingered in town. In something approaching a white fury, Elizabeth wrote the absent Robert, "Well I am independent of them, and as far as being lonely, I am not lonesome on their account."[26] If Elizabeth Humphreys and Cousin Mary slighted the Scotts' hospitable board and lodging, there was a constant procession of relatives, travelers, stockmen, and editorial visitors who did not. From overtones in family correspondence and from Robert Scott's official connections and reports, there was seldom a time when there were not guests at Locust Hill.[27]

4

The Social and Cultural Crusader

AT HEART Robert Wilmot Scott was a crusader, whether it be for building efficient farm gates, destroying noxious weeds, zealously promoting the cause of temperance, seeking peace among quarreling Baptist congregations, making a plea for the southern way of life, or establishing a Kentucky public school system. Throughout three quarters of a century he maintained the same zeal for learning which had motivated him as a student in Transylvania University. In most respects he was philosophically far removed from the Kentucky "relief" Jacksonian positions which had contributed materially to the stifling of the crusade for public education in the Commonwealth.

The Scotts had ample reasons for supporting the movement for public schools. Between September 12, 1832, and the birth of Preston Brown Scott and the birth of Henrietta Reese on July 20, 1849, there were nine children born to the couple.[1] From the outset this was challenge enough for a couple who wished to see their brood develop their minds and take their places in the world as cultivated persons.

When the Scotts moved from Frankfort to Locust Hill they took their young family into a culturally isolated vacuum. Frankfort was too far away for frequent access over rough and muddy roads, and even so Kentucky's capital city offered only remarkably limited cultural advantages. There was a cluster of old and aristocratic families who constituted a social enclave, but the general population was left almost destitute of genuine educational advantages. This was true for the entire Commonwealth of Kentucky in the decades prior to 1850. There was, however, a stirring of sentiment for public schools from 1818 onward, but there remained lack of both public policy and support in the appropriation of funds.[2]

Despite the severely limited but no less dedicated crusading for the organization of a genuinely operative public school system, the Kentucky General Assembly and the governors seemed to have been intellectually incapable of initiating legislation which would have caused the Commonwealth to assume its obligations for the education of the masses.[3] Finally, in 1838, there was enacted a detailed and philosophically poorly conceived law which clumsily attempted to outline the procedures by which public schools could be organized and administered locally. This law made emphatically clear that the Kentucky state government would make no attempt to initiate the establishment or support of such schools as might be organized.[4] This responsibility was left squarely up to local communities and concerned parents.

In the light of the law of 1838 the busy young father at Locust Hill took time out from livestock breeding, planting and harvesting crops, tending gardens and orchards, building fences and gates, and digging a fish pond to take an active role in the organization of a public school supported by local taxes on property in the eastern end of Franklin County. Fortunately, Robert Scott, the good Baptist in belief at least, was acquainted with Joseph J. Bullock, Herbert H. Kavanaugh, Ryland T. Dillard, and other Kentucky educational pioneers. From them he received encouragement and support to prevail upon his neighbors to cooperate in the organization of a school at the village of Jett. Unhappily for the sake of history only, Scott and his neighbors were denied the honor of having established the first public school under the new law in the Commonwealth.[5] Across the line in Woodford County progressive neighbors were forehanded in achieving the historic honor of organizing the first public school district.[6] In later years Robert Scott was as proud of his role in founding the Jett school as he was in the breeding of a distinct type of sheep.[7]

In time Robert Scott's educational interests reached far beyond the boundaries of Franklin County. As secretary of the earlier Kentucky Agricultural Society, he was active in 1838 in trying to persuade the General Assembly to establish an agricultural school and an experimental farm.[8] He continued active in this movement during the years of his secretariat, 1856-1858.[9] In 1860, Scott was appointed by Governor Beriah Magoffin to be a commissioner of the newly chartered institution for the training of feeble-minded children, and for several years he presided as president of this commission.[10] In another field he was active, both as innovator and peacemaker. While Baptist tempers flared and cooled over theological and secular issues, Scott served as a member of the Board of Trustees of Georgetown College, and for several years he was president of the Board of Trustees of the Baptist Theological Institute when it was located in Georgetown.[11]

Little could the young scholar who had impressed his adolescent cousin Priscilla Wilmot so deeply with his philosophical learning have imagined that his zeal for education would lead him along so many divergent paths in the future. In 1832, when Robert W. Scott closed his law office in Frankfort and embarked upon a farming career, the state of scientific agricultural knowledge in Kentucky was exceedingly low. A few progressive farmers in the Bluegrass read the classic sources in agricultural literature such as Liebig, Ruffin, Robinson, and others, but sources of advanced agricultural information were few and far between.[12] The region, however, was not without its successful farmers who used common sense in the breeding of livestock and the growing of field crops. It was true that generally among less well-informed and progressive farmers a majority exhausted their land, relied on antiquated tools, and were still bound by many ancient folk approaches to agricultural problems.[13]

In 1838, a small group of central Kentucky farmers, including Scott, had become aware of the fact that future improvements in Kentucky farming depended on concerted action by the farmers themselves. A call was sent out for interested persons to meet in Lexington to discuss the organization of a Kentucky Agricultural Society. Six farmers, including Dr. Elisha Warfield, Benjamin Gratz, Robert Aitcheson Alexander, J. G. Kinnaird, Robert W. Scott, and William Warfield met in the office of Benjamin Gratz.[14] They issued a call for a second meeting to be held in Frankfort on February 3 to prepare and begin procedures for seeking a charter of the Kentucky General Assembly.[15] Two months later the society was formally organized with Chilton Allen, an ex-congressman from Clark County, elected president, and Robert W. Scott recording secretary.[16] A number of objectives were outlined in the organizational meeting which were deemed to be of vital importance to the success of Kentucky farmers in the future. Among these were the gathering and publication of agricultural statistics, the organization of a Kentucky geological survey, the establishment of an agricultural school, and the contribution of financial support to the society by the General Assembly.[17] To date, except for the highly inadequate United States census data, no one in the Commonwealth had more than a vague idea of comparative agricultural production.

As a result of the second meeting of the society, James Guthrie of Louisville introduced a bill in the Senate proposing the establishment of an agricultural school and the purchase of an experimental farm. This bill, however, was defeated by a miserly and short-sighted House of Representatives.[18] The latter action left Kentucky farmers still in the dark ages of primitive educational and scientific matters. There was no certain way in 1840 of disseminating agricultural information or for systematically encouraging farmers to adopt advanced methods of cultivation, seed selection, and livestock breeding.[19] The Kentucky Society promoted the idea of offering cash awards for the best essays presented on the subjects of field crops and livestock. Four of these awards were won by Judge Adam Beatty of Mason County. The General Assembly authorized the printing and distribution of five thousand copies of the president's address, but adjourned without appropriating the necessary funds.[20] Thus neither the awards nor the publication of the Beatty address could be financed. Judge

Beatty's essays were privately printed in book form in 1844 at the press of Lewis Collins and Brown in Maysville.[21]

In writing a brief history of the Kentucky Agricultural Society, Robert W. Scott noted that the discouragement by the Kentucky General Assembly in 1840 caused the society to die a-borning, but not without having achieved some of its objectives.[22] A beginning was made in the gathering of agricultural statistics to be published in the state Auditor's Reports, provisions were made for organization of the first geological survey,[23] and the society supported the publication of the *Franklin Farmer* during its brief lifespan.[24] Robert Scott wrote the opening editorial for this periodical and contributed other materials to its columns during its two years of publication.[25] The great disappointment to the fledgling Agricultural Society, however, was the failure of the Kentucky legislators to favor the establishment of an agricultural college and to purchase an experimental farm where promising ideas and methodology could be given initial trials. This chronic short-sightedness of the legislators held Kentucky back for generations. Its farmers were left with the responsibility of conducting their own trial and error experiments. The thirty-two-year-old Scott was well aware of this fact, which largely accounted for his intense activities in livestock breeding and agricultural and horticultural activities at Locust Hill.[26]

The decade and a half from 1840 to 1856 was largely one of sterility where organized agriculture in Kentucky was concerned. State farmers operated almost independently so far as any cooperative associations were involved. They were unable to exert a unified influence to secure progressive legislation, to bring about general statewide improvements in livestock qualities, or to introduce new modes of cultivating and managing field crops. There was no public agency to disseminate even the meager scientific information available. Equally as important, the state no longer had a showcase for agriculture such as the earlier fairs had been. In 1853, Governor Lazarus W. Powell called attention to Kentucky's agricultural importance and needs in his annual message to the General Assembly.[27] He told legislators that "Heretofore, we have had very little, if any, legislation for the purpose of fostering and encouraging this numerous and meritorious class of our constituents. A large number of the states of the Union, for the purpose of encouraging and stimulating mechanical and agricultural industry, annually distribute state premiums at their industrial exhibitions, and the result has been most beneficial."[28] Two years later Governor Charles S. Morehead again emphasized the fact that Kentucky was an agricultural state and was obligated to give encouragement to its farmers.[29]

Responding to these admonitions from the two governors, six prominent bluegrass farmers met in Benjamin Gratz's office in Lexington on

January 1, 1856, to reactivate the Kentucky Agricultural Society. Present at this second meeting were Elisha Warfield, Benjamin Gratz, Robert W. Scott, Robert Aitcheson Alexander, William Warfield, and J. G. Kinnaird. A committee was appointed, with Scott as chairman, to prepare a general meeting to be held at the Kentucky capitol later that month.[30] In characteristic Scott prose, the heart of the one-page circular which was distributed read: "The agriculture of other States had experienced, for many years, the most genial impulses and most effective aid from the action of enlarged and powerful State organizations, the funds of which are supplied, chiefly or in part, from the public treasuries of those States. But Kentucky, the oldest Western State, the Farmer and Mechanic have been left to their own individual exertions, aided, in some cases, by small and local associations only. To relieve ourselves from this disadvantage, and to place us on equal ground in the field of improvement, is at present our aim."[31]

The gathering of Kentucky farmers took place in the capitol chambers on January 16.[32] Governor Morehead appointed James F. Buckner of Christian County to act as chairman, and Robert W. Scott and Philip Sweigert of Franklin County to serve as secretaries. Numerous sub-committees were appointed, with Scott a member of most of them. A resolution which struck home with the Master of Locust Hill was one which informed the Kentucky legislators that "any law which it might enact to diminish the dog population would be permanently wise and salutary, and would be cordially sustained by the people." This was indeed an overly optimistic statement because the average country Kentucky legislator knew full well that to lay legal hands on a Kentuckian's dog was to strike at one of the mainstays of a society where squirrel dogs were a cut above many members of families.

For the next two years Robert Scott of Franklin proved to be an industrious and attentive corresponding secretary. He promoted the revitalization of the Agricultural Society into a seminal force in Kentucky agriculture, helped to organize both state and local fairs, carried on a voluminous correspondence with the managers of local societies, wrote reports and special articles, and was a prime mover among his neighboring Franklin and Woodford county farmers.[33] In September 1857, he published an intelligent brief demographic article on his county which added significantly to an understanding of the resources and conditions of this outer Bluegrass area.[34]

A principal accomplishment of the second Kentucky Agricultural Society was the creation of an annual state fair. This required an enormous amount of organization work in the selection of a suitable place to hold the fair, the categorizing and planning of exhibits, arranging for the amounts of awards, and for social attractions. No doubt the selection of judges was the most tedious of Robert Scott's duties. This was potentially one which could create outbursts of tempers and animosities and bitter feuds which would destroy the fair. Aside from this responsibility for the state fair, the corresponding secretary was also entrusted with the solicitation of all the agricultural information from the local societies, an undertaking which yielded meager results.[35]

In a meeting of the Board of Directors of the Society in March 1857, Scott presented a carefully worded resolution saying again that Kentucky agriculture could profit from the establishment of an agricultural college. He cited the fact that this had proved true in states which had taken this step. The society adopted the Scott resolution proposing that the General Assembly be again encouraged to provide for such a school with full public support. It was emphasized that it would also be important to purchase and operate an experimental farm where information could be gathered without individual farmers having to engage in costly hit-and-miss individual experiments as Scott was having to do at Locust Hill.[36]

After two years of enormously demanding labors, Scott requested the Board of Directors of the Kentucky Agricultural Society on February 3, 1858, not to reappoint him corresponding secretary.[37] This request was honored, and later the directors presented him with a handsome sterling silver pitcher bearing an eloquent inscription of appreciation. Happily, this trophy, like so many of Robert Scott's papers and books, has survived the ravages of time and divisions of estates, and is now permanently the property of the National Society of Colonial Dames in the Commonwealth of Kentucky. As a valedictory Robert Scott prepared and published a 564-page report of his stewardship which is one of the better antebellum historic documents relating to Kentucky agriculture.[38] The compilation of this book was a monumental task of collecting, organizing, and presenting a cohesive volume, hardly an undertaking for an ordinary Kentucky "dirt" farmer devoid of the scientific interest and literary capability of Scott. Many a lesser man would have made the secretaryship of the Kentucky Agricultural Society a full-time job.[39]

The Southern Livestock Market

ROBERT SCOTT was not alone a model farmer and livestock breeder; he proved to be a highly competent salesman. The year he began farming at Locust Hill he staked claim to the Lower South as his market territory, and over the years he cultivated a responsive network of friends and customers. In the height of the antebellum era some of his sales forays were accomplished with a fanfare equal to that of a coming popular entertainment. He appreciated fully the importance of publicity and had an even better understanding of word-of-mouth advertising. Working from a broad experience of exhibiting choice animals at local and state fairs, he mastered the art of showing off sales stock.

Locust Hill documentary sources reflect that Scott held to a high standard of quality and refused to allow an inferior animal to go to market.[1] He assured customers he would replace animals which from reasons of improper breeding or raising proved less than satisfactory, or which died within a short time after their purchase.[2]

In the decades, 1840-1860, the lower southern livestock market was at best an unstable one, especially for purebred animals. It was still frontier in character, with central interests focused upon the growing of staple cotton and sugar cane.[3] The region's livestock heritage was one of primitive border drovers and yeoman farmers grazing rangy nature-bred hogs and cows. Farmers were more interested in purchasing cotton plow mules with which to cultivate cotton and cane fields. In that part of the antebellum South visited by Scott, there were only a few planters vitally concerned with improving their cattle and hog herds or with the introduction of sheep into a warm and humid climate where they were unduly exposed to diseases, parasites, and predators. This was indeed a difficult market to penetrate, not for the above reasons alone, but for the even more vital one that cash seems perennially to have been in short supply. Most often sales had to be made on the shaky credit terms which rose and fell with the rhythm of fortunes in crop seasons.[4]

The economic well-being of Locust Hill Plantation back in Franklin County depended in good part upon the income from southern livestock sales. Scott was forced to create a steady cash flow to maintain his standards of progressive farming and to sustain a comfortable way of life for his numerous family.[5] This necessitated extended absences from home over the spring and fall months of the year. Just as he had traveled south in 1835 on an investigative journey, he was to retrace the same route numerous times over in later years with the fixed objectives of exhibiting and selling choice farm animals.[6]

Fortunately for Scott and the small army of other seasonal livestock traders, they had a semblance of a clientele in the numerous Kentuckians who had emigrated to the emerging cotton belt. Through them they were able to make acquaintances which led to sales. Too, there seems to have been a small multitude of Scott and Brown relations well distributed throughout the region bordering on the Mississippi River. Robert and members of his family were forever visiting with "aunts," "uncles," and "cousins." These seemed to be fixed members of every steamboat's passenger list. These were mentioned only by first names or degrees of relationships with no indication of how close the blood relationships really were; no doubt many of them were as far removed in generations as those of ancient Hebrew kinships.

Occasionally there were mentions of Browns, Yergers, Lindsays, Rucks, Clarks, and others. It appears that most of these "relatives" enjoyed failing health and were ready to share their burdens of woe with "Cousin" Robert. Trapped aboard a steamboat he had to listen to family problems. In the spring of 1857 when he drifted south on the Ohio and Mississippi, all was far from being joyous and frolicsome. He wrote Elizabeth that he had made some pleasant extra-family acquaintances, one of whom was a Judge Lake to whom he had sold a Woburn-Irish cross-bred pig.[7] He remarked: "As might be expected among so many passengers we have some *oil* and some *water*; that is some which do not *mix* very well." He no doubt was referring to his "Cousin" Lucey and a Mrs. Johnson, the granddaughter of "Uncle" Ned, who were not speaking to each other. Scott wrote: "I am independent enough to talk to both, & perhaps loose something by my course, but I can not appreciate the loss, & will persist in bad taste, such as it is."[8]

Among the Memphis planters who invited Scott to visit their homes was the son-in-law of Colonel Abram Rennick, the famous cattle importer and breeder. On this occasion the affair was called a tea, which Robert wrote Elizabeth was "not exactly a *tea* either, but rather a cup of coffee, & the best fried oysters I ever ate, & as they were particularly good I ate a plate or two for you."[9]

Only infrequently on the southern sales ventures did Scott have to suffer "mean" hotelkeepers or tolerate their indifferent meals and services. He hardly reached the end of a Mississippi steamer's gangplank before hospitable "colonels" were on hand to invite him to make their homes his headquarters during his stay. So much of what transpired on these southern travels was taken so for granted that no precise record was made of the accommodations afforded members of the entourage. It is clear that Scott took along a herdsman, an assistant herdsman, and one or more slave attendants.[10] All of these apparently bedded down with the animals in livery stables.

Though Scott was too occupied with business during his subsequent travels to keep a journal, his letters to his wife Elizabeth are perhaps more intimate in their details than would have been the case with a diary. He traveled on some of the fanciest Ohio and Mississippi river steamboats, and even on some of the dreary "sandbar dawdlers." He took passage aboard such palaces as the *Southerner*, the *Baltic*, the *Sultana*, and the queenly *Eclipse*, and thoroughly enjoyed the excitement aboard. Sometimes the larger boats carried three to six hundred passengers. Gregarious by nature, and seasoned by travel experience, Scott readily made the acquaintances of planters, merchants, and even lowly Kentucky mule traders huddled on the lower decks. He also had a discerning eye for prominent Kentuckians and their families on the way south to visit in the Mississippi and Louisiana towns. Before he debarked he had gleaned generous amounts of information about social conditions in the towns, the economic state of cotton and sugar plantations, and he had gathered some notions of prevailing political views.

Letters written by Scott from aboard the steamboats glow with the excitement and socializing which went on. At times it seems the crowds of passengers literally vibrated the boats with emotions. Added to this were the bountiful meals served aboard. Ever a good trencherman, Scott found great satisfaction in the glorious repasts, and particularly in his prominent place at table. As indicated, Kentuckians were habitual travelers in good health and in ill, and almost every passenger list contained their names even unto the tottering oldest generation. Their sons and daughters added greatly to the excitement aboard. Not so high on the social scale, but no less colorful, were the deck passengers floating southward with their corrals of "cotton" mules which had been collected in the seasonal county court jockey row sales. These men were almost inexhaustible sources of information about monetary conditions, credit risks, the vagaries of cotton planters, and, of course, the livestock trade.[11]

The middle years of the decade from 1850 to 1860 were difficult ones for the Kentucky traders. They suffered losses of business and credit granted to planters in the recessions of 1855 to 1857. As an example, Robert Scott had sold purebred livestock to a Judge Rucks near Jackson, Mississippi, without securing proper financial guarantees. He wrote Elizabeth, "I regret to say Judge Rucks made no arrangement of his debts to me on which those protests received in consequence (I suppose) by his inability to sell his cotton farm." A year earlier, in 1853, Scott had met aboard the *Sultana* a company of Kentucky horse and mule traders who were in the depths of despondency. All of them had lost money because of slow sales and bed debts. He boasted to his wife, "From all I know I have done better than any of them." Despite recurring hard times Scott was able to secure orders for his livestock, a fact, he said, "I find my compensation in part."[12]

One of Robert Scott's most ambitious trading forays into the cotton South was made late in the fall of 1858. He left Locust Hill and Ducker's Station aboard a Louisville and Frankfort train with a full complement of family members, herdsmen, slave attendants, and assorted animals. Almost in the style of a circus manager, he appreciated the benefits of favorable newspaper publicity, and he was skilled in getting it. On November 24 he stabled his blue-ribbon selection of highly bred livestock in the Adams Livery Barn between Market and Main streets in Louisville. Hardly before the last pig was released from its box, W. N. Haldeman, editor of the Louisville *Daily Courier*, and George D. Prentice of the *Daily Journal* were on hand to gather notes for a story.

Haldeman described the Scott menagerie of prime blooded stock in detail even to mentioning many of their names of registry. There were fourteen thoroughbred Durham bulls, including Excelsior, a handsome roan; Capulet, a brilliant roan; and the sweetheart of the collection, the pure white heifer Snowflake who had recently won an award at the Southwestern Fair in Louisville. Keeping these aristocrats company were twelve "Improved Kentucky" sheep, four good milk cows, twenty Woburn-Irish, or "Hicklin," hogs, and some other stock. The *Courier* editor told his readers that Scott was "one of the most extensive and successful of the stock-raisers in Kentucky, and our southern friends among whom he has made frequent importations of his animals will form some idea of the superior quality of our stock." Haldeman was almost as much impressed by the fact that Scott was accompanied by his herdsman Reuben Sebrun, "an honest Democratic farmer" from Franklin.[13]

Not to be outdone by his rival, George D. Prentice ignored the Democratic allegiance of Robert Scott's Franklin County and puffed the Master of Locust Hill as "One of the most successful stockraisers in our state." He invited the people of Louisville to descend en masse upon Adams' Barn to see "some fine stock." "These," he wrote, "will be quite a procession to the stock raisers about Memphis." These flattering stories greatly inflated Robert Scott's ego. He wrote Elizabeth of his pleasure that both Louisville papers had given such generous attention to his passage through the city.[14]

One slight cloud blurred the Scott firmament in Louisville. He discovered while marching his procession aboard the *Southerner* that his overseer Trimble had put two common meat hog barrows in a box instead of purebred boars.[15] These he was practically forced to give away for fifty cents each. Otherwise, in his view everything was "pleasant and successful."[16]

Scott and his party reached Memphis aboard the fast *Southerner* on the morning of November 24, 1858, and true to George D. Prentice's prediction he, his men, and animals made quite a procession through the streets. The next day Robert wrote Elizabeth that he had just sent his son Preston and daughter Ella off to New Orleans aboard the *Eclipse* on a visit with Brown relatives in that city. Ella had traveled with him all the way from Frankfort, while Preston had come aboard the boat at Columbus, Kentucky, where he was attempting to establish a medical practice. "Yesterday morning," the elder Scott wrote Elizabeth, "before breakfast I headed our procession of Bulls, cows &c, & we marched through the streets up to a comfortable stable, without any disagreeable occurrences so far. I have had many acquaintances & some friends among the throng which has already called to pay respects to my English nobility." Quickly he sold the four grade milk cows for $75 each, and parted with Capulet for $300 on a crop season term of credit from four to six months. Two heifers went for $100 each, and a box of pigs sold for $50. At that point the Memphis market seems to have dried up. Actually, Scott had not collected a penny of hard cash.[17]

The western Tennessee livestock-planter gentry were obviously impressed with the fine Locust Hill collection of animals, but they were much longer on their hospitality than cash and a will to improve their own stock. After a time Scott sold all of his stock except twelve of the bulls, the heart of the collection. He sold a one-eyed bull yearling for only a hundred dollars and Snowflake was traded for a half-acre city lot valued at three hundred dollars. He then bargained for five adjoining acres to be paid for with livestock. He told Elizabeth, "If I succeed then so much has been done towards having a home here." There was a genuine tone of frustration in this latter note. "My stock attracts much admiration, but the planters say they are not ready for fine cattle, & they fear hog cholera. Cows and heifers would sell well."[18] With ample reasons Scott needed to be wary about some of the unsecured debts which he left behind in the Mississippi Delta, where fortunes were up one year and down the next with mercurial regularity, and where individual planters seemed to have habitually overburdened themselves with debts.

At Locust Hill Elizabeth was in need of ready funds with which to pay county taxes, to buy coal, and to meet daily operating expenses. Robert wrote her that he was sending her fifty dollars. But in a postscript he said that upon further examining the contents of his wallet, he found he could spare another forty, which he sent to her by registered mail.[19]

Throughout his lifetime Robert W. Scott managed his financial affairs with a frugal countryman's finesse. His year-to-year farming operations generated remarkably small cash returns as compared with the rather extensive activities in which he engaged himself. Accounts entered in the Locust Hill Farm Book document his meticulous attention to finances and the frugality of his nature. Measured by modern standards of values, Locust Hill made its most significant returns in the way of plantation life it sustained rather than in the volume of its cash returns. Fortunately, Elizabeth Brown Scott was every bit as good a manager as her husband. To all intents and purposes she was in charge of the farm when Robert was away. In 1858, after reading her letter describing some of her decisions, he wrote her from Memphis: "How proud and glad I was to have so smart a *business man* for my wife." During these periods Elizabeth was called upon to select pigs, bulls, cows, sheep, and goats for impatient customers, to fill orders, to supervise the making of crates, and to oversee Robert's precise shipping procedures. Scott, with his usual thoroughness, had worked out a shipping routine which, he boasted, had kept him from ever losing an animal in transit. Along with his crates of sheep and hogs he sent barrels of corn in the ear, chopped oats and hay, and directions for watering. Barrels which contained feed were capped in such a way that a hole was cut in the top just large enough for trainmen to insert their hands to withdraw feed. These holes were then "stopped" with hands of twisted hay to prevent spillage. When shipments were ready to depart Duckers, Elizabeth had to write factors Rowan, Cood, and Todd in Louisville to be on the lookout for them, and then to alert other factors in the southern cities that the animals were en route.[20]

In addition to the shipment chores, Robert asked Elizabeth to have his overseer Trimble mark all newborn pigs with identifying holes in their ears so he could relate them to the proper sows when he got home. He referred Elizabeth to the Farm Hog Book for additional instructions.[21]

Making preparations to embark upon a sales trip through the South demanded the expenditure of a good amount of energy. First, Scott had to select the animals he would take along, organize their registration papers, and then choose the managers he would need. There were always the problems of transportation to be arranged on trains and steamboats, the renting of space in livery stables, the preparation of advertising flyers describing the sales animals, and the making of credit arrangements with Colonel E. H. Taylor, Jr.'s, Frankfort bank.[22] Before Robert embarked on one of his journeys he made plans for the planting of various crops and the shearing of sheep and goats, established grazing schedules for the meadows, and left instructions as to the care and repair of fences and buildings. He made separate detailed entries in his various animal books and wrote out communications to the overseer and read them to him.

Periodically he would remind Elizabeth in his letters to have Trimble reread his instructions.[23]

A good example of the care which Robert Scott exercised for the direction of work in his absence was a set of instructions which he labeled "No. 10," dated March 16, but with no year indication. Scott reminded Trimble that the goats should be sheared in April if the weather was favorable. Then he outlined step-by-step instructions for handling both the animals and the wool clip. The sheep could be left in full coat until May, he wrote, when they would begin tagging their wool. He told Trimble, "Before shearing time I want you to single out one of the largest and finest formed ewes, & which has lost her lamb; & also one buck & one ewe yearling, of like qualities & when you are shearing leave these not shorn, as I want to have photographs taken when I get home."[24] One of Scott's prime selling exhibits was a collection of choice goat and sheep fleeces. Some of these he had placed on permanent exhibit in the Kentucky State Capitol. Thus it went, one crop year after another, with lambing, farrowing, calving, and foaling in season. One crop of young animals was rapidly reaching maturity as the older ones were shipped off to market.[25]

Outbreak of the Civil War disrupted, if it did not actually destroy, the lower southern market for finely bred Kentucky livestock. Breeding and grazing continued at Locust Hill throughout the war, but with a somewhat lesser tempo. No longer could Scott gather up a prime shipment of his herd book animals and set off downriver with a spectacular entourage of managers and helpers to draw in the cotton and sugar cane barons of the delta lands. Actually the record, like the dropping of autumn leaves, falls silent on what actually went on at Locust Hill during the war, except to indicate there was a continuity of farming activities. This was evident in the fact that, in 1866, the United States commissioner of agriculture included a section of Scott's sheep breeding in his *Report*.[26]

At the end of the conflict Scott directed his attention to opening a market for his stock north of the Ohio. In this he proposed to enter the territory of some of this strongest antebellum competitors. Somewhat in the old grand manner, he left Locust Hill in October 1865, and traveled up the Ohio. He stopped first in Cincinnati to display his goat and sheep fleeces in Dods and Shillito's stores and in some of the other "fashionable resorts." Merchants in these stores gave him encouragement whether they bought or not. On the steamer upstream from Louisville, pride got the better of him, and he exhibited his fine woolen samples to admiring passengers. He wrote Elizabeth, "I had a pleasant trip; made many acquaintances." In this lately closed land he experienced "nothing but politeness, kindness, & courtesy." Nevertheless, he wrote in the tone of a man venturing into a far distant and alien land. The people were polite and friendly, but Scott missed the warm hospitality which he had so enjoyed in the Old

South. He visited a "Mr. A" to whom he had consigned a shipment of animals, but was not invited to his house. He suspected that "Mrs. A." did her own cooking and that her husband waited upon the table. Household servant hire was much dearer above the Ohio than in Kentucky.[27]

Despite the new acquaintances he made aboard the steamboat and the cordial reception given him by the Cincinnati merchants, Scott met with devastating disappointment in Ohio. He found the animals he had shipped to his agent in such poor condition that they could not be sold at any price, and if they were disposed of they would only damage his reputation as a breeder. The goats and sheep were recrated, and shipped home for rehabilitation.

With radical changes in both market and labor situations, Robert Scott was forced to reduce his operations without compromising his high standards of breeding superior livestock.[28] For almost two decades following the war, he carried on with his usual thoroughness and attention to details, having much of the time to endure chronically poor health which necessitated his absence from Locust Hill for extended periods. He nevertheless maintained his reputation in the Bluegrass as a model farmer. From the standpoint of Kentucky farming, few, if any, local planters left behind so many documentary sources which bring into fairly clear perspective the yearly activities of so large and intensively operated bluegrass plantation.

Robert W. Scott's letters to his wife when he was away on sales trips were of a warm, personable nature of a farmer truly in close affinity with his land. In the mode of his earlier assessments of famous national personalities, the successful and self-assured Master of Locust Hill recorded a vivid sense of life in both Bluegrass Kentucky and in the more romantic years of the Lower South, when he sat in the elaborate salons of elegant Mississippi River steamboats, or in the handsome drawing rooms of planters, and made cherished acquaintances. It seemed to disturb Scott only mildly that the planter colonels of the cotton belt were far more proficient in producing "the most delicious fried oysters a man ever ate" than in producing negotiable cash with which to pay for their livestock purchases.

6

Descent into Babylon

ROBERT W. SCOTT was a decent, socially conscious man. As he nurtured his land, he involved himself in the betterment of the society about him. Existing within the shadow of Frankfort and the mainspring of Kentucky's ever-greening political hopes and frustrations, Joel and Robert Scott were pronounced partisans. As indicated they had consorted politically with the early Jacksonians. Later they and supported Lazarus Powell, Charles S. Morehead, and Beriah Magoffin for governor. As corresponding secretary of the Kentucky State Agricultural Society, Robert lobbied in succeeding sessions of the General Assembly for bills which promised to promote the interests of progressive farmers. Foremost among the legislation sought was the organization of a geological survey, establishment of an agricultural school, support of an experimental farm, passage of a more effective dog law, and dissemination of scientific agricultural information. Too, Scott was vitally interested in the enactment and application of more modern public school laws to break the stifling grip of illiteracy in the Commonwealth.[1]

Though politically concerned, Robert Scott only once offered himself for public office. In 1849, he entered the race for election as a delegate to the 1849 constitutional convention. After bickering over this issue, the voters in 1848 had favored the calling of a convention to revise the fifty-year-old document. Selection of delegates stirred intense interest throughout the state. There were at least a half-dozen matters of vital concern which demanded attention. One of these was the reduction of the number of elective officers in favor of the appointment of judges of the courts and some other officials. Slavery in general was a heated issue, but no aspect of this institution stirred emotions more readily than the possibility that a self-interested group might bring about the negation of the Non-importation Law of 1833 which forbade bringing slaves into Kentucky for resale to the Lower South.[2] Less explosive were questions of giving constitutional sanctity to the establishment and support of public schools, expanding the membership of the over-burdened Court of Appeals, and setting a limit on the accumulation of state debts within the context of anticipated annual tax income. The latter question had been brought to the fore largely by persons who feared that enthusiasm for public support of internal improvements would eventually bankrupt the Commonwealth.[3]

There was only one time previously in Kentucky history when the general emotions of the Kentucky electorate had been so vigorously stirred, and that was during the financial-political turmoil in the 1820s over the Old Court-New Court dispute. Indicative of this fact was voter participation. In 1848, Kentucky had the astonishingly small registration of 139,922 voters out of a population of 761,413 white persons. Yet, almost miraculously, 101, 828 of these voted to call a constitutional convention. Robert Scott based his candidacy on the issues of reducing the number of electoral officers and especially of appointing judges. He was opposed by Thomas N. Lindsay, an Irishman who had moved to Frankfort from Campbell County in 1835 to become a hotelkeeper. He was elected to the House of Representatives, and in 1849 was serving as commonwealth's attorney for Franklin County, a position which placed him at the core of the powerful courthouse ring. Lindsay made further appeal to the constituency of this river county by expressing favor for generous expenditures on internal improvements. Scott was defeated and never again sought public office.[4]

During the years 1856-57, when he was most active with the Agricultural Society, he was drawn into close association with the governors, especially Powell, Morehead, and, later, Magoffin. In 1860, Governor Magoffin appointed him president of the newly created commission for the Institute for the Feeble Minded, a position he held for three or four years.[5]

It was inevitable that Scott on his sales journeys in the Lower South prior to 1860 would become well-informed about the issues which stirred a rising sectional storm over staple crop economy and slavery. He learned from the cotton and sugar colonels something of the issues which had been discussed in the various southern conventions which had met during the decade. Scott was a slaveholder, and apparently he had some decided opinions of his own on the subject. As indicated earlier, there were twenty-six slaves at Locust Hill in 1850; a decade later, thirty-three.[6] These numbers had grown but not extensively. They did not, however, reflect Robert Scott's full involvement with the institution. His farm book contains numerous articles for slave hire owed to neighboring farmers.[7]

Management of slaves at Locust Hill seems to have fallen between being a system of intimate owner relationships and the use of an overseer. In the case of the latter it is difficult to discern how much authority Scott delegated to his overseer or farm manager. He seems to have set the workday schedule, and saw to its being carried out. Clearly, Scott retained in his and Elizabeth's hands control of their people. Strangely, in all the writing that he did he never discussed the subjects of politics or slavery.[8]

As indicated, when Scott was away from Locust Hill he left behind detailed instructions to be followed by the overseer. In none of these instructions which have survived is there mention of the precise relationship of the overseer's authority over the slaves. There are incidental notes which indicate that both Scott and his wife placed genuine trust in some, if not all, of their bondsmen and held them high in their affections.[9] Only one discordant note has survived which suggests that Scott was tempted to succumb to the insidious evil of the Kentucky interstate slave trade. He owned a slave named Billy who accompanied him on at least two of his trading journeys into the South. There is every indication he had confidence in this man because he entrusted him with the delivery of animals to purchasers. Apparently, he allowed Billy the utmost freedom of movement in a land where this was not done. At some point Billy committed an act of seemingly high indiscretion which angered Scott, who resolved to sell the man to a southern slavemaster. There followed an emotional confrontation, with Billy pleading not to be disposed of like a Locust Hill one-eyed yearling bull. Scott wrote Elizabeth: "Billy is still with me & begs & prays to return & makes fair promises, but has not confessed all as yet. He will be hard to sell at any price & I expect to sell him on a credit, & on trial perhaps as the best I can do, & will do the best I can."[10]

Billy must have confessed to whatever it was he had done because he was with his master on subsequent trading journeys. Two years later Robert wrote Elizabeth, from aboard the steamer *Philadelphia* on the Mississippi just above Vicksburg, about his good fortune in making connections with all the people with whom he had done business. He told her, "As I went from Greenville I met Billy coming, &c. &c. all good luck I have collected no money, but have taken steps to have both debts secured, & I think neither will be lost, & both paid, perhaps, soon."[11]

In Scott's absences from Locust Hill the slaves carried on with their usual tasks; in fact, some of them took pride in their ability to manage things while he was away. Simon, Lewis, Claiborn, and Cesar were sent to Versailles and Frankfort with stock and to run other errands. John and Anderson kept the house "wonderfully well" supplied with firewood. Eli, the carpenter, was kept busy building animal crates, and Siddy (Sidney) bustled about the kitchen preparing her sumptuous meals. All the other slaves, young and old, seem to have behaved and kept themselves reasonably well occupied with assigned tasks.[12] In January 1859, Elizabeth wrote: "Mr. Morton had all the hands taking up hemp yesterday evening and today as your father said there were about thirty acres that ought to be taken up. Mr. Morton is very industrious. I have never seen him but he is doing something (for I have been peeping about) altho I have nothing to do with their work, yet I wished to see whether he has taken an interest in our affairs, and from all I can see, I expect you have succeeded in getting a very industrious overseer. He blows the horn every morning at 5 and has breakfast at half past 6 at least the boys do, and I eat at seven, as I wish them to eat at the time Mr. Morton does."[13] There seems also to have been the same concern about the slaves' health as about that of members of the Scott family. Frequently in her letters Elizabeth referred to illnesses and doctors' visitations which seemed to have been related to the slaves. Certainly, she devoted personal attention to their welfare.

There were many reasons why Robert Scott empathized with the causes of the South in the decade from 1850 to 1860. He depended heavily upon the region's planters as purchasers of his fine blooded and premium-priced livestock. On his annual sales trips into the region he established an ever-widening circle of friends, and his and Elizabeth's families seemed to have generated concentric circles of relatives, of near and far kin, in the river South.

From 1835 onward Scott nurtured a dream that someday he might move his family either to the Lower South or to Texas. He was much interested in the bright promise of the rising new cities along the Mississippi, particularly Memphis.[14] He acquainted himself with the comparative growth statistics of the various port cities of the region, and speculated on their potentials for further growth. There is no doubt but what his political opinions and reactions were influenced by the numerous front porch and steamboat deck conversations he had with the planters and merchants who so generously extended their hospitality to him.

By the close of the 1850s, political cross-currents in Kentucky and the South had grown in intensity. Having once again to make political adjustments, Scott gave his support to John C. Breckinridge in the presidential campaign of 1860. He no doubt was disappointed in Breckinridge's defeat and the election of Abraham Lincoln, but was more concerned about the future course which Kentucky might pursue. From November 1860 on, Frankfort was more or less in a state of turmoil. The General Assembly had adjourned its regular session in February 1861, without having considered the secession crisis.[15] A special session was called to meet on May 6.[16] In the meantime there arose a complex and confusing splintering of political factions in the state. Extremist hotheads, centered largely in Louisville, raised a hue and cry for state's rights. The outspoken editor J. R. Johnson of the Frankfort *Commonwealth* called these people "Ophidians" and accused them of being thoughtless disciples of the headless horsemen George Nicholas Sanders and William Lowndes Yancey. They had rushed to the state capital to hold an early and abortive convention. Johnson said people of the town hardly had a chance to glimpse them before they were gone. In colorful medieval figure he wrote that the coming of the radicals was "Like an angel's wing through an opening cloud, Was seen and then withdrawn."[17] Frankly, the state's righters were quixotic in their efforts to stampede an already confused Kentucky public.

Working the opposite side of the spectrum from the extremist to gain the attention of the legislators were the old-line Whigs and Breckinridge Democrats, who sought a calmer and more tolerable solution to the Commonwealth's dilemma. They also called a meeting in Frankfort, delivered some pleasant oratory about Kentucky's glorious past, opposed the Sanders-Yancey rabble-rousers, elected Scott chairman of the convention, and went home.[18] Actually, the General Assembly was only a little more effective. In special session it adopted two laws strengthening the Kentucky militia and Home Guards, and then got down to the business in which, traditionally, Kentucky legislators have ever been proficient, that of enacting local and private legislation to placate constituents back home. The actions taken in this session, however, were reasonably reflective of the state of mind of Kentuckians in this era.[19] Legislators had been at home listening to constituents during a forty-day recess and returned to their legislative seats to make the usual petty political decisions. There was an exception to this overall fact, and that was the prevailing conviction that Kentucky should avoid becoming a geographical puck in the impending conflict.

With keen, but somewhat abrasive, insight, J. R. Johnson warned his readers about the States Rights leaders, saying that "If the people of Kentucky had handed the State over to the control of the ardent spirits last November, we would have been in a pretty pickle now, wouldn't we? We should have been by this time the border — the outside wall of a Southern confederacy. Our wits and our property would have been taxed for the purpose of paying the expenses of that paste board President Jeff Davis and his amusing cabinet of remarkable statesmen."[20] This was precisely the situation which Robert W. Scott and his more moderate Southern Rights colleagues wished to avoid.

Historically, the Southern Rights coalition achieved little, if anything. It sought between meetings of the General Assembly to whip up favorable public opinion to its arguments. It organized Southern Rights clubs and promoted the idea of pressuring the Assembly into calling a sovereignty convention, but none of this agitation bore fruit.[21] Robert Scott appears not to have been active on the tumultuous Kentucky political scene during the Civil War. Amazingly, there either were not created any documentary sources in this area or they have not survived. It is clear, however, that there was a remarkable continuity in the operation of Locust Hill Plantation.

Both of Scott's surviving sons, Preston Brown and John Orlando, served in the Confederate army as physicians. Preston, living at the time in Bolivar County, Mississippi, enlisted at the outset of the war. In November, he accompanied General Leonidas Polk on his invasion of

Preston Brown Scott, oldest son of Robert and Elizabeth

western Kentucky and found himself back in Columbus, where he had
begun his medical practice. He was present during the Battle of Belmont
in Missouri. The following year Dr. Scott became surgeon for the 4th Kentucky Regiment, 1st Brigade, and before the war ended served on the staff
of Ben Hardin Helm. After the Battle of Jackson, Mississippi, he was promoted to be medical director for Joseph E. Johnston's command. He then
transferred to the staff of General Leonidas Polk and was with that officer when Polk fell at Pine Mountain, Georgia, in 1864. Following that
incident Preston became medical director of military hospitals in Mississippi and Alabama, serving at times under the commands of Generals Stephen
D. Lee, Dabney Maury, and Dick Taylor.[22]

Robert Scott's second son, John Orlando, graduated from the Louisville Medical School in 1862 and went directly into the Confederate army
as an assistant surgeon in Cobb's Battery of the 2nd Kentucky Regiment.

He was present in the Battle of Stones River and was with General Roger Hanson when that officer was killed in January 1863. In later years the United Confederate Veterans of Texas promoted him to the rank of lieutenant colonel and made him chief surgeon of their organization.[23]

Surely, Robert and Elizabeth Scott spent uneasy years at Locust Hill during the war, with both of their sons actively engaged in military campaigning. Beyond attending to personal business Robert does not seem to have been active in public affairs, largely, no doubt, because of the lingering anxieties in and around Frankfort created by threats of military invasions. Too, the political situation during these years grew progressively more unstable.

John D. Scott, second son of Robert and Elizabeth

Scott survived the war with his Locust Hill estate intact, but he suffered from failing health. In 1865, in the months when the full impact of emancipation of his slaves fell upon him, he became ill almost to the point of being inoperative. In fact, he never again was to enjoy stable health, a fact which caused him to search anew for locations where he and Elizabeth could recover from their chronic afflictions.[24] Nevertheless, he was far from being oblivious to the swirling postwar struggle for power which went on about him. In 1866, he took an active part in calling a convention of Democrats in Louisville for the purpose of restoring that party to power in Kentucky. He was made a member of the Central Committee and subsequently presided as chairman of that body. As in the old days when he was a vigorous young member of the group which had organized, and later revived, the Kentucky State Agricultural Society, he served the Central Committee with vigor and aggressiveness. When he resigned this post he was given a warm vote of thanks. In working to restore the power and influence of the Democratic party, Robert Scott actually played a central role in opening the way for placing in state offices the Confederate brigadiers who would exercise enormous powers over the course of Kentucky political history throughout the remainder of the nineteenth century.[25]

At the peak of the Reconstruction chaos and confusion Scott submitted a long poem to J. R. Johnson of the *Commonwealth* in which he expressed with some poetic feelings his attitude toward what was happening. Three of the nine verses are illustrative of his state of mind:

"Oh! Jonathan, Jonathan, how could you dare
    To tell, in sweet numbers, a falsehood so bare?
I loved our dear Union far better than you,
    Or any one else of your 'free negro crew.'

          * * *

"And when at last, if the power you'd obtain'd
    We saw, at a glance, that our slaves you'd unchain,
'Compromise, Jonathan; guranteys give;
    And glorious Union forever shall live.

          * * *

"Oh, Jonathan, Jonathan, we forgive you the wrong;
    The wrong of the outrage, & thot of your song,
Then again let the Starspangled Banner float oe'r us,
    With all other blessings which it formerly bore us."[26]

In the years after 1870, Robert Scott became more interested in establishing his Florida home and modest citrus orchard than in politics. By the latter decade the old Kentucky order was fairly well reestablished, and his Confederate brigadier friends, including Joseph Desha Pickett, super-intendent of public instruction, firmly controlled state affairs.[27] Sons Preston and John had both returned safely from the war, Preston to prac-tice medicine in Louisville, and John in Owensboro. The slaves were freed at Locust Hill, and the history of Kentucky's livestock industry began a new chapter.[28] Before the state in general were the issues created by eman-cipation, the revision of the outmoded Constitution, the expansion of the political system, a new phase of internal improvements, and the establish-ment of the Kentucky Agricultural and Mechanical College along with its experimental farm. All of these were subjects which turned a still articu-late but aging man's thoughts into historical channels.[27]

7

We Are a United Family

LOCUST HILL PLANTATION was the seat of one of Kentucky's most interesting families. There existed under the roof of the stately mansion the ingredients of the good way of life, a mode of life which to a large extent was socially and economically self-sufficient in both human and material terms. The great house was a hospitable place to family and visitors alike. Robert W. and Elizabeth Brown Scott spent more than a half-century of their lives at Locust Hill dedicated to the raising of a numerous family, and projecting a dignified but affectionate image of parental concern. Just as Robert was dedicated to the upgrading of quality livestock, he made certain that his children would be given the cultural advantages which would enrich their lives as worthwhile human beings. Family correspondence and personal documents fairly shout a close-knit and durable family union. If there were family rifts, evidence of their occurrence was kept well out of the written record.

Early in January 1869 Robert W. Scott wrote his daughter Eleanor Green, "Though the past season had in it for us no serious disturbances, & the future is not obscured by any clouds of overwhelming threatening, still I have not grown more easy in my situation on the farm, nor has your mother in her domestic circle." The Locust Hill slaves had largely strayed away into the new-found freedom, and the master was left short-handed in the fields and pastures, and Elizabeth had only the aging and ailing Siddy (Sidney) upon whom she could depend. Robert realized the day was near at hand when Locust Hill would have to change hands. He was certain the coming year would exhaust his "forbearance" on the subject of changes which had occurred. He proposed that Lafayette Green purchase Locust Hill lock, stock, and barrel and move his operations to Franklin County.[1]

A month later Robert Scott wrote Eleanor and Lafayette that he and Elizabeth had reached the conclusion that farming no longer held profit or pleasure for them. He asked the Greens for $120 an acre for the 787½-acre plantation, including buildings and fencing. He would will Eleanor one-seventh of the property, and with other considerations they could reduce the $94,000 asking price to $30,834 for immediate payment. He would give his son-in-law three years in which to pay the latter sum.[2] Lafayette Green chose not to abandon his holdings at the Falls of the Rough, and Locust Hill remained in Robert W. Scott's hand for the next fourteen years, each year proving more burdensome than the last.

When Robert and Elizabeth had established their permanent home at Locust Hill, they had moved well beyond easy access to Frankfort churches and other social and cultural institutions. The Scotts, Joel and Robert, seemed to have been somewhat ambivalent in their church connections.[3] From childhood Joel had a leaning toward the Baptist Church, if he was not in fact a member. He was a member of the founding board of trustees of Georgetown College,[4] and during his years as keeper of the Kentucky Penitentiary he was active in a Baptist congregation in Frankfort, but it appears from his personal record that he did not actually join the church until 1834, when he moved out to his farm in Woodford County. Then he affiliated with the famous old pioneer Forks of Elkhorn Baptist Church. In 1843, Robert and Elizabeth joined this congregation. Robert, however, had organized before his marriage a Sunday school and served as teacher and superintendent in Frankfort. Later he was to do the same thing at the Forks of Elkhorn Church.[5]

Both religiously and morally, Robert W. Scott was a conservative man without being offensive in his actions. On his travels to the Northeast in his youth, he visited churches and was impressed by their architecture; he also observed church-related educational programs. But he made no mention in his journal of having attended church services. With the exception of Alexander Campbell, who was a member of the Virginia Constitutional Convention, he seems to have visited with no other minister of the gospel.[6] From his youth onward, Scott was an ardent temperance man, this despite the fact he wore the superficial mint-scented title of Kentucky Colonel, and wore it with pride. He never succumbed, however, to the popular attributes of this social and political rank.[7] As mentioned earlier, he denied his harvest hands the customary grog which was as much a part of the season as sunshine.

In personal appearance Robert dressed the part of the dignified plantation master. He was clean shaven and wore his hair in a high side roach. In his house his servants set a lavish table, and he took pride in the products of his orchard and vineyard (but not in fermented form). In like manner Elizabeth and her daughters conformed to the proper and conservative dress styles portrayed in *Graham's Magazine* and its colored fashion plates. Elizabeth was a subscriber to this arbiter of early nineteenth-century female fashions, and surviving bound volumes are inscribed with her name.[8] She patronized the dry goods stores in Frankfort, Lexington, and

Louisville, and bought piece goods which she made into dresses on her own patented sewing machine.[9]

Nine children, born in quick succession, created an extraordinary parental concern for their welfare and upbringing. Of the nine, seven survived to adulthood.[10] When the Kentucky General Assembly was stirred from its cultural lethargy in 1838 to enact a half-measure authorizing local communities to organize common schools, Preston Brown Scott, the oldest of the brood, was six years old and ready to begin his education. This fact stimulated Robert to assume leadership in organizing the school at Jett, where it seems all of his children in time received their foundation training.[11]

At times the Scotts either boarded female teachers or employed private tutors to instruct their children. On one of Robert's visitations into the South, "Lizzie" and Louisa wrote him what their mother called "pretty good letters." The fact was that Louisa's letter was an unusually mature one to come from a twelve-year-old child. In a living room discussion, a phlegmatic teacher named Miss Parke gave a poor account of her knowledge before her pupils. Elizabeth wrote Robert that "She does not care to take exercise because Miss P. does not like it." Louisa made the observation that the English did not enunciate the "h" sound in their casual conversations. When Miss Parke and Lizzie disputed this, Elizabeth had Louisa check her statement in the encyclopedia. The young girl found that she was right.[12]

Miss Parke disturbed Elizabeth in other ways. She said, "I hope Miss P. will see that she needs rubbing up to cope with her scholars or rather Louisa says, 'she gives up to her in French for she knows the most, but she can't stump her at history, geography & Arithmetic,'" she told Robert, "but Father [Joel] told her to behave and respect Miss P. or she would catch her a heap of times. I hardly know what to do, but she seems to do her best poor as it is. She told me the other day if Miss Wright left — Mr. Rogers — she did not know what she should do. I told her I never kept an unwilling bird, and if she was unhappy to go — but she said she would stay the session out." Repeatedly, Elizabeth wrote of her children's educational progress.

There was a good family library at Locust Hill. Robert Scott was a constant and mature reader, and he cultivated throughout life his youthful desire to own books. As nearly as it is now possible to reconstruct, there was in the Locust Hill library a rich variety of books which gave the Scott children ready access to a much better than average well-to-do family library. Definitely the Locust Hill book collection was not the traditionally superficial assortment of antebellum southern drawing-room ornamentation of show-case standard sets of ancient and English classics. On this score the cultural and intellectual environment at Locust Hill was far superior to most homes in the nineteenth-century Bluegrass.[14]

Unfortunately for the modern historian, nineteenth-century Kentucky was such a thoroughly masculine age that none of the contemporary biographical encyclopedic sources contains sketches of women. There does not appear to be a record of Elizabeth Brown Scott's educational background, except in a casual note to her grandson Willis Green when she mentioned the stern instructions of an aunt.[15] Nevertheless, there exists ample documentation that she had some sound background instruction in the use of the English language and that she was almost as capable as Robert in making and describing business transactions. Her letters were cast in a clear, good English style which reflected so graphically her personality. Her handwriting so closely resembled that of her husband's that, with the exception of the formation of two or three letters, it is difficult to distinguish between them.

The Scotts' sons, Preston, John, and Joel, quickly outgrew the elementary level of instruction offered in the Jett school. The Reverend James Eells tutored Preston in preparation for admission to Georgetown College, of which both his grandfather and father served as trustees. Preston graduated in 1851 at the head of his class.[16] He then went to Knoxville to study under the watchful eye of his uncle, Judge William Brown Reese. Apparently Judge Reese was a part-time professor in what is now the University of Tennessee. When Preston had completed his work in Knoxville, he entered the Medical Department of the University of Louisville; he graduated in 1856.[17] Interestingly, Preston did much of his medical studies in the office of his distant relative Lewis Rogers, who in turn was a student of Preston's great-uncle Samuel Brown.[18] Brother John went from the Jett elementary classes to the B. B. Sayre Institute in Frankfort, and then to Centre College, where he graduated in 1856. He followed Preston to the University of Louisville, where he too graduated in medicine, in the second year of the Civil War.[19] The middle son, Joel, attended the Military Academy at Drennon's Springs, and then entered Georgetown College. His letters to his father reveal a close bond between the two. They also give enlightening glimpses of student life in a small Baptist college in a Kentucky county seat town. Joel was endowed with his father's observant talents, and his comments on his landlord Dr. Gano and his relations with his slaves give an insight into slave-master accommodations in antebellum Kentucky. Joel and his roommate had to fetch their own water and firewood, and to perform other chores which they thought the slaves should attend to for them. He begged his father to allow him to change boarding houses.[20] Under the rules of the College, a boy could not make such a change without written parental consent.[21] He found Greek a difficult subject and contemplated dropping it, but by dogged determination he became rather proficient in the subject. Unhappily, this bright young boy died in 1855 during his junior year, a serious blow to the Scott family.[22]

Like their mother, the five Scott daughters gave evidence in their letters of having bright minds. They seem to have received good instruction in the use of English, and they demonstrated distinct capabilities in discussing more substantive topics than the current gossip which so entranced most women in their social circle. Louisa especially wrote long and informative letters. So did Ellie from her elegant mansion at the Falls of Rough oasis in the mid-Kentucky backwoods. Writing in a comparable vein of an English country lady from the confines of a bountiful country estate, Ellie described the primitive social and cultural state of her rural neighbors. None of the personal letters, nor any other family records, gives even a hint of what advanced formal education the Scott daughters may have received beyond their attendance at the Jett community school and from private tutors.

As indicated, family life at Locust Hill was socially comfortable and rich in expressions of mutual affections. The Scott children seem to have fitted into the rhythm of a thriving farm life as a matter of course, without being bored by its daily and seasonal routines. The three sons were employed from time to time in farming tasks which required them to assume responsibilities. The girls grew up as active and articulate parts of their family circle, but appear to have kept themselves separate and apart from the workaday operations of the farm, with its earthy pastures and stables. Their letters reveal interests in parties and visits with relatives and friends. Like their Brown kinsmen, they became an accepted part of the social life of the Kentucky capital city.[23]

Although Robert and Elizabeth Scott were devout Baptists who by their own upbringing had a strict sense of social propriety, they appear not to have been stern in their attitudes toward their children's participation in social activities, including dancing. The girls went to house parties in Louisville, Cincinnati, and Frankfort. They were popular with other young people. Just on the eve of matrimony Louisa paid an extended visit to relatives, perhaps in Louisville. She attended a fashionable dance where she refused to participate in some of the more forward dances. Her father wrote her: "I sit down to write you a few lines, determined that you shall not make so long an absence from home without having at least one written evidence of my affection for you. And first I desire to commend your sense of propriety in not dancing the hugging dance at some ball or party which I have heard you attended. Of course you were slighted & neglected on account of so great a breach of etiquette & fashion, & to soothe your mortification I enclose you five dollars, with which to purchase the best and handsomest standard work on female deportment you can find for that sum." Scott encouraged Louisa to make plans to return home before she wore out her welcome. He also informed her that there was to be a "Calico Ball" at the Capital Hotel and that she should be at home for that party. Evidently a "calico ball" was not the "hugging" kind.[24]

All the Scott daughters, except one, escaped the fate of so many members of proud Bluegrass families, for they found husbands of unusually good social and economic standing. In light of the prevailing social customs it could hardly be said that Scott girls rushed heedlessly into early marriages. Mary Brown was twenty-three when she married Frankfort native

S.I.M. Major, husband of Mary Brown Scott

Samuel Ire Monger Major, who boasted a proper Virginia ancestry. He was a man after Robert's own heart. Major was educated at the B. B. Sayre Institute and by private tutors. In 1852, he became printer to the Commonwealth and editor of the *Kentucky Yeoman*. He served several terms in the Kentucky General Assembly and was four times mayor of Frankfort. In the latter position he was instrumental in the creation of the city school system. Colonel Major and Mary prospered, and acquired a handsome home on Ann Street in a select neighborhood. In fact, the Major house bespoke a comfortable way of life similar to that of Locust Hill.[25]

Eleanor Rebecca (Ellie) was said to have been a leading Kentucky belle in 1866, when she married Lafayette Green of the Falls of Rough in Grayson-Breckinridge counties. She met him when he came to Frankfort as a state senator. He and his family possessed one of Kentucky's largest landholds, spread over Grayson, Breckinridge, and Ohio counties. Lafayette Green was born in Illinois of Virginia parentage and inherited his estate

Lafayette Green, the husband of Eleanor Rebecca (Ellie) Scott

from his acquisitive pioneer surveyor uncle Willis Green. Willis was a member of the Kentucky House of Representatives, 1836-1837, and then of the United States House of Representatives, 1839-1840.[26]

On their isolated barony the Greens conducted a multiplicity of businesses which ranged from large-scale farming to an important water-powered milling industry. There was between Robert Scott and his son-in-law a shared interest in the breeding of livestock. Lafayette Green bred horses and mules, and was famous for his shetland ponies. Ellie presided over the twenty-room Green mansion with the grace of a grand dame at the head of so impressive a country estate. It was said that her dining table was seldom without guests who came either to transact business with her husband or to make extended family visits.[27]

In many respects Louisa had more social verve than her sisters. She was handsome, spritely in conversation, and stylishly dressed. She married Edward Rumsey Wing of Owensboro and Louisville in 1865, almost immediately after he was discharged from the Union army. He had been engaged in the Battle of Perryville and attended General S. Jackson as an aide when that officer was mortally wounded. Wing was a graduate of Centre College, with a reputation as a superb debater. As a practicing attorney in Louisville, he played an active role in Republican politics. In

Louise Scott Wing

1868, he lost the race for state treasurer to that great financier James W. ("Honest Dick") Tate. President Ulysses Grant appointed him minister to Ecuador in 1870; he died in Quito four years later.[28]

Louisa later became the third wife of her distant cousin William Campbell Preston Breckinridge of Lexington. Colonel Breckinridge was almost the obverse of the coin of her first husband. He had a distinguished career as a Confederate officer, was an attorney of note and editor of the Lexington *Observer and Reporter* (and subsequently of the Lexington *Herald*), and was a congressman. Yet Louisa's second marriage did not prove to

W.C.P. Breckinridge, second husband of Louise Scott

be a felicitous one. Colonel Breckinridge became deeply involved in the widely publicized Madelaine Pollard breach-of-promise case in 1894, which no doubt caused him to be defeated for reelection to Congress.[29] This scandal was so emotionally unsettling for Louisa that those who knew her in later years were of the opinion that she never regained her composure after the scandal.[30]

    The fourth and last Scott daughter to marry was Henrietta or "Etti." She and Elizabeth Brown had remained single and at Locust Hill partly entrusted with the care of the farm after Robert was forced to go away to Florida for the winters. On occasion they too went south to make extended visits to their parents, where apparently Etti carried on at least one flirtation. In her thirty-fourth year, and in the year prior to Robert's death, she married First Lieutenant D. D. Mitchell of St. Louis and the United States Army. Mitchell first met Etti in 1867, when he was a cadet in the Kentucky Military Academy at Franklin Springs, five miles southeast of Frankfort, and near Locust Hill.[31] At that time he proposed marriage to her, but she refused his hand. Sixteen years later he again saw her in Louisville and renewed his suit, this time successfully. Lieutenant Mitchell wrote Robert in proper Victorian fashion asking for Henrietta's hand in marriage, even though she was of an age to be an entirely free agent. He gave a brief biographical sketch of himself, noting even the fact that he had been a failure in business, and included two character references.[32] At that time, March 29, 1883, Robert was almost too ill and feeble to raise an objection if he had one. He was delayed in answering Mitchell's letter because of illness and by the fact that Henrietta was away in Jacksonville. When Etti wrote her father that she had consented to marry the

Henrietta (Etti) Scott Mitchell, wife of David Dawson Mitchell

Lieutenant, Scott replied: "I have no reason why you should not be taken as an equal & beloved member of a united family, in which Mrs. Scott also concurs."[33] Henrietta was married on September 18, 1883, from the Episcopal Church of the Ascension in Frankfort, and went immediately to live with her new husband on the army post at Fort Randall in Dakota

Territory.[34] David Dawson Mitchell was later mortally wounded in the Philippines in 1900, and it was his daughter, Henrietta Mitchell Wiley, a resident of Buffalo, New York, who preserved the valuable collection of personal letters of the Scott family.[35]

The affections of Robert Scott's children for him were as warm and tender as their mother's was for her husband. The surviving correspondence between Robert and Elizabeth contains a distinct Browning-esque element of an ever-burgeoning romance. There never crept into any of Elizabeth's letters even a hint that "Mr. Scott" was less than lord and master of Locust Hill Plantation and of her life as well. Robert in turn reciprocated her love almost to the point of being maudlin about missing her when he was away on his numerous trips.[36] Unhappily, the entire Scott tribe seem to have been of the opinion that time stood still; most of their letters bear only a day date with no indication of the year.

On one of his many forays into the Lower South, Robert was aboard a steamboat on a Saturday night, and he missed Elizabeth mightily. He wrote her, "We have many persons on board, but I miss *you*. I wish for *you*, & I think of *you* all the time, & I dream of *you* all the night. How I do wish you were here to be my Queen among her maidens."[37] There was aboard the boat a newly married couple who reminded Robert of that day in 1831 when he married Elizabeth. The couple, he said, were "so much like ourselves when we first went to Cin. that on looking at them I found a thousand sweet memories passing through my frame, & my heart, to be with you again, & then how much I wish you were here." In his best saccharine collegiate verse he wrote,

> "But while far away from thee I roam,
> I think of her I left at home,
> And for your sake the strangers greet."

As the boat made its way out of the Ohio into the Mississippi, Robert awoke to a bright Sunday morning and added more expressions of affection to his letter. "Nothing to hug but my pillow! Nothing to kiss but your sweet image on my heart. But now what a blessing is the memory of the past, & the hope of the future. Again our souls are holding sweet communion together. Again fond arms embrace each other, & again lips meet lips & a _____ I have a pleasant sneeze." With the exception of the "pleasant sneeze," Robert's letters for a half-century literally throbbed with the tenderest sentiments for his wife and children.[38]

There springs from Elizabeth's letters a personal image of a proud, mature woman whose numerous brood gathered about her with full trust in her counsel. She was equally as poetic in her expression of affection for Robert as he was of her. When he won her hand in marriage, he also won her heart for good. On December 8, 1858, she received at one time three letters from Robert, after a fortnight of wondering if he still existed.

She wrote him immediately: "Just to think I have letters from my own dear husband after having waited two long weeks in awful suspense. The first letter I read over and over, much to the amusement of the children who no doubt thought I would wear it out in service. I wish I had your flowing pen darling to tell you all I felt about perusing your first letter written on the boat. I would fairly make the paper sing with raptuous words, but you know love that still waters run deepest, and my love is deeper in my heart for you than yours for me, but I am proud of your love and proud to be your wife, and proud to find how high you stand in the estimation of people here."[39]

Elizabeth's letters were filled with news of her children, of the physical condition and behavior of the slaves, and of the comings and goings of overseers and visitors to Locust Hill. She was teacher to her children, confidante to their thoughts and ambitions, and always their tender nurse when they were ill. Locust Hill was the focal center of her world, and she seldom ventured far beyond its boundaries. Occasionally she visited Lexington and Louisville, or she drove into Frankfort to shop and visit with her numerous relatives. But, for the most part, the outside world came to Elizabeth as the hostess of a hospitable mansion. Visitors came in almost-continuous procession; they came to discuss agricultural problems, to further the causes of improved farming and livestock breeding, to view Robert's plant and livestock experiments, to buy purebred animals, and to rent pasture space. Too, there were the editors and farm reporters who came to enlist Robert's aid in promoting their projects, and to gather notes and graphic materials for their publications.

Elizabeth's one big visit, before she and Robert went to Florida after the Civil War, was a trip to Nashville and Knoxville to visit her brother and sister and other relatives. She set out from Ducker's Station in high style, dressed in her best silks, with the prevailing fashionable two-puff sleeves. In Louisville, her distinguished cousin, the famous Dr. Lewis Rogers, was awaiting her arrival with his carriage. She was hustled off to the Rogers home to greet an assembly of members of the best old families in the city and to make further travel arrangements. She was immediately showered with invitations from relatives to come and stay with them. She was accompanied by an unidentified lad named William Nichols, who no doubt was a Nashville cousin. William served as her outside eyes and ears in gathering travel information and making arrangements. In the meantime Elizabeth was the center of a gathering of Pirtles, Prestons, Helms, and other kinfolk. They sat up until after eleven o'clock gossiping and catching up on family news. The next morning William gave her the disturbing information that he had just talked with a man who had spent four hard days trying to reach Louisville from Nashville aboard a Cumberland River steamboat. Both the Cumberland and Ohio were too low, he said, to permit satisfactory navigation. Added to this, the man had complained that the food aboard the boat was even more miserable than the vessel's progress.

News of the dismal prospect of river travel determined Elizabeth to take passage aboard a lumbering fourteen-passenger stagecoach going over Kentucky's indifferent roads. Passengers were seated ten inside this vehicle with another four atop. Dressed in her voluminous silks with wide puffed sleeves, she was made terribly uncomfortable. She suffered from the dust, heat, and the jostling.[40] At Nashville, her arrival was made unhappy by a family tragedy. A young cousin, Percy Brown, son of James Brown, had fallen out of a mulberry tree and died as a result. Too, there was a siege of white caterpillars which crawled everywhere and seemed to have had a special affinity for Elizabeth. She wrote Robert that after the terrible stagecoach ride, the young cousin's death, and the caterpillar horde, she felt that the wrath of the Lord had been visited upon her in the same measure as upon Pharaoh.[41] Despite the grievous tragedy there were family gatherings of Browns, Rucks, and their kith and kin, all of which flattered Elizabeth's vanity.[42]

On the second leg of her journey Elizabeth again set forth to Knoxville aboard a stagecoach. She was on her way to visit her sister Henrietta, who was married to Judge William Brown Reese. Never before had Elizabeth seen mountains, and Knoxville in the Great Smoky foothills impressed her as a geographical curiosity. She wrote of Knoxville to Robert that "It is up hill and down hill, and hills all around, a curious sort of town."[43] The society of Knoxville greatly flattered Elizabeth by its hospitable attention to her. She wrote Robert: "We have visitors every day since I came, and once I have spent the evening out — today several called, and one of my stage friends Mr. Charles Coffin sent me word he was coming this evening and would bring his wife. Lou said she had not seen so many persons here in a year before, and she hoped I would stay a good while as she got so many notices." Before she arrived at Knoxville, she continued, her relatives had feared that "I would be lonesome, and would not be called upon by the citizens."[44]

Away in "up-and-down-hill" Knoxville, Elizabeth's thoughts turned constantly to Robert, her children, and the comforts of Locust Hill. She told her husband that "last night I dreamed so much about you and I was so happy in your arms — now do not show this, burn it." Fortunately, Robert disregarded her instructions, and the letter has survived to convey a rich note of family history. Elizabeth told her husband that she and Henrietta had been discussing the old times when the Brown girls were young and popular. Henrietta said to Elizabeth: " 'If you had not been so deeply in love with Mr. Scott you might have been a dashing widow. . . .' I knew this was all gammon and asked what she meant. 'Oh you know James Breckinridge would have married you had you not been in such a hurry to marry Robert.' 'Well,' says I, 'does that follow of course that I would have married him, Mr. B., but then he had so much money, but that made no difference to me if I did not love him, besides he [did] not propose, but Herewith if Mr. B. had a million & offered it to me I would not have him unless I loved him, for *not to love* & marry an old man appears like *prostitution* and I could not be happy — but [with] Mr. Scott I could be happy without anything, for my love for him is based in esteem.' But between you and I Love, I don't think there is much love here yet[,] not like yours and mine."[45]

Robert and Elizabeth's letters contained warm expressions of great affection for each other, and for their children. Beyond this they seem to have been related to prominent families in central Kentucky and in the South, even as far east as South Carolina, Virginia, and Maryland. They cherished these connections, and in some way knew the locations of their kinsmen even unto third and fourth cousins. To them, family connections and ties were sacred. When they went traveling they seldom lodged in hotels and boarding houses, but with uncles and cousins, or relations of relations. With them, southern hospitality was a natural way of life rather than a myth. At Locust Hill they dispensed their own hospitality with generosity, and accepted that of others as a matter of course.

The Scott daughters went on extended visits to places as far away as New Orleans. On many of his livestock trading ventures, Robert was accompanied by daughters and a son. The girls seem to have attended social events far and wide, and they visited with kinfolk. There were visitations between the Scotts and the Greens at Falls of Rough, and the Greens came frequently to Frankfort. Ellie remained close to her family, and her husband maintained a close tie with them; Robert expressed a fondness for his son-in-law and admired his business acumen.

There were, of course, more prominent bluegrass families than the Scotts, but it is doubtful that any lived with greater internal harmony and affection or with greater social decorum. No member of the family aspired to high political office or got caught in the entangling web of gritty partisan in-fighting. None of the children aspired to riches, but they were far from being poor. Robert Scott himself was never a man of appreciable financial means. He, however, possessed wealth in land and farming skill, and in public esteem. His credit rating, as demonstrated in frequent borrowings, was good. He paid his debts, gave every appearance of being scrupulously honest in his dealings, especially in the sale and warranty of his livestock. None of his children became involved in breaches of the law or in scandals. They all honored their parents to the end of their days.

The impress of Elizabeth Brown Scott upon her children was an indelible one. She blended motherly love and concern with firm discipline, and she set and maintained proud social standards. She administered to her children's physical and emotional needs as nurse in their illnesses, drilled them in their school work, encouraged them to read books in the family library, and made many of their clothes.[46] She was quick to compare, with satisfaction, the educational progress of her children with that of their cousins. Ella and Etti were advanced in their music, while Louisa, despite her groaning, became a sharp student of French who expressed the hope she could visit France and speak the language with the natives. On the visit in Nashville Elizabeth overheard William Nichols say that Ella especially was well read in literature. This prompted her to admonish Robert to see that the girls read from the collection of Cowper and Addison in the library.[47]

There was never any question as to who was the dominant personality in the Locust Hill household. Robert presided over his family with the assurance of a successful nineteenth-century Kentuckian who was lord of all he surveyed. He gave, however, every indication of being a benevolent head of household. His letters to his children were gentle in tone, always maintaining a respectful parental barrier between them. When he expressed an opinion to them concerning their problems, he did so without nagging or scolding. When they were negligent in writing, he became upset about them, and sent off inquiries about their welfare.[48]

Through economic crises, ill health, civil war, and political confusion in the postwar years, the Scott family remained united. It kept its intimate records, giving a rare insight into the social and economic workings of a Bluegrass family living on the land in what the Kentucky romanticist might consider "better times." How much of the family still survives is not known, but through at least three generations its members maintained high social and professional standards.

In the Course of Time

BY ALMOST EVERY social and physical criterion, Locust Hill Plantation in Franklin County was one of the most pleasantly located homesteads
in nineteenth-century Kentucky. Atop a commanding hill, the mansion
site was well drained, amply exposed to sanitizing sunlight and pleasant
breezes throughout the year. Yet as pleasant as the location and the way
of life in the great house were, there hung over the place a miasmic cloud
of ill health. Some of this may have been brought to the place. Early in
the 1830s Robert W. Scott abandoned the practice of law to become a
farmer for reasons of health. Throughout the remainder of his life, he and
members of his family seem to have experienced undue illnesses. Two of
the three daughters suffered from systemic disturbances; on one occasion
Elizabeth took Eleanor to Louisville and Preston's home to have her examined thoroughly by Dr. Lewis Rogers.[1] It was thought at first that Ellie
suffered from an obstruction of the bowels, but after further examination
and observation Dr. Rogers concluded that she suffered from pleurisy.
Elizabeth herself was a victim of recurring headaches. She wrote Robert
in December 1858: "I suffer more from headache than I ever did."[2]

The slaves at Locust Hill also seem to have been almost constantly
ill. They suffered from colds, or from suspected consumption; on one occasion apparently there was an outbreak of typhoid fever. Drinking water
was drawn from two wells, while human sanitation relied upon two privies
located in the garden and orchard. Dr. Mitchell of Frankfort was a frequent visitor to Locust Hill either to treat members of the Scott family
or the slaves.[3]

At the end of the Civil War Robert Scott's health declined markedly.
He suffered from blinding headaches, as well as "catarrh" and digestive
troubles. Later he fell victim to tumors about the face and mouth, skin
rashes, hemorrhoids, and phlebitis which severely limited his mobility.
In September 1867, and in the beginning of the busy harvest season, he
was compelled to go off to the Crab Orchard Springs in Lincoln County
to seek relief by taking the mineral waters of that place. This resort had
long been popular with bluegrass families and had even attracted a good

patronage from malaria-ridden southern communities. By 1867, however, the several Kentucky mineral springs resorts had begun to wane in popularity, although there still were large numbers of people who had faith in the therapeutic properties of the various impregnated waters which bubbled upward from subterranean mineral beds along the western face of the Kentucky Knobs region. Scott, accompanied by his daughter Mary Major, made the round-about rail journey from Preston's home in Louisville to Crab Orchard. He arrived feeling "wearily and feeble."[4] Soon after dinner he took his first treatment from the Brown Spring, a vile oozing of earth minerals which were distasteful enough to make even the most confirmed invalid question their medicinal qualities.

The family gatherings at Crab Orchard were highly social affairs. Kentucky bluegrass colonels paraded their beautiful daughters, and their wives gossiped the days away, while the colonels talked about crops, horses, cows, and politics. It did not take Scott long to discover that he was among kindred souls and that the porches of the rambling hotel were but extensions of the steamboat saloons which he had enjoyed so thoroughly on his visits to the South. He wrote Elizabeth, "I find a number of old friends who greet me cordially, & I feel in congenial society with Dr. [Christopher Columbus] Graham, Dr. Elliott, Mr. Benjamin Casseday & Mr. Bridgeford of Lou. & Mr. & Mrs. Pitman, &c, &c." His ego was vastly improved because "Several other gentlemen have known me by reputation & after the formalities of introduction we felt easy with each other." Robert did not explain how he, an ardent temperance man, tolerated the jovial tippling which was such an essential part of the gatherings on the hotel porches. He assured Elizabeth that he would not burden her by reviewing business matters, but he hoped she, the overseer, and the hands would do their best. To cheer her he said, "I have already begun to operate & hope to sell enough stock to pay the expenses of this trip."[5]

The nauseous water treatments, the convivial company, and the landlord's bountiful table seemed to work their magic. Both Robert and Mary were relieved of their headaches, and he was able to sleep soundly. The Crab Orchard cure, however, was at best momentary in nature. Worry and strenuous demands at Locust Hill took their toll. Before the decade of the 1870s had dawned, Robert had come to realize that his years as an active farmer were drawing to a close.[6]

Neither Scott nor his wife fared happily in the Kentucky weather. Their chronic illnesses were such that they were forced to find a milder climate in which to spend the winters. This meant that Robert had to give up most of his activities as farmer and stock breeder and depend upon inferior farm management. The economic times in Kentucky in 1871 were stringent. Money was hard to come by, and farm products and quality livestock brought low prices; even the most successful farmer was pinched

to make economic ends meet. One readily senses the reluctance with which
Scott had to accept the impelling fact of poor health. He agonized over
the decision to sell Locust Hill. He organized a meticulously careful sales
broadside on which he offered the plantation, then containing 780 acres,
the mansion, and the livestock, for immediate sale.[7] His purebred Durham
cattle herd had dwindled to fifteen to twenty animals; all of them, however,
had distinguished herd book pedigrees. There remained a hundred "Improved Kentucky" sheep, and the same number of angora goats, all in
fine wool. Besides these, there were a hundred fattening hogs, and forty
horses which were rapidly consuming the last crop of corn. A year later
Scott wrote Rumsey and Louisa Wing, "My sheep & goats now constitute
my largest stocks, & they are favorites because they require no grain, while
one hundred head of fattening hogs eat about four barrels [of corn] daily;
& they will consume a large part of my present crop which is of average
quality."[8]

Locust Hill in 1871 was still well fenced with good gates, and the land
was in a prime state of cultivation. There remained in the field at that
date a hundred acres of corn from the previous season, and the sheds were
stuffed with an abundance of hay and oats. One senses in this extensive
advertisement, cast in characteristic Scott prose, that the nostalgic master
sat in his observatory atop the mansion and cast a soulful eye over the
scene of happier days. In lyrical style he described the attractive features
of this corner of the bluegrass country which for the past half-century
had been the hearthstone of his family's way of life.[9] Sadly, neither of
Scott's surviving sons revealed any desire to follow in their father's
footsteps, nor did any of the girls marry a farmer husband, except Eleanor
Rebecca, who married Lafayette Green, master of the imperial holdings
of the Green family at the Falls of Rough in Grayson County. Not one
of the large Scott brood was capable of relieving the aging patriarch of
the responsibilities for the large farm. Like Abraham of old, he had grown
rich in both age and knowledge, in flocks and herds, but he was too feeble to manage them or to lay a furrow on the land.

There was no lack of wishful inquirers about the price of the land
or terms of purchase, but none could raise the necessary capital to purchase Locust Hill. They came with dancing dreams in their eyes only to
have them dashed to pieces by overcautious bankers.[10] Thus the enfeebled
Scott was forced to struggle on as best he could, having to tolerate tri-
fling managers and their careless ways. He was made wholly dependent
upon these indifferent, if not rascally, overseers to run the farm for him
during a decade and a half.[11]

In August 1871, after he had publicly offered Locust Hill for sale the
preceding June, Scott purchased from Richard Marks approximately 160
acres of potential citrus lands in Orange County, Florida. This property

was located on the St. Johns River, near Lake Monroe and Orlando. A year later he acquired an additional tract of 172 acres, paying for the two parcels $437. The deeds of grant give no indication that there were other cash or credit considerations. This land was located near the village of Mellonville and the Fort Reid Post Office.[12]

Although Robert Scott was a semi-invalid, he was stirred by the spirit of adventure in developing his Florida property. He built on the shore of Silver Lake a nine-room dwelling, a barn, a combination carriage and henhouse, and two privies. The setting of this estate was radically different from that of Locust Hill. In a subsequent letter to John W. Cannon, the bedsheet and towel manufacturer of Concord, North Carolina, Scott said the residence "Is conceded to be the handsomest and prospectively the most valuable residence on any of the three lakes, Silver, Crystal & Golden."[13] It was constructed of logs mounted on lightwood piers five or six feet off the ground. Outside walls were battened over with vertical pine planking, and the interior was ceiled with planking covered with paper. The numerous windows were shaded by venetian blinds. Scott offered, unsuccessfully, to sell the North Carolina textile manufacturer this place at the depressed 1875 price of four thousand dollars.[14]

American farmers everywhere in these stringent years had to manage capital astutely in order to maintain possession of their farms. An instability of market conditions almost chronically depressed prices for farm products and livestock. Undaunted by his inability to sell the Silver Lake property, Scott set about with usual thoroughness planting orchards, a pasture, a field, and the grounds immediately surrounding the house, just as he had done at Locust Hill in the 1830s. He planted every foot of ground before Silver Lake in orange, lemon, lime, citron, and banana trees. He had muck hauled from the lakeshore and spread over the sterile sandy soil in the grove and crop areas. Ever the dedicated dirt farmer, he planted corn, two kinds of millet, pumpkin, and sweet potatoes. His vegetable garden was tended as carefully as the one had been cared for in Kentucky. To finish off his adjustments to the Florida agricultural environment, Scott had milk cows shipped from the Locust Hill herd to supply milk and butter.[15]

On the second tract of Florida land, Scott had sixteen plots of slightly more than ten acres which he offered for sale to invalids and sun-seekers who wished to flee the northern winters. These lots were precisely surveyed and illustrated on a carefully drawn map which not only located the Scott holdings, but those of neighbors on several hundred acres of surrounding properties, along with roads and streets, the post office, and public centers.[16]

Along the St. Johns, Robert and Elizabeth Scott made a host of friends, many of whom seem to have been Kentuckians. Among them, as usual, was a sprinkling of kinsmen. They entertained frequent visitors, their home sometimes serving as a base for guests who came to Florida to bask in the sun, eat their fill of citrus fruit, and see the sights. So far as he was physically able to do so, Scott tended the garden and orchard the year-round, in the winter in Florida, and in the summer in Kentucky.[17]

Unsettled and ill, Scott was tortured by restlessness the latter part of his life. In Florida he was disturbed by the bitter political conflict between the local Democrats and the radical extremists of Reconstruction.[18] Nationally, he was out of harmony with the politics of the Grant and Hayes administrations, and was uncertain earlier whether he wished to support Horace Greeley for president. At the base of his worry were the economic instabilities of the depressive years. Tortured further by dependence upon barely literate Kentucky farm managers, he could obtain information about Locust Hill only with the greatest difficulty. His sons and daughters were little more responsive correspondents, so he and Elizabeth were left to worry about the welfare of their children, if in fact they still lived.[19] There was one stalwart source of information which turned up in Florida with the regularity of the mails, and that was his son-in-law Major's Frankfort *Yeoman*. Scott read this paper almost omnivorously.[20]

In December 1876, Robert Scott wrote his maiden daughter Elizabeth Brown, almost pleadingly, for her to supply him with information about the activities at Locust Hill. He told her that the Kentucky farm, "which is the source of my temporal welfare," was much on his mind. He could have added that it was also a central force in his emotional welfare.[21] It is difficult at times to determine who was in charge at Locust Hill. Apparently, there were at least three or four persons responsible for its operation either as overseers or tenants. One or two of them may have been, in fact, purchasers of some of the land for which they were paying on a delayed plan. Robert wrote that, for all he knew, one of them, a Mr. Hockersmith, might have departed and that Locust Hill was rapidly reverting to its primeval cover of haw bushes, iron weeds, and ground-hog holes. Lizzie seemed no more attentive in her correspondence than the phlegmatic, if not illiterate and devious, Hockersmith.

In his letter to his daughter, Robert left space for Elizabeth to write an incisive letter describing their rather difficult situation, which at best seemed somewhat precarious. In part, the letter was addressed to Mary Major. She said the preceding October storm had cut the orange crop in half, and a freeze had damaged the remaining fruit. None could be shipped without the prepayment of express charges. The limes and bananas were lost, and the geraniums were frazzled and dead. Even the cabbage crop, "the staple commodity here," had suffered, first from the late summer drought, and then from the cold. Adding further to the Scott household woes was the fact that the cook did not know how to make biscuits anywhere near "Moriah's" standards, the stove was burnt out and they could not bake cakes, and in all other phases of housekeeping they were thrust upon the mercies of green twelve-dollar-a-month black help.[22]

Aside from the limited human associations about Silver Lake, there was little excitement. On one occasion Elizabeth and Robert ventured across the Florida pine barrens to visit in Tallahassee, "but," Elizabeth wrote, "Mr. Scott got impatient to be at home, and only a day after we came home we had the cold spell." She asked Mary to secure some money from the ubiquitous Hockersmith with which to pay a seamstress and a "taylor," and to pay twenty-five cents for the repairs of a satchel.[23]

Except for the generally prevailing mild and sunny climate, Florida for the Scotts was not a haven of psychological and physical peace. They were eternally short of money enough to permit them to live comfortably in a style of the past. A perpetually nagging problem in these years of greatest financial need was the sale of Locust Hill. In April 1879, the couple was almost ready to make their annual springtime journey back to Kentucky, but they had insufficient funds with which to purchase railway tickets. Robert had requested his overseer Lester to sell fifty barrels of corn and to send him $100 by return mail. Receiving no reply, he ordered Lester to increase the sale to a hundred barrels and to send the money immediately. Lester replied that he had in hand $306.75, but he failed to send it to Scott, who by then was desperate for money to pay their fare home. He wrote Etta, "I yet hope, almost without hope, to have the remittance, in a few days. He [Lester] had said $100.00 would be all the money for corn he could spare; &, if so, I will be compelled to borrow money from the Bank of Ky. to go home on . . . as my credit here is thread bare, & I am ashamed to ask it of them who are in our service."[24]

Lizzie and Etta kept the Locust Hill mansion after a fashion during the winter months, and the managers and workhands tended the land in their slovenly, careless ways. In some years Scott had been able to rent some of the fields for six dollars an acre.[25] Happily, the sheep and goats were able largely to fend for themselves as long as they were protected from predators and the ewes given some attention at lambing time. In the face of frustrations and ineffective management, dilatory correspondents, and other setbacks. Robert Scott remained ever a loyal Democrat. He pinned his hopes for better times on the election of Grover Cleveland in 1884 and the uplift of the national economy.[26]

Just as he remained a dyed-in-the-wool Democrat, he never ceased to be a farmer at heart and intellectually. From time to time the daughters at Locust Hill bundled up the inflow of mail which came to their father and sent it off to Florida. He remained an avid reader of the farm journals, and his name appeared in all sorts of subscriber lists. One journal, however, irritated him. He asked Etta especially to return the *California*

Farmer unopened, because it was being forced upon him unsolicited. In a brighter vein he told Etta that he had read in the Cincinnati *Commercial* that she had appeared at a big social dance a-sparkle with diamonds, jewels which she had borrowed from a sister. "I am thankful," he wrote, "you have a kind loving sister who will loan them to you. I wish I could afford to give you such things, & I am the more grieved that I cannot supply you with spending money. We are living here with all possible economy consistent with decency, & we hope for better times."[27]

As the years went by, Robert Scott's bodily afflictions became more debilitating. His mouth and face were subject to outbreaks of boils and tumors, much of the time forcing him to remain in bed. The annual trips between Kentucky and Florida began to make heavy physical inroads on both the Scotts. Elizabeth's headaches became more frequent and intense. She imagined that if she could get home to Locust Hill and into a quiet room upstairs where she could sleep as late as she pleased, her malady would go away. When they came home in spring 1882, Robert still had made no progress in the sale of his farm. He got out a copy of the 1871 broadside and brought the data on it up to date. By then he had sold the land down to 440 remaining acres, an area which was reduced further in the next two years to 378 acres. The fish pond had either been choked

Elizabeth Brown Scott during the Florida years, circa 1883

with silt or dried up and was overgrown. Only the mansion, a large barn, and stables were listed among the buildings. No longer were the orchards and gardens in productive condition. There remained in the pastures only ten or twelve head of thoroughbred registered Durham cattle, a hundred head each of sheep and goats, a few "practical farm grade" sows and pigs, and six or eight horses. Scott's report to the census taker in 1880 was only a thin facade of the farm's operation and animal population in the flush years before the Civil War. In fact, it is difficult to reconcile the agricultural census report with statements made by Scott in his more intimate personal documents.[28]

Conditions at Locust Hill in 1882 were a far cry from those promising years when Scott paid the Northern Kentucky Importing Company of Bourbon County $2,000 for the Durham bull Senator 2nd, and was the first Kentucky breeder to sell a native-bred sire for as much as $1,610. The lowing and bellowing of such pasture aristocrats as Constellation, Senator 2nd, Frederick, Prince, Ed Taylor, Hetty Haggin, Fair Maid of Frankfort, Alcanza, Rubiano, and others were but the dying echoes of a fading past. In a plea to history itself, Scott had his son-in-law's printing firm, Major, Johnson, and Barrett, organize and produce a sales catalog in which were included not only the revised 1871 advertisement of Locust Hill but his essays on Short-Horn Durham Cattle, "Improved Kentucky" sheep, Hogs for the Farm or Plantation, and Cashmere and Angora Goats. In essence, this booklet was a sorrowing valedictory to the closing career of one of nineteenth-century Kentucky's most progressive farmers and livestock breeders. Scott had become a prisoner of time and ill-fortune trapped in a physical and economic world over which he lacked stamina and spirit enough to condition the course of his life or to control it. The receding gardens and orchards, the weed- and-brush-choked fence rows, the deterioration of the barns, and the shrinking numbers of quality animals were but ghostly imitations of the well-ordered past in which an imaginative and industrious farmer once had operated, but was now held immobile by pain.[29]

Robert Scott made one other appeal to history in his declining years. He prepared a historical account of the struggles which he and his neighbors had undergone in the opening of the first Kentucky public schools under the provisions of the law of 1838. He submitted this document to his old "brigadier" Democratic friend Joseph Desha Pickett, with a request that it be included in the next annual report of the superintendent of public instruction. Unhappily, this was not done. Otherwise, it would have brightened considerably the dull and unimaginative recitation of educational statistics which had neither reality nor relevance to the actual condition of public education. Scott's essay, if published, would have given historians a keen insight into the workings of the rural Kentucky agrarian mind, popular resistance to public education, and the lack of leadership on the part of Kentucky officials toward lifting the Commonwealth out of its morass of illiteracy.[30]

During the summer of 1884, Robert became too ill even to think of returning to Florida. Elizabeth and her daughters moved him from Locust Hill to the Majors' home on Ann Street in Frankfort where medical care could be more immediately available. By October his condition had deteriorated to the point that it was necessary for someone to sit by his

Elizabeth Brown Scott, circa 1884

bedside and watch him around the clock. Two years before, he had made his will designating Preston to be his executor.[31] Elizabeth in this moment of anxiety turned to her son for advice and assistance in making decisions relating to Locust Hill. She still hoped to find an overseer-caretaker more responsive and reliable than she and Robert believed Hockersmith to be. More than anything else she wished to find a purchaser for the farm. A Mr. Pepper of Scott County had come to see her and said he thought the place to be worth a hundred dollars an acre, a price he seemed willing to pay if he could dispose of his own land. Mr. Pepper told her, however, that no Kentucky farmer at that time could pay $44,000 in ready cash for land; it would be necessary for him to pay an amount down in cash and give a long-term mortgage for the rest. Pepper said Hockersmith had been such an indifferent farmer that he had allowed the land and animals to reflect his shameful neglect. In the sale of the livestock, only the horses

Robert W. Scott on the eve of his death

Scott's death occurred in the home of S.I.M. and Mary Brown Scott Major on Ann Street in Frankfort

had sold well.[32] Robert's pride, the sheep and fine-fleeced goats, had sold for disappointing prices.[33]

In a letter to her daughter Ella Green, Elizabeth Scott blamed herself for leaving her husband's bedside to eat breakfast on the morning of November 8, 1884. When she returned to his room, Robert was in the throes of death. Lizzie held his hand as Mary lay beside him and held his head, while his wife Elizabeth sat by and helplessly saw his life ebb away in a gentle slumberlike peace. He died in the home of son-in-law S. I. M. Major in the rambling brick house on Ann Street, within sight of the gateway to the Kentucky Penitentiary where his father had made history as its warden. Only a few doors away was the Governor's Mansion, and nearby Gideon Shryock's noble Greek temple, the Statehouse. Robert W. Scott's life ended almost at the very spot where he had begun his journey to the East in the fall of 1829.[34]

That day in 1829 the young Jacksonian had ridden out into the larger national world with bright promise before him, and with an eagerness to see what made Jacksonian America progress. Behind him he had left an immediate chapter of troubled Kentucky history. Not far from his home Jeroboam Beauchamp had murdered Solomon P. Sharp in cold blood. Angry relief and antirelief legislators had challenged one another in furious debate over issues which had brought on the great financial panic of 1819. Across the Louisville, Frankfort, and Lexington railway tracks, there was the enclave of historic homes tucked in the elbow cul-de-sac of the Kentucky River where Robert had gone to parties and courted Elizabeth, and where the Brown clan had dominated the social scene. Life for Robert had come full circle, but in between the beginning and the end had blossomed a brilliant career as scholar, farmer, and public man.[35]

A long procession followed Scott's casket up the eastern Frankfort hill to the state cemetery, where it was deposited in a grave dug on the narrow berm of the Kentucky Palisades overlooking the river and the narrow valley beyond. A few steps to the north were the final resting places of Daniel and Rebecca Boone. In time, most of his and the Brown family members were to be gathered here about him. In death as in life, they remained a united family.

Kentucky's newspapers devoted generous space to Robert W. Scott's biographical sketch and obituary. "Marse Henry" Watterson's *Courier-Journal* reviewed his constructive career as agricultural statesman, practical farmer, stock-breeder, and public citizen. It spoke appreciatively of Scott's role in the Southern Rights Party and as a moving force in the restoration of Democrats to power. Other state editors were equally as appreciative in their praise.[36]

There was a grievous element of tragedy in the fact that so imaginative and innovative a farmer had to be so treacherously stricken at a time when the Commonwealth of Kentucky so desperately needed his kind of leadership in strengthening the field of scientific agriculture. For Scott personally, it was traumatic to have to stand by and see his fine bluegrass plantation deteriorate under the ill-management of sloppy and uncaring supervisors. He was never able to find an overseer who could be trusted, let alone who possessed knowledge and energy enough to operate a modern farm. Buildings, fences, orchards, and other improvements on such a farm are fragile things when not given constant care. The gentle ridges and valley swales became choked with weeds and brush, finely bred goats and sheep dragged their silky coats through trash growth befouling their fleeces with damaging debris, a thing which was anathema to Scott. No attempt was made to breed up the dwindling cattle herd, or to improve the drove of ravenous hogs. This was the main source of the tortuous anxiety so often expressed in the letters of Robert and Elizabeth.

In the longer and more durable range of Kentucky history, few if any bluegrass farmers of the nineteenth century articulated so clearly the necessity for adopting the newer findings in scientific agriculture. Certainly, none left behind a more graphic historical document which described early national and local political personalities, or such a large volume of intimate personal documentary sources. The Locust Hill mansion itself still stands a time-defying monument of stately dignity atop its pleasant site. It faces off into a sprawling suburban Frankfort with its warrens of shopping centers and subdivisions. Before its door an endless procession of traffic roars by furiously on a four-lane federal interstate highway which connects the Falls of the Ohio with the Port of Norfolk from which Robert sailed in the fall of 1829 for New York. The right-of-way of the road slashes mercilessly through the once-sylvan pastures and fields where aristocratic livestock grazed contentedly and where once slaves spread thousands of shocks of hemp to rot, or where they shucked almost countless bushels of corn. With all the changes, Locust Hill, now called Scotland,[37] stands an honest landmark to another, and perhaps more romantic, age of an agrarian way of life in the Kentucky Bluegrass. Beyond this, it was the homeseat of a numerous family drawn into close unity by bonds of abiding filial affection and devotion.

BOOK ONE
MEMORANDA ITINERIS

1. Robert Wilmot's grandfather was John Scott, a Georgetown, Kentucky, farmer and merchant. He came to the Elkhorn Valley in 1785 from Madison County, Virginia. The "single lady" was Elizabeth Watts Brown, whom he married October 20, 1831. The Scott-Major genealogy is in possession of Mrs. Hartley Ferguson, Richmond, Kentucky; the Scott-Green genealogy is in the manuscript collection of Western Kentucky University, Bowling Green, Kentucky. Biographical sketch of Robert Wilmot Scott, in *The Biographical Encyclopedia of Kentucky* (Cincinnati, 1878), 222-27.

2. Samuel M. Wilson said there were only 240 Indians at the most, and 182 Kentucky officers and men. *The Battle of the Blue Licks* (Lexington, 1927), 73-74. The battle was fought August 19, 1782. Lewis Collins said there were five hundred warriors. Sixty Kentuckians were killed, among them Daniel Boone's son Israel, Stephen Trigg, John Bulger, Levi Todd, and Silas Harlan. Lewis and Richard H. Collins, *History of Kentucky* 2 vols. (Covington, Ky., 1874), 2:657.

3. Greenup County was formed in 1803. Greenupsburg was incorporated February 14, 1818, and the name was not changed until March 13, 1872. Kentucky *Acts* (1871-72), 4.

4. There was located in Greenup County the Laurel, Hummell, Bellefonte, Pennsylvania, Clinton, Raccoon, Caroline, and Buffalo furnaces. Robert Peter identified seven varieties of iron ore with one variety yielding 40.56 percent iron per ton of ore. Collins, *History of Kentucky*, 2:299-300; A. M. Miller, *The Geology of Kentucky* (Frankfort, 1919), 314-15; David Dale Owen, *Fourth Report of the Geological Survey in Kentucky* (Frankfort, 1861), 166-72. Scott recorded an accurate general description of the process of smelting iron ore.

5. Count Francesco Arese wrote in 1837, "I reached Guyandotte. The region I went through and the valley of the Kanawha are very well cultivated and scattered with charming and rich farms. As Guyandotte, at the extreme western tip of Virginia, I left that beautiful country, not indeed with tears in my eyes, but certainly with great regret." Count Francesco Arese, *A Trip to the Prairies and in the Interior of North America* [1837-1838] Trans. Andrew Evans (New York, 1934), 39.

6. Charleston, Virginia, was founded in 1794 in Kanawha County on the northern bank of the Great Kanawha River. In 1829 it had a population of 9,326. Few travelers of note visited interior western Virginia in the earlier years. Count Arese wrote, "I took in the pretty little town of Charleston, west Virginia." *Ibid.*, 38; Fifth United States Census, 88.

7. Arese described almost the identical view of the salt works, in his *Trip to the Prairies*, 38. See also Elizabeth Goodall, "The Manufacture of Salt — Kanawha's First Commercial Enterprise," *West Virginia History* 26 (1964-65): 234-50; James G. Jones, "The Early History of the Natural Gas Industry in West Virginia," *ibid.* 10 (1948-49), 49:79-81; James Laing, "The Early Development of the Coal Industry in the Western Counties of Virginia, 1800-1865," *ibid.* 27 (1965-66):144-46.

8. "I went to see the Falls of the Kanawha, which are pretty enough without being anything remarkable. There is plenty of water but it falls only 15 or 20 feet," Arese, *Trip to the Prairies*, 38.

9. Greenbriar County was divided into Kanawha County in October 1788, and provisions were made to construct a road to the Little Kanawha, and another from the Kanawha to Lexington, Kentucky. W. W. Hening, *The Statutes at Large; being a Collection of all the Laws of Virginia, . . . 1619-1792*, 13 vols. (New York and Philadelphia, 1809-23), 12:282-83, 669-71. The bridge over the Gauley River was begun in 1821 and was completed in 1824. This road was used frequently by Kentucky hog drovers, and West Virginia salt haulers. On July 11, 1826, vandals destroyed the original bridge in order to protect their ferry business. The uncovered wooden structure over which Scott crossed the river was constructed in 1828. It cost a thousand dollars a year to maintain the road from Lewisburg to the Falls of the Kanawha, hence the high toll. J. M. Callahan, *Semi-Centennnial History of West Virginia* (Morgantown, W. Va., 1926), 95-96.

10. Robert W. Scott was almost fanatical about drink and the temperance movement which in 1829 was gathering momentum throughout the nation. The movement was begun in 1808 by Dr. Billy Clark in Moreau, New York. It made little headway until 1825 when Protestant evangelists took up the cause. What Scott saw in 1829 was a gathering of forces. John A. Krout, *The Origins of Prohibition* (New York, 1925), and Daniel Dorchester, *The Liquor Problem in all Ages* (New York, 1884).

11. The main spa was located on Howard's Creek. It was one of many in the cluster of popular Virginia mineral springs in this area. The discovery of the White Sulphur Spring was of uncertain date, possibly as early as 1778. Log cabins were built on the site in the 1784-1786 period. It was said to have been well known to the Shawnee Indians. White Sulphur became popular after 1820 and Scott was there in a period of expansion. One of the ridges which Scott saw, Kate Mountain, was named for a legendary Indian maiden. The springs are 2,000 feet above sea level, and the water holds at 62° Fahrenheit. William Burke, *The Mineral Springs of Virginia, with Remarks on Their Use, and the Diseases to which they are Applicable* (New York, 1842), and Charles Daubeny, *Journal of a Tour Through the United States, and in Canada, made during the years 1837-38* (Oxford, England, 1843).

12. Other visitors agreed with Robert Scott that the western Virginia mountains and streams were beautiful. Among them were Caroline Gilman, *The Poetry of Traveling in the United States* (New York, 1838), 348-69; Harriett Martineau, *Retrospect of Western Travel*, 2 vols. (London, 1838), 1:270-76; and an anonymous foreign traveler quoted in Henry Howe, *Historical Collection of Virginia* (Charleston, S.C., 1845), 456-57.

13. Located in present Greenbriar County, West Virginia, in the confluence of two narrow valleys about five miles from Warm Springs. This is also a thermal spring. See *Appleton's Illustrated Handbook of American Travel* (New York, 1857), Virginia Section.

14. Warm Springs, also in Greenbriar County, is in a picturesque setting.The Rock or lookout on the mountain is 2,700 feet above sea level as estimated by Paul Nicklin, *Letters Descriptive of the Virginia Springs; the Roads Leading Thereto, and Doings Thereat* (Philadelphia, 1835), 20-46.

15. The Blowing Cave is located on a ledge overlooking Cow Pasture Creek west of the village of Millboro. The semi-circular entrance is about four feet high, and was in 1829 forty feet above the road. The blowing sound resulted from changing temperatures.

16. The original owner of the 151 acres surrounding the Natural Bridge was Thomas Jefferson. The bridge was discovered by Thomas Sallings in 1734, and acquired as a royal grant by Jefferson in 1774. See Marshall Fishwick, ed., *Rockbridge County, Virginia* (Richmond, 1852), 40, 112; Howe, *Historical Collections*, 57-60. "This bridge, called 'Natural' because nature made it might perhaps with even better reason be called the supernatural bridge, so large is it and so sublime in its savage beauty." Arese, *Trip to the Prairies*, 28;

Thomas Jefferson, *Notes on the State of Virginia* (Richmond, 1853; orig. pub., 1785), 18, 34-38.

17. Scott apparently made only a brief stop in Lexington. He referred to Washington College, established in 1776. The town itself was founded on twenty-six and three-quarters acres of land in 1778 and named for Lexington, Massachusetts. Fishwick, *Rockbridge County*, 39; Howe, *Historical Collections*, 448-49.

18. Lexington, Virginia, was a stronghold of Scotch Presbyterianism. The citizens of the town were puritanical and conservative according to Howe, *Historical Collections*, 453-55.

19. John Edward Caldwell, *A Tour through Part of Virginia, in the Summer of 1808* . . . (New York, 1809), 23-26; Henry Tudor, *Narrative of a Tour in North America* . . . , 2 vols. (London, 1834), 1:457-66.

20. The Virginia General Assembly chartered the University of Virginia, February 21, 1818. After much debating and political maneuvering the institution was located in Charlottesville. When Scott visited the campus the buildings were still under construction. At the time of Jefferson's death six of his planned buildings had been constructed, and in 1830 the plant was valued at $333,095.12. There were 120 students enrolled. Philip Alexander Bruce, *History of the University of Virginia, 1818-1919*, 2 vols. (New York, 1920-21), 1:90-287.

21. The town of Richmond was surveyed in 1737 by Colonel William Byrd, II, incorporated in 1742, and became the capital of Virginia in 1779. John P. Little, *Richmond* (Richmond, 1851).

22. The Eagle Tavern was one of Richmond's most popular inns. It, however, suffered from changes in ownership, and loss of much of its prestigious clientele. A Colonel Radford was proprietor, and an "Old Citizen" said he "was of as grand dimensions as was his house's and of great resort." *Richmond in By-gone Days by an Old Citizen* ([Richmond?], 1859), 172. Later the house was owned by Esme Smock. It was in the Eagle that John Marshall began his examination of Aaron Burr. *Ibid.*, 131. Not all the Eagle's patrons were enamored of its hospitality. Ralph Izard of Charleston, South Carolina, wrote his mother, "Of all the Taverns I ever was in that yclept Eagle is the worst." Ralph Izard to Alice de Lancey Izard, communicated to Helen G. McCormack, Charleston Historical Society. Also, Mary Wingfield Scott, *Old Richmond Neighborhoods* (Richmond, 1950), 131-32.

23. Scott could not have chosen a more historic moment to arrive in Richmond. This was the beginning of a truly significant state constitutional convention which convened October 5, 1829, when James Monroe escorted James Madison to the presidential chair. Richmond *Enquirer*, October 6, 1829. Delegates included those who were both locally and nationally famous. Certificates of their elections are contained in papers filed by the clerks of the convention, and are now in the Virginia State Archives where the author examined them in August 1985.

24. The Richmond *Enquirer* during the latter months of 1829 carried full accounts of the convention. The judiciary committee made its report on Saturday, October 24, 1829.

25. W. P. Palmer and H. W. Fournoy, eds., *Calendar of Virginia State Papers*, 11 vols. (Richmond, 1875-93), 10: 518, 571. Philip Pendleton Barbour was forty-six years of age. He had practiced law for a brief time in Bardstown, Kentucky, but returned to Gordonsville in Orange County, Virginia. He was a member of Congress from 1814-1825, and from 1827 to 1830, when he resigned. *Biographical Directory of the American Congress, 1774-1949*, (Washington, D. C., 1950), 813-14; Dumas Malone, "Philip Pendleton Barbour," *Dictionary of American Biography*, 1:594-96.

26. Scott added an initial to Andrew Stevenson's name. There is no city directory for Richmond for these years, and it is not possible to locate precisely the site of the Stevenson home. Stevenson was Speaker of the United States House of Representatives in 1829. *Biographical Directory of Congress*, 1863. Near the time Scott called on the Madisons, Anne Royal also visited with them. She wrote, "There is more indulgence in her eyes than any

mortal's." Katherine Anthony, *Dolly Madison: Her Life and Times* (New York, 1949), 316-17.

27. Dolly Madison was sixty-eight years of age, eighteen years younger than James. Maud W. Goodwin, *Dolly Madison* (New York, 1896), 216; J. B. Cutts, *Memoirs and Letters of Dolly Madison* (New York, 1886), 5; Anthony, *Dolly Madison*, 9.

28. John Bryce was born in Goochland County, May 31, 1784, practiced law in Richmond and Lynchburg, and was master in chancery under John Marshall. He became a Baptist minister in 1822. In 1827 he moved to Georgetown, Kentucky, where he was minister and original board member of Georgetown College. J. H. Spencer, *A History of Kentucky Baptists from 1769-1885*, 2 vols. (Cincinnati, 1885), 2: 294-98; B. O. Gaines, *The B. O. Gaines History of Scott County*, 2 vols. (Georgetown, Ky., 1904), 1:78-79, 2:58-59.

29. Scott erred in his guess as to Madison's age. He was born March 5/6, 1750/1751. Irving Brant, *James Madison: The Virginia Revolutionist, 1751-1780* (Indianapolis, 1941), 29-30.

30. This description conforms with Harriett Martineau's. See *Retrospect of Western Travel*, 2:2-4.

31. A delegate from Augusta, Rockbridge, and Pendleton counties. *Calendar of Virginia State Papers*, 10: 353; original clerk returns of election results, Virginia State Archives.

32. John Marshall represented nine James River counties. *Ibid.*

33. James Monroe presided over the convention until December 12, 1829. He represented Loudon and Fairfax counties. *Ibid.* He was born April 28, 1758, and was seventy-one in 1829. W. P. Cresson, *James Monroe* (Chapel Hill, N.C., 1946), 493-95, 478-81; Harry Ammon, *James Monroe: The Quest for National Identity* (New York, 1941), 540, 563-66. The following November Philip Hone saw Monroe in New York and described him as being feeble, in ill health, but mentally alert. *The Diary of Philip Hone, 1825-1851*, 2 vols. (New York, 1889), 1:25.

34. John Randolph represented Charlotte, Halifax, and Prince Edward counties. He was born June 2, 1773. Hugh A. Garland, *The Life and Times of John Randolph of Roanoke*, 2 vols. (New York, 1850), 2:4.

35. W. B. Giles represented six middle eastern counties including Petersburg. *Calendar of Virginia State Papers*, 10:353.

36. Alexander Campbell, a founder of the Disciples Church, represented the four western Ohio River counties. *Ibid.*, 354; Robert Richardson, *Memoirs of Alexander Campbell*, 2 vols. (Philadelphia, 1868, 1870).

37. The museum was erected in 1817 in the southeastern corner of the Capitol Square facing Twelth Street by Richard Loring, a painter. It quickly collected twenty thousand objects ranging from natural curiosities to paintings. Scott, *Old Richmond Neighborhoods*, 104; "Old Citizen," *Richmond in By-Gone Days*, 285-89.

38. The Virginia Penitentiary was built in 1797-1800. Scott, *Old Richmond Neighborhoods*, 206. It was located on Oregon Hill in South Richmond.

39. Between the years 1815 and 1818 the United States purchased twelve armory and arsenal sites. Richmond was one of these. Thomas H. S. Hamersby, *Complete Regular Army Register of the United States for One Hundred Years, 1779-1879* (Washington, D. C., 1880), 802. In 1831 the Richmond Arsenal was listed among the eight important installations in the country. U. S. House of Representatives, *Executive Documents* (Washington, D. C., 1831), 1:145.

40. The Eagle Tavern was built in 1787 on the south side of Main Street, at Twelfth and Thirteenth streets. Scott, *Old Richmond Neighborhoods*, 131-32.

41. The Virginia State Library was provided for by law January 23, 1823. It is interesting that the library was organized ostensibly to aid in the editing, publication, and sale of Hening's *Statutes*. In 1829 the Library spent $7,005.61, much of which went to purchase books. *First Annual Report of the Virginia State Library for the Year ended June 30, 1904* (Richmond, 1904), 4-11.

42. On the night of December 26, 1811, a fire occurred in a theatre which resulted in the loss of seventy lives. Citizens of Richmond decided that a church would best memorialize this tragedy, and the famous architect Robert Mills of South Carolina was employed to design the building. It was completed in 1814. Although an Episcopal church, it was used largely as a community institution. Scott, *Old Richmond Neighborhoods*, 102-3.

43. All of these paintings except those of Judge Bushrod Washington and the Duke of Sussex still hang in the Virginia capitol. However, the Virginia State Library has no record that the state has ever owned portraits of Daniel Boone and Judge Robert Trimble (who had died the year Scott visited Richmond). Robert Trimble was an associate justice of the United States Supreme Court. *Portraits and Statuary of Virginians* (Richmond, 1977), 41, 73, 75. It may have been that Chester Harding's famous portrait of Daniel Boone was once on temporary exhibit.

44. Scott was mistaken — the Richmond Society for the Promotion of Temperance was organized January 7, 1829. The meeting he attended had been called to discuss the admission of women and to re-elect the officers. *The First Annual Report of the Richmond Society for the Promotion of Temperance* (Richmond, 1830), 2, 15.

45. Charles Joseph Latrobe traveled over the James from Norfolk to Richmond at a slightly earlier date. He wrote, "The ascent of the James River was interesting, though the scenery is rarely of a bold character." See Charles Joseph Latrobe, *The Rambler in North America*, 2 vols. (London, 1836), 2:4. Captain Basil Hall descended the James on his tour. He said, "In the evening we reached the town of Norfolk after a voyage of 150 miles in the steam boat. The whole expenses of our party, which consisted of three grown-up persons and one child was 12½ dollars, breakfast, dinner, and tea included. Thus we traveled for very little more than two cents, or about a penny a mile." Basil Hall, *Travels in North America, in the Years 1827 and 1828*, 3 vols. (London, 1829), 3:81.

46. Fort Powhatan was built by early Virginia settlers on the south side of the James and near a modern village named Little Brandon. Hamersby, *Complete Army Register*, 149; Francis R. Heitman, *Historical Register and Dictionary of the United States Army* (Washington, D. C., 1903), 535.

47. Fortress Monroe was located on the site of Old Point Comfort. It was begun in 1818 on the tongue of land bounded by the waters of the Chesapeake Bay and Hampton Roads. Hamersby, *Complete Army Register*, 145.

48. Colonel James House was a member of the 1st Artillery. *Ibid.*, 521.

49. See Joseph Martin, *A New and Comprehensive Gazetteer of Virginia and the District-Columbia* (Charlottesville, 1835), 247-48.

50. Norfolk was a busy entrepot for Virginia and Chesapeake Bay area. The coastal shipping also furnished virtual shuttle service between Virginia and New York. At one time Norfolk had a virtual monopoly on the West Indies trade. *Ibid.*

51. Fort Norfolk was located on the east side of the Norfolk Harbor a mile north of the city, and on the right bank of the Elizabeth River. The United States Navy had assumed charge of it in 1824. Hamersby, *Complete Army Register*, 147; Heitman, *Historical Register*, 529.

52. The Rip Raps were partly built in 1818 by Elijah Mix. The awarding of this contract by Secretary of War John C. Calhoun had resulted in a public scandal. Work on the artificial island was halted in 1822. See *American State Papers: Military Affairs*, 2; 431-49, 715. Also *Niles Weekly Register* 22 (June 15, 1822): 251-56; (June 29, 1822): 279-82.

53. "The Washington, the Waverley, the Mansion House, the American, the Carleton, the Globe, and the Athenaeum, are all species establishments of the same nature. . . ." James Silk Buckingham, *America, Historical, Statistic, and Descriptive*, 3 vols. (London, 1841), 1:47.

54. The Peale Museum in New York was developed by Reuben Peale. It was opened to the public on October 26, 1825, the same day the Erie Canal was opened to traffic. Located

in the Parthenon on Broadway opposite the city hall, the collection ranged from paintings to mineral and animal curiosities. Charles Coleman Sellers, *Charles Willson Peale* (New York, 1969), 383.

55. The editor has been unable after a diligent search to identify the Susan and Deborah Tripp whom Scott described. The New York newspapers seem not to have noticed their presence in the city. They may have been the two obese children from Hyde Park, or Duchess County. Americans of the era seemed to be interested in abnormally large human beings. Hezekiah Niles noted the passing of the Irish giant Charles Hammon who stood seven feet, six inches barefooted. His place in the news was taken by a young woman named Melius, a well formed and beautiful girl, though seven feet high; she was said to be a native of South Carolina, "18 years old, remarkable in the symetry of her form and fairness of complexion." Then there was the Pitna, Switzerland, nineteen year old giant who stood nine feet three inches tall. *Niles Weekly Register* 37 (October 31, 1829):153, 217.

56. At the time Scott visited New York both American and European inventors and scientists were making advances in microscopic construction and magnification. The amount of magnification Scott mentions seems a bit extravagant. He did not record enough information to identify the microscope and its maker, but it seems likely that he saw the work of Charles Spencer, Edward Thomas, or Alden Allen. Most likely it was that of Spencer.

57. Isaac Chauncey, born in Connecticut, was a prominent naval officer. William B. Weaver, *United States Official Register of all Officers and Agents Civil, Military, and Naval in the Services of the United States on the Thirtieth of September 1833* (Philadelphia, 1834), 121. "In company with a most intelligent and kindly friend, who was lately mayor of the city, I visited the Navy Yard at Brooklyn. Commodore Chauncey, the commander, is a fine specimen of an old sailor of the true breed. He has a good deal of the *Benbow* about him, and one can read his open weatherbeaten countenance, that it has braved both the battles and the breeze." Thomas Hamilton, *Men and Manners in America*, 2 vols. (Philadelphia, 1833), 1:152.

58. The *United States*, built 1779-1797, commissioned July 1, 1797, 1,576 tons. Jack Bauer, *Ships of the Navy, 1775-1869* (Troy, N.Y., 1969), 1, 13.

59. The *Ohio*, built 1817-1820, 2,757 tons, complement of 820 men, built in New York, and at the time the finest "74" in the world. *Ibid.,* 6.

60. The *Brandywine* had a rugged history. It was a vessel of 1,708 tons and carried a complement of 480 men. It had been the *Susquehanna* until 1823. *Ibid.,* 18-19.

61. The *Fulton* was an experimental ship of 2,475 tons, and 153.2 feet long. Its designer and builder, Robert Fulton, created this catamaran type of ship to protect the New York Harbor. It had on board hot shot furnaces, and plans were to use 100 columbiads. It was built in the New York Navy Yard, and was propelled by center paddle wheels, and was the first power-driven warship in world history. Peter Kemp, ed., *The Oxford Companion to Ships and the Sea* (New York, 1976), 98. The *Fulton* was destroyed in an accidental explosion on June 4, 1829. *Niles Weekly Register* 36 (June 18, 1829): 252.

62. The Brooklyn Navy Yard was located on the eastern bank of the East River, and was the main ship building facility of the United States Navy. Kemp, *Oxford Companion,* 593.

63. The *United States* was a regular coastwise vessel whose comings and goings were not listed in the ship arrivals by the New York papers.

64. First settled April 18, 1638. George L. Clark, *A History of Connecticut and Its People and Institutions* (New York, 1914), 17; United States *Fifth Census*, 27.

65. Jeremiah Day was president of Yale College. Scott visited the school in one of its stirring historical moments. Its faculty had just published the famous seminal report on teaching and higher education which was to have such an impact in America. Its principles were just being applied at Yale in 1829. Reuben A. Holden, *Profiles and Portraits of Yale University Presidents* (Freeport, Maine, 1968), 63-68.

66. "The principal edifices of Yale College, four stories in height, face the entire length of the western boundary of the green presenting an imposing aspect. Yale College from which New Haven derives much celebrity, was founded in 1700, and is one of the oldest and most distinguished literary institutions in this country. . . . The mineralogical cabinet, another large building, is situated in the rear of the line of college edifices. It contains the great cabinet of Colonel Gibbs, consisting of 10,000 specimens, collected by him in Europe during the revolutionary period there, at the commencement of the present century, together with very large subsequent additions." John Haywood, *A Gazetteer of the United States of America* (Hartford, Conn., 1853), 467-77. An illustration of Yale University as it appeared at the time of Scott's visit appears in Clark, *A History of Connecticut*, 60.

67. On the road from New Haven to Hartford Scott passed through Cheshire, Southington, and Farmington, a distance of thirty-seven miles. See *An Accompaniment to Mitchell's Reference and Distance Map of the United States* (Philadelphia, 1835), 223.

68. In 1792 the General Assembly appointed a committee to have a statehouse built in Hartford. The building was completed in 1795. In 1763 a new statehouse was built in New Haven, and was replaced by a new one in 1827. Hartford did not become the sole capital of Connecticut until 1875. Clark, *A History of Connecticut*, 60.

69. The Hartford Convention was made up of delegates from five New England states. It met December 15-January 1815 to discuss problems confronting the section which arose out of the War of 1812. Theodore Dwight, *History of the Hartford Convention* (New York, 1933), 1-2, 368-98.

70. Scott was mixed up in his Connecticut history. The charter issued to the colony in 1662 by Charles II was in danger of being withdrawn by Sir Edmund Andros in 1687. It was said that the charter was spread out on a table below the New England colonial governor when the light was blown out. When the candles were relighted the charter was gone. Captain Joseph Wadsworth had fled with the document and hid it in a hollow oak tree near Westogue Brook. The oak became a revered symbol of Connecticut's independence as a chartered colony. W. H. Gocher, *Wadsworth or the Charter Oak* (Hartford, Conn., 1904), 251-354.

71. The city of Providence had a population of 16,833 in 1830. It was founded in 1636, and began operating as an organized town in 1701. In 1830 it depended upon manufacturing and shipping as a source of support. Welcome Arnold Greene, *The Providence Plantations for Two Hundred and Fifty Years* (Providence, 1886), 21-23, 67-77; Abstract, *United States Fifth Census* (Washington, 1832), 6.

72. Thomas Hamilton wrote of his arrival in Providence, "On reaching the hostelry, however, its external appearance was far from captivating. There was no sign board, nor did the house display any external symbol of the hospitality within." Hamilton, *Men and Manners*, 1:80-81.

73. Providence in November 1829 was a city of many church steeples, and each one had a bell. None, however, rang out so boomingly as the 2,215 pound monster in the First Baptist Church belfry. This bell was cast in London, and when it cracked in 1787 it was recast in America. Greene, *Providence Plantations*, 143-46.

74. The Arcade, a commercial landmark erected in 1827, fronting on Westminster and Weybosset Streets, was a Greek Revival or Federalesque structure, 188 x 216 feet, and cost $145,000. It was owned by the Arcade Corporation and Cyrus Butler. *Ibid.*, 76. Thomas Hamilton was less than enchanted by the structure. He wrote, "The only building which makes any pretension to architectural display is the arcade, faced either extremity with an Ionic portico. Judging by the eye, the shaft of the columns is in the proportion of the Grecian Doric, an order beautiful within itself, but which, of course, is utterly barbarized by an Ionic entablature. By the way, I know not anything in which the absence of taste in America is more signally displayed than in their architecture." Hamilton, *Men and Manners*, 1:82-83.

75. This institution had its beginnings in 1764 as the College of Rhode Island. In 1804 its name was changed to Brown University in honor of Nicholas Brown. Greene, *Providence Plantations*, 57-58.

76. This school opened for classes November 8, 1784. It was partially endowed by the textile manufacturer Moses Brown. *Ibid.*, 172-73.

77. The *Chancellor Livingston* was a regular commuter boat between Providence and New York. In May 1831 it accidentally rammed and destroyed the commuter *Washington*. *Ibid.*, 129. "In a sea-port," wrote Thomas Hamilton, "one generally takes a glance at the harbour, to draw some conclusions, however, uncertain, with regard to traffic of the place. The guide-books declare, that Providence has a good deal of foreign commerce. It may be so, but in the bay I could only count two square-rigged vessels, and something under a score of sloops and schooners." Hamilton, *Men and Manners*, 1:83.

78. Sam Patch (1807-1829) may have worked briefly in one of the Pawtucket cotton mills. At least he was born in Rhode Island. He was a foolhardy stunt man who specialized in jumping off cliffs, bridges, scaffolds, and all other high places. He made his final jump into the Genessee Falls in Rochester, New York, November 13, 1829. In mid-air his body took an unexpected twist; on March 17, 1830, it was found frozen in a block of ice at the mouth of the Genesee River. S. A. Ferrall, *A Ramble of Six Thousand Miles in the U. S. A.* (London, 1835), 27.

79. James Silk Buckingham said, "The Tremont House is nearly as large as the Astor House in New York , and much more agreeable, because it is more quiet and less crowded." *America*, 3:306. "Most gratifying is it to a traveller in the United States, when, sick to death of the discomforts of the road, he finds himself fairly housed in the Tremont Hotel. The establishment is on a large scale, and admirably conducted." Hamilton, *Men and Manners*, 1:88.

80. "The Tremont [Theatre] is the largest, most expensive, and most fashionable. It is little inferior in size or elegance to Drury Lane or Covent Garden in London; but, except when some prominent actor or actress is engaged, it is but thinly attended." Buckingham, *America*, 3:372.

81. This was the English-Jewish actor Junius Brutus Booth (1796-1852). He played various major and minor Shakespearean roles and was popular on the American theatrical circuit. Asia Booth Clarke, *The Elder and Younger Booth* (Boston, 1882), 3:109; Noah M. Ludlow, *Dramatic Life as I Found It* (St. Louis, 1880), 619.

82. Boston had a succession of museums. Buckingham described the one Scott visited, "A third was erected on the same spot, and opened the same year [1807]; but in 1825 it was sold for $5,000 to a new body of proprietors, who established the New England Museum, which is the one now existing, and was opened in 1818." *America*, 3:274-75.

83. In 1793 Boston named a square for Benjamin Franklin, and Charles Bullfinch erected an urn in honor of this famous citizen. A monument was erected over the graves of Franklin's parents. James Parton, *Life and Times of Benjamin Franklin*, 2 vols. (New York, 1864), 2:633.

84. "The college buildings are agreeably situated, and surrounded with lawns and trees. University Hall, which is built of granite, is 104 feet long by 50 broad, and 42 feet high. The separate colleges, of which there are six, are of brick, but substantially built, and furnished with every requisite accommodation, as well as with a library of 30,000 volumes, and a most complete philosophical apparatus for experiments." Buckingham, *America*, 3:326-27.

85. Scott was correct in saying that he viewed a large and valuable collection of minerals. This collection was begun in the 1780s, and was placed on public exhibit in the period around 1793. Today it numbers approximately 100,000 minerals and approximately 400,000 rock samples. They are on display in 125 cases containing over 8,000 mineral specimen. William Metropolis to author, January 3, 1983. "Mineralogical and Geological Museum," in *Harvard Museums, Their Locations and Guides* (Cambridge, Mass., n.d.).

86. Josiah Quincy (1772-1864) was elected president of Harvard University January 29, 1829, and served in that office until August 27, 1845. Edmund Quincy, *Life of Josiah Quincy* (Boston, 1867), 429-54.

87. At the time Scott visited the monument work had been suspended on it. It had cost to date $57,000 and it was estimated it would take $81,835 to finish it. The obelisk had not been constructed to its full height of 230 feet and the Association was broke. *Niles Weekly Register* 31 (July 11, 1829): 518-19.

88. It seems that everybody who visited Boston in this era went to see the penitentiary. It was considered a moral prison. One observer wrote, "This penitentiary is extremely well conducted. The attention which is paid to the state, and to the excellent chaplain to whose care they are confined." William Crawford, *Report on the Penitentiaries of the United States Ordered by the House of Commons* (London, 1854), 57-67.

89. The Boston Navy Yard was located in Charlestown, and was one of the major United States building and maintenance facilities. Bauer, *Ships of the Navy*, xi.

90. "Two noble vessels, of the latter class [of the line] lay alongside the yard, there being water enough for the largest ships to lie close to the wharves at low-water springtides, and never touch the ground. These ships were the Columbus and the Ohio, both fitting out for foreign stations; and these we were invited to inspect. The Ohio was built in New York, in 1820; the Columbus in Washington in 1819. They are both called 74s, but, like our ships carry more guns than they are rated at." Buckingham, *America*, 3:382.

91. The Marine Railway, an invention of Commodore Rogers, was intended for propelling ships into and out of the water. It was merely an inclined plane. Balthasar H. Meyer, ed., *History of Transportation in the United States before 1860* (Washington, D. C., 1917), 586.

92. Technically Jerome Bonaparte, the spoiled member of the Bonaparte family, was absent without leave from the French navy. On Christmas Eve in 1803 he married Elizabeth Patterson, daughter of the wealthy shipping merchant of Baltimore. Jerome was heedless enough to have shot a horse. He and Elizabeth went on a delayed honeymoon up the Hudson and to Niagara Falls. Eugene L. Didier, *The Life and Letters of Mme. Bonaparte* (New York, 1879), 3-11; Alice Desmond, *Bewitching Betsy Bonaparte* (New York, 1858), 12-24. The episode Scott mentions sounds more like one of Jerome "Bo" Bonaparte's capers. "Bo" was the son of Elizabeth and Jerome. His grandfather Patterson had him entered as a student at Harvard. Because of a roisterous society party, President John Thornton Copeland suspended him. Desmond, *Betsy Bonaparte*, 204-10.

93. Mr. Stepherd is unidentified, but there is reason to believe he was connected with one of the Northhampton textile mills. One of the larger mills of that place employed fifty laborers, had an investment of fifty thousand dollars, but turned out only twenty-two yards of superfine broadcloth a day. Victor S. Clark, *History of Manufactures in the United States, 1607-1860*, 3 vols., rev. ed. (Washington, D. C., 1929), 1:563. At the time of Scott's visit, the New England woolen industry was suffering from the restrictions of the famous tariff of "abominations" 1828. *Niles Weekly Register* 31 (July 11, 1829):518.

94. This may have been Francis Lee, an assistant quartermaster. Hambersby, *Complete Army Register*, 575. The United States maintained eight "important" arsenals and six minor ones. There were three principal ones. *Executive Documents of the House of Representatives*, 1:144-45.

95. The manufacturing process which Scott described was developed largely by the yankee "whittler" Thomas Blanchard, who developed the process of multiple manufacture of wood and metal objects by employing templates and mechanical cutters. Blanchard introduced his gun stock cutting machine in 1819 and it was constantly being perfected after that date. The same principles were applied to all materials. William H. Doolittle, *Inventions in the Century* (London, 1903), 342-46. Also, Clark, *History of Manufactures*, 1:421-22.

96. Chicopee Falls was a site of abundant water power, and large cutlery and textile manufacturing plants took advantage of this resource. Clark, *History of Manufactures*, 1:523, 551.

97. The process is described in James Montgomery, *The Cotton Manufacturers of the United States and Great Britain* (New York, 1970), 25,111.

98. Massachusetts in 1831 led the country in the number of mills, capital invested, number of spindles, and yards of cloth produced. There were 256 mills which employed 10,378 females at an average of $2.25 a week. *Ibid.*, 160-62.

99. In 1830 Springfield had a population of 6,784. United States Fifth *Census*, 18-19.

100. From Northampton Scott traveled south to Springfield, and from the latter place the distance was slightly less than one hundred miles. *An Accompaniment to Mitchell's Reference*, 217.

101. Albany in 1830 had a population of 24,209. See *An Accompaniment to Mitchell's Reference*, 10; Abstract United States Fifth *Census*. "The towns look new and handsome. A barren rock over which we traveled is named Lebanon; . . . this, I observe, accords with a point of national character, which shows itself in a love of striking, of ancient, and of hard names." Henry Bradshaw Fearon, *A Narrative of a Journey of Five Thousand Miles through the Eastern and Western States of America* (London, 1819), 125.

102. Characteristic of a state capital town, Albany had more hotels than mere travelers and casual visitors justified. There were fifteen or twenty so-called principal hotels of which Drake's American was one. Heywood, *Gazetteer of the United States*, 266.

103. George Clinton (1739-1812) served seven terms as governor of New York. Frank Monaghan, "George Clinton," *Dictionary of American Biography*, 4:225-26. "Of the other prominent buildings, the Capitol, or Legislative Hall, is one of the most prominent . . . and in the interior are two halls of legislation. . . . The state Library consisting of 30,000 volumes. . . . The various rooms are well proportioned . . . with portraits of Washington, and of the several governors of the State also, with portraits and busts of other public characters of America." Buckingham, *America*, 2:319; Hall, *Travels in North America*, 2:30.

104. Scott was mistaken. The portrait was of Abraham Van Vetchen (1762-1837), who was called "the father of the New York bar." Richard B. Morris, "Abram Van Vetchen," *Dictionary of American Biography*, 19:218.

105. "The Academy is on the north side of the public square; is a fine building, constructed of Nyas stone, three stories high and ninety feet front; cost at the city charge, $90,000, exclusive of the site and some important donations. The *Albany Institute* has commodious apartments in the Academy. Its library contains about two thousand volumes, and its museum more than ten thousand specimens in geology, mineralogy, botany, coins, engravings, cats, &c." John W. Barker and Henry Howe, *Historic Collections of the State of New York* (New York, 1841), 49.

106. Perhaps the first screw dock was placed in operation in June 1829 at Ramsey's Wharf, Fells Point, Baltimore. The brig *Catherine* was raised above the water for repairs. *Niles Weekly Register* 3 (July 4, 1829): 298.

107. Scott was in Albany at a moment when there was some entertainment available in an otherwise staid puritan city. Buckingham wrote, "The winter is the period when Albany is fullest of residents and strangers, for at this season of the year the legislature and the courts are in session; and at that time, besides the families of legislators, and the numbers of the bench and the bar, a great number of families come in from the country to stay for the winter. There is somewhat more gaity than in the summer, though even then there is less than in most other cities." *America*, 2:329.

108. In his annual message, 1793, President Washington recommended the establishment of a training facility to strengthen the national militia. It was not until 1802 that it was actually opened to receive cadets, and it was not until the appointment of Major Sylvanus

Thayer as superintendent that the academy began to thrive. James D. Richardson, *A Compilation of the Messages and Papers of the Presidents of the United States, 1789-1908*, 10 vols. (Washington, D. C., 1909), 1:140.

109. The plan of West Point from the Villefranche map, and general description of the site. John Crane and James F. Keiley, *West Point "The Key to America"* (New York, 1947), 1-35.

110. Sylvanus Thayer (1785-1872) was a military engineer educated at Dartmouth College and the Military Academy. He was appointed superintendent in 1817 at the age of thirty-two. Considered the "father of West Point," he retired as superintendent in June 1833. Hamersby, *Complete Army Register*, 803.

111. Fort Clinton was located six miles below West Point. *Ibid.*, 128. In writing of events of 1778, Washington Irving said, "Fort Clinton had subsequently been erected within rifle shot of Fort Montgomery, to occupy ground which commanded it. A deep ravine and stream called Peplopep's Kill, intervened between the two forts, across which there was a bridge." See Washington Irving, *Life of George Washington*, 3 vols. (New York, 1859), 3:223.

112. Tadeusz Bonaventure Kosciusko (1746-1817) joined the American cause in 1776. He was highly successful as a defense engineer in planning fortifications on the Delaware River, Mount Defiance in New York, and at Saratoga. In the spring of 1778 he was placed in charge of fortifying West Point on the Hudson. Frank Monaghan, "Kosciusko," *Dictionary of American Biography*, 10:497. "The spot where Kosciusko dreamed is still a place where the young man may still see visions not less exalted than those of the liberty-loving Pole." Edgar Mayhew Bacon, *The Hudson River from Ocean to Source* (New York, 1910), 385. Hamersby, *Complete Army Register*, 2, 179.

113. West Point cadets erected the monument to honor Kosciusko in 1828. Crane and Keiley, *West Point*, [71].

114. *Ibid.*, [28-29].

115. Fort Putnam was located on Mount Independence. Heitman, *Register and Dictionary*, 356; Hamersby, *Complete Army Register*, 150. "Fort Putnam is one of the most celebrated and, in some respects the most attractive of military remains of the Revolutionary period at the point. It was built upon a spur six hundred feet above the level of the river, and so situated that it commands an extensive view of the water and of the Highlands on both sides." Bacon, *Hudson River*, 384-85; Crane and Keiley, *West Point*, [17].

116. Major John Andre was sent by Sir Henry Clinton under a flag of truce in September 1780 to arrange details with Benedict Arnold regarding the surrender of West Point. Andre was arrested and hanged as a spy. He had papers hidden in his stockings which gave the Arnold plot away. Andre violated Clinton's orders by going on the mission in civilian clothes. *Webster's Military Biography* (Springfield, Mass., 1978), 14; Andre was captured September 23, 1780, and was shot as a spy on October 2, 1780. Crane and Keiley, *West Point*, [27].

117. James Carnahan was chosen president of the College of New Jersey May 13, 1823. Scott was correct in saying the college was in feeble condition. It had a president and two professors. The budget was approximately seven thousand dollars and forty-four students were enrolled, 1829-1830. John McClean, *History of the College of New Jersey*, 4 vols. (Philadelphia, 1877), 2:247, 278-92.

118. *Ibid.*, 1:7-8, 147; 2:283, 292.

119. Strangely, Scott did not know this was the Battle of Trenton which had followed Washington's crossing of the army over the Delaware on Christmas night at McKonkey's Ferry. This battle had greatly revived American hopes. Claude Halsted Van Tyne, *The American Revolution, 1776-1783* (New York, 1905), 130-32.

120. Scott traveled down the Delaware River. Joseph Bonaparte, or Count de Survelliers, former King of Spain, had a home on the east bank of the Delaware in New Jersey. Fearon, *Narrative of a Journey*, 132-33; Hamilton, *Men and Manners* 1:206-8.

121. "This person has purchased an estate in the neighborhood [Philadelphia], and by his simplicity and benevolence of character, has succeeded in winning golden opinions from all classes of Americans. He often visits Philadelphia, and mingles a good deal in the society of the place." Hamilton, *Men and Manners*, 1:207. "On our way from New York, we made a visit, by invitation, to the Count de Survelliers, elder brother of the later Emperor Napoleon, and formerly King Joseph of Spain, who has resided for some years at this country seat, near Bordenstown, in New Jersey." Hall, *Travels in North America*, 2:138.

122. This was Thomas Abthorpe Cooper (1776-1849), the English born actor who for thirty years was perhaps the most conspicuous actor on the American stage. He was especially good in Shakespearean and classical Roman roles. Ludlow, *Dramatic Life as I found it*, 227-28, 288-89.

123. These no doubt were Bristol, Willingboro, and Ardmore.

124. There was an active interest in things Oriental in Philadelphia at the time of Scott's visit. Nathan Dunn's Chinese Museum was near the Fairmount Water Works. The main building was of Chinese design, and so was the tower or pagoda. Edwin Wolf, II, *Philadelphia: Portrait of an American City* (Philadelphia, 1911), 2:175.

125. The velocipede or swift walker was imported from Europe in 1819. It first appeared in New York, May 19, 1819, and three months later the Common Council passed a law forbidding its use in public places. Joseph N. Kane, *Famous First Facts, a Record of First Happenings, Discoveries, and Inventions in the United States* (New York, 1964), 107.

126. "The Waterworks at Fair Mount may take rank with the Girard Collge, if not for architectural taste, yet for its charming situation, its agreeable prospects, and its combination of beauty, simplicity, and utility of the highest degree." Buckingham, *America*, 2:45-48.

127. This was Beck's Shot Factory located at Arch and Schuylkill streets. "Lists of Institutions, Public Buildings," in Robert DeSilver, *Philadelphia Directory and Strangers' Guide* (Philadelphia, 1829).

128. William Ellis Tucker began the search for an American clay which would take the proper glazing for the making of porcelain. In 1825 he established his kiln in the old Philadelphia Water Works plant. He succeeded and it was said his product compared favorably with that of the Royal Manufactory at Secres, France. When Scott visited the American Porcelain Manufactory it was located at Chestnut and Schuylkill streets. Samuel Hazard, ed., *The Register of Pennsylvania* 12 (1833): 291-94; Robert DeSilver, *Philadelphia Directory and Strangers' Guide* (Philadelphia, 1830), 199.

129. Everybody who visited Philadelphia in this period seems to have gone through the penitentiary. The most comprehensive view of this institution is contained in William Crawford's *Report on the Penitentiaries of the United States*, 1-14. Thomas Hamilton wrote, "During this interval I visited the Penitentiary. It stands about two miles from the city, but owing to the depth of snow, the sleigh could not approach within a considerable distance of the building. . . . I did, however, reach the Penitentiary at last. It is a square granite building of great extent, with a tower at each angle, and the walls enclose a space of ten acres. In the center of the area stands an observatory, from which it is intended that seven corridors shall radiate, but three only have been completed. The cells are arranged up either side of these corridors, which may be opened at pleasure from without." *Men and Manners*, 1:184-85; Buckingham, *America*, 2:167-68.

130. The Pennsylvania legislature authorized the construction of a new jail in Philadelphia, February 26, 1773. This was the Walnut Street Jail at Walnut and Sixth streets. It was ready for occupancy in 1776 and was used by the revolutionary government as a military prison. In 1780 it was sold back to the city. It was a solid stone structure, the best in the colonies. F. F. Watson, *The Annals of Philadelphia and Pennsylvania in the Olden Times as revised by Hazard*, 3 vols. (Philadelphia, 1898); 3:77ff; Harry Elmer Barnes, *The Evolution of Penology in Pennsylvania: A Study in American Social History* (Indianapolis, 1927), 70.

131. See Barnes, *Evolution of Penology*, 134-37, 156, 163-168.

132. See Crawford, *Report on the Penitentiaries of the United States*, 11.

133. See *ibid.*, 1-14.

134. At the time Scott visited the Eastern Pennsylvania Penitentiary it had only recently been completed and placed in operation on October 25, 1829. Barnes, *Evolution of Penology*, 141-46, 168-69.

135. See Crawford, *Report on the Penitentiaries of the United States*, 8.

136. The United States Mint in Philadelphia was established by an act of Congress in April 1792. It commenced operation in 1793. The original structure was at Chestnut and Juniper streets. The structure under construction which Scott saw was the Greek Revival building facing on Chestnut Street. *Illustrated History of the United States Mint with a Complete Description of American Coinage* (Philadelphia, 1886), 17.

137. See *ibid.*, 21-35.

138. In 1828 there were 124 inmates of the Deaf and Dumb Institute which included 77 in the Pennsylvania Asylum. Hazard, *Register of Pennsylvania*, 2:352; "The Asylum for the Deaf and Dumb is situated in Broad Street, and in a fine airy space. The building is neat and most commodious, and all its internal arrangements are well adapted to the wants of the pupils. It was first established in 1821, with a grant from the state of 8,000 dollars, as a building fund, and a further grant of 160 dollars for each indigent child that it might receive subsist, and educate." Buckingham, *America*, 2:119.

139. The Peale Museum was the idea of Charles Willson Peale to establish a great national museum. He began thinking about this in 1784. When organized, the museum contained both artistic and natural objects, a world in miniature. From 1784 to 1829 it emerged as a famous institution. When a company was formed to build "The Philadelphia Arcade" the third floor became the museum. Sellers, *Charles Willson Peale*, 204-5, 331, 394, and Sellers, *Charles Willson Peale; Later Life, 1790-1827*, 2 vols. (Philadelphia, 1947), 2:395-96.

140. This institution was located at Chestnut between Tenth and Eleventh streets. It was founded in 1807, and housed an invaluable collection of paintings. Robert DeSilver, *The Stranger's Guide in Philadelphia to all Public Buildings . . . &c* (Philadelphia, 1858), 126.

141. The Atheneum in Philadelphia was organized in 1814 as a reading room by a group of young men. When Scott visited the institution it was located in a part of the American Philosophical Building on Fifth Street below Chestnut. It specialized in newspapers, magazines, charts, maps, and other materials. *Ibid.*, 110.

142. The Arch Street Theater was opened in 1828. It was designed by the famous architect William Strickland. Wolf, *Philadelphia*, 114.

143. Catherine Yohe ran a boarding house known as the Washington Hotel at 6-8, N. 4th Street. DeSilver, *Philadelphia Directory and Stranger's Guide* (1829), 218.

144. This was the Chesapeake and Delaware Canal which was being opened to full use after having been given up in 1823 as a hopeless enterprise. Meyer, ed., *History of Transportation*, 218-20; this canal had been authorized by the Maryland General Assembly in 1799, but was not opened to Delaware City until 1829. Wilson Floyd Bevan and E. Melvin Williams, *History of Delaware Past and Present*, 2 vols. (New York, 1929), 2:755. This waterway was designed to accommodate bay vessels and had a depth of eight feet. *Niles Weekly Register*, 36 (May 16, 1829):187.

145. Barnum's Hotel was built in 1825 by D. Barnum, W. Shipley, and J. Phillips, Jr. Robert Vexler, *Baltimore: A Chronological and Documentary History, 1639-1970* (New York, 1975), 30. It was operated by David Barnum, and was located on Monument Square and North Calvert streets. *Mitchell's Baltimore Directory . . . Containing an Engraved Plan of the City . . .* (Baltimore, 1829), "Bar" page.

146. James Brown (1766-1835) had lived in Frankfort and served as secretary of state under Isaac Shelby. In 1803 he moved to the Louisiana Territory, and served as secretary

of the Louisiana Purchase Commission. In 1823 he was appointed by James Monroe as minister plenipotentiary to France and remained in that position until 1829. When Scott saw the family on the boat, Mrs. Brown was suffering from cancer. James Brown was Elizabeth Brown Scott's uncle and within the year she had married Robert. Charles E. A. Gayarre, *History of Louisiana*, 4 vols. (New York, 1854-57), 1:275, 380, 358; *Biographical Encyclopedia of Kentucky*, 14; *Biographical Directory of the American Congress, 1774-1971*, 648-49.

147. This is a fairly accurate description of the Carrolton Viaduct over the Guymas Falls. This structure was completed in December 1829, and still stands. It is 312 feet long, and 51 '9" above the water at the main arch. It was built wide enough for two tracks. James Lloyd was the architect. E. L. Hungerford, *The Story of the Baltimore and Ohio Railroad, 1827-1927*, 2 vols. (New York, 1928), 1:63-64.

148. What Scott saw was the first of several experimental runs from Mount Clare to President Street, a distance of approximately eight miles. Charles Carroll (1737-1832) was a member of the Board of Directors of the railroad. He had laid the foundation stone, July 4, 1828. Kate Mason Rowland, *The Life of Charles Carroll of Carrollton*, 2 vols., (New York, 1898), 2:360-61. Hungerford, *The Baltimore and Ohio Railroad*, 1:73-74. A party of twenty-seven attended the occasion and were drawn in one car, by a single horse, at the rate of 9 or 10 miles an hour, to the end of the rail-line, and with much apparent ease. Another car, one of Winan's, in return, carried thirty-seven passengers, among them several ladies — one horse being only used, which galloped off with his load with great ease. It was thought that he might have drawn a second car so filled, at the same rate of speed. *Niles Weekly Register*, 37 (December 25, 1829):273.

149. During the interval December 21, 1829 to January 1, 1830, the railroad company conducted several excursion runs. The formal opening occurred January 1, 1830, when the Postmaster General of the United States was whisked over the finished tracks in less than six minutes. Hungerford, *B & O Railroad*, 1:73-74.

150. Ross Winan was a New Jersey horsetrader who came to Baltimore to sell horses to the railroad company. He invented the system described by Scott by which flanged wheels were mounted on revolving axles, thus greatly increasing the drawing power of the horse. Charles Carroll was still a company director. *Ibid.*, 1:76-80.

151. See Meyer, ed., *History of Transportation*, 397-98.

152. Scott visited the Baltimore Glass Manufactory. *Mitchell's Baltimore Directory* (1829), "Industrial section."

153. The Maryland Penitentiary was opened for reception of prisoners in January 1812, when fifty-one convicts were moved from the state's public road camps. The eastern wing was completed in 1829 with 320 solitary cells. Crawford, *Report on the Penitentiaries of the United States*, 94-101.

154. "The walls, which are of stone, 18 feet high, and surmounted by a wooden parapet, enclose a square of four acres. . . . The cells are five stories high, built on arches . . . . No distinction is made in the treatment of coloured from other prisoners. The numbers of each are nearly equal, notwithstanding the difference of numbers between white and black population." *Ibid.*, 94, 96.

155. Labor began at sunrise and quit a half hour before sunset. In 1829 profits amounted to $17,053. Women prisoners spun, knitted, washed wool and clothes, and fabricated shoes. The men made combs and shoes, and sawed marble. *Ibid.*, 95-97.

156. "Here all are obliged to labour while they have health and strength; and tasks assigned to them are rigidly exacted, and under penalties sufficiently severe to enforce their performance. The principle kind of labour is weaving, which all understand or can soon be taught." Buckingham, *America*, 1:407.

157. See Crawford, *Report on the Penitentiaries of the United States*, 96.

158. See *ibid.*, 95.

159. A plan of the prison appears in Crawford's *Report,* opposite page 94.

160. "The government of the prison is vested in twelve directors resident in Baltimore, who are appointed annually by the executive council of the State; and these appoint a resident keeper, sixteen deputy keepers and guards, a book-keeper, a clerk, and a physician." Buckingham, *America,* 1:407.

161. A drawing of the monument made about 1829 appears in Matthew Page Andrews, *Tercentenary History of Maryland,* 2 vols. (Chicago, 1925), 1:744.

162. The cornerstone of the famous Baltimore Washington Monument was laid July 4, 1815, in Howard's Park. Vexler, *Baltimore,* 26; Andrews, *Tercentenary History of Maryland,* 1, illustration. "This monument is a noble Doric column of marble, rising from a base of ample dimensions, 50 feet square and 20 feet high. The shaft of the column is 160 feet, its diameter 20 feet, and the statue of Washington, which stands on the summit, is 13 feet in height." Buckingham, *America,* 1:421.

163. City Spring was located on the west side of Charles Street near Camden. No doubt this was James Cortlan Tin and Sheet Iron Manufactory at no. 10 Baltimore Street. The medical college was located opposite Peale's Museum on Holiday Street. *Matchett's Baltimore Directory* (Baltimore, 1829), 61, 212, advertisement.

164. Richard M. Johnson (1781-1850) of Georgetown. Scott's family had been neighbors to the Johnsons, Richard M. and James. *Biographical Encyclopedia of Kentucky,* 297-98. Gadsby's Tavern was a popular political boarding house of the Jacksonian persuasion. In 1829-1830 Scott was able to see most of the prominent politicians of the new administration. Marquis James, *Andrew Jackson: Portrait of a President* (Indianapolis, 1937), 99, 108, 210.

165. Scott revealed the fact that anyone who cared to call at the White House could expect to gain access to the president. Unfortunately he did not give a detailed description of Andrew Jackson, who had been in office less than a year.

166. Martin Van Buren (1782-1862) of Kinderhook, New York, was a bitter opponent of John Quincy Adams. A bachelor and Jackson's secretary of state, he became deeply involved in the O'Neale-Eaton affair.

167. John Henry Eaton (1790-1856) was from Tennessee and was Jackson's secretary of war. His marriage to Margaret (Peggy) O'Neale was to create a bitter social storm in Washington, and resulted in a reorganization of Jackson's cabinet, and some considerable national political repercussion.

168. Samuel Delucenne Ingham (1779-1860) was from Bucks County, Pennsylvania, and was a member of Congress from 1813-18, 1822-29. Jackson appointed him secretary of the treasury. Like everybody else in the Jackson administration, he and his wife became involved in the social snarl over the O'Neale affair. *Biographical Directory of the American Congress, 1774-1949,* 1358; James, *Portrait of a President,* 183, 228-36.

169. John Caldwell Calhoun (1782-1850) had behind him in December 1829 a highly successful career as secretary of war and United States senator. He had been elected vice president. When Scott called on him he was on the threshold of one of the bitterest challenges of his life, the explosion in the administration over the O'Neale affair. Charles Wiltse, *John C. Calhoun, Nullifier, 1829-1839* (Indianapolis, 1949); James, *Portrait of a President,* 266-82; James Parton, *Life of Andrew Jackson,* 3 vols. (Boston, 1866), 3:184-309.

170. William Taylor Barry (1784-1835) was a Virginian by birth, raised in Jessamine County, Kentucky, and a lawyer in Lexington. He was a Kentucky politician of the first order, but lost the governor's race in 1828. *Biographical Encyclopedia of Kentucky,* 310-11.

171. Matthew St. Clair Clarke of Pennsylvania was re-elected clerk of the house December 3, 1827. *Biographical Directory of the American Congress, 1774-1949,* 157; *Congressional Debates* 20th Congress, 1st Session, December 7, 1829.

172. The Jacksonian levees often appeared as much mob scenes as formal parties. Thomas

Hamilton wrote, "On the following evening I attended the levee. The apartments were already full before I arrived, and the crowd extended even into the hall. Three — I am sure that there were not four — large saloons were thrown open on the occasion, and were literally crammed with the most singular and miscellaneous assemblage I had ever seen. The numerical majority of the company seemed of the class of tradesmen or farmers, respectable men, fresh from the plough or the counter, who accompanied their wives and daughters, came forth to greet the President, and enjoy the splendours of the gala . . . ." Hamilton, *Men and Manners*, 2:70.

173. Isaac Hull (1773-1843), a native of Massachusetts, commanded the *Constitution* when it defeated the British *Guerriere* on August 19, 1812. He had various commands in the United States Navy including the Boston Navy Yard, the Portsmouth Navy Yard, and the Pacific Station. In 1830 he was in command of the Washington Navy Yard. Gardiner W. Allen, "Isaac Hull," *Dictionary of American Biography*, 9:360-62.

174. A highly corroborative account of the excesses of the Jacksonian "King Mob" scene appears in Nathan Sargent, *Public Men and Events from the Commencement of Mr. Monroe's Administration in 1817 to the close of Mr. Fillmore's Administration in 1853*, 2 vols. (Philadelphia, 1875), 1:122-64.

175. This was Thomas Abthorpe Cooper (1776-1849), who was first a Shakespearean and star character actor on the American stage. In 1830 he was fifty-five years of age. William C. Young, *Famous Actors and Actresses of the American Stage*, 2 vols. (New York, 1975), 1:213-15.

176. Cooper was born in Harrow Hill, England, December 16, 1776. He first appeared in America at Baltimore and Philadelphia in Shakespearean roles. He later played the theatrical circuit out in the country. "In April 1827, Mr. Thomas A. Cooper played in Mobile an engagement of ten nights, appearing in this usual round of characters, viz.: MacBeth, Virginius, Damon, (each of the last two characters twice), Richard III., Leon ('Rule a Wife'), Hamlet, Rolle, (in 'Pizarro'), Beverly ('Gamester'), with Petruchio. His engagement was a success." Ludlow, *Dramatic Life as I found It*, 288-89. In 1830 Cooper's popularity was on the wane, but not from age. Oral S. Coad, "Thomas Abthorpe Cooper," *Dictionary of American Biography*, 4:416-17.

177. C. D. E. Bangeman Huygenses, E. E., and M. P., presented his credentials, August 26, 1825. Adelaide Hasse, *Index to United Documents Relating to Foreign Affairs*, Part II, *1828-1861* (Washington, D. C., 1919), 1129. The Huygenses became involved in the Peggy O'Neale affair. James, *Portrait of a President*, 230; Wiltse, *Calhoun*, 37. It is uncertain what Scott meant by *in effigie*. Mrs. Huygens told John Quincy Adams at Ambassador Krudeners's party she would not attend President Jackson's supper if Peggy O'Neale was present. She refused to send the Eatons an invitation to her New Year's party. Allan Nevins, ed., *Diary of John Quincy Adams* (New York, 1929), January 3, 1830, 298-99.

178. This canal was projected in 1791. The company was incorporated by Congress May 1, 1802. *Statutes at Large of the United States of America, 1789-1873*, 17 vols. (Washington, D. C., 1850-73), 2:175-78. In 1830 transportation on the waterway had declined. Cornelius W. Heine, "The Washington City Canal," *Records of the Columbia Historical Society of Washington, D. C.* Vols. 53-56 (Washington, D. C., 1959), 2-3, 12-13.

179. This was one of three principal United States arsenals. *Executive Documents of the House of Representatives*, 24th Cong., 1st Sess. (November 20, 1835), Doc. no. 2,1:145, 236.

180. Georgetown University was founded as "The Academy of Georgetown, Patomack River Maryland," by John Carroll. In 1815 the Congress approved a new charter making it a college. The bill was signed by James Madison. *Annals of Congress*, 13th Cong., 3rd Sess. 116, 1122; *New Catholic Encyclopedia*, 4:356-58.

181. Carusi's Saloon was the fashionable gathering place in the age of Jackson. "We attended a concert given by Madame Caredari Allan at Carusi's Saloon, where, it was said,

all the beauty and fashion of Washington was present." Buckingham, *American*, 1:342.

182. This portrait was by Thomas Sully. Scott was correct in considering it a poor one. Marquis James, *Andrew Jackson: The Border Captain* (Indianapolis, 1933), 40.

183. "It is only fair to state, however, that during my stay in Washington, I never heard the President's levee mentioned in company without an expression of indignant feeling on the part of the ladies, at the circumstances I have narrated. To the better order of Americans, indeed, it cannot but be painful that their wives and daughers should be compelled to mingle with the very lowest people." Hamilton, *Men and Manners*, 2:72.

184. Mrs. Hannah Price ran a boarding house in Frankfort at the corner of Washington and Broadway, and next door to George M. Bibb. An unsigned and undated manuscript in the news clipping file in the Kentucky Historical Society, Frankfort. This was the manuscript copy of a story which appeared in the *Frankfort Ledger*. Also see the United States Fifth *Census*, manuscript schedule, 1830.

185. Tristam Burgess (1770-1850) entered the opening debates over the famous Foote Amendment. On January 7, 1830, consideration of the bill dealing with the distribution of public lands was disrupted by discussion of an issue over southern Indian affairs. Burgess spoke on the public land bill on January 12 and 13. He favored distribution of lands in such a way as to benefit all the states in the fields of education and other social areas. In the Senate, in the meantime, the great debate was beginning between Robert Y. Hayne and Daniel Webster. *Congressional Debates*, 20th Cong., 1st Sess., 6:11-16, 501-30. "Mr. Hunter was evidently a man of cleverness, with a tolerable command of words, and a good deal of wordly sagacity. He occasionally made a good hit, and once or twice showed considerable adroitness in parrying attack; but he was utterly wanting in taste and imagination; nor could I detect a trace of any single quality which could be ranked among the higher gifts of an orator." Hamilton, *Men and Manners*, 2:54; *Biographical Directory of the American Congress, 1774-1971*, 68.

186. James Buchanan (1791-1868) was a member of the Judiciary Committee of the House of Representatives. He had been active in Jacksonian politics, and soon was to be appointed minister to Russia. *Biographical Directory of the American Congress, 1774-1971*, 659.

187. The Inghams, Calhoun partisans, were caught up in the O'Neale social storm. In April 1831, Ingham was forced to resign from the secretary of the treasury position in the Jackson cabinet. James, *Portrait of a President*, 275; Parton, *Life of Andrew Jackson*, 3:352.

188. Sam Houston (1793-1863) had just left his Tennessee wife and the governorship of Tennessee and was living with the Cherokee Indians west of the Mississippi River. This was one of several visits to Washington.

189. In December 1829, Houston and two Indian companions slipped away from Arkansas to Washington to protest abuses in the payment of Indian annuities in paper instead of gold. The Indians knew little or nothing of the worth of the paper and were shamelessly cheated by traders, liquor dealers, and other sharpers. The arrival of the three in Washington created a sensation when they arrived January 14, 1830. Houston wore an Indian blanket trimmed with metal baubles, and caused quite a tinkling of trophies and Washington tongues. Marquis James, *The Raven: A Biography of Sam Houston* (Indianapolis, 1929), 124-33; Llerena Friend, *Sam Houston, The Great Designer* (Austin, Texas, 1954), 26-27.

190. January 16, 1830, was a Saturday and the House of Representatives was in adjournment from the evening of the fifteenth until the morning of the eighteenth. *Congressional Debates*, 21st Cong., 1st Sess., 6:537. The Columbian Institute for the Promotion of Arts and Sciences was conceived by Dr. Edward Cutbush, a naval surgeon stationed at the Washington Naval Yard. The institute was formed in 1816 with eighty-nine members, most of whom were cabinet members and congressmen. It was first housed in Blodget's Hotel along with the Patent Office and the General Postoffice. In 1824 it was removed to the large room under the Library of Congress, and it was here that Scott heard Edward Everett's lec-

ture. *Report of the National Museum*, Bulletin 101, 4-5, 7-9, 11, 37, 67-74, 229; Max Meisel, *A Bibliography of American Natural History: The Pioneer Century, 1769-1865*, 3 vols. (Brooklyn, N.Y., 1924-29), 228.

191. Edward Everett (1794-1868) was a Unitarian minister who had a reputation as an excellent orator. He was from Charlestown, Massachusetts, and served the Middlesex District five terms in Congress. *Biographical Directory of the American Congress, 1774-1949*, 1141.

192. Provisions were made in the construction of official buildings in Washington for executive and legislative branches but not for the judiciary. The court was located first in the room which it occupied until 1808. Charles Warren, *The Supreme Court in United History*, 2 vols. (New York, 1937), 1:171. "The room was hardly up to the dignity of the Court. It was also a robing chamber." Corroborating Scott's descriptions are those of O. H. Smith, *Early Indiana Trials and Sketches: Reminiscences by Honorable O. H. Smith* (Cincinnati, 1858), 155-56, and Hamilton, *Men and Manners*, 2:66-67.

193. Robert Scott visited the Supreme Court chamber in a transitional moment in its history. Though seven justices sat in a row flanking Chief Justice John Marshall, behind the scenes a bitter tug of war was occurring. It is not entirely clear what case was being argued on that occasion. It is almost certain, however, that it was either *Craig* v. *Missouri*, which involved the fundamental constitutional issue of whether a state had the privilege of issuing bills of credit, or the case of the *Cherokee Indians* v. *Georgia*. Both issues were basic ones. In the Missouri case Justices Johnson, Thompson, and McLean wrote dissenting opinions which in a sense marked the end of the solidarity of the Marshall Court. Marshall had five years to live, but in that time he saw the Jacksonian influence dilute his conservative leadership. Albert J. Beveridge, *Life of John Marshall*, 4 vols. (New York, 1916-17), 4:508-15, 539-49, 567-88.

194. An excellent description of the court is contained in Ben: Perley Poore, *Perley's Reminiscenses of Sixty Years in the National Metropolis*, 2 vols. (Washington, D. C., 1886), 1:83-87.

195. See Warren, *Supreme Court*, 1:465-71.

196. See David Paul Brown, *The Forum; or Forty Years of Full Practice at the Philadelphia Bar* (Philadelphia, 1856), 562.

197. Scott was vague in this statement. He seems to refer to the congressional debates then in progress in both the House and the Senate over the famous Foote Amendment to the public land bill. He, however, mentioned Charles A. Wickliffe of Bardstown as a lawyer in the important case of *Craig* v. *Missouri*. William Wirt, a former United States attorney general under John Quincy Adams, had returned to private practice. J. P. Kennedy, *Life of William Wirt* (Philadelphia, 1856), 2:240-67.

198. Thomas Hart Benton (1782-1858), United States senator from Missouri, had angered New Englanders generally, and John Quincy Adams particularly, in accusations that they wished to prevent further expansion on the western frontier, and that Adams had given away a large block of American territory in the Adams-Onis Treaty of 1819. *Congressional Debates*, 21st Cong., 1st Sess., 6:22-41; Nevins, ed., *Diary of John Quincy Adams* (February 10, 1830); William M. Meigs, *Life of Thomas Hart Benton* (Philadelphia, 1904).

199. Edward Livingston (1764-1836) was born at "Clermont," Columbia County, New York. He moved to New Orleans in 1803, and became a major political figure in Louisiana, served in Congress, and was elected to the Senate in 1828. He spoke against the Foote Amendment on January 19, 1830, saying it would not be in the interest of his state to check the sale of public lands. *Cong. Debates*, 21st Cong., 1st Sess., 30-31; *Biographical Directory of the American Congress, 1774-1949*, 1467-68.

200. John C. Calhoun (1782-1850) was forty-two years of age in 1830. The Chester Harding portrait of 1832 shows him as having a fairly long, angular, clean-shaven face with a shock of black hair. Wiltse, *Calhoun*, 96; *Biographical Directory of the American Congress, 1774-1949*, 937.

201. Daniel Webster (1782-1852) was born in Franklin, Massachusetts, and was educated at Phillips Exeter Academy and Dartmouth College. He served in Congress, beginning in 1813, and in the United States Senate starting in 1827. He was sometimes called "Black Dan" because of his somber appearance. *Biographical Directory of the American Congress, 1774-1949,* 1987.

202. Littleton Waller Tazewell (1774-1860) was a member of Congress from 1800 to 1801, was in the Virginia House of Delegates, was a member of the Virginia constitution convention, and served as United States senator from 1824 to 1832. Scott knew him from his meeting with Tazewell in Richmond in late 1829. *Ibid.,* 1902.

203. Andrew Stevenson (1784-1857), a graduate of William and Mary College, a Richmond lawyer, and a Virginia legislator, first served in Congress in 1821, and was Speaker of the House of Representatives from 1827 to 1834. It was his house where Scott visited the Madisons in Richmond. *Ibid.,* 1863.

204. George McDuffie (1790-1851) was forty years of age in 1830. He served in Congress from 1821 until he resigned in 1834. In 1830 he had just begun his fifth term in that body. He favored abolishing the tariff, and was deeply involved in the South Carolina controversy. He had been a Jacksonian until 1829, and was a confirmed dyspeptic. *Ibid.,* 1533; Thomas Perkins Abernathy, "George McDuffie," *Dictionary of American Biography,* 12:34-36.

205. John Randolph of Roanoke (1773-1833) was born at the mouth of Appomattox Creek or River, Prince George County, Virginia. At age twenty-six he was elected to Congress where he served from 1799 to 1831. He opposed numerous proposed laws, but none more so than legislation favoring the fraudulent Yazoo land speculation. He and Henry Clay fought a duel, and Randolph was a truculent debater. He died in Philadelphia after what he told a doctor had been a lifetime of illness. Scott's somewhat whimsical suggestion of Anne Royall and John Randolph is interesting. Garland, *John Randolph,* 2:*passim.*

206. Phillip Pendleton Barbour (1783-1841) was one of the young politicians who opposed the Clay-Calhoun views. Scott had seen him in Richmond in the past October. Soon after this Barbour was appointed to a federal judgeship for the eastern district of Virginia. *Biographical Directory of the American Congress, 1774-1949,* 813-14.

207. Anne Newport Royall was born in Maryland, June 11, 1769. She was a servant in the household of William Royall, a Revolutionary soldier. In 1797 he married her, and when Royall died in 1824 Anne embarked on a career of traveling, writing, and bookselling. She had both a sharp eye and an acid tongue and pen. In Washington she was regarded as a woman to avoid if possible, if not to treat with discretion. See S. H. Porter, *The Life and Times of Anne Royall* (Cedar Rapids, 1909). Anne Royall had visited Kentucky and described the state in her *Letters from Alabama on Various Subjects,* (Washington, D. C. 1830). She no doubt expected adverse reactions to her comments. See Thomas D. Clark, ed., *Travels in the Old South: A Bibliography,* 3 vols. (Norman, Okla., 1956), 3:95-98.

208. In 1829 the Library of Congress contained approximately 15,000 volumes. It had suffered losses in two fires. After considerable in-fighting Congress enacted a law, January 20, 1815, to purchase Thomas Jefferson's library of 6,487 volumes for $23,950. A special room was prepared in the capitol at a cost of $1,520.77 for housing the library. The Jefferson books arrived in the spring of 1816 packed in boxes containing three tiers of shelves. The ends of the boxes were removed and the books were already shelved. David Mearns, *The Story Up to Now, 1800-1945* (Washington, D. C., 1946), 16-27.

209. On June 13, 1830, Congress adopted a resolution granting access to the library by the secretary of state, treasury, war, navy, postmaster general, secretary of the Senate, clerk of the House, and the chaplain. *Ibid.,* 39.

210. The building which housed the Post Office Department and the Patent Office was somewhat a catch-all structure. It had been built as a hotel to be given as a lottery prize. Congress had met in the building after the British burned the city. It had also housed the

Library of Congress and other offices. *Ibid.*, 27. The constitutional provision relating to patents was introduced August 18, 1787. President Washington in his first annual message in 1790 asked that provisions be made to protect American inventors. The patent law was to stimulate American inventive genius, and all sorts of mechanical ideas were sent to the patent office in the form of working models. There exhibits constituted a grand national curiosity shop. William B. Kerkman, "Some Historical and Current Reflection on the American Patent System," *Centennial Celebration of the American Patent System, 1836-1936* (Washington, D. C., 1937), 8-9; William B. Bennett, *The American Patent System: An Economic Interpretation* (Baton Rouge, 1943), 64-73.

211. On March 3, 1829, at 9 p.m. John Quincy Adams left the White House for Meridian Hill, the home of his son John. It was here that Scott visited him. Nevins, ed., *Diary of John Quincy Adams*, 390; Marie B. Hecht, *John Quincy Adams: A Personal History of an Independent Man* (New York, 1972), 490-92. M. A. Elliott, *Washington Directory* (Washington, D. C., 1830) listed J. Q. Adams as living near St. John's Church in 1830.

212. The interest which John Quincy Adams evinced in Russia stemmed from his direct association with that country. From 1809-1814, he was United States Minister to the court of the Czar. In his second annual message, December 5, 1826, he informed the two houses of Congress that because of the recent death of Emperor Alexander the United States had been deprived of "a long-tried, steady, and faithful friend." There had existed between the emperor and the United States mutual agreement over several issues, including the independence of the South American states. Nicholas I had promised to continue this relationship. Richardson, *Messages and Papers of the Presidents*, 2:350-51.

213. In this connection Adams referred to a rather complex situation in the change of rulers in Russia, and he perhaps had no real knowledge of what had happened. On the death, December 14, 1825, of Alexander I under mysterious circumstances, the country was left without a ruling head. Possible heirs were Constantine, Nicholas, and Michael. Large numbers of Russians, especially the military officers, preferred Constantine, and when he refused the crown there was organized a conspiracy or uprising against Nicholas which had to be put down in a bloody resistance before he could fully assume the emperorship. The Grand Duke Michael was regarded only as a weak possibility to succeed to the crown, but nevertheless he held great potential for possibly bringing about the defeat of Nicholas by leading a Guard uprising. Constantine de Gruenwald, *Tsar Nicholas I*, trans. Brigit Patmore (New York, 1955), 1-18.

214. President Jackson wrote the House of Representatives, January 19, 1830, that he had been presented a gold medal by the Republic of Colombia commemorating that country's liberation by President Simon Bolivar. He expressed great admiration for General Bolivar, and was personally gratified by the gift, but he felt that under the Constitution he could not accept it, and asked that Congress make suitable disposition of it. Richardson, *Messages and Papers of the Presidents*, 2:466-67.

215. Adams as secretary of state and later president had shown warm friendship to the emerging Latin American states. Venezuela and Colombia were especially grateful for the support of the United States, and its willingness to send Richard C. Anderson as a delegate to the Panama Mission in 1823. Hecht, *John Quincy Adams*, 427.

216. It is difficult to determine any facts about this lost shipment in the literature relating to Washington Irving. There is a hint about a "late shipment" in Pierre E. Irving, *Life and Letters of Washington Irving*, 2 vols, (London, 1908), 2:406.

217. A biographer said of Adams, "His manner was cold, contentious, headstrong. As a result, his circle of friends was small, the roster of his enemies large and studded with the politically powerful. Andrew Jackson, his successor as President, was in Adams' estimation 'a barbarian who could scarcely spell his name.'" Leonard Falkner, *The President Who Wouldn't Retire* (New York, 1967), 12-13.

218. Charles King was a portrait painter whose gallery was located between E and F streets, Pennsylvania Avenue. Elliot, *Washington Directory* (1830), 47.

219. Washington was visited by many Indian delegations during the early years of the Jackson administration. They came from the South and the West. Three major issues faced the government in the administration of Indian affairs — removal of the southern Indians to beyond the Mississippi River, the Cherokee dispute with Georgia, and the readjustment of land cessions in the West. *Public Statutes at Large*, 4:411-412; *Niles Weekly Register*, 38 (March 20, 1830): 67.

220. Paul Baron de Krudner, the Russian Minister plenipotentiary, served in that post from 1827 to 1838. He was a bachelor, supported the Jacksonians in the Eaton affair, and became a somewhat comic actor in this social storm. Hasse, *Index to U. S. Documents*, Pt. II, 867; Parton, *Life of Andrew Jackson*, 3:289-90.

221. Brent Robert Gustaf Stacleberg presented his credentials as Minister from Holland on November 14, 1819, and took leave of that position in 1832. Hasse, *Index to U. S. Documents*, 1564, 1586.

222. The American Colonization Society was organized June 1, 1817, with Judge Bushrod Washington as its president. He served in this position until his death in 1829. Henry Clay was vice president. The meeting which Scott attended was at about the peak of the organization's popularity. Early Lee Fox, *The American Colonization Society, 1817-1840* (Baltimore, 1919), 50-51, 75-79, 90.

223. Charles Fenton Mercer (1778-1858) was from Leesburg, Virginia, and a member of Congress. He was an active leader in the colonization society. Scott had seen him earlier in the Virginia constitutional convention. *Biographical Directory of the American Congress, 1774-1949*, 1399.

224. Scott had the extremely good fortune of being present to hear one of the greatest orations ever delivered in the United States Senate. This oration was three hours long, and was delivered January 26, 1830. *Cong. Debates*, 21st Cong., 1st Sess., 6:58-75.

225. As noted earlier, Benton antagonized the easterners in his blunt accusitive speeches. John Quincy Adams confided to his diary, February 10, 1830: "Thomas Hart Benton, a liar of magnitude beyond the reach of Ferdinand Mendez de Pinto." Adams accused Benton of being obsessed with the idea that he as an eastern president had given away a large block of American territory in the treaty with Spain in 1819, Nevins, ed., *The Diary of John Quincy Adams*, 400.

226. Thomas Hart Benton served five terms in the United States Senate. *Biographical Directory of the American Congress, 1774-1949*, 584. He spoke on February 2-3, 1830, in four installments. At this time he was sharply critical of easterners for trying to block western expansion. *Congressional Debates*, 21st Cong., 1st Sess., 6:1830.

227. Robert Young Hayne (1791-1839), son of a prosperous rice planter, a railroad president, state legislator, and pro-Calhoun partisan, was elected to the United States Senate from South Carolina in December 1828. He opposed the tariff and in the great debate favored a southern-western alliance. Ulrich B. Phillips, "Robert Young Hayne," *Dictionary of American Biography*, 8:456-59; *Biographical Directory of the American Congress, 1774-1971*, 1093.

228. The Webster-Hayne debate was one of the most dramatic moments in United States senatorial history. The Foote Resolution was introduced December 29, 1829, in connection with the consideration of the public land bill. The debate proper began January 18, 1830, when Hayne spoke on January 25th. Webster replied in a three hour speech on January 26. *Cong. Debates*, 21st Cong., 1st Sess., 6:22, 43-58, 58-80. Ben: Perley Poore wrote later, "When Mr. Webster went to the Senate chamber to reply to General Hayne, on Tuesday, January 20th, 1830 [sic], he felt himself master of the situation. Always careful about his personal appearance when he was to address an audience, he wore on that day the Whig

uniform, which had been copied by Revolutionary heroes — a blue dress coat with bright buttons, a buff waist coat, and a high white cravat." Poore, *Reminiscences*, 116.

229. No doubt Scott agreed heartily with Thomas Hamilton's observation that in 1830, "In Washington, there is little to be done in the way of sight-seeing." Much of his long walk was over the undeveloped mud flats of the Potomac-Anacosta area. It is little wonder that he forgot the name of the girl he hoped to see in Georgetown.

230. Apparently Miss Hart was the daughter of Samuel Hart, a naval "constructor" who entered the naval service in 1818 and retired in 1839, and was stationed at the Washington Naval Yard. Edward W. Callahan, ed., *List of Officers of the United States Navy Marine Corps* (New York, 1969), 250. The general naval and marine base occupied the area in the southeastern or peninsula quadrant of Washington between the Potomac and Anacosta rivers.

231. Mrs. B. H. Blake's Boarding House was one of many in Washington which catered to congressmen and visitors. On March 12, 1821, Henry Clay received a receipt for three months' board. Clay Files, Papers of Henry Clay Project, University of Kentucky. This house was located on Pennsylvania Avenue between 13th and 14th streets. Elliott, *Washington Directory* (1830), 15.

232. The monument of American sailors who fell before Tripoli in 1804 was erected in 1808 by subscriptions from American naval officers. This was one of the first monuments, if not the first monument, established in Washington. *Report of the National Museum*, 10.

233. The prison which Scott saw had just been constructed on a tract of land projecting into the Potomac River opposite Alexandria. It contained about forty convicts of both sexes. Crawford, *Report on the Penitentiaries of the United States*, 102-5.

234. At the moment Robert Scott visited the Supreme Court chambers, a hot debate was taking place in Congress and the administration over the reorganization of the court. President Jackson's appointment of John McLean and John Bannister Gibson had stirred partisan feelings in Congress. Beyond this there was a long smouldering desire to enlarge the court, and possibly to reduce the power exercised by Chief Justice John Marshall. Specifically, proposals were made to add two to three additional justices. Arguing in favor of this proposition were Charles A. Wickliffe, James Buchanan, James Knox Polk, and other westerners. *Cong. Debates*, 21st Cong., 1st sess. (January 14, 19, February 16, 17, March 10, 1830), 530-37, 542-51, 560-75, 598-605. When the court opened its new term in January 1830, it had so many cases ready to be reported that Richard Peters was unable to include them all in a single volume of his *Reports* or *Statutes at Large*. There was not a landmark case among them.

235. William Wirt was engaged in two major cases at this time. There were the impeachment proceedings against Judge James Hawkins Peck (1790-1836), over a harsh contempt citation in a western land case. The other was the famous Cherokee Nation against Georgia. Kennedy, *Life of William Wirt*, 2:240-85.

236. Stilson Hutchins and Joseph West Moore wrote of Washington streets and life: "Every one who lived in what was called the 'court end' of the city kept a carriage of some kind, and it was said 'many persons would even ride to church when the distance was not more than a hundred paces . . . .' Outside of its fashionable life, however, the city was apparently in a 'long dead calm of fixed repose,' and its development year-by-year was very slow. It was not until 1830 that Pennsylvania avenue, the central thorofare, was paved, and then done cheaply and badly." *The National Capital Past and Present* (Washington, D. C., 1885), 60.

237. On August 24, 1814, the British had marched on Bladensburg. Brigadier General William Winder galloped out from the Washington Naval Yard at the head of a green civilian militia force, but by late afternoon the British had defeated the Americans and the road to Washington was clear. John K. Mahon, *The War of 1812* (Gainesville, Fla., 1972), 298-300; John F. Biddle, "Bladensburg — An Early Trade Center," *Records of the Columbia Historical Society of Washington, D. C.*, 53-56: 309-26.

238. There was an Irish immigration to Maryland and the District of Columbia during the building of the Chesapeake and Ohio Canal, and of the railroads. Poore, *Reminiscences*, 1:126.

239. The Roman Catholic Cathedral, the seat of the first American Archbishop, John Carroll, was designed by Benjamin Latrobe and completed in 1821. Francis F. Bierne, *Baltimore, a Picture History, 1858-1958* (New York, 1957), 11. "The first [church], in size and importance, is the Metropolitan Catholic Cathedral, which occupies a commanding situation on one of the most elevated summits of the town, at the corner of Cathedral and Mulberry streets. It was designed by Mr. Latrobe, but his original plans, which were very beautiful, were obliged to be abandoned for less expensive ones, the restriction in funds obliging him to reduce his building, in size and decoration, to match humbler standards than was at first intended." Buckingham, *America*, 1:408.

240. This museum, opened in 1814 by Rembrandt Peale, was based on the ideas which had made the Peale Museums in New York and Philadelphia popular. The collections consisted of paintings, and mastodon bones and other natural objects; the Peales and guests gave lectures on varying subjects. Sellers, *Charles Willson Peale*, 2:276-79.

241. The Baltimore Merchants Exchange was located on Gay Street, and was designed by Benjamin Latrobe and Maxmillian Godefroy. For half a century it was the most significant structure in the city. Here the bodies of Henry Clay and Abraham Lincoln were to lie in state on their passages through Baltimore. Bierne, *Baltimore*, 21.

242. George Beltzhoover's Indian Queen Hotel was located on the southeast corner of Baltimore and Hanover streets. *Matchett's Baltimore Directory* (1829).

243. A later traveler wrote, "The landing place on the southern bank [Susquehanna River] is the town of Havre de Grace, which was a witness to some of the naval evolutions of the late war. It is very prettily situated on a high sloping bank, and commands a noble prospect, both of land and water." Alex MacKay, *The Western World; or Travels in the United States, 1846-1847*, 2 vols. (Philadelphia, 1849), 1:104.

244. Elkton, Maryland, was just above the mouth of the Susquehannah River, and at the head of Chesapeake Bay on Elk River, in Cecil County. It was from this place that General Washington launched his southern campaign in June 1781. The town is located eighty-eight miles from Washington. James Truslow Adams, ed., *Atlas of American History* (New York, 1943), 71, 80; *Accompaniment to Mitchell's Reference*, 48.

245. Newcastle is in Newcastle County, Delaware, which in 1830 had a population of 2,463. *Ibid.*, 100.

246. Darby in Delaware County, Pennsylvania, had a population of 1,085. *Ibid.*, 54.

247. Brandywine and Christina rivers supplied the water power for much of the colonial industry centered in this area. There was concentrated along these streams 130 mill seats which at the peak of their operation ground 400,000 bushels of wheat annually. Clark, *History of Manufactures*, 1:64. "The next morning I walked to Brandywine, to see the grist mills, which are said to be the best in the United States." William Priest, *Travels in the United States of America beginning in the year 1795 and Ending in 1797* (London, 1802), 21.

248. Mrs. Catherine Yohe's boarding house was one of many in Philadelphia. It was located at 6-8, North 4th Street. DeSilver, *Philadelphia Directory* (1830), 218. James Silk Buckingham wrote, "The boarding houses are about the same, in character and in quality, as those in two other cities named. The same inconveniences attach to them in quite as large degree. The hour of breakfast is half past seven, and before eight the table is entirely cleared. The dinner is at two: and before half past two, the greater number have finished and departed. The sleeping room of boarders, is their only sitting room, in which they can be alone by day . . . ." *America*, 2:31.

249. Franklin V. Merrick of the Philadelphia Gas Works encouraged the organization in 1824 of the Franklin Institute for the promotion of American industry by awarding medals

and premiums to inventors, manufacturers, and mechanics. The Institute held meetings to discuss scientific and technological issues, and issued a journal. Wolf, *Philadelphia*, 149. The speaker possibly was David Hopkins, 321 Chestnut Street. DeSilver, *Philadelphia Directory* (1830).

250. Many who visited Philadelphia went to the Navy Yard to view the United States naval ships in various stages of construction. The central attraction, 1822-1837, was the *Pennsylvania*. This was a graceful 74 ship of the line designed by Samuel Humphreys. Its keel was laid in November 1822, and the vessel was launched July 8, 1837. It probably was the most graceful ship in the world to date, and was the largest built for the United States Navy. The vessel was 210 feet long, and 59.6 feet of beam, and 3,241 tons. It accommodated a hundred men and more than a hundred guns. At sea the *Pennsylvania* proved difficult to trim and was a poor sailor. She spent most of her time in Norfolk Harbor as a receiving ship. Bauer, *Ships of the Navy*, 1:5.

251. "In company of one of these gentlemen, I visited the Navy Yard, and went over a splendid line of battle ships, the Pennsylvania. She is designed to carry a hundred and forty-four guns; and is, I believe, the largest ship in the world. I likewise inspected a magnificent frigate, called the Raritan. Both of these vessels are on the stocks, but I was assured would suffice at any time to make them ready for the sea. They are completely covered in from the weather; and every apperture of the wood is filled with sea salt to prevent decay." Hamilton, *Men and Manners*, 1:200.

252. Scott was traveling over the route of the old Forbes Road, and the main connecting highway between Philadelphia and the head of the Ohio. Norristown had a population of 1,300, Pottsgrove 1,302, Reading 1,001, Harrisburg, 4,312. He traveled by stage coach over the southern route which was advertised to take three and a half days. United States Fifth *Census; Accompaniment to Mitchell's Reference* (Pennsylvania sections); Hazard, *Register of Pennsylvania*, 4:318.

253. The Schuylkill Canal was part of an interconnection of streams with the Pennsylvania Canal system which connected eastern and western Pennsylvania. This project was first promoted in 1814. Meyer, ed., *History of Transportation*, 209-10. The western section of arterial canal connection from Johnstown was completed in 1830. The Juniata Division was completed in 1832. Stefan Lorant, ed., *Pittsburgh: The Story of an American City* (Garden City, N.Y., 1964), 94-95; Archer Butler Hulbert, *The Great American Canals* (*Historic Highways of America*) 2 vols. (Cleveland, Ohio, 1905), 1:169-215.

254. The Union Canal Company was organized in 1811 to build seventy-seven miles of canal and improved sections between Middletown on the Susquehanna and a point on the Schuylkill a short distance below Reading. Meyer, ed., *History of Transportation*, 214-15.

255. "The Germans compose about one quarter of the population, and chiefly reside in the counties of Philadelphia, Montgomery, Bucks, Dauphin, Lancaster, York, and Northampton . . . . Farms within a few miles of the city [Philadelphia], on the road leading to Pittsburgh are managed in a very superior manner; they consist of from fifty to 200 acres and are worth £ 45 sterling an acre. The farmers are chiefly Dutch and Germans, and their descendants, who are a quiet, sober, and industrious set of people, and are most valuable citizens. They are almost all wealthy, and have fine dwellings, substantial barns, and excellent breed of cattle." *View of the United States of America*, 420, 426.

256. Harrisburg was first located on the Susquehanna River by John Harris who operated a ferry at this important crossing. In 1785 John Harris, Jr. platted a city on the spot, and in 1812 it became the capital of Pennsylvania. In 1830 it had a population of 4,312. George H. Morgan, *Annals of Harrisburg* (Harrisburg, 1852), 1, 23: Haywood, *Gazetteer of the United States*, 285-86.

257. The crossing of the Susquehanna at Harrisburg was a major point on the road between Philadelphia and the west. By 1830, a covered bridge had replaced John Harris'

ferry. No traveler has left a more graphic description of this structure than Charles Dickens. "We crossed the river by a wooden bridge, roofed and covered on all sides, and nearly a mile in length. It was profoundly dark: perplexed, with great beams crossing and recrossing it at every possible angle; and through the broad chinks and crevices in the floor, the rapid river gleamed, far down below, like a legion of eyes. We had no lamps; and the horses stumbled and floundered through this place, towards the distant speck of dying light, it seemed interminable. I really could not at first persuade myself as we rumbled heavily on, filling the bridge with hollow noises, and I held my head down to save it from the rafters above, but that I was in dream; for I have often dreamed of toiling through such places, and often argued, even at the time, 'this cannot be reality.' At length, however, we emerged upon the streets of Harrisburg . . . ." Charles Dickens, *American Notes and Reprinted Pieces* (London, 1861), 64.

258. Carlisle was a historic village in the path of the spreading American frontier in mid-eighteenth century. The defeat of Braddock in July 1755 exposed this outpost to serious attack from the Indians and French. The village was the western terminus of the wagon road and the beginning of the packhorse trail west. It became the post of the famous Indian fighter Colonel John Armstrong. By 1830 it had grown to a town of 3,707. Edmund Kimball Alden, "John Armstrong," *Dictionary of American Biography*, 1:553-54; Charles Coleman Sellers, *Dickinson College: A History* (Middletown, Conn., 1973); United States Fifth *Census*, 61.

259. Chartered September 9, 1783. Sellers, *Dickinson College*, 4.

260. Scott said he was a member of the Union Philosophical Society. It had a chapter at Transylvania University. John D. Wright, *Transylvania University: Tutor to the West*, rev. ed. (Lexington, Kentucky, 1980), 96, 127. The chapter at Dickinson College was founded in 1789. Sellers, *Dickinson College*, 12.

261. A decade later Charles Augustus Murray in his *Travels in North America*, 2 vols. (London 1839), 2:185-98, described the same journey, and corroborated Scott's observations.

262. Scott's "lovely maid" was educated in Hagerstown, Maryland. There was no Hagerstown, Pennsylvania.

263. Hazard, *Register of Pennsylvania*, 5:80, reported at the end of January: "The Schuylkill is frozen over and the boys are amusing themselves by skating upon it, and those who have ice houses are now seizing the opportunity to fill them."

264. Scott was confused about the name of the place. This was Brushy Run, the place where Henry Bouquet at the head of a small command of Royal Americans and Highlanders coaxed the Delaware and Shawnee Indians from cover by pretending to retreat and then fell upon them in a bloody bayonet attack. William Smith, ed., *Historical Account of Bouquet's Expedition Against the Ohio Indians in 1764 with preface by Francis Parkman, Translation by Dumas* (Cincinnati, 1868), 16-20.

265. "Brown" is unidentified. He might have been one of the younger Browns from Frankfort, but more likely he was an acquaintance Scott made on the stage coach.

266. Pittsburgh became famous for its glass of several grades. Henry Bradshaw Fearon wrote, "At Messrs. Page and Bakewell's glass warehouse I saw chandeliers and numerous articles in cut glass of a very splendid description; among the latter was a pair of decanters, cut from a London pattern, the price of which will be eight guineas." Fearon, *Narrative of a Journey*, 204. "Pittsburgh, for instance, has extensive glass works; and as fuel, a most important article in that manufactory, may be had at a price scarcely worth naming." Hazard, *Register of Pennsylvania*, 4:288; Leland D. Baldwin, *Pittsburgh: The Story of a City* (Pittsburgh, 1937), 148-49.

267. See Hazard, *Register of Pennsylvania*, 5:167-70.

268. The Western Penitentiary was erected in 1820, and was opened for reception of prisoners in 1827. It was somewhat comparable to the Eastern Penitentiary in Philadelphia. There were forty convicts in 1830. Crawford, *Report on the Penitentiaries in the United*

States, 15; Barnes, *Evolution of Penology*, 138-41. The warden's name was Joseph Patterson. Hazard. *Register of Pennsylvania*, 5:170.

269. "The main line of the [Pennsylvania] canal crossed the Allegheny River over a leaky wooden acqueduct and followed what is now Eleventh Street to Liberty . . . ." Baldwin, *Pittsburgh*, 193. "This was the western terminus of the Pennsylvania Canal which was carried over the Allegheny River by a 1100 foot acqueduct." Lorant, ed., *Pittsburgh*, 94.

270. The English painter Joshua Shaw made a sketch of Pittsburgh in 1825 in which the covered Monongahela Bridge appears. A decade later Leander McCandless painted a view of the Monongahela Wharf in which two-thirds of the bridge is portrayed. These paintings are reproduced in Lorant, ed., *Pittsburgh*, 82, 85.

271. Christopher Cowan introduced the first steam powered rolling mill in Pittsburgh in 1812. By 1830 all types of iron smelting and forging was handled by steam-powered machinery. Lorant, ed., *Pittsburgh*, 93; Baldwin, *Pittsburgh*, 221.

272. The editor of the Cincinnati *Advertiser* wrote in April 1830, "On Saturday morning last, we were shown on board the Waverly, by Captain M'Knight with that politeness which characterises him. Damask Table Cloths, manufactured at Pittsburgh, for the use of the Waverly, of the most beautiful patterns and large size, which among other ornaments contained a perfect likeness of the boat, and the name *Waverly* in large handsome and distinct letters under it, the whole raised in bold relief on the cloth." Hazard, *Register of Pennsylvania*, 3:15, 144; 4:256; *View of the United States of America*, 421; Clark, *History of Manufactures*, 1:531.

273. A city ordinance in 1824 provided for the construction of a new waterworks, and the plant was placed in operation in 1828. The reservoirs which Scott saw were located on Grant's Hill. Baldwin, *Pittsburgh*, 206-7; Lorant, ed., *Pittsburgh*, 102.

274. Almost every traveler who passed through Pittsburgh in this era noted the dismal appearance of the place. Tyrone Power, the Irish actor, said, "I entered the smoky Pittsburgh, more than ever charmed with the scenery admist which it is seated, still beautiful despite the ravages of the miner and the pollution of steam, smoke, and all the other useful abominations attendant upon the manufacture of iron, glass, pottery, etc. . . . The greatest ravages which I had to mourn, because it appeared to a wanton heedless extent, was the havoc everywhere making with barbarous and indiscriminate zeal amongst the neighboring timber . . . ." Of the city itself he wrote, "Even the short distance I had to explore on the line of the principle street, I found beset by perils; loose pavement, scaffold poles, rubbish, and building materials of all kinds blocked the trottoir in several places, which were to be avoided by instinct, for light there was none." *Impressions of America During the Years 1833, 1834, and 1835*, 2 vols. (London, 1836), 1:312, 325. The Pittsburgh Academy was chartered in 1787 at the instigation of H. H. Brackenridge, and was rechartered in 1819 as the Western University of Pennsylvania. It was located on Third Street until a fire destroyed its buildings in 1845. Baldwin, *Pittsburgh*, 215; Lorant, ed., *Pittsburgh*, 51-52. A reproduction of Russell Smith's painting of this institution appears in Lorant, ed., *Pittsburgh*, 88.

275. The Pittsburgh *Gazette*, February 9, 1830, said, "On Saturday morning Feb. 9, at 6 o'clock the thermometer stood at 10 degrees below zero in this city. This was the coldest weather we have experienced for 9 or 10 years past." Quoted in Hazard, *Register of Pennsylvania*, 5:125.

276. Steubenville is located in Jefferson County, Ohio. In 1830 it had a population of 3,696. Located in the town were a paper mill, woolen and cotton mills, copper and coal mines, and other industries. It was seventy-one miles below Pittsburgh. Wellsburgh is seven miles down stream on the east bank in Brooks County, Virginia (West Virginia), and a point of frontier embarkations. This was a shipping port for flour sent to the New Orleans market and for earthenware. In 1830 it had a population of slightly more than a thousand inhabitants. Samuel Cuming, *The Western Pilot*, revised and corrected by Charles Ross and John Klinefelter (Cincinnati, 1848), 14-15.

277. Alexander Campbell (1788-1866) was a native of County Antrim, Ireland. Scott had seen him in Richmond when he visited the Virginia constitutional convention in October 1829. In 1830 Campbell had just begun publishing the *Millenial Harbinger*, and had established himself as founder of one branch of the Disciples of Christ Church.

278. Robert Owen (1771-1858), the New Lanark Mill operator, British socialist, and organizer of New Harmony Community on the Wabash in Indiana. Campbell and Owen engaged in a week-long debate, April 13-20, 1830, in Cincinnati on the truth or falsity of organized religions. Frances Trollope, *Domestic Manners of the Americans*, ed. Donald Smalley (New York, 1949, orig. pub. 1832), 146-53.

279. Hills surrounding Wheeling contained rich deposits of coal, and a large amount of this fuel was used by local manufacturing plants. Martin, *Gazetteer of Virginia and the District of Columbia*, 406-7.

280. This raid occurred September 2, 1777. Reports differ as to what Mrs. Carpenter said to the Shawnee warriors. Whatever it was lacked a scriptural basis. A. B. Tomlison, "First Settlement of Grave Creek," *American Pioneer*, 2 vols. (Cincinnati, 1844), 2:347-57.

281. Wheeling was laid out as a village in 1873. Originally it was the site of Wheeling Fort. Located on the eastern high bank of the Ohio, ninety-four miles below Pittsburgh, it had in 1830 a population of 5,222. For a considerable period Wheeling was the western terminus of the National Road. For this reason it became an unusually busy port town serving both water and land transportation. Martin, *Gazetteer of Virginia and the District of Columbia*, 406-8.

282. Two paper mills in Wheeling industries employed 1,300 men, and used one million bushels of coal. *Ibid.*, 406-7. Mrs. Trollope wrote of Wheeling, "It has many manufactories, among others, one for blowing and cutting glass, which we visited. We were told by the workmen that the articles finished there were equal to any in the world; but my eyes refused their assent . . . . Wheeling has little of beauty to distinguish it, except the ever lovely Ohio, to which we were bid adieu, and a fine bold hill, which rises immediately behind the town. This hill, as well as every other in the neighborhood, is bored for coal. Their mines are all horizontal." Trollope, *Domestic Manners of the Americans*, 155.

283. Scott was still 419 miles away from home. The *LaGrange*, a 130 ton boat, was built in Wheeling in 1827. Timothy Flint, *A Condensed Geography of the Western United States*, 2 vols. (Cincinnati, 1828), 2:518.

284. Wheeling Island, immediately opposite the town, was located between the mouths of Wheeling Creek on the Virginia side, and Wheeling Indian Creek on the Ohio shore. Cumings, *Western Pilot*, 16.

285. Marietta is located at the mouth of the Muskingum River, 179 miles below Pittsburgh. In 1830 the town had a population of 1,915. In 1787 it was laid out as the seat of the famous Ohio Company, and became one of the most important of the early Ohio settlements. The geographical situation, however, was not conducive to expansion. The lowland along the Ohio River overflowed periodically, and the hinterlands were not really fertile. John S. C. Abbott, *The History of the State of Ohio* (Detroit, 1874), 297-304; Archer Butler Hulbert, *The Ohio River: A Course of Empire* (New York, 1902), 168-70.

286. Gallipolis in Gallia County, Ohio, had a population of 1,093. It was settled by French immigrants fleeing the French Revolution. They were victimized by the sharp dealings of representatives of the Scioto Land Company in 1791-92. Richard E. Banta, *The Ohio* (New York, 1949), 196-97; Hulburt, *Ohio River*, 263-65.

287. In 1830 Cincinnati had a population of 24,831. *Accompaniment to Mitchell's Reference*, 33. Cincinnati was the victim of several outbreaks of yellow fever and smallpox, and the city had several ordinances pertaining to the spread of epidemic diseases. Certainly the city wanted no publicity but in the era of Scott's trip, there was a great deal of concern about the outbreak of epidemics. See Alan I. Marcus, "In Sickness and Health: The Mar-

214 / Footloose in Jacksonian America

riage of the Municipal Corporation to the Public Interest and the Problem of Public Health, 1820-1870" (Ph.D. dissertation, University of Cincinnati, 1973), copy in the Cincinnati Public Library.

288. James Haggin was a native of Mercer County, Kentucky, and was a close friend of governors John Adair and Joseph Desha. An ardent "relief" partisan and Jacksonian, he was appointed an associate judge in the "New Court." H. Levin, ed., *The Lawyers and Lawmakers of Kentucky* (Chicago, 1897), 496; Arndt M. Stickles, *The Critical Court Struggle in Kentucky, 1819-1829* (Bloomington, Ind., 1929), 61, 105.

289. This farm contained 378 acres and was located just east of the village of Jett. Presently the estate is called Scotland, but Scott cherished the name Locust Hill. On the east side it was bounded by the Frankfort-Versailles Turnpike, and the Lexington Turnpike. A brief description of the farm appeared in Robert Scott's *Sale Catalog,* 1884, 1-2.

290. William P. Duval (1784-1854) was born in Henrico County, Virginia, and as a young man emigrated to Kentucky where he studied law under Judge Brodnax. Duval then served as county attorney in Hardin County, was elected to Congress from that district in 1812, and in 1822 James Monroe appointed him territorial governor of Florida. He died in Washington, D. C., in 1854. *Biographical Encyclopedia of Kentucky,* 166.

291. The governor was basically correct in the descriptions of the artifacts and remains of Fort St. Lewis which stood near his dwelling Tallahassee. One of the cannon was missing its muzzle, but was fired at times in the future. There are good descriptions of the ruins in John Lee Williams, *A View of West Florida* (Gainesville, 1976, orig. pub. 1827), 32-34. Also, Mark F. Boyd, "Spanish Mission Sites in Florida," *Florida Historical Quarterly* 17 (1939): 264-69; Mark F. Boyd, Hale G. Smith, and John W. Griffin, *Here they Once Stood, the Tragic End of the Apalachee Missions* (Gainesville, 1951), 140-41.

292. John Brown (1757-1837) was born in or near Staunton, Virginia, and moved to Kentucky in 1782 or 1783. In 1789 he was sent to Congress to represent the District of Kentucky, and after 1792 was three times elected United States senator. In 1805, he retired to practice law in Frankfort. *Biographical Encyclopedia of Kentucky,* 14.

293. In this period Daniel Boone was trading in ginseng which was sold by way of Philadelphia. In 1788 Daniel, Rebecca, and Young Nathan went to Berks County on horseback to visit the Boone family. John Bakeless, *Daniel Boone: Master of the Wilderness* (New York, 1939), 333.

294. This is an interesting note on Daniel Boone, as much for its source as for the gossip it passes on. John Brown no doubt heard most of the stories going around in the western country in the early years. Biographers of Daniel Boone deal only vaguely with the subject of Daniel's reunification with Rebecca. They have relied upon Boone's statement to John Filson that, "Shortly after the troubles at Boonesborough, I went to them, and lived peaceably there until this time. The history of my going home, and returning with my family forms a series of difficulties, an account of which would swell a volume, and being foreign to my purpose, I shall omit them." John Filson, *Kentucke and the Adventures of Col. Daniel Boone* (Louisville, 1934, orig. pub. 1784), 73. In 1929 the editor of this journal saw in the Lewis and Richard H. Collins Library in the old Kentucky State Library a note on paper of contemporary make and ink of the same vintage a manuscript which contained substantially John Brown's story. With the disassembling of the Collins Collection the whereabouts of this note is unknown. Fortunately there is a copy of it in the Special Collections of the Margaret I. King Library, University of Kentucky, Lexington.

295. Worthington Landing was located on the east bank of the Mississippi River in present Washington County, Mississippi, and near Lake Washington. Cuming, *Western Pilot,* 105-6.

296. In 1836 Washington County, Mississippi, was an emerging delta cotton-growing area which had a white population of approximately 600, and a slave population of 7,000. At the time Scott visited there its swamps sustained approximately 20,000 cows, and 7,000

hogs. Its cleared lands yielded approximately 12,000 bales of cotton. This region attracted many Kentucky farmers who wished to change from general and livestock farming to growing cotton. United States Sixth *Census*, 56-60, 227-28.

297. This was a case of a passenger in an out-of-the-way landing place catching the first steamboat he could persuade to land and take him aboard. Donaldsville in Louisiana was in Ascension Parish, Louisiana, on the west side of the Mississippi River at the mouth of Bayou LaFourche. Cuming, *Western Pilot*, 123.

298. This tomb was located above a plantation boat landing, but no other traveler seems to have seen it. The lone grave seems to have touched the homesick Kentuckian, but not so much as did the approach of spring in that far-off southern region. It is possible that Scott was viewing a sacred monument erected before the Convent of Sacre Coeur. J. H. Ingraham, *The Southwest*, 2 vols. (New York, 1835), 1:250.

299. "I think I have remarked, in a former letter, that the plantations along the river extend from the levee to the swamps in the rear; the distance across the belt of land being, from one to two or three miles. These plantations have been, for a very long period, under cultivation for the production of sugar crops." *Ibid.*, 248.

300. "Bishop's Hotel; so designated from its landlord, has been recently constructed, and is one of the biggest in the Union. The Tremont possesses more architectual elegance; and Barnum's, the pride of Baltimore, is a handsome structure. In the appearance of Bishop's, there is nothing imposing but its height . . . . A peculiarity in this hotel, and in the one or two others here, is the exclusion of ladies from among the number of boarders: it is properly, a bachelor establishment." *Ibid.*, 182, 184.

301. This was indeed a lavishly appointed house. A reproduction of an engraving of its interior appears in Oral Summer Coad and Edwin Mims, Jr., *The American Stage*, vol. 14, *The Pageant of America Series* (New York, 1929), 14, 166. "The interior of the house was richly decorated; and the paneling in the interior of the house was composed of massive mirror plates, multiplying the audience with fine effect. The stage was lofty, extensive, and so constructed, either intentionally, as to reflect the voice with unusual precision and distinctness. The scenery was in general well executed: one of the forest scenes struck me as remarkably true to nature, both in colouring and design. While surveying the gaudy interior, variegated with gilding, colouring, and mirrors, the usual cry of 'Down, Down Hats Off.' warned us to be seated." Ingraham, *The Southwest*, 1:222-23. "Notwithstanding Mr. Caldwell took a formal leave of the stage, both as actor and manager, we find him, according to his own statement laying the corner-stone of a large theatre on the 9th of May, 1835, which he opened on 30th of November of the same year . . . seven months, lacking nine days, from the laying down of the corner stone." Ludlow, *Dramatic Life as I Found It*, 464.

302. George "Yankee" Hill (1809-1899) was a popular character actor of the period who specialized in portrayal of the Yankee in various comical roles. Garf B. Wilson, *Three Hundred Years of American Drama and Theatre* (Bloomington, Ind., 1966), 169; Ludlow, *Dramatic Life as I Found It*, 423, 431, 498; and Glenn Hughes, *A History of the American Theatre 1700-1850* (New York, 1951), 143, 160. There is an interesting account of George N. Hill by J. Childs of Covent Garden, London, 1838, as a frontispiece in Coad and Mims, *American Stage*.

303. Ingraham, *The Southwest*, 1:222-23.

304. "One of the curiosities which all strangers should see — and which too many of them visit without seeing — is the public burying ground, about a half mile from the city." Hamilton, *Men and Manners*, 2:110. "The wall which surrounds, or is to surround the four side of the burial ground, (for it is yet uncompleted), is about twelve feet in height, and ten in thickness. The external appearance on the street is similar to that of any other high wall, while to the beholder within, the cemetery exhibits three stories of oven-like tombs, constructed *in* the wall, and extending on every side of the grave-yard. Each of these tombs

is designed to admit a single coffin . . . ." Ingraham, *The Southwest*, 1:153-54.

305. John Lightfoot Waller, a native of Woodford County, was an outstanding but highly controversial Baptist minister. He edited several Baptist publications, but much of his fame rested on the debates with Nathan Rice on infant baptism. He also debated with John T. Hendrick and Robert G. Grundy on doctrinal questions, and with E. M. Pingree of Cincinnati on the subject of universalism. He was the leading Baptist controversialist of his day. Waller was a member of the Kentucky Constitutional Convention in 1849, and wrote a history of the Baptist Church in Kentucky. *Biographical Encyclopedia of Kentucky*, 344; *Report of the Debates and Proceedings of the Convention for the Revision of the Constitution of the State of Kentucky*, (Frankfort, 1849), 925-30.

306. On February 16, 1838, the Kentucky General Assembly enacted an extensive but vague common school law in which the responsibilities for the organization of local district schools were left with district leadership. Robert Wilmot Scott was an active leader in the organization of a public school in the district lying about the village of Jett just east of Frankfort. This district surrounded Scott's Locust Hill Plantation. Kentucky *Acts* (1838), 274-83. Joseph J. Bulloch was a Presbyterian minister in Louisville. He was overlooked by the compilers of Kentucky biographical volumes. On September 13, 1845, he gave the commital prayer over the remains of Daniel and Rebecca Boone in the Frankfort Cemetery. Collins, *History of Kentucky*, 2:251-52. He was succeeded in office of the state superintendent of schools by Benjamin Bosworth Smith, a graduate of Brown University, and a bishop in the Episcopal Church. He served in office 1840-42. *Biographical Encyclopedia of Kentucky*, 257.

BOOK TWO
THE LIFE OF
ROBERT WILMOT SCOTT

1. The Master of Locust Hill

1. Book II is included in the Jennie Green Collection, Kentucky Library, Western Kentucky University. Robert W. Scott prepared these books either for the course in sophomore themes or declamation in Transylvania University, 1824. See the Transylvania University *Catalog* (1824), 19.

2. Scott enrolled in a course entitled "Galla Majors," which introduced him to the works of Socrates. *Ibid.*, xx.

3. Henry Niels Sonne, *Liberal Kentucky, 1780-1828* (New York, 1939), 171-90; John D. Wright, Jr., *Transylvania: Tutor to the West*, rev. ed. (Lexington, 1980), 99-116.

4. Sonne, *Liberal Kentucky*, 186-90; Wright, *Transylvania*, 102-7.

5. *Biographical Encyclopedia of Kentucky* (Cincinnati, 1878), 222.

6. Though a conservative man, Robert W. Scott had an intellectual liberality which he demonstrated throughout his life.

7. William Taylor Barry was a professor of law in Transylvania University and one of Lexington's and Kentucky's best-known citizens. He was to play an active role in Democratic politics, first in Frankfort, and later in Washington. *Biographical Encyclopedia of Kentucky*, 310-11. Joel Scott and his son Robert were well acquainted with their fellow Relief partisans, and they knew John Adair (1820-24) and Joseph Desha (1824-28).

8. George W. Ranck, "The Press," in Robert Peter, ed., *History of Fayette County, Kentucky* (Chicago, 1882), 366-67. A chronology of events which appeared in Lexington newspapers is contained at the Lexington Public Library in an index file of historical events, created by Charles R. Staples.

9. George W. Ranck, "The Bar of Lexington," in Peter, *History of Fayette County*, 343-45.

10. Joseph Desha (1768-1842) served as governor from 1824 to 1828. *Biographical Encyclopedia of Kentucky*, 37.

11. Carl Russell Fish, *The Rise of the Common Man, 1830-1850* (New York, 1927), 1-12; Arthur M. Schlesinger, Jr., *The Age of Jackson* (Boston, 1945), 132-43.

12. William C. Sneed, *A Report on the History and Mode of Management of the Kentucky Penitentiary, from Its Origin in 1798 to March 1, 1860* (Frankfort, 1860), 217-18; U. S. Census Schedule, Scott County, 1810; *Biographical Encyclopedia of Kentucky*, 222.

13. *Biographical Encyclopedia of Kentucky*, 222.

14. *Ibid.*, 217.

15. *Ibid.*, 218.

16. Robert W. Scott prepared a biographical sketch of his early Wilmot ancestor. This material may be found in the Archives of the National Society of Colonial Dames in the Commonwealth of Kentucky, Orlando Brown House, Frankfort (hereinafter referred to as NSCD Archives).

17. Kentucky *Acts* (1798), 157-59; Lewis and Richard H. Collins, *History of Kentucky,* 2 vols. (Covington, Ky., 1874), 2:771; Joan Wells Coward, *Kentucky in the New Republic: The Process of Constitution Making* (Lexington, 1979), 124-81.

18. Sneed, *Report on the Kentucky Penitentiary,* 218.

19. Kentucky *Acts* (1824-25), 119-27.

20. Sneed, *Report on the Kentucky Penitentiary,* 114-17.

21. Robert Gunn Crawford, "A History of the Kentucky Penitentiary System, 1865-1937" (Ph.D. dissertation, University of Kentucky, 1957).

22. Kentucky *Acts* (1824-25), 122-23.

23. Sneed, *Report on the Kentucky Penitentiary,* 166, 173.

24. *Ibid.,* 169.

25. Preston S. Loughboro was a professor of law in Transylvania University in 1824 when Scott was a student. Transylvania University *Catalog* (1824), 2. Born in Mercer County in 1780, Judge James Haggin moved to Lexington in 1810 to practice law. In 1824 he was appointed a judge on the Court of Appeals, the "New Court" bench. He died in Frankfort in August 1835. Lexington *Observer and Reporter,* September 2, 1835; Ranck, "The Bar of Lexington," 242.

26. Kentucky *Acts* (1821-22), 247-48; (1822), 119-24, 230-31. Earlier legislation relating to banks and the crises of 1819 can be located in Kentucky *Acts* (1817-19), 693-96, and *ibid.,* (1821), 452, 469-70.

27. Kentucky *Acts* (1824-25), 278.

28. See, for example, Robert Penn Warren, *World Enough and Time* (New York, 1950); William Gilmore Simms, *Beauchamp: Or, The Kentucky Tragedy. A Tale of Passion* (Philadelphia, 1842); Jeroboam Beauchamp, *Beauchamp's Confessions . . .* (Philadelphia, 1830).

29. Scott kept a meticulously recorded set of legal notes which was bound in with the original journal of his travels in 1829-1830. Special Collections, University of Kentucky Library, Lexington.

30. Prisilla Wilmot to Robert Wilmot Scott, February 22, 1827, NSCD Archives.

31. Dr. Preston W. Brown, 1775-1826, was the youngest son of Reverend John and Margaret Brown of Virginia. He practiced medicine in Woodford, Franklin, and Jefferson counties, Kentucky. After his death in 1826 his widow and five children moved back to Frankfort. Bayless E. Hardin, "Dr. Preston W. Brown, 1775-1826; His Family and Descendants," *Filson Club History Quarterly* 19 (1945): 3-28. A genealogical chart of the Brown and Scott families may be found in the NSCD Archives. See also Alice Trabue, *A Corner in Celebrities* (Louisville, 1922), *passim.*

32. Dr. Preston Brown was shot by Randall W. Smith on September 22, 1826, as Brown attempted to break up a fight between Smith and his father-in-law, a Mr. Christopher. Smith fired on Christopher with a gun heavily loaded with slugs and accidentally hit Brown. Frankfort *Commentator,* October 2, 1826; Washington, D. C. *National Intelligencer,* October 7, December 4, 1826; Henry Clay to James Brown, October 8, 1826, in James F. Hopkins, Mary W. Hargreaves, and Robert Seager II, eds., *The Papers of Henry Clay* (9 vols. to date, Lexington, 1959-), 5:760.

33. H. Levin, ed., *The Lawyers and the Lawmakers of Kentucky* (Chicago, 1897), 496; Lexington *Observer and Reporter,* September 2, 1835. Although Haggin's momentary fame as a judge on the "New" Kentucky Court of Appeals won him a line in state history, he was in many ways a tragic figure. That particular court was dissolved by legislative act, and it was doubtful that his law practice yielded an appreciable income. When he died in 1835 he left his family in debt. This no doubt accounts for the fact that Robert W. Scott was able to purchase his livestock, and his farm east of Jett. In January 1841, Haggin's widow, Hetty, and her children sought relief of the Kentucky General Assembly in adjudicating the judge's debts. They asked that an administrator be appointed to sell his remaining property and to care for the widow and heirs. Kentucky *Acts* (1840-41), 107.

34. Schedule of the United States Census, Franklin County, Kentucky, 1840; Frankfort *Weekly Kentucky Yeoman*, November 11, 1884. Elizabeth's wedding dress along with other items of personal clothing are preserved in the collection of the National Society of Colonial Dames, Orlando Brown House.

35. Winston J. Davie wrote in 1879 of "Colonel Robert W. Scott, of Franklin County, Kentucky, who is one of the best educated and most scientific farmers in the state, and whose farm is near Frankfort." *Second Annual Report from the State Bureau of Agriculture and Horticulture & Statistics* (Frankfort, 1879), 288. "Every one here has long recognized Mr. Scott as one of the most painstaking and successful farmers in the state, while to great practical judgment he adds highly cultivated and refined taste, which has shown itself in superior improvements, and pleasing hedges, shrubs, garden, orchard, and woodland which everywhere meets the eye." Frankfort *Weekly Kentucky Yeoman*, quoted in Robert W. Scott, *Pedigrees, Descriptions, Testimonials, Essays, &c., Short-Horn Durham Cattle, "Improved Kentucky" Sheep* . . . (Frankfort, 1884), 8.

36. Sneed, *Report on the Kentucky Penitentiary*, 218; *Biographical Encyclopedia of Kentucky*, 225.

37. Robert Wilmot Scott's land transactions were somewhat complicated, and are now difficult to document. On December 30, 1834, John R. Scott bought of James Brown a tract on South Elkhorn and a part of the Lewis military survey. Franklin County Deed Book P, 370. Robert W. Scott was meticulous in all things apparently except one. He seems not to have believed in recording his deeds. The author has spent hours searching for the Scott deeds in both the Franklin and Woodford County courthouses without discovering some of the entries for his properties. Yet the recorded deeds of properties belonging to his neighbors refer to the Scott lands and their boundaries. On September 19, 1843 Robert W. Scott bought of John Wiggs and wife a tract of James Brown land, and another part of the Lewis military survey, Franklin County Deed Book R, 237. In October 1838 Scott bought of Samuel Churchill 87½ acres. The deed to the Hardin tract is no longer obtainable due to one of Kentucky's most infernal archival problems — it has been removed from Franklin County Deed Book R, 237, by vandalism. The record of these deeds was graciously supplied by Anita Gantley of the Franklin County Clerk's Office, March 10, 1984.

38. Scott purchased the Hardin land in 1834. He said he paid "about $9,000 for 205 acres." This deed is now unobtainable as explained above. Scott moved his family directly to this farm. In his 1871 broadside (Archives, Western Kentucky University, Bowling Green) offering Locust Hill for sale, he indicated there was one brick house of early construction. The Scott record is silent on which house the family first occupied. See S. I. M. Major Collection, Townsend Room, Eastern Kentucky University, Richmond. Willard Rouse Jillson indicates that there was a log house near the site of the future Locust Hill mansion. Jillson, *Early Frankfort and Franklin County* (Louisville, 1936), 50. The disposal of the lands of James Haggin is an interesting footnote to Kentucky's tangled economic-political situation in the decades 1810-1830. Judge Haggin borrowed $4,541.45 of Charles Humphrey of Lexington in 1832 to pay off a mortgage or note due the Bank of the United States. Security for this note were Terah T. Haggin of Jefferson County and John Haggin of Mercer County. They in turn accepted the Haggin lands near the Forks of Elkhorn as security. It was the settlement of this indebtedness which resulted in the sale of the lands to Robert W. Scott. Haggin to Humphrey, Franklin County Deed Book 3 (May 2, 1832), 352, and Deed Book O (October 8, 1832), 259.

39. Franklin County Deed Book 37 (October 11, 1838), 337-39, in Franklin County Clerk's Office, Frankfort.

40. Generally, the Locust Hill Plantation was bounded on the west by the Versailles-Frankfort Turnpike, on the east by the L C. and L. Railroad. The Woodford-Franklin county boundary crossed it about an eighth of a mile back of the house site. Scott may have accumu-

lated one thousand acres, as he said. The agricultural section of the United States Census Schedules, 1850 and 1860, do not indicate so large a holding. On January 9, 1856, Scott sold to his neighbor Walter N. Ayers 220 acres of Woodford County land which was a contiguous part of the Locust Hill tract, at eighty dollars an acre. Woodford County Deed Book Z, p. 455, Woodford County Clerk's Office, Versailles. That same year he bought from Thomas I. and Fanny Ficklin 300 acres of Woodford County land for which he paid $24,067. *Ibid.*, 450. On April 3, 1860, Robert and John Scott transferred 180 poles of land along the Leestown Road to the trustees of the Elkhorn Baptist Church to be held by them in perpetuity as a church ground. *Ibid.*, 20.

41. Scott, *Pedigrees*, 6.

42. Jillson, *Early Frankfort and Franklin County*, 50.

43. Scott, *Pedigrees*, 6.

44. *Ibid.*

45. Locust Hill Farm Book (No. 1), 12-13, 23-29, 45-48. This book is part of the Jennie S. Green Collection, Filson Club, Louisville. See also *Western Farmer and Gardener* 2 (August 1841): 254.

46. Lewis F. Allen, *History of the Short-Horn Cattle and Their Origin, Progress and Present Condition* (Buffalo, 1872), 169; *Western Farmer and Gardener* 2 (August 1841): 241. The pedigrees of the Scott herd were published in the *Franklin Farmer* 2 (December 2, 1838): 103.

47. This book (No. 1) covers the antebellum years, and contains details of the planting of field crops, gardens, orchards, and of the breeding of farm animals. It also contains labor accounts, rental returns from pasturage, slave hire, wages paid other workers, and general credit accounts. A second farm book covering later years, to 1880, is in the Green Collection at Western Kentucky University, Bowling Green (hereinafter Green Collection, WKU).

48. An example of the care he exercised in records was his experiment with Baden and Chinese corn. *Franklin Farmer* 2 (September 23, 1837): 25. He kept detailed records in various bull, hog, sheep, and goat books, none of which is known to have survived.

49. United States Census, Slave Schedules, District 1, 8, Franklin County, Kentucky, 1850, p. 8; *ibid.*, 1860, p. 5. There are numerous slave hire entries in the earlier Locust Hill Farm Book. See pp. 102, 110, 112-14, 120.

50. Although Scott kept full labor records it is often difficult to tell who were common laborers and who among the workers might have been overseers. Pitcher's accounts were recorded in the Locust Hill Farm Book (No. 1), 52-57.

51. *Ibid.*, 52-57, 61. Ebernezer Morton's account appears at *ibid.*, 78-81.

52. Specifically, Elizabeth to Robert, December 2, 7, 1858, NSCD Archives.

53. Locust Hill Farm Book (No. 1), 3, 41, 49.

2. The Complete Farmer

1. *Ibid.*, 45-48.

2. *Ibid.*, 18.

3. *Ibid.*, 20-21.

4. *Ibid.*, 22-23.

5. *Ibid.*, 36, 40-41, 49.

6. *Franklin Farmer* 3 (August 31, 1839): 1; (September 28, 1839): 12.

7. Allen, *History of the Short-Horn Cattle*, 199-200; Alvin H. Sanders, *Short-Horn Cattle: A Series of Historical Sketches, Memoirs and Records of the Breed and the Development in the United States and Canada* (Chicago, 1901), 254-59.

8. Allen, *History of the Short-Horn Cattle*, 161-71; Sanders, *Short-Horn Cattle*, 215-24;

Otis Rice, "Importation of Cattle into Kentucky, 1785-1860," *Register of the Kentucky Historical Society* 49 (1951): 35-54.

9. Lewis Sanders to Robert W. Scott, January 1, 1853, NSCD Archives; *Western Farmer and Gardener* 3 (October 1841): 2.

10. Robert W. Scott to John Duncan, October 17, 1883, NSCD Archives.

11. *Franklin Farmer* 1 (November 4, 1837): 78.

12. This is one of the most adequately documented facts in Kentucky history. Lewis Sanders to Robert W. Scott, January 1, 1853, NSCD Archives; Allen, *History of the Short-Horn Cattle*, 155-77, 252-60; Lexington *Observer and Reporter*, September 2, 1855; *Western Farmer and Gardener* 2 (January 1840): 83; Sanders, *Short-Horn Cattle*, 173-80.

13. Allen, *History of the Short-Horn Cattle*, 162-65; Sanders, *Short-Horn Cattle*, 173-90; E. P. and O. M. Healy, *A Record of Unfashionable Crosses in Short-Horn Cattle Pedigrees* (Bedford, Iowa, 1883), 6-7, 121, 130.

14. Pedigree no. 36555 in Healy and Healy, *A Record of Unfashionable Crosses in Short-Horn Cattle Pedigrees*, 171; Allen, *History of the Short-Horn Cattle*, 45-46. The question of registering Kentucky short-horns became a highly controversial issue. The point of dispute was essentially whether the animals springing from the 1817 importation and before the publication of the English *Herd Book* should be subject to registration. In 1840, a committee of three — Dr. Samuel D. Martin, Captain Benjamin Warfield, and Robert W. Scott — was appointed to organize the Kentucky Herd Book. Martin, in particular, worked on the organization of the registry; in March 1846, he wrote Scott that it was ready for publication. The manuscript consisted of a generous number of plates and 175 pages of text which Martin asked Scott to check; Martin also requested assistance in finding a printer. Samuel D. Martin to Robert W. Scott, March 24, 1846, NSCD. This herd book was never published because of the disputes among breeders. Allen, *History of the Short-Horn Cattle*, 252-53.

15. Robert W. Scott to John Duncan, October 17, 1883, NSCD Archives.

16. *Western Farmer and Gardener* 3 (October 1841): 2.

17. Elizabeth Brown Scott to Robert W. Scott, January 11, 1859, NSCD Archives.

18. *Western Farmer and Gardener* 3 (October 1841): 2.

19. *Ibid.*, 2 (August 1841): 241.

20. *Ibid.*, 241-42.

21. *Ibid.*, 242.

22. Locust Hill Farm Book (No. 1), 205-8.

23. Scott, *Pedigrees*, 15-18.

24. *Ibid.*, 15-18.

25. There no doubt was at least one exception to the above. Scott bred his mare Sea Gull to the famous Kentucky stallion Medoc. Medoc was owned by Scott's neighbor, Colonel William Buford of Woodford County. Medoc, the son of Eclipse, was foaled in Virginia. The mare breeding record for Locust Hill is a fairly extensive one. Locust Hill Farm Book (No. 1), 190-200, 209-12.

26. Robert M. Ireland, *Little Kingdoms: The Counties of Kentucky, 1850-1891* (Lexington, 1977), 90-100.

27. Locust Hill Farm Book (No. 1), 184.

28. Scott hired numerous slaves, as indicated above. An entry in his Farm Book, 184, noted: "Pays $75.00 down in a credit note or note for negro hire which he holds & the rest to be paid on delivery of mules."

29. The problem of dogs running at large was a serious deterrent to sheep raising, especially near populous communities. Locust Hill was fairly well isolated from Frankfort and its dog packs. Nevertheless, Scott had his worries on this score. On January 16, 1856, the Kentucky General Assembly was requested to enact a stricter dog law. See Robert W. Scott, Corresponding Secretary Kentucky State Agricultural Society, *[First] Report, Kentucky*

Agricultural Society (Frankfort, 1857), 11. There was on the statutes a law permitting any person to slay a sheep-killing dog and then to become a competent witness justifying his act. Richard H. Stanton, ed., *The Revised Statutes of Kentucky* . . . 2 vols. (Cincinnati, 1860), 1:223. The General Assembly enacted an additional law, February 15, 1858, which permitted Shelby and Hardin county officials to collect a tax of $1.00 from owners of more than one dog. Kentucky *Acts* (1857-58), 117-18.

    30. Charles Foster, editor of the *Western Farmer and Gardener*, was a visitor (June 1842, 3:213). Adam Beatty came frequently on his way to attend meetings in Frankfort of the State Historical Society. In fact there seem to have been few months when there was not an agricultural visitor at Locust Hill.

    31. A Kentuckian writing under the pseudonym "Umbra" published a series of essays on sheep in Kentucky in the *Western Farmer and Gardener* 2 (April 1841): 156-59; (July 1841): 224-26; and (August 1841): 260-63. See also Robert W. Scott, "Improved Kentucky Sheep," *Report of the United States Commissioner of Agriculture for the year 1866* (Washington, D. C., 1867), 334-40, and Scott, *Pedigrees*, 22.

    32. *Report, United States Commissioner of Agriculture*, 335-36.

    33. Scott, *Pedigrees*.

    34. *Ibid.*

    35. *Ibid.*, 23.

    36. Scott, *[First] Report, Kentucky Agricultural Society*, 53.

    37. Scott, *Pedigrees*, 32.

    38. *Ibid.*

    39. Plates XXIV, XXV.

    40. Scott, *Pedigrees*, 30.

    41. Pp. 287-91.

    42. Scott, *Pedigrees*, 34-35.

    43. Davie, *Second Annual Report from the State Bureau of Agriculture*, 290.

    44. *Ibid.*

    45. Locust Hill Farm Book (No. 1), 14-15.

    46. *Western Farmer and Gardener* 2 (October 1840): 9-10; 2 (March 1841): 122-23; 2 (June 1841): 211-16; 2 (September 1841): 280-82; 3 (October 1841): 5-11; 3 (January 1842): 94-96; 3 (February 1841): 102-3.

    47. Locust Hill Farm Book (No. 1), 15.

    48. *Ibid.*, 14-16; Scott, *Pedigrees*, 33-34.

    49. Scott, *Pedigrees*, 33-34.

    50. *Ibid.*, 34.

    51. Elizabeth Brown Scott to Robert W. Scott, December 7, 1858, NSCD Archives.

3. An Idyll of the Land

    1. Scott, *Pedigrees*, 32.

    2. Elizabeth Brown Scott to Robert W. Scott, December 7, 1858, NSCD Archives.

    3. Scott, *Pedigrees*, 9.

    4. *Western Farmer and Gardener* 2 (April 1841): 149.

    5. Scott, *Pedigrees*, 12-15.

    6. *Ibid.*, 13.

    7. *Ibid.*, 14.

    8. *Ibid.*, 14.

    9. Elizabeth Brown Scott to Robert W. Scott, December 9, 1858, NSCD Archives.

    10. *Ibid.*

11. *Ibid.*

12. *Ibid.,* December 2, 1858.

13. Allen, *History of the Short-Horn Cattle,* 252.

14. It is difficult to know whether all of Scott's essays have been located. He wrote a generous number which appeared in farm journals, government publications, stock books, and newspapers.

15. Davie, *Second Annual Report from the State Bureau of Agriculture,* 288.

16. *Western Farmer and Gardener* 2 (March 1841): 125.

17. Locust Hill Farm Book (No. 1), 66.

18. "It may well be said, that no man who can make a set of *draw bars,* should ever have a *slip gap;* and be as truly said, that no man who can make a gate should ever have draw bars, (except in some peculiar cases where bars answer better than a gate.)" Thomas Afleck wrote in response, "Generally speaking the farms in Kentucky are admirably provided with gates — well hung and properly latched. But we must be *even* with one noted stock breeder, not quite a hundred miles from Louisville on the Bardstown Road, who had the clumsiest *slip-gap* we ever laid down, every one, with a fractious horse in the buggy, one very hot morning before breakfast. Whew! we haven't got over it yet." *Western Farmer and Gardener* 2 (August 1841): 254-55.

19. *Ibid.,* 2 (March 1841): 125.

20. *Ibid.,* 2 (April 1841): 149.

21. *Ibid.,* 2 (February 1841): 117. Locust Hill Farm Book (No. 1), 24-39.

22. *Western Farmer and Gardener* 2 (February 1841): 125.

23. Scott experimented with all kinds of animals and fowls. He became interested in Poland ducks, and at least one contemporary hand drawn illustration shows ducks before the Locust Hill mansion. E. S. Washington to Robert W. Scott, January 8, 1846, and Scott to Elizabeth Brown Scott, July 20, 1866, NSCD Archives. Scott also experimented with corn varieties. See *Franklin Farmer* 2 (December 2, 1837): 105; Locust Hill Farm Book (No. 1), 22-23. He published a series of five articles on the principles of breeding cattle in the *Franklin Farmer* 1 (March 3, 1838): 223; (April 7, 1838): 246; (April 14, 1838): 259; (May 12, 1838): 287; and (May 19, 1838): 310. Also interested in bee-keeping, Scott published an extensive essay on the troublesome bee moth and its control. *Ibid.* (October 14, 1837): 1.

24. Robert W. Scott to Thomas Afleck, July 5, 18, 1841, NSCD Archives; *Western Farmer and Gardener* 2 (August 1841): 254.

25. Elizabeth Brown Scott to Robert W. Scott, (undated), NSCD Archives.

26. *Ibid.,* January 11, 1859.

27. The Browns seem to have been frequent visitors, as were farm editors, stockmen, animal painters, agricultural society people, Kentucky politicians, and all other wayfarers.

4. The Social and Cultural Crusader

1. Hardin, "Dr. Preston W. Brown," 1-28.

2. C. W. Hackensmith, *Out of Time and Tide: The Evolution of Education in Kentucky* (Lexington, 1970), 1-35; Alvin Fayette Lewis, *History of Higher Education in Kentucky* (Washington, D. C., 1899), 328-35.

3. The question of instituting a system of public education in Kentucky was raised at intervals. It was only a minor issue, if in fact an issue at all, in the Second Constitutional Convention in 1799. See especially Coward, *Kentucky in the New Republic,* 22, 85-86.

4. Kentucky *Acts* (1837-38), 274-83.

5. Robert W. Scott, "Early History of the Common School System of Kentucky," in NSCD Archives.

6. It is difficult to determine factually claims of "firsts." Scott believed his school was first. A fairly creditable sketch of public school beginnings is Lewis, *History of Higher Education in Kentucky*, 331-35.

7. *Biographical Encyclopedia of Kentucky*, 225.

8. Scott, *[First] Report, Kentucky Agricultural Society*, 7; *Franklin Farmer* 1 (February 10, 1838): 177-78; 2 (February 16, 1839): 162-64, 206.

9. Robert W. Scott, *[Second] Report of the Kentucky State Agricultural Society*, (Frankfort, 1857) contains throughout materials prepared by the corresponding secretary. On February 13, 1858, the Society adopted a resolution to purchase a fifty dollar sterling silver pitcher "To be presented to Mr. Scott as a testimonial of regard for the valuable services rendered by him to the Society," *ibid.*, 146. The pitcher bearing an eloquent inscription is now the property of the National Society of Colonial Dames, Orlando Brown House.

10. "Report of the Superintendent of the Institution for the Education and Training of Feeble-minded Children in Response to a Resolution of the House, adopted January 24, 1861," in *Kentucky Documents* (Frankfort, 1861).

11. This was the branch of the Western Baptist Theological Institute which was separated from the Covington institution. About $25,000 in funds was transferred to the Georgetown branch, which was made a part of Georgetown College. William H. Perrin, *History of Bourbon, Scott, Harrison, and Nicholas Counties, Kentucky* (Chicago, 1882), 199-200.

12. The identifiable remains of Robert W. Scott's extensive library reflect a wide range of scientific and literary interests. This library, which in 1886 Dr. Preston Scott paid W. H. Cleveland twenty-three dollars to list (not found), has become badly scattered. Some of the books have found their way into the libraries of the University of Kentucky, both Eastern Kentucky University and Western Kentucky University, Berea College, and some remain the private property of Marion Burnam and James Ferguson, Madison County. The settlement record of the Robert W. Scott Estate filed by Preston Brown Scott, December 5, 1886, in the Settlement Book, Franklin County Clerk's Office, Frankfort. Two lists compiled by James Ferguson of the Scott-Major libraries were prepared when the books were offered for sale.

13. This fact is made evident in the United States decennial *Census Reports*, 1830-1860, and in the Kentucky *Auditor's Reports*, and after 1878, in the annual *Reports* of the Bureau of Agriculture, Horticulture, and Statistics. These contain reports from the individual counties.

14. Winston J. Davie, *Kentucky: Its Resources and Present Condition: The First Annual Report, the State Bureau of Agriculture, Horticulture, and Statistics* (Frankfort, 1878), 209-11; Scott, *[First] Report, Kentucky Agricultural Society*, 5-12.

15. Scott, *[First] Report, Kentucky Agricultural Society*, 10; *Franklin Farmer* 2 (February 3, 1838): 172.

16. Scott, *[First] Report, Kentucky Agricultural Society*, 18-24.

17. *Franklin Farmer* 2 (February 16, 1839): 164, 206.

18. Scott, *[First] Report, Kentucky Agricultural Society*, 7.

19. In 1840, those Kentucky farmers who read anything about the science of agriculture did so in essays in highly limited circulation in outside agricultural journals, and for a brief time in the *Franklin Farmer*. The state's newspapers were almost altogether devoted to political and unusual news. There was no central body of materials relating to the results of agricultural experimentation or other scientific farm information. The Kentucky General Assembly even reneged on financing the publication of the State Agricultural Society's prize essays. Kentucky *Acts* (1840-41), 276, indicate legislative indifference to the subject.

20. *Ibid.*

21. Adam Beatty, *Essays on Practical Agriculture including His Prize Essays Carefully Revised* (Maysville, Ky., 1844).

22. Davie, *Kentucky: Its Resources and Present Condition*, 210; Scott, *[First] Report, Kentucky Agricultural Society*, 18-22.

23. Kentucky *Acts* (1837-38), 357; *Franklin Farmer* 2 (September 16, 1837): 22; Resolutions, Kentucky State Agricultural Society (January 16, 1838): 19; (January 14, 1839), 6; *Franklin Farmer* 2 (January 26, 1839): 163; 2 (February 16, 1839): 206.

24. *Franklin Farmer* 2 (January 26, 1839): 163.

25. "The Importance of Agricultural Publications," *Franklin Farmer* 1 (August 12, 1837): 1.

26. This fact is strongly implied in entries in the Locust Hill Farm Book (no. 1), and in Scott's articles on corn varieties, the breeding of cattle and sheep, and on combating noxious weeds. There are numerous articles by Scott in the *Franklin Farmer*. One which appeared in the *Western Farmer and Gardener* on pasture care and control of noxious weeds is enlightening as to the author's progressive approaches to farming. Much of Scott's influence is reflected in the two reports of the Kentucky Agricultural Society, and in the article on sheep which appeared in the *Report of the United States Commissioner of Agriculture* (Washington, D. C., 1866).

27. Kentucky *Senate Journal* (1853-54), 22-23.

28. *Ibid.*, 23.

29. *Ibid.*, (1855-56), 7.

30. Scott, *[First] Report, Kentucky Agricultural Society*, 9.

31. *Ibid.*, 10.

32. *Ibid.*, 10-12; *Franklin Farmer* 1 (February 10, 1838): 176.

33. Scott was president of the Franklin County Agricultural Society. *Franklin Farmer* 1 (August 12, 1837): 7.

34. Scott, *[First] Report of the Kentucky Agricultural Society*, 540-41.

35. *Ibid.*, 354-58.

36. "Resolutions on the Erection and Endowment of an Agricultural School for Kentucky," *Franklin Farmer* 2 (January 12, 1839): 162-64; "Memorial to the Legislature of Kentucky — A School of Agriculture," *ibid.*, 156-57.

37. Scott, *[Second] Report of the Kentucky State Agricultural Society*, 146.

38. The *Report* was published in Frankfort in 1857.

39. In none of his correspondence and notes did Scott indicate how much time he gave the State Agricultural Society, but obviously it was a prodigious amount. In 1856, he was paid $300 for his services, but he collected $11,334 for the Society.

5. The Southern Livestock Market

1. Scott, *Pedigrees*, 9-10.

2. *Ibid.*, 14.

3. Frank L. Owsley, *Plain Folk of the Old South* (Baton Rouge, 1949), 23-77; Lewis Gray, *History of Agriculture in the Southern States to 1860*, 2 vols. (Washington, D. C., 1933), 2:853-57. The editor of the *Southern Agriculturist* (Charleston ed.), in 3:201, quoted a letter written in 1842 from Mississippi describing Scott's sale of shorthorns in that state.

4. In Robert W. Scott to Elizabeth Brown Scott, February 2, 1853, he said: "I regret to say Judge Rucks made no arrangements of his debts . . . ." This was almost a steady refrain in the years to come. NSCD Archives.

5. Scott's financial fortunes, like those of every other Kentucky farmer, depended upon the felicity of the seasons. There possibly was never a moment in his long farming experience when he was free of a financial pinch. Robert to Elizabeth, November 30, [1858?], *ibid.*

6. Although the family correspondence does not make precisely clear how many selling trips Robert made to the Lower South between 1840 and 1860, he seems to have gone approximately every two years. His letters to his wife in this period are fairly explanatory of heroic attempts to introduce pure-bred livestock to the region.

7. Nearly all the exchange of letters between Robert W. Scott and his wife Elizabeth Brown mentioned relatives. On February 2, 1855, and March 14, 1857, for example, Robert wrote that he had seen "Cousin Emile's family," "Cousin Mary," "Cousin May Ann," and "Cousin Lucey." He also saw Rucks, Yerkes, Sykes, and other relatives. NSCD Archives.

8. Robert to Elizabeth, March 14, 1857, *ibid.*

9. *Ibid.*, December 8, 1856.

10. *Ibid.*, December 4, 8, 1858, November 30, 1857.

11. *Ibid.*, February 2, 1855.

12. *Ibid.*

13. November 24, 1858.

14. *Ibid.*

15. The carelessness of the overseer Trimble was one of the crosses which Scott had to bear throughout his farming career. He never really found a wholly dependable man for that responsibility.

16. Robert to Elizabeth, November 24, 1858, NSCD Archives.

17. *Ibid.*, November 30, 1858.

18. *Ibid.*, December 4, 1858.

19. *Ibid.*, November 30, 1858.

20. *Ibid.*, December 4, 1858.

21. *Ibid.*

22. *Ibid.*, December 8, 1858.

23. *Ibid.*, undated.

24. Scott's Order No. 10, March 16, 1857, NSCD Archives.

25. Locust Hill Farm Book (No. 1), and contents of family correspondence.

26. *Report, United States Commissioner of Agriculture, 1866*, 334-40.

27. Robert to Elizabeth, October 29, 1865, NSCD Archives.

28. Sales broadside, 1871, Major Collection.

6. Descent Into Babylon

1. *Franklin Farmer* 1 (December 23, 1837): 101-2.

2. Kentucky *Acts* (1832-1833), 258-61; *Report of the Debates and Proceedings of the Convention for the Revision of the Constitution of the State of Kentucky* (Frankfort, 1849), 923-52.

3. Internal improvements was a hotly debated issue in the Constitutional Convention. *Kentucky Constitutional Debates and Proceedings, 1849*, 36, 977, 1094.

4. Scott announced his candidacy from the steps of the Franklin County Courthouse and made at least one fiery speech in support of his views. However, he was bucking the united Whig party and the local courthouse ring. Frankfort *Commonwealth*, June 5, 1849. In the August election Scott withdrew on the first day of a three-day election. He drew 188 votes to Lindsay's 1,097. *Ibid.*, August 14, 1849.

5. "Report of the Superintendent of the Institution for the Education of Feeble Minded Children, January 24, 1861," in *Kentucky Documents* (Frankfort, 1862).

6. United States, Slave Schedule, District 1, Franklin County, 1850, 8.

7. Locust Hill Farm Book (No. 1), 84-114.

8. Scott had numerous overseers, among them John Pilcher, Thomas Kirwin, Simeon Cane, and John Buckley. *Ibid.*, 52-57, 66, 89, 92, 129-34, 45.

9. Elizabeth Brown Scott to Robert Wilmot Scott, December 9, 1858, January 11, 1859, NSCD Archives.

10. *Ibid.*, February 2, 1855.

11. *Ibid.*, March 27, 1857.

12. *Ibid.*, January 11, 1859. In this case some of the slaves boasted that they could manage just as well with Scott away as with him present.

13. *Ibid.*

14. *Ibid.*, September 1, 1858.

15. Kentucky *Acts* (1861), Kentucky *House Journal* (1861), 3-41, contains various messages on the subject from Governor Beriah Magoffin for the various adopted resolutions. See Kentucky *Acts* (1861), 47-52.

16. Kentucky *Acts* (May 1861), 1.

17. The House of Representatives voted March 20, 1861, to allow the State Rights Convention to be held in its hall. Kentucky *House Journal* (1861), 323-24; Frankfort *Commonwealth*, March 23, 1861.

18. Frankfort *Commonwealth*, April 1, 1861.

19. Kentucky *Acts* (1861), 6-7.

20. Frankfort *Commonwealth*, March 14, 1861.

21. E. M. Coulter, *Civil War and Readjustment in Kentucky* (Chapel Hill, 1926), 36-37.

22. J. Stoddard Johnston, *Memorial History of Louisville*, 2 vols. (New York, 1896), 2:445.

23. *The Sunbeam* (Sun Life Insurance Company House Organ), 10 (July 1901):1 (copy in the NSCD Archives).

24. Scott visited the Crab Orchard Springs in July 1866 and again in September 29, 1867. He suffered from a condition he called "catarrh" which must have had a much more serious implication of respiratory infection. Robert W. Scott to Elizabeth Brown Scott, July 20, 1866, September 29, and one undated letter, 1867, Green Collection, WKU. Sometime in these years Scott carried out a long nurtured dream and purchased land in Texas. He bought a full section of 640 acres near Llanos, Texas, for an undisclosed price. In addition, he acquired possession of 172 acres of Florida land on August 1, 1871. Registered deed, Marks to Scott, August 1, 1871, in Orange County, Florida, Deed Book A, 152-54 (copy in Green Collection, WKU).

25. Louisville *Courier-Journal*, November 11, 1884.

26. Original text in Green Collection, WKU.

27. Coulter, *Civil War and Readjustment in Kentucky*, 287-311; "Report of the Superintendent of Public Instruction," in *Kentucky Documents* (1880-82) (Frankfort, 1882).

28. Preston re-established his medical practice in Louisville where he lived until his death on September 21, 1900. John practiced medicine in Owensboro until 1878, when ill health forced him to seek a milder climate in Sherman, Texas. He died in that city in 1907. Hardin, "Dr. Preston W. Brown," 1-28; undated newspaper clipping in NSCD Archives; *The Sunbeam* 10 (July 1901):2.

29. J. Allen Smith, *The College of Agriculture of the University of Kentucky, Early and Middle Years, 1865-1951* (Lexington, 1981).

7. We Are A United Family

1. Robert W. Scott to Mr. and Mrs. Lafayette Green, January 30, 1869, Green Collection, WKU.

2. *Ibid.* Also Scott, *Pedigrees*, 1, 5-8.

3. Sneed, *Report on the Kentucky Penitentiary*, 218; J. Robert Snyder, *A History of Georgetown College* (Georgetown, Ky., 1979), 7; Frankfort *Yeoman*, November 11, 1884; Dr. Howard Smith, "Robert W. Scott," an unidentified newspaper clipping in NSCD Archives; Genealogy of Dr. Preston W. Scott, Robert W. Scott, and Joel Scott, vol. 2, organized by Mrs. S. I. M. Major, and now in the possession of James and Marion Burman Ferguson, Winter Creek Farm, Madison County, Kentucky.

4. Scott was a trustee of Georgetown College from 1841 to 1861. J. Robert Snyder to author, February 19, 1981.

5. Smith, "Robert W. Scott."

6. See entry for October in Scott Travel Journal, 99.

7. There seems to be no record as to which governor commissioned Scott a Kentucky Colonel, but it most likely was Lazarus Powell, who served from 1851 to 1855.

8. A part of her file is still intact and in the possession of James and Marion Burnam Ferguson, Winter Creek Farm, Madison County, Kentucky.

9. Elizabeth Brown Scott to Robert W. Scott, December 7, 1859, NSCD Archives.

10. Manuscript genealogical chart, *ibid.*; Hardin, "Dr. Preston W. Brown," 14-18.

11. Robert W. Scott, "History of the Organization of the First Kentucky Common School," Green Collection, WKU.

12. Elizabeth Brown Scott to Robert W. Scott, December 2, 1858, *ibid.*

13. *Ibid.*

14. Book lists made by James Ferguson in 1865 and revised in 1981. As indicated, the Scott library, or parts of it, were combined with the Major and Green libraries, and now many of the books are in various Kentucky university and college libraries.

15. Elizabeth Brown Scott to Willis Green, October 6, 1881, Green Collection, WKU.

16. Johnston, *Memorial History of Louisville*, 2:444.

17. *Ibid.*

18. "Lewis Rogers," *Biographical Encyclopedia of Kentucky*, 175-76; Johnston, *Memorial History of Louisville*, 2:431-32.

19. *The Sunbeam* 10 (July 1901):1; undated and unidentified newspaper clipping, NSCD Archives.

20. Joel Scott to Robert Scott, June 6, 1853, NSCD Archives.

21. Snyder, *Georgetown College*, 41.

22. Joel Scott to Robert W. Scott, March 4, 1854. Joel died August 1855. D. R. Campbell to Robert W. Scott, September 5, 1855, NSCD Archives; Hardin, "Dr. Preston W. Brown," 15; tombstone inscription, the Frankfort Cemetery.

23. Scott was accompanied on some of his southern trips by one or more of his children. Elizabeth to Robert, undated; also, C. V. Waters to Robert W. Scott, undated, NSCD Archives.

24. Robert W. Scott to Louisa Scott, February 16, 1865, *ibid.*

25. *Biographical Encyclopedia of Kentucky*, 552.

26. *Biographical Directory of the American Congress, 1774-1971* (Washington, D. C., 1971), 1030.

27. Undated and unidentified newspaper notice of Lafayette Green's death, NSCD Archives.

28. *Biographical Encyclopedia of Kentucky*, 369.

29. Colonel Breckinridge and Louisa were married secretly in Washington in April 1893. W. C. P. Breckinridge to Preston B. Scott, May 14, 1893, and Louisa to Ellen Green, July 26, 1893, Green Collection, WKU. See also Agnes Parker, *The Real Madeline Pollard: A Diary of Ten Weeks Association with the Plaintiff in the famous Breckinridge-Pollard Suit* (New York, 1894), 127-28. Louisa was not entirely happy with her marriage to "Cousin Billy." She may have had emotional tendencies which influenced her behavior at times. See also James C. Klotter, *The Breckinridges of Kentucky, 1760-1981* (Lexington, 1986), 161-70, 182-83.

30. Robert revealed his anxieties about Louisa in several of his letters.

31. David Dawson Mitchell to Robert W. Scott, March 29, 1882, NSCD Archives.

32. *Ibid.*

33. Robert W. Scott to David Dawson Mitchell, April 11, 1883, *ibid.*

34. Copies of the Scott-Mitchell wedding invitation, NSCD Archives; Hardin, "Dr. Preston W. Brown," 18. Hardin was mistaken as to the date of the wedding.

35. John G. Putnam, Jr., to Director, Orlando Brown House, January 27, 1979. Also, John G. Putnam, Jr., to Mrs. Louis Cox, February 14, 1979, NSCD Archives.
36. Elizabeth Brown Scott to Robert W. Scott, "June 25, I believe," *ibid.*
37. Robert W. Scott to Elizabeth Brown Scott, undated, Major Collection.
38. *Ibid.*
39. Elizabeth Brown Scott to Robert W. Scott, December 9, 1858, NSCD Archives.
40. *Ibid.*, undated.
41. *Ibid.*
42. *Ibid.*, "June, I believe."
44. *Ibid.*
45. *Ibid.*
46. *Ibid.*, December 2, 1858. See also letter from Elizabeth who had taken Louisa to Louisville to be examined by "Cousin" Lewis Rogers, December 9, 1858, *ibid.*
47. Elizabeth Brown Scott to Robert W. Scott, Nashville, undated, *ibid.*
48. Robert W. Scott to his daughters Etta, Mary, and Lizzie, March 1 (no year); Scott to Louisa, February 16, 1865; Scott to Lizzie, December 12, 1878, NSCD Archives.

8. In the Course of Time

1. Elizabeth Brown Scott to Robert W. Scott, *ibid.*
2. *Ibid.*, "December."
3. *Ibid.*, December 9, 1858.
4. Robert W. Scott to Elizabeth Brown Scott, "Tuesday Night," July 1866, Major Collection.
5. *Ibid.*
6. Robert W. Scott advertised Locust Hill for sale June 22, 1871. Broadside, Major Collection.
7. *Ibid.* See also Scott, *Pedigrees.*
8. Robert W. Scott to Rumsey and Louisa Wing, September 27, 1872, NSCD Archives.
9. See Broadside, Major Collection, and Scott, *Pedigrees.*
10. Elizabeth Brown Scott to her son Dr. Preston Brown Scott, October 1884, NSCD Archives. Locust Hill was finally sold on September 22, 1885. The acreage had been reduced to 378.08 and was disposed of at the ridiculously low price of $65.00 an acre for a total of $24,575, payable in four annual installments of $6,043.80 bearing 6 percent interest. The purchasers were H. P. Mason, Charles E. Hoge, S. D. Gooch, and W. F. Dandridge. Franklin County Deed Book 23, 157-58.
11. Robert W. Scott to Willis Green, October 6, 1881, Green Collection, WKU.
12. Copies of registered deeds are included among the Scott papers, *ibid.* These include deeds from Marks to Scott, August 1, 1871 (Deed Book A, Orange County, Florida, 152-54); and Stedman to Scott, October 3, 1872 (*ibid.*, 303-4).
13. Robert W. Scott to John W. Cannon, March 22, 1875, NSCD Archives.
14. *Ibid.*
15. Robert W. Scott to his daughter Etta Scott, February 25, 1878, *ibid.*
16. A plat of the Florida lands is included in the Green Collection, WKU.
17. In both Robert's and Elizabeth's Florida letters they mention entertaining company. Specifically, Robert W. Scott to his daughter Lizzie Scott, December 1, 1876, *ibid.*
18. Robert W. Scott to his daughter Etta, March 3, 1884, and Scott to his son-in-law and daughter Rumsey and Louisa Wing, September 27, 1872, *ibid.*
19. Robert wrote with faithfulness and the greatest parental tenderness to his children, and his letters reveal both his physical and financial conditions. *Ibid.*
20. *Ibid.*, December 12, 1876.
21. *Ibid.*

22. Elizabeth Brown Scott to Etta Scott, February 25, 1878, NSCD Archives.

23. *Ibid.*, December 12, 1876.

24. March 16, 1879.

25. Robert W. Scott to his daughter Etta, March 1882. All through his letters to his children, 1869 to 1884, Scott wrote of the problems of trying to manage the affairs of Locust Hill in his absence. As early as January 9, 1869, he wrote Ella Green, "The day is not far distant when all must change hands in this homestead, & the change is hastened by the consideration that I can make it better than anyone can for us. After this year will exhaust the last of my forbearance on the subject." He hoped that Lafayette Green would consent to buy Locust Hill and live on the plantation. Green Collection, WKU.

26. Scott read the Democratic newspapers, especially his son-in-law's passionately Democratic Frankfort *Yeoman.* There was irony in the fact that the issues which announced Democratic victories in 1884 also announced Robert's death.

27. Robert W. Scott to his daughter Etta Scott, February 25, 1878, Green Collection, WKU.

28. United States Census Schedules, Elkhorn District, Franklin County, Kentucky, 1850, p. 8; 1860, pp. 3, 5; Scott, *Pedigrees*, 6-7, 15-20, 32-34.

29. Scott, *Pedigrees.*

30. "Early History of the Common School System in Kentucky," NSCD Archives.

31. Elizabeth Brown Scott to her son Dr. Preston Brown Scott, October 1884, *ibid.*; Frankfort *Weekly Yeoman*, November 11, 1884; Will Book, 1882-1884, Franklin County, County Clerk's Office, July 12, 1884, pp. 94-97. Scott left all his property "of every description . . . at all personal or mixed" to his wife Elizabeth Brown Scott. Following her death the residue was to be divided into eight equal parts, with each child receiving one part (with the exception of Elizabeth, or Lizzie, who was to have two parts). Scott's daughters were instructed to receive and hold their shares separate and apart from their husbands.

32. Elizabeth Brown Scott to her son Dr. Preston B. Scott, October, 1884, Green Collection, WKU.

33. The last of the Locust Hill livestock was sold on October 24, 1884, just a fortnight before Robert's death. Hogs brought at public auction $4.80 a hundred weight, yearling colts $100, cattle $40 a head. No one bid on the farm. Frankfort *Weekly Kentucky Yeoman*, October 28, 1884. Dr. Preston B. Scott presented his father's will for probate on December 1, 1884 (Will Book, 1882-1884, Franklin County, 94-97). Final settlement of the estate was made October 31, 1886. The executor paid all obligations which amounted to $35,065.42. This left Elizabeth a net sum of $1,224.89 plus the sale price of Locust Hill, the Florida properties, and the Texas lands. Sale of the Texas land was handled by John O. Scott and John C. Oatman, Llanos, Texas. Oatman to Preston B. Scott, February 18, 1887. The Florida land perhaps was sold by James B. Ingraham. Ingraham to Preston B. Scott, December 1, 1884. Both in Green Collection, WKU. Elizabeth Brown Scott died December 25, 1886. Tombstone inscription, Frankfort Cemetery.

34. See also Elizabeth Brown Scott to Eleanor Green, December 1, 1884, Green Collection, WKU.

35. Frankfort *Weekly Frankfort Yeoman*, November 11, 1884. The graves of most of the members of the Scott-Brown clan are lined up in the Frankfort Cemetery near the high limestone ledge overlooking the Kentucky River and the State Capitol.

36. Scott served as a member, and often as chairman, of the Central Committee of the postwar Democratic party in Kentucky. He had helped initiate the call of the reorganizational convention in 1865. He received special commendation when he retired as chairman of the Central Committee. Louisville *Courier-Journal*, November 11, 1884.

37. When Mason, Hoge, Gooche, and Dandridge purchased Locust Hill in 1885, they changed its name to Scotland, presumably in honor of its former owner. Ermina Jett Darnell, "Happy Days at Jett," Manuscript, 76-81, courtesy of Jacob C. Darnell, Frankfort.

Bibliography

Archival Collections

Miraculously a significant portion of the archival materials pertaining to Robert W. Scott and his family has survived family divisions and estate settlements. The family manuscripts, like the Locust Hill library, have become widely separated. Henrietta Dawson Wiley preserved a good number of the intimate Scott family correspondence, and upon her death an intelligent attorney, John G. Putnam, Jr., sensed the importance of the bundle of papers found in Mrs. Wiley's desk and, perhaps against her wishes, entered into correspondence with Mrs. Louis Cox of Frankfort about returning them to Kentucky. These papers, along with several articles of clothing and silverware, are now the property of the National Society of Colonial Dames in the Commonwealth of Kentucky, and are a part of the archival collection in the Orlando Brown House, Frankfort. The rest of the Scott-Green-Major family papers are deposited in the Filson Club, Western Kentucky University, and Eastern Kentucky University archives in Louisville, Bowling Green, and Richmond, respectively. The library has become widely divided with some of the books deposited in the University of Kentucky, Berea College, and Western Kentucky University libraries, while a good portion of it is still the property of the Ferguson family in Madison County, Kentucky. The important Scott travel diary along with Robert W. Scott's legal studies notes are the property of the Special Collections Division of the University of Kentucky Library. Marion Burnam and James Ferguson generously deposited the good collection of family photographs in the archival collection of the Kentucky Historical Society. The Fergusons are still in possession of the extensive collection of genealogical materials compiled by Mrs. S. I. M. Major, some of which relates directly to the history of the Robert W. Scott family. Miss Jennie Green, a Scott granddaughter, gave the highly significant collection of papers relating to her family and life at the Falls of Rough to the Kentucky Library, Western Kentucky University. This collection consists of personal correspondence and the business records of this important Kentucky family. It contains Robert W. Scott's second farm book which is in fact a complete record of labor and furnishing accounts for Locust Hill after 1865.

The Writings of Robert Wilmot Scott

Albert Gallatin Hughes, publisher of the Frankfort *Commonwealth* and the *Kentucky Farmer*, wrote in 1859 that if the state had many farmers like Robert

W. Scott Kentucky would be amply rewarded with able writers on agricultural subjects. Scott demonstrably was one of the Commonwealth's most literate farmers. The list which follows is one of his discovered essays. There may be others. Essays which appeared in the *Kentucky Farmer*:

"Cross Breeding of Livestock," April, 1859, 154.
"Essay on Breeding Cattle," March 1859, 130-32.
"Feeding Stock of Store Cattle in Winter," January 1859, 105.
"Hemp Breaking," March 1859, 138-39.
"How to make an Asparagus Bed," February 1859, 121-22.
"Husking Shock Corn," November 1858, 74.
"Sheep Husbandry in the West," January 1859, 186-88.
"Sowing Grass Seeds," March 1859, 136.
"Sowing Wheat. Preparation of Seed, &c." October 1858, 59.
"Spreading Hemp while it is in the Straw," December 1858, 90.
"Taking up Hemp," January 1859, 105-6.
"The Quantity of Seed which should be sowed to the Acre on Rich and on Poor Land," January 1859, 104.
"To the Friends of Agricultural Improvement in Kentucky," June 1859, 185.

Essays which appeared in the *Franklin Farmer*:
"Badin Corn,"1 (December 2, 1837): 105.
"Foreign Seeds — A Caution," 2 (February 16, 1839): 242.
"Franklin Agricultural Society," 1 (November 20, 1837): 101.
"Pedigree of Frederick," 1 (October 12, 1837): 78.
"The Bee Moth," 1 (October 14, 1837): 37.
"The Importance of Agricultural Publications," 1 (August 12, 1837): 1.
"The Principles of Breeding Cattle," (in five numbers) 1 (1838): 223, 245-46, 258-59, 287, 310, 341.
"To the Breeders of Sheep," 1 (April 14, 1837): 262.

"Improved Kentucky Sheep," *Report of the United States Commissioner of Agriculture for the Year, 1866*, Washington, D. C., 1867.
"Sheep Husbandry in Kentucky," *Second Report of the Kentucky Agricultural Society*, Frankfort, 1860, 206-17.
"On Breeding Cattle," *Ibid.*, 55-64.
"Memorial to the Members of the House of Representatives," *Kentucky Legislative Documents*, Document 1, December 16, 1837.
"Angora Goats," *Second Annual Report from the State Bureau of Agriculture, Horticulture, and Statistics*, 287-91.
Pedigrees, Descriptions, Testimonials, Essays, &c., Short-horn Durham Cattle, "Improved Kentucky" Sheep and of Woburn, Irish-Grazier, White Bedford, Yorkshire, Berkshire, and China Hogs Blended, Frankfort, 1884.
First Annual Report of the Kentucky State Agricultural Society to Legislature of Kentucky for the Years 1856 and 1857. Frankfort, 1857.

Public Records

Deed Book B-6, Fayette County Clerk's Office, Lexington, Kentucky.
Deed Books 23, 37, Franklin County Clerk's Office, Frankfort.
Deed Books E, Z, Woodford County Clerk's Office, Versailles.
Deed Book A, Orange County Clerk's Office, Stanford, Florida.
Will Book 1882-1884, Franklin County Clerk's Office, Frankfort.
Estates Settlement Book, 1882-1886, Franklin County Clerk's Office, Frankfort.

Published Legal Sources

Henning, W. W. *The Statutes-at-Large; being a Collection of all the Laws of Virginia, 1619-1792.* 13 vols. New York and Philadelphia, 1809-23.
Kentucky *Acts,* 1820-1861.
Kentucky *House Journal,* 1861.
Kentucky *Legislative Documents,* 1830-1870.
Morehead, C. S., and Mason Brown. *A Digest of the Statute Laws of Kentucky, of a Public and Permanent Nature.* Frankfort, 1833.
Palmer, W. P., and H. W. Fournoy, eds. *Calendar of Virginia State Papers.* 11 vols. Richmond, 1875-93.
Peters, Richard, Jr. *Reports of Cases Argued and Adjudged in the Supreme Court, 1828-1843.* 17 vols. Boston, 1844.
Register of Debates in Congress, 21st Congress. Washington, D.C., 1830.
Report of the Kentucky State Agricultural Society to the Legislature of Kentucky for the Years 1856 and 1857, and for the Years 1858 and 1859. Frankfort, 1857, 1860.
Report of the Debates and Proceedings of the Convention for the Revision of the Constitution of the State of Kentucky. Frankfort, 1849.
Stanton, Richard H., ed. *The Revised Statutes of Kentucky.* 2 vols. Cincinnati, 1860.
United States House of Representatives. *Executive Documents.* Vol. I. Washington, D.C., 1831.

Indexes, Papers, and Reports

Annual Reports, Kentucky Commissioner of Agriculture and Labor. Frankfort, 1878-1884.
The First Annual Report of the Richmond Society for the Promotion of Temperance. Richmond, Va., 1830.
First Annual Report of the Virginia State Library for the Year ended June 30, 1904. Richmond, 1904.
Hasse, Adelaide. *Index to United States Documents relating to Foreign Affairs, 1828-1861.* Part II. Washington, D.C., 1919.
Hopkins, James F., and Mary Wilma Hargreaves, eds. *The Papers of Henry Clay.* Vol. III. Lexington, 1963.

Owen, David Dale. *Fourth Report of the Geological Survey in Kentucky.* Frankfort, 1861.

Portraits and Statuary of Virginians. Richmond, 1977.

Richardson, James D., compiler. *A Compilation of the Messages and Papers of the Presidents of the United States, 1789-1908.* 10 vols. Washington, D.C., 1909.

Second Report of the Kentucky State Agricultural Society of the Legislature of Kentucky for the Years 1858 and 1859. Frankfort, 1860.

Van Cittert, P. H. *Descriptive Catalog of the Collection of Microscopes in Charge of the Utrecht Museum with an Introductory Historical Survey of the Resolving Power of the Microscope.* Gronigen, Holland, 1934.

Works Progress Administration, Writers Program. *Fairs and Fair-Makers of Kentucky.* Vol. I. Frankfort, 1942.

Travel Accounts and Memoirs

Appleton's Illustrated Handbook of American Travel. New York, 1857.

Arese, Count Francesco. *A Trip to the Prairies and in the Interior of the United States* [1837-1838]. Translated by Andrew Evans. New York, 1934.

Brown, David Paul. *The Forum; or Forty Years of Full Practice of the Philadelphia Bar.* Philadelphia, 1856.

Buckingham, James Silk. *America, Historical, Statistic, and Descriptive.* 3 vols. London, 1841.

Burke, William. *The Mineral Springs of Western Virginia, with Remarks on Their Use, and the Diseases to which they are Applicable.* New York, 1842.

Caldwell, John Edward. *A Tour Through Part of Virginia, in the Summer of 1808, in a Series of Letters, Including an Account of Harper's Ferry, the Natural Bridge, the New Discovery called Weir's Cave.* New York, 1809.

Cornelius, Elias. *Tour in Virginia, Tennessee, Etc. Etc.* London, 1820.

Daubeny, Charles. *Journal of a Tour Through the United States, and in Canada, made during the Years 1837-38.* Oxford, England, 1843.

Dickens, Charles. *American Notes and Reprinted Pieces.* London, 1861.

Fearon, Henry Bradshaw. *A Narrative of a Journey of Five Thousand Miles through the Eastern and Western States of America.* London, 1819.

Ferrall, S. A. *A Ramble of Six Thousand Miles in the U. S. A.* London, 1835.

Flint, Timothy. *Condensed Geography of the Western United States.* 2 vols. Cincinnati, 1828.

Gilman, Caroline. *The Poetry of Traveling in the United States.* New York, 1838.

Hall, Basil. *Travels in North America, in the Years 1827 and 1828.* 3 vols. London, 1829.

Hamilton, Thomas. *Men and Manners in America.* 2 vols. Philadelphia, 1833.

Ingraham, J. H. *The Southwest.* 2 vols. New York, 1835.

Jefferson, Thomas. *Notes on the State of Virginia.* Richmond, 1853.

Latrobe, Charles Joseph. *The Rambler in North America.* 2 vols. London, 1836.

Ludlow, Noah M. *Dramatic Life as I Found It.* St. Louis, 1880.

McKay, Alex. *The Western World; or Travels in the United States, 1846-1847.* 2 vols. Philadelphia, 1849.

Martineau, Harriet. *Retrospect of Western Travel.* 2 vols. London, 1838.
Murray, Charles Augustus. *Travels in North America.* 2 vols. London, 1839.
Nicklin, Paul. *Letters Descriptive of the Virginia Springs; the Roads Leading Thereto, and Doings Thereat.* Philadelphia, 1835.
Parker, Agnes. *The Real Madeline Pollard, A Diary of Ten Weeks Association with the Plaintiff, the Famous Breckinridge Suit.* New York, 1894.
Pencil, Mark. *The White Sulphur Papers, or Life at the Springs of Western Virginia.* New York, 1839.
Poore, Ben Perley. *Perley's Reminiscences of Sixty Years in the National Metropolis.* 2 vols. Washington, D.C., 1886.
Power, Tyrone. *Impressions of America, During the Years 1833, 1834, and 1835.* 2 vols. London, 1836.
Priest, William. *Travels in the United States of America beginning in the Year 1795, and ending in 1797.* London, 1802.
Royall, Anne. *Letters from Alabama on Various Subjects: to which is Added an Appendix, Containing Remarks on Sundry Members of the 20th and 21st Congress, and Other High Characters, etc., etc., at the Seat of Government.* Washington, D. C., 1830.
———, ———. *Sketches of History, Life and Manners in the United States.* New Haven, 1826.
Trollope, Frances Anne. *Domestic Manners of the Americans, Edited with a History of Mrs. Trollope's Adventures in America.* New York, 1949.
Tudor, Henry. *Narrative of a Tour in North America; comprising Mexico, the Mines of Real del Monte, the United States, and the British Colonies.* 2 vols. London, 1834.
Withers, Alexander Scott. *Chronicles of Border Warfare, or a History of the Settlement by the Whites of Northwest; and of the Indian Wars and Massacres . . . Virginia.* Clarksburg, Va., 1831.
Worcester, Joseph Emerson, *A Geographical Dictionary or Universal Gazetteer Ancient and Modern.* 2 vols. Andover, Mass., 1817.
———, ———. *Worcester's Outline Maps, to be filled in by Younger Students in Geography.* Boston, 1829.

Periodicals

Boyd, Mark F. "Spanish Mission Sites in Florida." *Florida History Quarterly* 17 (1939): 264-69.
Franklin Farmer. I, II (Frankfort, 1837-1839).
Gage, Simon Henry. "Microscopy in America (1830-1945)." Edited by Oscar W. Richards. *Transactions American Microscopical Society* 83, No. 4 Supplement, 1964.
Goodall, Elizabeth. "The Manufacture of Salt — Kanawha's First Commercial Enterprise." *West Virginia History* 26 (1964-65): 234-50.
Hardin, Bayless. "Dr. Preston W. Brown, 1775-1826. His Family and Descendants." *Filson Club History Quarterly* 19 (1945): 3-28.

Heine, W. "The Washington City Canal." *Records of the Columbia Historical Society of Washington.* Vols. 53-56. Washington, D.C., 1959.

Jones, James G. "The Early History of the Natural Gas Industry in West Virginia." *West Virginia History* 10 (1948-49): 79-81.

Kerkam, William B. "Some Historical and Current Reflections on the American Patent System." *Centennial Celebration of the American Patent System, 1836-1936.* Washington, D.C., 1937.

Laing, James. "The Early Development of the Coal Industry in the Western Counties of Virginia, 1800-1865." *West Virginia History* 27 (1965-66): 144-46.

Niles Weekly Register. Vols. 35-37 (1827-1830).

Rice, Otis. "Importation of Cattle into Kentucky." *Register of the Kentucky Historical Society* 49 (1951): 35-54.

Tomlison, A. B. "First Settlement of Grave Creek." *American Pioneer.* 2 vols. Cincinnati, 1844.

"The Columbian Institute for the Promotion of Arts and Sciences." *National Museum Bulletin*, 101, Washington, D.C., 1917.

Western Farmer and Gardener. 6 vols. Cincinnati, 1841.

Newspapers

Frankfort *Commentator*, 1826.

Frankfort *Commonwealth*, 1849-1861.

Frankfort *Weekly Yeoman*, 1880-1884.

Lexington *Observer and Reporter*, 1835.

Louisville *Courier*, 1858.

Louisville *Courier-Journal*, 1868-1884.

Louisville *Daily Journal*, 1858.

Richmond *Enquirer*, 1829-1830.

Washington (D.C.) *National Intelligencer*, 1826.

Atlases, Dictionaries, Directories, and Gazetteers

Adams, James Truslow, ed. *Atlas of American History.* New York, 1943.

Accompaniment to Mitchell's Reference and Distance Map of the United States. Philadelphia, 1835.

Bauer, Jack. *Ships of the Navy, 1775-1869.* Troy, N.Y., 1969.

Biographical Directory of the American Congress, 1774-1949. Washington, D.C., 1950.

Biographical Encyclopedia of Kentucky of the Dead and the Living of the Nineteenth Century. Cincinnati, 1878.

Callahan, Edward W., ed. *List of the Officers of the United States Navy and Marine Corps.* New York, 1969.

Cullum Memorial Edition, 1960, Register of Graduates and Former Cadets, 1802-1960, of the United States Military Academy. West Point, 1960.

Cumings, Samuel. *The Western Pilot.* Cincinnati, 1848.

DeSilver, Robert. *Philadelphia Directory and Stranger's Guide.* Philadelphia, 1829, 1830.

Elliott, S. A. *The Washington Directory.* Washington, D.C., 1829, 1830.

Hamersby, Thomas H. S. *Complete Regular Army Register of the United States for One Hundred Years, 1779-1879.* Washington, D.C., 1880.

Heitman, F. B. *Historical Register and Dictionary of the United States Army.* Washington, D.C., 1903.

Heywood, John. *A Gazetteer of the United States of America.* Hartford, Conn., 1853.

Hazard, Samuel. *The Register of Pennsylvania, devoted to the Preservation of Facts and Documents and Other Kinds of Useful Information Respecting the State of Pennsylvania.* Vols. IV-VI. Philadelphia, 1829-30.

Kane, Joseph N. *Famous First Facts: A Record of First Happenings, Discoveries, and Inventions in the United States.* New York, 1964.

Kemp, Peter, ed. *The Oxford Companion to Ships and the Sea.* New York, 1976.

Levin, H., ed. *Lawyers and Lawmakers In Kentucky.* Chicago, 1897.

Martin, Joseph. *A New and Comprehensive Gazetteer of Virginia and the District of Columbia.* Charlottesville, 1835.

Matchett's Baltimore Directory. Baltimore, 1829.

Mitchell's Baltimore Directory, corrected up to June 1829. Containing an Engraved Plan of the City of Baltimore. Baltimore, 1829.

Register of Graduates and Former Graduates of the United States Military Academy, 1802-1879. West Point, 1979.

The Strangers Guide in Philadelphia to all Public Buildings, Places of Amusements, Commercial, Benevolent, and Religious Institutions, and Churches, Principal Hotels, &c. &c. &c. Philadelphia, 1858.

View of the United States of America; Forming a Complete Emigrant's Directory Through Every Part of the Republic. London, 1820.

Weaver, William B. *United States Official Register of all Officers and Agents Civil, Military, and Naval in the Services of the United States on the Thirteenth of September 1833.* Philadelphia, 1834.

Webster's Military Biography. Springfield, Mass., 1978.

Local and State Histories

Abbott, John S. C. *The History of The State of Ohio, 1805-1875.* Detroit, 1874.

Andrews, Matthew Page. *Tercentenary History of Maryland.* 2 vols. Chicago, 1925.

Baldwin, Leland D. *Pittsburgh: The Story of a City.* Pittsburgh, 1937.

Barker, John W., and Henry Howe. *Historic Collections of the State of New York.* New York, 1841.

Bevan, Wilson Floyd, and E. Melvin Williams. *History of Delaware Past and Present.* 2 vols. New York, 1929.

Bierne, Francis F. *Baltimore: A Picture History, 1858-1958.* New York, 1957.

Callahan, James Morton. *Semi-Centennial History of West Virginia.* Morgantown, W. Va., 1926.

Clark, George L. *A History of Connecticut and Its People and Institutions*. New York, 1914.
Collins, Lewis, and Richard H. Collins. *History of Kentucky*. 2 vols. Covington, Ky., 1874.
Coulter, E. Merton. *The Civil War and Readjustment in Kentucky*. Chapel Hill, 1926.
Coward, John Wells. *Kentucky in the New Republic: The Process of Constitution Making*. Lexington, 1979.
Filson, John. *Kentucke and the Adventures of Col. Daniel Boone*. Louisville, 1934.
Fishwick, Marshall. *Rockbridge County, Virginia*. Richmond, 1852.
Gaines, B. O. *History of Scott County*. 2 vols. Georgetown, Ky., 1904.
Gayarre, Charles E. A. *History of Louisiana: The French Dominion*. 4 vols. New York, 1854-57.
Greene, Welcome Arnold. *The Providence Plantations for Two Hundred and Fifty Years*. Providence, 1886.
Howe, Henry. *Historical Collections of Virginia* . . . Charleston, S. C., 1845.
Hutchins, Stilson, and Joseph W. Moore. *The National Capitol: Past and Present*. Washington, D.C., 1885.
Ireland, Robert. *Little Kingdoms: The Counties of Kentucky, 1850-1891*. Lexington, 1977.
Jillson, Willard Rouse. *Early Frankfort and Franklin County*. Louisville, 1936.
Johnston, J. Stoddard. *The Memorial History of Louisville*. 2 vols. Chicago, 1896.
Little, John P. *Richmond, Capital of Virginia: Its History*. Richmond, 1851.
Lorant, Stefan, ed. *Pittsburgh: The Story of an American City*. Garden City, N.Y., 1964.
Miller. A. M., *The Geology of Kentucky*. Frankfort, 1919.
Morgan, George H. *Annals of Harrisburg, Comprising Memoirs, Incidents and Statistics from the Period of its First Settlement*. Harrisburg, 1852.
Perrin, W. H., G. C. Kniffen, and J. H. Battle. *Kentucky: A History of a State*. Louisville, 1888.
Perrin, William H. *History of Bourbon, Scott, Harrison, and Nicholas Counties, Kentucky*. Chicago, 1882.
Peter, Robert, ed. *History of Fayette County, Kentucky*. Chicago, 1882.
Pruett, Rebecca K. *The Browns of Liberty Hall*. Shelbyville, Ky., 1966.
Richmond [Virginia] in By-gone Days by an Old Citizen. Richmond, 1859.
Scott, Mary Wingfield. *Old Richmond Neighborhoods*. Richmond, 1950.
Smith, O. H. *Early Indiana Trials and Sketches; Reminiscences by Honorable O. H. Smith*. Cincinnati, 1858.
Sharpless, Isaac. *Two Centuries of Pennsylvania History*. Philadelphia, 1900.
Sonne, Henry N. *Liberal Kentucky, 1780-1828*. New York, 1939.
Spencer, J. H. *A History of Kentucky Baptists from 1769-1885*. 2 vols. Cincinnati, 1886.
Stannard, Mary Newton. *Richmond and Its People*. Philadelphia, 1923.
Stickles, Arndt M. *The Critical Court Struggle in Kentucky, 1819-1829*. Bloomington, 1929.
Trabue, Alice. *Corner in Celebrities*. Louisville, 1922.

Vexler, Robert. *Baltimore: A Chronological and Documentary History, 1639-1970.* New York, 1975.

Watson, F. F. *The Annals of Philadelphia and Pennsylvania in the Olden Times. As Revised by Hazard.* 3 vols. Philadelphia, 1898.

Williams, John Lee. *A View of West Florida.* Gainesville, 1976.

Wilson, Samuel M. *A Battle of the Blue Licks, August 19, 1782.* Lexington, 1927.

Wolf, Edwin II. *Philadelphia: Portrait of an American City.* Philadelphia, 1911.

Biographies

Ammon, Harry. *James Monroe, The Quest for National Identity.* New York, 1941.

Anthony, Katherine. *Dolly Madison: Her Life and Times.* New York, 1949.

Bakeless, John. *Daniel Boone, Master of the Wilderness.* New York, 1939.

Beveridge, Albert J. *The Life of John Marshall.* 4 vols. New York, 1916-19.

Brant, Irving. *James Madison: The Virginia Revolutionist, 1751-1780.* Indianapolis, 1941.

Clarke, Asia Booth. *The Elder and Younger Booth.* Boston, 1882.

Cresson, W. P. *James Monroe.* Chapel Hill, 1946.

Cutts, J. B. *Memoirs and Letters of Dolly Madison, Wife of James Madison President of the United States.* New York, 1886.

Desmond, Alice. *Bewitching Betsy Bonaparte.* New York, 1858.

Didier, Eugene L. *Life and Letters of Mme. Bonaparte.* New York, 1879.

Falkner, Leonard. *The President Who Wouldn't Retire.* New York, 1967.

Friend, Llerena. *Sam Houston, the Great Designer.* Austin, 1954.

Garland, Hugh A. *The Life and Times of John Randolph of Roanoke.* 2 vols. New York, 1850.

Goodwin, Maud W. *Dolly Madison.* New York, 1896.

Gruenwald, Constantine de. *Tsar Nicholas I.* New York, 1955.

Hecht, Marie B. *John Quincy Adams: A Personal History of an Independent Man.* New York, 1972.

Holden, Reuben A. *Profiles and Portraits of Yale University Presidents.* Freeport, Me., 1968.

Irving, Pierre E. *The Life and Letters of Washington Irving.* 2 vols. London, 1908.

Irving, Washington. *Life of George Washington.* 3 vols. New York, 1856.

James, Marquis. *Andrew Jackson.* 2 vols. Indianapolis, 1933, 1939.

———, ———. *The Raven: A Biography of Sam Houston.* Indianapolis, 1929.

Kennedy, J. P. *Life of William Wirt, Attorney General of the United States.* Philadelphia, 1856.

Klotter, James C. *The Breckinridges of Kentucky, 1760-1981.* Lexington, 1986.

Meigs, William M. *Life of Thomas Hart Benton.* Philadelphia, 1904.

Meyer, Leland Winfield. *The Life and Times of Colonel Richard M. Johnson of Kentucky.* New York, 1932.

Nevins, Allan, ed. *The Diary of John Quincy Adams.* New York, 1929.

Parton, James. *Life of Andrew Jackson.* 3 vols. Boston, 1866.

———, ———. *Life and Times of Benjamin Franklin.* 2 vols. New York, 1864.

Porter, S. H. *The Life and Times of Anne Royall.* Cedar Rapids, Iowa, 1909.

Quincy, Edmund. *Life of Josiah Quincy*. Boston, 1867.

Richardson, Robert. *Memoirs of Alexander Campbell, Embracing a View of the Origin, Progress and Principle of the Religious Reformation which He Advocated*. 2 vols. Philadelphia, 1868. 1870.

Rowland, Kate Mason. *The Life of Charles Carroll of Carrollton*. 2 vols. New York, 1898.

Sargent, Nathan. *Public Men and Events from the Commencement of Mr. Monroe's Administration in 1817 to the Close of Mr. Fillmore's, in 1853*. 2 vols. Philadelphia, 1875.

Sargent, Winthrop. *The Life and Career of Major John Andre*. New York, 1902.

Schlesinger, Arthur M., Jr., *The Age of Jackson*. Boston, 1945.

Sellers, Charles Coleman. *Charles Willson Peale*. 2 vols. Philadelphia, 1947.

_____, _____. *Charles Willson Peale*. New York, 1969.

Wiltse, Charles. *John C. Calhoun, Nullifier, 1829-1839*. Indianapolis, 1949.

General Works

Allen, Lewis F. *History of the Short-Horn Cattle and Their Origin, Progress and Present Condition*. Buffalo, 1872.

Bacon, Edgar Mayhew. *The Hudson River from Ocean to Source*. New York, 1910.

Banta, Richard E. *The Ohio*. New York, 1949.

Barnes, Harry Elmer. *The Evolution of Penology in Pennsylvania; A Study in American Social History*. Indianapolis, 1927.

Beatty, Adam. *Essays on Practical Agriculture*. Maysville, Ky., 1844.

Bennett, William B. *The American Patent System: An Economic Interpretation*. Baton Rouge, 1943.

Cherrington, Ernest Hurst. *The Evolution of Prohibition in the United States of America*. Westerville, Ohio, 1920.

Clark, Victor S. *History of Manufactures in the United States*. 3 vols. Rev. ed. Washington, D.C., 1929.

Clift, Glenn. *Kentucky Obituaries, 1787-1845*. Baltimore, 1979.

Coad, Oral Sumner, and Edwin Mims, Jr. *The American Stage. The Pageant of America*. Vol. 14. New York, 1929.

Dellinger, W. H. *The Microscope and Its Revelations*. London, 1891.

Doolittle, William H. *Inventions in the Century*. London, 1903.

Dwight, Theodore. *History of The Hartford Convention with a Review of the Policy which Led to the War of 1812*. New York, 1933.

Fish, Carl Russell. *The Rise of the Common Man, 1830-1850*. New York, 1927.

Fox, Early Lee. *The American Colonization Society, 1817-1840*. Baltimore, 1919.

Gage, Simon Henry. *The Microscope: An Introduction to Microscopic Methods and Histology*. New York, 1920.

Gocher, W. H. *Wadsworth or the Charter Oak*. Hartford, Conn., 1904.

Gray, Lewis. *History of Agriculture in the Southern States to 1860*. 2 vols. Washington, D.C., 1933.

Hackensmith, C. W. *Out of Time and Tide. The Evolution of Education in Kentucky*. Lexington, 1970.

Healy, E. P. and O. M. *A Record of Unfashionable Crosses in Short-Horn Cattle Pedigrees.* Bedford, Iowa, 1883.

Hughes, Glenn. *A History of the American Theatre, 1700-1850.* New York, 1951.

Hulburt, Archer Butler. *The Great American Canals* (Historic Highways of America). Vol. I. Cleveland, 1905.

———, ———. *The Ohio River: A Course of Empire.* New York, 1902.

Hungerford, E. L. *The Story of the Baltimore and Ohio Railroad, 1827-1927.* 2 vols. New York, 1928.

Kendall, John S. *The Golden Age of the New Orleans Theatre.* Baton Rouge, 1952.

Krout, John A. *The Origins of Prohibition.* New York, 1925.

Lewis, Alvin Fayette. *History of Higher Education in Kentucky.* Washington, D.C., 1899.

Mahon, John K. *The War of 1812.* Gainesville, Fla., 1972.

Masters, Frank M. *A History of the Baptists in Kentucky.* Louisville, 1953.

Mearns, David. *The Story up to Now, 1800-1945.* Washington, D.C., 1946.

Meisel, Max. *A Bibliography of American Natural History: The Pioneer Century, 1769-1865.* 3 vols. Brooklyn, N.Y., 1924-29.

Meyer, Balthasar H., ed. *History of Transportation in the United States before 1860.* Washington, D.C., 1917.

Montgomery, James. *The Cotton Manufacturers of the United States and Great Britain.* New York, 1970.

Owsley, Frank L. *Plain Folk of the Old South.* Baton Rouge, 1949.

Sanders, Alvin H. *Short-Horn Cattle: A Series of Historical Sketches, Memoirs and Records of the Breed and Its Development in the United States and Canada.* Chicago, 1901.

Simms, William Gilmore. *Beauchamp: or, The Kentucky Tragedy. A Tale of Passion.* Philadelphia, 1842.

Smith, J. Allen. *The College of Agriculture of the University of Kentucky, Early and Middle Years, 1865-1951.* Lexington, 1981.

Smith, William, ed. *Historical Account of Bouquet's Expedition . . .* Cincinnati, 1868.

Van Tyne, Claude Halstead. *The American Revolution, 1776-1783.* New York, 1905.

Warren, Charles. *The Supreme Court in United States History.* 2 vols. Rev. ed. New York, 1937.

Warren, Robert Penn. *World Enough and Time.* New York, 1950.

Wilson, Garf B. *Three Hundred Years of American Drama and Theatre.* Bloomington, 1966.

Young, William C. *Famous Actors and Actresses of the American Stage.* 2 vols. New York, 1975.

Institutional Histories

Bruce, Philip Alexander. *History of the University of Virginia, 1818-1919.* 2 vols. New York, 1920-21.

Crane, John, and James F. Keiley. *West Point: "The Key to America."* New York, 1947.

Crawford, William. *Report on the Penitentiaries of the United States Ordered by the House of Commons.* London, 1854.

McClean, John. *History of the College of New Jersey from Its Origins in 1746 to the Commencement of 1854.* 4 vols. Philadelphia, 1877.

Sellers, Charles Coleman. *Dickinson College: A History.* Middletown, Conn., 1973.

Sneed, William C. *A Report on the History and Mode of Management of the Kentucky Penitentiary from Its Origins in 1798 to March 1, 1860.* Frankfort, 1860.

Snyder, Robert. *A History of Georgetown College.* Georgetown, Ky., 1979.

Wright, John D., Jr. *Transylvania University: Tutor to the West.* Rev. ed. Lexington, 1980.

Index

A

A & M College. *See* Kentucky A & M College
Abbe, Licard, 58
Academy of Fine Arts, 58, 199
Adams, Chilton, 138
Adams, John Quincy, 6, 10, 12-13, 72, 80, 206
Adams Livery Stable (Louisville), 145
Afleck, Thomas, 124, 133-34
Albany, N. Y., 8-9, 41-42, 196
Alexander, Robert Aitcheson, 120, 123, 138, 140
Alexander, Thomas, 9
Allegheny Canal Aqueduct, 15, 94-95
Allegheny River, 63
Allen, Edward, 127
Allen, Robert, 127
Allen's American Short Horn *Herd Book*, 123
American Centennial Exhibition (Pa.), 125
American Colonization Society, 83, 207
American Hotel (N. Y.), 30
Arch Street Theater (Phil.), 58, 199
Armstrong, John, 9
Atheneum (Phil.), 58, 199
Austin, William, 36
Ayres, W., 123

B

Baldwin, Henry, 74
Baltimore, 10-11, 17, 60, 64-65, 87-88, 209
Baltimore and Ohio Railroad, 10, 60-61, 200
Baltimore County Artillery, 109
Baltimore Exchange, 88
Baltimore Museum, 88
Bank of Kentucky, 179
Baptist Theological Institute, 137
Barbour, Philip P., 24, 78, 189, 205
Barnum's Hotel (Baltimore), 60, 199
Barry, Walker, 9

Barry, William T., 11, 13, 65, 108, 201, 217
Battle Monument (Baltimore), 65
Battle of Blue Licks, 4, 187
Battle of Jackson, Miss., 155
Battle of New Orleans, 11, 68
Battle of Perryville, 166
Battle of Stone's River, 156
Beatty, Adam, 124, 138
Beauchamp, Jeroboam, 111, 185
Beltzhouver's Tavern, 88
Benton, Thomas Hart, 12, 74, 84-85, 204, 207
Bishop House (La.), 18, 103, 215
Blackburn, W. C., 124
blacks, 83, 116, 122, 134, 147, 150, 153, 157, 174
Bladensburg, Md., 87
Blanchard, Thomas S., 8, 38-39, 195
Bledsoe, A. T., 9
Blowing Cave, 22
Blue Ridge, 5
Bolivar, Simon, 80
Bolivar County, Miss., 154
Bonaparte, Jerome, 38, 195
Bonaparte, Joseph, 10, 45, 197
Boone, Daniel, 18, 20, 28, 101, 214
Boone, Squire, 101
Booth, Junius B., 34, 194
Boston, 7, 8, 34-37
Boston Navy Yard, 37, 195
Boston Neck, 37
Bourbon County, Ky., 109, 127
Boylston Market, 37
Brandywine, frigate, 31, 192
Breckinridge, James, 172
Breckinridge, John C., 153
Breckinridge, W. C. P., 166-67, 228
Breckinridge County, Ky., 165
Breeds Hill, 35
Brooklyn, N. Y., 7, 30
Brooklyn Navy Yard, 6, 30-31, 192
Brown, Elizabeth Watts, 3, 17, 111-12

post-war years, 174-76; Princeton, N.J.,
44; purchase Locust Hill, 115; Rhode
Island, 33-34; Richmond, Va., 5, 23-25;
southern livestock trade, 142-49;
Springfield, Mass., 38; travel on canals,
59-60; travel to New Orleans, 100-103;
U.S. Supreme Court, 73-74; Va. caves,
aᵣd springs, 4, 22-23; Washington,
11-13, 62-88; Webster-Hayne Debates,
83-85; West Point, 9, 42-44; West Va.,
4-5; "Yankee" manufactures, 9, 33-41;
Scott County, Ky., 107, 109
Second Ky. Const. Convent., 109
Screw dock, 42
Shakers, 121, 127
Sharp, Solomon P., 111, 185
sheep, "Improved Kentucky," 125-26
Shillito's dept. store, 148
Shirley, Lewis, 127
Shryock, Gideon, 110, 184
Silver Lake, Fla., 179
slaves, 116, 122, 134, 147, 150, 153, 157,
174
Smith, B. B., 103
Smith, Thomas, 108
Springfield, Mass., 37-38, 41, 196
Springfield Paper Manufacturing, 98
South Carolina, 84, 172
Southern, steamer, 146
Southern rights club, 154
Southern rights party, 185
Springfield, Mass., 38
Stackleberg, Baron, 82, 207
states rights, 154
Steubenville, Ohio, 15, 96-97, 212
Stevenson, Andrew, 24, 76, 189, 205
Stoner Creek, 109
Story, Joseph, 73
Sumner Forest, 114, 116
Supreme Court, U. S., 13, 72-73, 87, 204,
208
Susquehanna River, 91, 211
Sutton, David, 121
Sweigert, Philip, 140

T

Taliafero, John, 24
Tallahassee, Fla., 101, 179
Tate, James W., 166
Taylor, Dick, 155
Taylor, E. H., Jr., 147
Tazewell, Littleton W., 76, 205
temperance, 21, 28, 188, 191
Tennessee livestock, 146
Texas, 153
Thayer, Sylvanus, 43, 197
theater, 18, 34, 58, 103, 199, 215

Thompson, Duncan, 133-34
Thompson, Smith, 13, 74
Todd, Colonel, 20
Townsend, John W., Library, 16
Transylvania University, 3, 7, 107-8, 110,
136
Tremont House (Boston), 34, 37, 194
Tremont Theater, 34
Trenton, N.J., 45
Tripp, Deborah, 30
Trollope, Frances A., 19
Tucker, William E., 46
Turtz, Maurice, 81

U

Union Canal, 9
Union Philosophical Society, 14, 91
Union Stage Lines, 87
United Confederate Veterans of Texas,
156
United States, ship, 31, 192
United States; Bank, 57; Bureau of Agri-
culture, 126; Congress, 65; House of
Representatives, 70, 72, 165; Military
Academy, 42-43; Mint, 10, 56, 199
United States Hotel (Hartford, Conn.), 33
United States Military Academy. *See*
West Point
United States Supreme Court. *See*
Supreme Court, U.S.
United States *Telegraph*, 73
University of Tennessee, 162
University of Virginia, 5, 23, 189

V

Van Buren, Martin, 65, 201
Vanceburg, Ky., 3, 20
Van Dusen, R., 124, 126
Van Vetchen, T., 42
Velocipede, 45
Versailles, Ky., 16
Virginia, 165, 172; armory, 28, 190;
caves and springs, 4, 22-23; constitu-
tional convention, 12, 160, 189;
library, 28, 190; penitentiary, 27, 190

W

Walleck, Henry, 9
Waller, John L., 103, 216
Walnut Street Prison (Phil.), 54-55,
198-99
Warfield, Elisha, 121, 138, 140
Warfield, William, 140
Warm Springs, Va., 22, 188
Washington College, Va., 4, 23, 32-33,
189
Washington County, Miss., 17, 215

Washington, D. C., 1, 11-13, 62-88, 112, 208
Washington Monument, Baltimore, 64-65, 201
Washington Navy Yard, 66, 85-86
Watterson, Henry, 185
Webster, Daniel, 12, 76, 82-85, 205
Webster-Hayne Debate, 13, 83, 207
Webster, Wirt, Wickliffe, and Bronston, 74
Wells, Basel. 97
Wellsburg, Ohio, 97
Western Pennsylvania Penitentiary, 15, 93, 212
West Point, N. Y., 9-10, 42, 196-97
Weyer's Cave, Va., 4, 23
Wheeling, W. Va., 15, 17, 97-98, 213
White House, 66, 68, 82, reception, 67-70
White Sulphur Springs, Va., 21, 188
Whitney, Eli, 8
Wickliffe, Robert, 108
William Penn, steamboat, 59

Wilmington, Del., 14, 59, 89
Wilmot family, 109
Wilmot, Priscilla, 111, 137
Wilmot, Robert, 108-9
Wilmot, Sarah Ridgely, 108
Winan's Car, 10, 62
Wing, Edwin Rumsey, 166
Wing, Louisa, 166
Wirt, William, 87, 208
Wood, Samuel, 47
Woodburn Farm, Ky., 120
Woodford County, Ky., 112, 114, 124
Worcester *Atlas and Gazette*, 8, 16
Worcester, Mass., 37
Worthington Point, Miss., 18, 101, 215

Y

Yale College, 7, 15-16, 32, 192-93
Yancey, William Lowndes, 153
Yohe, Catherine, 14, 59, 199, 209-10
York River, Va., 28

Printed by BoD˝in Norderstedt, Ge